American Public Policy

American Public Policy

The Contemporary Agenda

Steven G. Koven
UNIVERSITY OF LOUISVILLE

Mack C. Shelley, II
IOWA STATE UNIVERSITY

Bert E. Swanson
UNIVERSITY OF FLORIDA

HOUGHTON MIFFLIN COMPANY   Boston   New York

Sponsoring editor: *Melissa Mashburn*
Associate editor: *Lily Eng*
Senior project editor: *Rosemary Winfield*
Production/design coordinator: *Deborah Frydman*
Manufacturing coordinator: *Andrea Wagner*
Marketing manager: *Sandra McGuire*

Cover design by Melissa A. Molusis

Printed in the U.S.A.

Library of Congress Catalog Number: 97-72507
ISBN: 0-395-71388-9

123456789-DH-00 99 98 97

Contents

Preface

American Public Policy: The Contemporary Agenda both develops a framework for understanding public policy and expands the range of policy domains that are typically addressed in political science and public administration courses. In developing this new framework, we have looked at how underlying determinants influence policy and have avoided a strategy of merely describing the actions of political institutions. In augmenting the range of conventional policy domains, we have included topics such as urban decay, general educational decline, and environmental degradation, which we feel represent critical policy challenges for the nation as it enters the new millennium.

SPECIAL FEATURES OF THE BOOK

The application of a policymaking model that emphasizes the roles of rationality, power, and ideology—the *rationality, power, ideology (RPI) model*—sets this text apart from others that either stress the policy process or fail to illustrate how specific models explain substantive issues of public policy. The RPI model considers how public policy is influenced by rationality, power, and ideology inputs on substantive issues such as economic and budget policy; environmental policy; rural, agricultural, and small-town policy; urban policy; education policy; health policy; family and welfare policy; crime policy; and "intermestic" policy. We believe that discussing these factors leads to a more comprehensive grasp of the underlying currents that influence policy.

In addition, the text attempts to engage students' interest in public policy and enhance the perceived relevance of public policy. Each chapter includes an *opening vignette,* which depicts a policy decision and how it can have far-reaching local and national repercussions; a *Case Study,* which examines a particular issue, such as education, illustrated by a specific state's approach to the policy problem; and a *Contemporary Controversy* box, which presents both sides of the argument on issues such as drug legalization, spiraling health costs, and equitable tax burdens.

A further distinguishing characteristic of the book is the incorporation of topics that have not received extensive coverage in other public policy texts—interactions between domestic and international policy, consolidation in the agricultural economy, economic viability of small towns in rural areas, as well as family issues such as recognition of same-sex marriages, interpretations of pornography, and the definition of life itself (abortion). While the discussion of urban problems has declined in policy texts as memories of the riots of the 1960s have faded, we believe that recent events fully justify an extensive reexamination of this policy issue. To grasp how these contentious issues as well as others will be resolved in the near future, we are convinced that it is essential for students to understand the uses of rationality in American society, society's power relationships, and society's value and ideological positions.

We support the view that values and ideologies influence policy preferences, and we realize that each of us brings his or her own biases to the table. Nevertheless, we have emphasized a balanced presentation of views and place discussions within a framework of enhancing policy understanding rather than advocating personal policy positions. We accept full responsibility for failures in our efforts to achieve balance in the eyes of our readers.

ACKNOWLEDGMENTS

We would like to thank the many people who helped to carry this project forward to fruition. At Houghton Mifflin, Jean Woy, Fran Gay, Paul Smith, Lily Eng, Leah Strauss, Melissa Mashburn, and Rosemary Winfield provided encouragement and advice. Thoughtful comments, which greatly improved on earlier drafts, were provided by the following reviewers: Gary L. Gregg, Clarion University; John A. Hird, University of Massachusetts, Amherst; Arthur P. Lupia, University of California, San Diego; Don F. McCabe, Southern Illinois University at Edwardsville; Glenn McNitt, State University of New York, New Paltz; Keith Mueller, University of Nebraska; Phillip Roeder, University of Kentucky; Christine Rossell, Boston University; Michael J. Scicchitano, University of Florida; Richard T. Sylves, University of Delaware; and Mark E. Tompkins, University of South Carolina. We greatly appreciate the useful suggestions and recommendations of these scholars. Finally, we are indebted to our families, who have supported us throughout our careers and through the difficult times when we were struggling with the development of this manuscript: Andrea, Eli, Faye, Edith, Kathy, Anne, and Will.

S. G. K.
B. E. S.
M. C. S.

1

American Public Policy: The Contemporary Agenda

INTRODUCTION

Public policies touch every aspect of human existence, from protecting citizens against foreign invasion to determining the street corner on which to install a traffic light. Policies reflect specific means that have been adopted by leaders in order to attain sweeping goals, such as those described in the preamble to the United States Constitution:

> We the People of the United States, in Order to form a more perfect Union, establish Justice, insure domestic Tranquillity, provide for the common defense, promote the general Welfare, and secure the Blessings of Liberty to ourselves and our Posterity, do ordain and establish this Constitution for the United States of America.

Since guarantees of noble goals such as justice, tranquillity, defense, welfare, and liberty are not preordained, specific behavior can either promote or forsake these ends. Over the past two hundred years, numerous critics have proclaimed the deficiencies of American governance, yet a number of achievements are evident. In the twentieth century, American policies managed to curtail the power of enormous corporations, improve the working conditions of child as well as adult laborers, defend American ideals during two world wars, put astronauts on the moon, build a massive interstate highway network, promote civil rights, win the Cold War, develop sophisticated technology for civilian as well as military products, and set the nation in the forefront of world leadership.

Of course, many profound problems remain. Those who are homeless or jobless or who lack adequate health care, have subpar educations, and are at the bottom of the economic strata with little hope of changing their plight may not be inclined to celebrate America's triumphs. Problems such as the fragility

1

of American financial institutions, international competitiveness in world trade, sustaining the agricultural "bread basket" to the world, pervasive inequities between the affluent and the poor, hostilities between races, and a host of unmet needs of citizens continue to plague and challenge the nation. These problems must be addressed by public policy.

A goal of this book is to provide insights into how policies are created and how problems are addressed in the public sector. The book formulates a model that identifies various influences on policymaking institutions.

PUBLIC POLICY: WHAT IS IT?

Public policies come in various forms, ranging from congressional resolutions about future goals, municipal proclamations, precedent-setting decisions of the U.S. Supreme Court, and administrative regulations defining how public services should be delivered. Public policies determine qualifications for activities such as driving an automobile, practicing medicine, obtaining an abortion, or qualifying for food stamps. Government can also prohibit certain types of behavior such as aggravated assault, public intoxication, and mail fraud. Governments establish penalties for illegal actions. Table 1.1 describes various definitions of public policy.[1]

While relatively simple definitions of public policy have been formulated, many scholars also recognize that public policy is difficult to study systematically. Factors that influence policy are difficult to pinpoint; environments in which policies are formulated are changing; actors move in and out of the process; and a large number of participants with different goals are involved. Some powerful actors want to be hidden from view; weaker actors may give the false impression that they are essential players; actors posture or rhetorically advance positions that they do not really support; a large number of poorly defined alternatives compete for acceptance; and players support policy options simply to prevent others from arising.[2]

In democracies and in what political scientists call pluralist systems (a system where power is not exclusively held by the few but is spread out to a larger number of actors), policy is not a constant to be enforced by the powerful few against the wishes of the many. In democratic societies, policy is dynamic and is influenced by political forces.[3] Therefore, factors such as public opinion, political philosophy, and interest-group behavior all shape policies. Under the pluralist paradigm, governmental leaders must balance competing demands for specific benefits. For example, businesses in the community may pressure state leaders to reduce payments for workers' compensation benefits. Labor leaders, on the other hand, may lobby to maintain or increase benefit levels for their members. At the national level, groups may pressure environmental officials to set aside certain forests as a preserve for future generations. Representatives of paper companies as well as employees of logging companies, however, may

TABLE 1.1 Definitions and Examples of Public Policy

Definitions	Examples
1. Actions intended to accomplish an end	1. Action of mandating school integration with the end of providing equal access to a quality education
2. Whatever governments choose to do or not to do	2. Choice of state governments to raise speed limits to 65 miles per hour or to keep it at 55 miles per hour
3. An authoritative allocation of values through government activity	3. Government funding of abortions conveys and promotes certain values
4. All government action	4. Any official action of personnel on the government payroll—delivering mail, putting out fires, arresting violators of the law
5. A program of goals, values, and practices	5. Welfare program with goal of self-sufficiency, values of individualism and limited government, practice of time limits for eligibility
6. Standing decision on the part of those who make it and those who abide by it	6. Decision to invite big donors to a political campaign for coffee, handshakes, and personal pictures with high-level officials

seek to protect their interests and pressure leaders not to set aside additional acreage for preserves. Local leaders must also balance the demands of competing interests. For example, the interests of pro-growth citizens who advocate expansion of airports and highways conflict with the interests of community residents who would be displaced by such development. Some analysts reject the pluralist paradigm, claiming that a small "ruling class" actually dominates decision making on major policy issues.[4]

A classic study of the 1940s identified competing goals of American policies as including external security (protection against other groups), internal order (establishing reasonable expectancies about what is to be done and by whom), justice (fairness for all), general welfare (protection of the health, safety, morals, comfort, and convenience of the public), and freedom (opportunity for free development of personal desires for expression).[5]

Competing goals constantly confront policymakers who must balance disparate desires. One can see, for example, that drafting citizens into the military helps preserve the very existence of the nation from international threats (external security) but interferes with personal freedom. One would assume that many citizens would like to be free to tell their draft boards that they are sorry but that they will not participate in the military because it intrudes upon their freedom to do other things. Similarly, the goal of internal order may necessitate the banning of assault weapons, an act which some citizens consider to be an infringement upon their freedom. The goal of general welfare (convenience for travelers) in the case of airport expansion also must be weighed against the goals of justice and protecting the rights of displaced citizens. The balancing of competing interests therefore is a major responsibility of policymakers.

THE POLICY PROCESS

Policy is usually studied in its institutional setting, that is, in the various branches of government: the legislative branch, where laws are enacted; the judicial branch, where the constitutionality of laws is decided; the bureaucracy, where policy is implemented; and the executive branch, where laws are signed or vetoed. At the national level, policymaking can be observed in the halls of Congress, in Supreme Court pronouncements, in the actions of the president, and in the behavior of federal bureaucrats. The national media pay the most attention to these actors and follow the details of the dramas in the Senate or the House of Representatives, the ceremonies in the Rose Garden of the White House, and the decisions of the Supreme Court. Institutional actors at other levels of government such as state legislators, city councilors, aldermen, governors, mayors, judges, police chiefs, school principals, teachers, and police all play roles in the formulation and implementation of public policies.

Congress and the Policy Process

Congress plays a major role in the writing, debating, and passing of legislation that either directly or indirectly affects all American citizens. Congress goes through a regularized procedure for enacting legislation. This process includes: (1) introducing bills (introducing similar bills into both the Senate and House of Representatives), (2) committee action (referring the bill to the appropriate committees), (3) floor action (sending the bill to the floors of both chambers), and (4) conference action (referring related bills to a conference committee to work out differences between House and Senate versions).

The ability of Congress to make policy is demonstrated in the large number of well-paid lobbyists and others roaming congressional halls. Members of Congress are often contacted by advocates of special interest groups (usually paid lobbyists) who attempt to shape or even write legislation. Such behavior is pursued to establish special advantage for one group. Lobbying may also arise to prevent legislation that would be harmful to special interests. The high salaries paid to lobbyists, public relations firms, and others who attempt to influence congressional behavior are one indication of the value of political influence. Congress is a major policy actor, yet others such as the president, the courts, and the bureaucracy also contribute to the process.

The Executive and the Policy Process

The particular holder of an executive office often makes a difference in the thrust and scope of public policy. In the 1930s, a strong president was able to gain acceptance of the idea that government had a role to play in the social and economic welfare of the nation. Franklin Roosevelt's New Deal philosophy of proactive intervention in the economy replaced the view that government should adopt a "hands off" attitude. Harry Truman's Fair Deal and Lyndon Johnson's Great Society further expanded the public sector's role in addressing issues of the day. More recently, presidential policy initiatives have ranged from Ronald Reagan's efforts to revitalize the military to Bill Clinton's plans for reshaping health care.

The formal powers of the president described in Article II of the U.S. Constitution include the powers of the president alone, for example those of commander-in-chief of the armed forces; powers shared with the Senate, such as the power to make treaties; and powers shared with the entire Congress, such as the power to approve legislation. Broad interpretation of specific phrases in the Constitution have also increased the policymaking power of American presidents.

The ability of presidents to shape policy depends upon the type of policy in question. The president holds more power in defense and foreign policy matters than in domestic affairs. It has even been proposed that America has two presidencies: one presidency for domestic affairs and the other for defense and foreign policy. Presidents are able to exercise more power in the foreign policy arena for a number of reasons: the greater need for speed in dealing with international crises, the power of the president to command the armed forces, the relatively low level of public understanding about international problems, and the general reluctance of members of Congress to stand up to the president on foreign policy issues.[6] Presidential power in foreign policymaking also includes the "rally around the flag" effect, or the tendency of the people to support the nation's leader in periods of danger. The process of policymaking in crisis periods appears in speeches before Congress, addresses to the nation, and endorsements by congressional leaders. Franklin Roosevelt's address to Congress following the Japanese attack on Pearl Harbor in 1941, John Kennedy's address to the nation twenty years later during the Cuban Missile Crisis, and George Bush's address to the nation following Iraq's invasion of Kuwait indicate how presidents can operate in periods of foreign policy crisis.

Today, presidents are expected to respond to policy emergencies; propose solutions to the country's social, economic, and political ills; and redeem campaign promises. As the nation's chief executive, the president is accountable to the people for the success or failure of national initiatives. Presidential power to make policy, however, is limited in the American system of checks and balances. The courts act as a major constraint on the power of some branches of government to make policy arbitrarily.

The Courts and the Policy Process

The judicial system in the United States was described by Alexander Hamilton as the weakest of the three departments of power, since it had "no influence over either the sword or the purse." The role played by the courts in the policy process, however, has grown since the founding of the nation. Landmark Supreme Court decisions such as *Brown v. Board of Education of Topeka, Kansas* (1954) and *Roe v. Wade* (1973) left an indelible mark on the nation in shaping both education and abortion policy. In *Brown v. Board of Education,* the Supreme Court declared that racial segregation violated the Fourteenth Amendment's equal protection clause, which rendered the policy of "separate but equal" schools inoperative. This decision effectively struck down segregated schooling in the United States and led to the busing of children to achieve racial balance in public schools. In *Roe v. Wade* (1973), the court struck down a Texas law banning abortion, except when the life of the mother was threatened. The *Roe v. Wade* decision contended that the Constitution extended a right of privacy that protected a woman's freedom to choose to have an abortion in the first three months of pregnancy.

The courts act as the final arbiter in the process of public policymaking. The legislative branch passes laws outlining the dimensions of public policy; the executive branch proposes, vetoes, or signs legislation; the judicial branch of government determines whether those are in accordance with or in violation of the U.S. Constitution. By approving or disapproving their behavior, the courts are a postaudit for policymakers.

Courts in the American political system are both subject to external influences and designed to be insulated from direct pressure. Judges generally either are elected (at the state and local level) or appointed (at the federal level). Selection is usually influenced by political pressure. A time lag often exists, yet public opinion and political philosophy affect the nature of courts. At the national level, the election of Presidents Nixon, Reagan, and Bush helped to establish a more conservative Supreme Court when contrasted to the philosophies of the Supreme Court of the 1960s.

The courts have become involved in various policy disputes in recent years. For example, in the area of education financing, state courts have addressed the issue of unequal funding levels for wealthy and poor school districts. In 1988, a trial court judge in Kentucky ruled that the state's financing system violated the Kentucky Constitution by providing inferior education to children in poorer school districts. As a result of this ruling, the governor and state legislature overhauled the state's education system in 1990. In 1989, the Texas Supreme Court declared that their state's system for education financing violated the Texas Constitution. The Texas legislature subsequently enacted education finance reform that was acceptable to the courts. In 1988, a New Jersey judge ruled that the state's school financing law did not comply with its constitution.[7]

These examples represent only a few of the instances where courts have become involved in the policy process. The important job of implementing public policy and delivering public sector services normally falls in the domain of the bureaucracy. Bureaucrats, particularly "street-level" bureaucrats such as policemen and teachers, have a tremendous impact on the day-to-day delivery of public policies.

The Bureaucracy and the Policy Process

Thousands of administrators are engaged in the implementation stage of the policy process. Administrators, or bureaucrats, hold power through their possession of technical skills, expertise, specialization, and access to information. All of these enable them to mold the views of other participants in the policy process.[8]

Implementation of policy is assigned to bureaucrats who often have to interpret vague directives. Legislators often write broad language into laws and omit details concerning how policies are to be implemented. Administrative agencies then define public policy through their interpretation of directives.

Bureaucracies have become adept at disregarding directives that they do not support. A number of maneuvers are employed by seasoned bureaucrats who have learned how to avoid compliance. Bureaucratic maneuvers that influence policy include not passing on orders, changing "cosmetics" but not reality, doing something else, delay, and obeying the letter but not the spirit of an order. Bureaucratic resistance undermines policies and negates the intent of legislation. Bureaucratic inaction occurs in both small details and major initiatives. Bureaucrats have resisted directives in trivial issues such as the naming of naval ships as well as more substantive policy matters such as school integration.[9]

Bureaucrats influence policy through the use of discretion, which is the ability of employees to choose how policy is implemented. In some cases, discretion of workers may be quite broad while in others discretion is severely limited. For example, it was reported that in 1971 in the city of San Antonio, there were 274,053 police reports, nearly a quarter of a million properties on the tax roll, 42,000 tons of asphalt allocated, and 125,000 new books ordered.[10] Bureaucrats had considerable discretion in prioritizing police cases, and in deciding which properties to assess, which potholes to fill, and which libraries would receive how many books. Discretion was somewhat limited by "decision-rules" of government organizations, which were defined as a rough mixture of professional norms, rules, and loose perceptions of needs.

"Street-level bureaucrats," such as teachers, social workers, parole officers, and police officers who deal with clients on the "street level," exercise a considerable amount of discretion.[11] Teachers have a prescribed curriculum yet may choose to emphasize certain elements of instruction, and police may choose to ignore some illegal actions but not others.

Congress, the executive, the courts, and the bureaucracy represent the major institutions that address issues of public policy. The institutional perspective, however, presents only one conception of policymaking. Public policy creation can also be viewed from other frames of reference. For example, policy can be viewed as an orderly process that follows a specific patterned sequence or as a more chaotic, random, and disorderly process.

NONINSTITUTIONAL VIEWS OF THE POLICY PROCESS

Policy as an Orderly Process

Some scholars contend that policymaking flows from an ordered sequence of activities. Initially, questions or problems are defined. A sufficient number of people then conceive of the question/problem as representing a real dilemma. These people are fairly well organized and have access to decision makers who place the question/problem on the policy agenda. Proposals are then formulated, support is generated, and if sufficient support exists, money is allocated. Following budget allocation, policies are implemented and finally evaluated. On the basis of evaluations, policies are adjusted, expanded, or terminated.[12]

An alternative description of the policy process identifies five distinct stages of activities: (1) problem identification and agenda setting, (2) formulation, (3) adoption, (4) implementation, and (5) evaluation.[13] Stage 1 (agenda setting) involves getting the government to consider action on a problem. The focus here is on agenda setting—that is, identifying and specifying the problems that may become the targets of public policies. In this stage, one asks why some conditions become public problems and others do not get placed on the policy agenda. Stage 2 (policy formulation) asks what is proposed to be done about the problem. This stage encompasses the creation or identification of proposed courses of action for resolving or ameliorating public problems. Stage 3 (adoption) involves deciding which proposed alternative, including taking no action, will be used to handle a problem. In American legislatures, proposed alternatives are adopted after they have been passed by a majority vote. The implementation stage (stage 4) is synonymous with administration. Attention focuses upon what needs to be done to carry a policy into effect. Often, further development or elaboration of policies occurs at this stage. Finally, stage 5 (policy evaluation) asks whether or not the policy worked. Activities are carried out at this stage to measure what a policy is accomplishing, whether it achieved its goals, or whether it had other consequences.[14]

The conceptual framework of *iron triangles* also explains the process of public policymaking. An iron triangle involves a pattern of stable relationships among (1) congressional committees or subcommittees, (2) an administrative agency or two, and (3) the relevant interest groups.

A relatively stable relationship has existed for many years between the congressional committees on veterans affairs, the Department of Veterans Affairs, and the American Legion. These three parts of the triangle (congressional committees, administrative agency, and interest group) form a tight, mutually advantageous alliance that works together to manage the flow of policy affecting veterans. Iron triangles have traditionally been viewed as a dominant, if not the dominant, explanation of policymaking. This concept, however, has been attacked in recent years as incomplete, and newer conceptualizations have been developed.[15]

Policy as a Disorderly Process

A newer concept of policymaking suggests that disorder is ever present in policymaking. In contrast to the orderly arrangements of iron triangles, the newer concept of issue networks posits that many more participants (public officials, interest group representatives, political activists, and policy experts from universities) are involved in the policy process. Within these "issue networks," direct material benefits are secondary in importance to intellectual or emotional rewards. Issue networks include numerous activists who wish to publicize issues in order to achieve change. This view stands in sharp contrast to the iron triangle perspective in which a few actors work quietly with trusted partners to obtain material rewards. The notion of iron triangles presumes small circles of participants, while issue networks comprise a large number of participants that move in and out of the networks constantly. In issue networks, no one appears to be in control of policies, and material interests are secondary in importance to intellectual or emotional commitment. Passion, ideals, and moral dedication replace material gain as a motivation for policy involvement. Actors in issue networks also try to keep problems complex in order to gain power and influence. Issue networks foster division, spawn extremists who support narrow interests, and thrive by keeping arguments brewing (see Table 1.2).[16]

Another contemporary view of public policy suggests that policy is produced through the connection of largely unrelated streams flowing through the system: (1) streams of problems, (2) streams of policies, and (3) streams of politics.[17] These three streams are believed to be largely independent of one another with each following its own rules. At some critical juncture, the three streams are joined. This coupling produces the greatest changes in public policy.

In regard to the first stream (problems), problems are brought to the attention of people in and around government by systematic indicators, events like crises or disasters, or by feedback from the current programs. Problems are identified by comparing current conditions with other periods of time or by comparing one government's performance with that of others.

In regard to the second stream (policies), many ideas are possible and float around in a "policy primeval soup." In this "soup," policy specialists try out their ideas in a variety of ways such as introducing bills, making speeches, testifying, publishing papers, and talking to others. In this "policy stream" proposals are floated; they come into contact with one another; they are revised; they are combined with other ideas; and they are reconsidered. To be seriously

TABLE 1.2 Issue Networks versus Iron Triangles

	Iron Triangle	Issue Network
Actors	Small stable group	Dispersed, numerous players
Interests	Economic gain	Intellectual and emotional gain
View of issues	Simple	Complex
Goals	Consensus, compromise, closure of debate	Division, zealotry, keep arguments boiling

considered, proposals must be technically feasible, must fit in with the dominant values, must be congruent with the current national mood, must have workable budgets, and must have political support.

The third stream (political) is composed of factors such as swings of national mood, interest group pressure, and legislative turnover. Agenda items are more likely to gain favor if they meet the following conditions: (1) they are consistent with the current national mood; (2) they are supported by interest groups or lack organized opposition; and (3) they fit orientations of the current administration or Congress.

The three separate streams (problem, policy, and political) come together at critical times. During these periods, solutions are coupled to problems, and both solutions and problems are connected to favorable political forces. The policy analyst John Kingdon has asserted that the coupling of policy streams is most likely when "policy windows" or opportunities for pushing pet proposals are open. Windows open either with the appearance of compelling problems or with events in the political stream. Agendas are set by problems or politics (streams one and three) and alternatives are generated in the political stream (stream two). People who are willing to invest their resources in pushing pet proposals or problems (policy entrepreneurs) are responsible for both prompting important people to pay attention and for coupling streams together.[18]

Disorder and untidiness are inherent to this "policy stream" perspective of policymaking. The "untidy" perspective of policymaking has long been recognized by major historical figures such as Otto von Bismarck, first chancellor of the German Empire, from 1871 to 1890. Bismarck characterized policymaking as being very similar to making sausage, a very messy process that can nevertheless produce very favorable outcomes.

A MODEL OF POLICYMAKING

The above descriptions of conceptions of the policy process provide some insight. They do not, however, tell the whole story, since they do not give adequate attention to other aspects of policymaking. In an effort to present a broader conceptualization, this book presents a model that focuses upon how the constructs of Rationality, Power, and Ideology influence policymaking. This model does not deny the relevance of political institutions (such as Congress, the executive, the courts, and the bureaucracy) but asserts that policy analysts should also consider less visible (Rationality, Power, and Ideology) influences on public policy.

What Is a Model?

What is a model, and how can it help us to understand the complex process of public policymaking? Can a policy model help in understanding why public sector officials choose to enact policy A, instead of policy B, or policy C? This is the fundamental question of public policy.

To address this question, this book develops a policymaking model that serves as a framework for discussing substantive policy issues such as budgeting, agriculture, environmental, urban, "intermestic" (linkage between international and domestic policies), education, health, family, and welfare policy.

A model is an abstraction or representation of political life that serves to (1) order and simplify reality, (2) identify what is significant, (3) provide meaningful communication, (4) direct research, and (5) suggest explanations.[19] Models are conceptual frameworks or lenses to view a series of events. Each conceptual framework or lens consists of a cluster of assumptions, which influence problem identification, data collection, and analysis. Models also help to select which policies should be chosen.

Another definition of a model maintains that the term is most appropriately applied in connection with scientific theory couched in certain styles. Under this definition, one system is a model of another system if the study of the first system is useful for understanding the other.[20]

The Rationality, Power, Ideology (RPI) Model

The RPI model provides the framework for the text. It departs from the traditional institutional focus as it examines the influences of three policy inputs. This model posits that the institutional perspective is not so much inappropriate as incomplete. Analysts also need to understand the less visible influences that are exerted on official policymakers. Reduced to its most fundamental elements, the RPI model contends that the policy inputs (rationality, power, ideology) influence American institutions that produce official public policies. Policy outputs in turn feed back to affect inputs. Rationality, power, and ideology are not independent but interact with each other to exert policy influence.

It is necessary to develop new models of studying public policy, since traditional perspectives are showing signs of age.[21] The institutional approach is not an invalid means of studying policy, but it is incomplete. It does not tell the whole story, a story that is greatly enriched by discussion of how factors such as rationality, power, and ideology influence public policy.

Institutional analysis provides images of policy outputs but doesn't provide background information about why those policies were enacted. In a baseball analogy, one may watch a ballplayer hit a home run but not really understand how he did it. The visible act is clear enough, but the details behind the scenes are not. How many hours a day did he practice batting? Did he lift weights over the years to build strength? How much weight could he lift? Did he study the pitcher's repertoire? Did he prepare mentally through positive thinking? What preparation, conditioning, and behavior prepared him for his day in the sun?

In such a manner, it is useful to understand influences on policymaking. One can readily observe the end product of policy (the output), but it is more difficult to understand background inputs. The RPI model presents the opportunity for learning more about such inputs.

Rationality, Power, Ideology

At times, rationality can influence public policy. Policy "experts" often are called to testify about specific issues. Policy analysts within government organizations monitor program effectiveness using rational techniques and make recommendations for periodic changes. Experts serve in advisory roles to political decision makers who consider many other factors in the course of their deliberations. Rationality contends that it is technically possible to define goals and to objectively measure the utility of programs. Calculation and consideration of benefits, as well as costs, are important components of rationality. The rationality input relies heavily on empirical analysis and methodological tools such as statistics, scientific procedures, and experimental designs.[22] From the perspective of rationality, policy is a matter of (1) defining one's goals, (2) listing all options for achieving those goals, (3) evaluating the effectiveness of each, and (4) choosing the best option.

Policy can also be studied from a perspective of power. Interest groups, citizens, and influential individuals influence policy through lobbying, voting, shaping public opinion, or contributing to political campaigns. Struggles exist between various interests in society. Health care providers, environmentalists, moralists, gun owners, and tobacco growers represent just a few of the players actively involved in contemporary policy disputes. Examination of the relative power of such actors is useful in understanding policy.

Assumptions and views of the world shape the policy process as well. Policy can be studied in order to gain insight into the relevance of specific philosophical viewpoints. Policy reflects values or coherent sets of beliefs of members of societies since policy actors consciously or unconsciously respond to philosophical guideposts. The input of ideology therefore can be a useful tool for explaining policy. Examples of how ideology affects policy abound. If one assumes that welfare payments reduce incentive and create dependency, one might advocate limits on the number of years someone is qualified to receive welfare payments. However, if one assumes that welfare payments provide necessary relief for individuals in times of stress and are a minimum support level for humane societies, then one may advocate a different position. Investigation of the ascendancy or decline of specific sets of assumptions is therefore useful in understanding public policy.

CONCLUSIONS

In this book, we have chosen to focus attention on the three policy inputs of rationality, power, and ideology. We do not wish to suggest that these are the only factors that influence policy. We do assert, however, that these factors, individually and in concert with each other, influence policy. All three influences are identifiable in high-profile issues such as abortion.

Rationality appears in the abortion issue in regard to the definition of a "viable" fetus. Acceptance or rejection of "rational" definitions, however, is usually a function of bias toward one highly emotional set of convictions or another. Terms such as "choice" or "life" are surrogates for deeply held ideological positions. Interaction between inputs develop as groups supporting either "choice" or "life" positions (ideological groups) place pressure on institutions by presenting favorable data (rational input), by lobbying (power input), and by proselytizing their view (ideological input). The commingling of inputs muddles and obfuscates the policy process.

Public policy is like the blind man and the elephant. It can be many things to different people. Various blind individuals, separately feeling the elephant's tail, ears, tusks, legs, and body, will have different images of the animal. Acquiring an understanding of public policy can be even more puzzling. Students of public policy are not blind, but they choose to focus upon certain aspects of policy and not others. They incorrectly believe that in their analysis they are getting the "full scoop," and they ignore aspects of public policy that may be of larger importance.

A policymaking model that identifies underlying influences on policy creation is a helpful guide to understanding American public policy and serves as a hub around which the rest of the book will revolve. Chapter 2 will describe in detail the policymaking model. Chapters 3 through 11 discuss individual policies through the lens of the policymaking model. The concluding chapter discusses enduring policy challenges as well as forces that are likely to shape the future.

Suggested Readings

Dunn, William. *Public Policy Analysis: An Introduction.* Englewood Cliffs, NJ: Prentice-Hall, 1981.

Easton, David. *A Framework for Political Analysis.* Englewood Cliffs, NJ: Prentice-Hall, 1965.

Jones, Charles. *An Introduction to the Study of Public Policy.* Belmont, CA: Wadsworth, 1970.

Kingdon, John. *Agendas, Alternatives, and Public Policies.* Boston: Little, Brown, 1984.

Lindblom, Charles E. *The Policy-Making Process.* Englewood Cliffs, NJ: Prentice-Hall, 1968.

Mazmanian, Daniel A., and Paul A. Sabatier. *Implementation and Public Policy.* Glenview, IL: Scott, Foresman, 1983.

Rourke, Francis. *Bureaucracy, Politics and Public Policy,* 2nd ed. Boston: Little, Brown, 1976.

Notes

1. James Anderson, *Public Policymaking,* 2nd ed. (Boston: Houghton Mifflin, 1990); Clarke Cochrane, Lawrence Mayer, T. R. Carr, and N. Joseph Cayer, *American Public Policy: An Introduction,* 4th ed. (New York: St. Martin's Press, 1993; Thomas Dye, *Understanding Public Policy* (Englewood Cliffs, NJ: Prentice-Hall, 1995); Heinz Eula and Kenneth Prewitt, *Labyrinths of Democracy* (Indianapolis: Bobbs-Merrill, 1973); David Easton, *The Political System,* 2nd ed. (New York: Knopf, 1965); Charles Jones, *An Introduction to the Study of Public Policy,* 3rd ed. (Monterey, CA: Brooks/Cole, 1984); Harold Lasswell and Abraham Kaplan, *Power and Society* (New Haven, CT: Yale University Press, 1970).

2. George Greenberg, Jeffrey Miller, Lawrence Mohr, and Bruce Vladeck, "Developing Public Policy Theory: Perspectives from Empirical Research," *American Political Science Review* 71 (4), pp. 1532–1543.

3. John P. Heinz, Edward O. Caumann, Robert L. Nelson, and Robert Salisbury, *The Hollow Core: Private Interests in National Policy Making* (Cambridge, MA: Harvard University Press, 1993).

4. G. William Domhoff, *The Power Elite and the State: How Policy Is Made in America* (New York: Aldine DeGruyter), p. 165.

5. Charles Merriam, *Systematic Politics* (Chicago: University of Chicago Press, 1945), pp. 31–55.

6. Aaron Wildavsky, "The Two Presidencies," *Transaction* 4 (2), December 1966.

7. Christopher Smith, *Courts and Public Policy* (Chicago: Nelson Hall Publishers, 1993), p. 91.

8. Frances Rourke, *Bureaucracy, Politics and Public Policy,* 3rd ed. (Boston: Little, Brown, 1984), pp. 15–18.

9. Morton Halperin, *Bureaucratic Politics and Foreign Policy* (Washington, DC: Brookings Institution, 1974), p. 280.

10. Robert Lineberry, *Equality and Urban Policy: The Distribution of Municipal Services* (Beverly Hills: Sage, 1977), p. 154.

11. Michael Lipsky, *Street Level Bureaucracy* (New York: Russell Sage Foundation, 1980), p. 13.

12. Charles Jones, *An Introduction to the Study of Public Policy,* 3rd ed. (Monterey, CA: Brooks/Cole, 1984), pp. 27–28.

13. James Anderson, *Public Policymaking,* 2nd ed. (Boston: Houghton Mifflin, 1994), p. 38.

14. Ibid.

15. Hugh Heclo, "Issue Networks and the Executive Establishment," in *Public Administration,* ed. R. Stillman, 5th ed. (Boston: Houghton Mifflin, 1992), pp. 429–439.

16. Ibid.

17. John Kingdon, *Agendas, Alternatives, and Public Policies* (Boston: Little, Brown, 1984), p. 19.

18. Ibid., p. 20.

19. Thomas Dye, *Understanding Public Policy,* 8th ed. (Englewood Cliffs, NJ: Prentice-Hall, 1995), pp. 40–41.

20. Abraham Kaplan, *The Conduct of Inquiry: Methodology for Behavioral Science* (New York: Crowell, 1964), p. 263.

21. Paul Sabatier, "Toward Better Theories of the Policy Process" *PS* 24 (June 1991), pp. 147–156.

22. William Dunn, *Public Policy Analysis,* 2nd ed. (Englewood Cliffs, NJ: Prentice-Hall, 1994); and Lawrence Mohr, *Impact Analysis for Program Evaluation* (Pacific Grove, CA: Brooks/Cole, 1988).

2

A Policymaking Model: Rationality, Power, Ideology (RPI)

INTRODUCTION

Policy is influenced by numerous forces and actors who interact with one another in complex relationships. To understand more fully how policy is made, it is important to identify the key actors who influence the policy process. This chapter describes a model that focuses on the impacts of rationality, power, and ideology on public policy. The model posits that explanations of how the three inputs operate will provide readers with a fuller understanding of public policy. The model focuses upon the less visible, noninstitutional forces that influence policy. A virtue of this model is that it identifies underlying pressures on "official" actors, whose activities are reported frequently in the media and appear to represent the real policy action. Forces that exert pressure just below the surface, however, are also meaningful and may be even more salient than the official forces. This less visible component is explained in the RPI model that is developed throughout this book.

A Model for Understanding Policy (RPI Model)

Models provide insights and simplify complex phenomena. The model developed in this book assesses how the three policy inputs of power, rationality, and ideology affect public policy. In short, the RPI model contends that institutions do not exist in a vacuum but are influenced by numerous outside forces. Rationality, power, and ideology focus attention on what we believe to be key forces that affect American public policy. In focusing attention on these forces, we do not wish to imply that other factors are not important. We believe, however, that investigation of RPI factors will contribute greatly toward a more extensive understanding of how public policy is made in the United States.

Typically, public policy is studied through analysis of institutions. Such analysis, however, only examines the most visible manifestations of underlying forces ' in society. Institutional analysis therefore represents only the tip of a formidable iceberg, an iceberg whose underpinnings include inputs from rational analysis, philosophical thought, and powerful interests. The relationships among the inputs of rationality, power, ideology, the major American institutions, and policy outputs are presented in Figure 2.1.

Figure 2.1 describes the interrelationship between power, rationality, ideology, political institutions, and public policy. The model presented in the figure represents an open system in which policy outputs interact with the three inputs. In explaining how such interaction occurs, it could be argued, for example, that the lack of popular support for some of the outputs of Lyndon Johnson's Great Society program undermined ideological support for those policies. This lack of support eventually led to the election of presidents and congressional representatives who held more conservative positions and who consequently passed more conservative legislation. Similarly, use of analytical tools to pursue the war in Vietnam (implemented by Secretary of Defense Robert McNamara) undermined the credibility of rational policy analysis. The power of military contractors diminished as perceptions of public policies filtered through the environment. Negative perceptions of the military in turn eroded the power of military contractors to push for higher levels of spending. Subsequently, the public policies of lower defense spending and perceptions of American vulnerability (especially following the Iran hostage crisis of 1979) produced a backlash

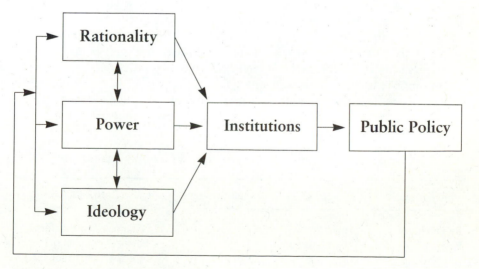

FIGURE 2.1 RPI Policymaking Model

and a new shift in the policy pendulum. When Ronald Reagan was elected in 1980, defense spending grew, states tied to the defense industry prospered, and defense contractors enjoyed "fat" times.

Figure 2.1 depicts the interaction between the three inputs of the RPI model as well as the direct impact of the three inputs on institutions. In the example of policies associated with the Vietnam War, discrediting McNamara's rational policies (witnessed in body counts, computer printouts, and targeted bombing) reduced the credibility of the rational input. Perceived policy failure also weakened the acceptance of the philosophical underpinnings supportive of the war effort. The "domino theory," or belief that small countries could fall to Communism like dominos and that America was defending freedom and democracy against the growth of totalitarianism, fell into disrepute. An ideology that justified opposition to the war grew in popularity.

The RPI model of policymaking identifies various factors that shape policy through political institutions. These factors possess some similarities (e.g., they all influence policy) as well as some differences (e.g., power attempts to shape policy for personal gain while ideology attempts to implement a "correct" vision.) The model allows us to note differences between the three inputs in terms of the types of actors that dominate each input, the desired type of environment for each input, and the desired payoff. Table 2.1 identifies distinct differences.

As described in Table 2.1, the rationality input is linked to actors who are recognized as "experts." These so-called experts wish to wrap themselves in cloaks of objectivity and purport to produce policy that will maximize the collective benefit or benefits to all, for a given amount of resources. In contrast, the power input is linked to self-interested actors who wish to acquire personal benefits. These actors have an interest in operating within a relatively closed, stable structure as they seek to maximize personal rewards. The ideology input is linked to polemical actors who try to polarize issues in efforts to foster what they believed to be "correct" behavior for society. The ideological input is associated with emotional rather than material rewards and with polarized environments involving many actors engaged in continuous debate.

Both power and ideology exert strong independent influences on policy. The independent effect of rationality appears to be more muted since rationality is often utilized to enhance the positions of the other two inputs. Vested interests

TABLE 2.1 Actors, Environments, and Desired Payoffs for Policy Inputs

Policy Inputs	Actors	Environments	Desired Payoff
Rationality	Experts	Objectivity	Maximize benefits for all
Power	Self-interested	Closed	Personal material gain
Ideology	Polemicists	Polarized	"Correct" vision for society

or ideological forces often sponsor rational studies in order to promote their personal gain or their vision of the "good" society. Numerous access points exist for powerful forces to assert themselves in policy debates. Campaign contributions can ensure a place at the table when policy matters are discussed. Certain groups lobby for their policy preferences and at times subvert the wishes of the general public. The failure of the Clinton administration to garner adequate support for passage of sweeping health care reform attests to the ability of powerful groups to block policy initiatives that they believe would be harmful to their interests.

Ideology also can affect policy through the intellectual battle for the "hearts and minds" of both elites and average citizens. Ideology is disseminated through the media, through control of research foundations, or through teaching that is conducted at major universities. Policy experts claim to be unbiased scientists, but their biases are often unavoidable. Critics of the rational policy perspective contend that it may be impossible to conduct studies rationally, or that even if it were possible to conduct studies rationally, results would be distorted to fit the needs of powerful forces in society.

Rational, power, and ideological perspectives are discussed in greater detail below to illustrate further how they influence policy. These three influences on public policy are integral parts of a framework that guide this book.

THE CONCEPTS OF RATIONALITY, POWER, AND IDEOLOGY (RPI)

Rationality

The Rational-Comprehensive Perspective

Public policymaking can be viewed as an outcome of rational decisions made to maximize the use of scarce public sector resources. The rational-comprehensive theory of policymaking is grounded in the scientific approach, which prioritizes objective analysis or analysis that is untarnished by the personal biases of individual researchers. The rational-comprehensive method, or what has been termed the root method, involves a number of specific steps such as: clarifying values, developing means to accomplish goals, and choosing the most appropriate means to achieve desired results. In the root method, (1) objectives are clarified and values are considered, (2) the means to reach specific goals are investigated, (3) decisions are evaluated on the basis of attaining some specific objective, (4) every important relevant factor is taken into consideration, and (5) theory is heavily relied on.[1]

From time to time, government agencies have engaged in what appears to be rational analysis. Department of Defense studies aimed at choosing which military bases to close provide interesting examples of rational decision making. In 1990, in an effort to produce findings that were grounded in rationality,

Congress passed the Defense Base Closure and Realignment Act. This Act established very specific criteria for evaluating the termination or continuation of military bases. The Army used a two-phased approach in evaluating bases for possible closure, on the basis of their mission category and military value. To evaluate military value, the Army developed measures of merit and assigned weights to indicate the relative importance of bases. The Air Force and Navy also devised their own rational approaches to base-closing recommendations.[2]

The rational-comprehensive perspective tries to place public policy within a framework of order, objectivity, and businesslike proficiency. A description of rational action includes the following:[3]

1. *Goals and objectives.* These are translated into "payoffs" that represent the value of alternative consequences. All sets of consequences are ranked and side effects of alternatives are considered.
2. *Alternatives.* Rational actors choose from sets of alternatives displayed before them in a particular situation.
3. *Consequences.* A set of consequences is attached to each alternative.
4. *Choice.* The alternative whose consequences rank the highest, according to the decision makers' calculations, is chosen.

Rationality is a powerful concept because it can account for behavior in terms of a few simple assumptions about goals people are trying to achieve. The concept of rationality, however, is complex for a number of reasons. One factor adding to its complexity is the idea that there is not one discrete type of rationality but there are multiple bases of rationality, including:

1. *Technical rationality,* which involves the comparison of alternatives according to their capacity to promote solutions for public problems;
2. *Economic rationality,* which involves the comparison of alternatives according to their cost;
3. *Legal rationality,* which involves comparison of alternatives according to their legal conformity to established rules and precedents;
4. *Social rationality,* which considers alternatives according to their capacity to maintain or improve social institutions.[4]

Limits of Rationality

Criticisms of the rational-comprehensive framework abound. One author states:

> Unfortunately, comprehensive rationality remains a utopian ideal for most policy areas. The model is extremely demanding, as it requires high levels of consensus and knowledge base unlikely to be attained very often. For example, the model requires initially that decision makers agree on the precise nature of the problem they face. There is no guarantee, however, that a particular problem will be perceived at all, or that all actors will necessarily define it the same way. There are no commonly accepted criteria for distinguishing legitimately public problems from private concerns. . . .

Finally, the rational model presumes a capacity to estimate accurately the consequences of all relevant alternatives that is often beyond the reach of policy makers.[5]

Other critiques of the rational-comprehensive method state that optimal choice and the rational-comprehensive model are unrealistic because:

1. Policymakers do not have the time, money, or information to investigate all alternatives to existing policy;
2. Policymakers accept the legitimacy of previous policy because of the uncertainty of completely different policies;
3. There may be heavy investment in existing programs that precludes radical change;
4. Only small changes are politically expedient;
5. People are practical in terms of investing time and energy into looking for solutions that may not be significantly better than the situation at hand; they rarely search for the one best solution;
6. In the absence of agreed upon societal goals, it is easier for government to continue existing programs.[6]

Because of perceived problems with the rational-comprehensive approach, a strategy of piecemeal, marginal choice has been advanced. In such a strategy, instead of spelling out all the possible causes and consequences of alternative policy options, policymakers proceed in small steps. "Satisficing" is achieved, rather than maximizing, due to the fact that policymakers aim for tolerable levels of satisfaction in their choice of alternatives. The fundamental premise of satisficing holds that the first alternative encountered that meets or exceeds the decision maker's minimum expectations will be chosen. If a satisfactory alternative is not found after an initial search, the decision maker's expectations and the minimum standards will decline.

Satisficing is practiced because rationality is bounded. Herbert Simon stated that human beings satisfice because "they do not have the wits to maximize." Whereas economic man maximizes (selects the best alternative from among all those available to him), his cousin, administrative man looks for a course of action that is "good enough." Economic man deals with the complexity of the "real world," while administrative man interprets the world as a drastic simplification of reality. Administrative man is content with simplification because he believes that most facts of the real world do not relate to him. Administrative man makes choices using a simple picture of the situation that takes into account just a few of the factors that are considered to be most relevant and crucial.[7]

While the rational-comprehensive method has been attacked as unrealistic, analysts constantly strive to achieve its goals. The presence of the rational approach is witnessed in the emerging field of public policy analysis. Public policy analysis is employed to improve the quality of public policy decisions and has found its way into traditional social science disciplines such as economics, sociology, and political science. Many view it as a growth field in both academics and the public sector.

Public Policy Analysis

Policy analysis represents a systematic and data-based alternative to intuitive policymaking. As a tool for decision makers, it includes numerous analytical techniques and sophisticated forms of analysis.[8] These methodologies are designed to identify solutions to public policy problems. The destruction of the U.S. spacecraft *Challenger* in 1986 represents the type of problem that is readily addressed through policy analysis. This situation demanded answers to specific questions such as: Why did the spacecraft explode? What design changes could prevent future disasters? How quickly could the changes be made? How much would they cost? To what extent would future risks be reduced? These questions and others are directly addressed in policy analysis.

Policy analysis of one sort or another can trace its roots back to the beginning of modern time. In nineteenth-century America, the development of public policy was viewed as a product of bankers, industrialists, and the Victorian middle class. These interests believed that new methods of inquiry were necessary to meet novel challenges. A specific motivator of policy analysis during this period was uncertainty over the new class of industrial workers that populated large cities. Policy questions were very pragmatic: How much money did urban workers need to maintain themselves and their families? How much money did they have to earn before they could be taxed? How much money did they have to save to pay for medical treatment and education? How much would the government need to invest in day care facilities to allow a significant number of mothers of young children to work? How much investment in public works projects (sanitation, sewage, housing) was needed to maintain adequate public health and to protect the middle and upper classes from infectious diseases? Social scientists responded to these questions by generating specific, quantitative, and policy-relevant information.

The twentieth century was marked by the professionalization of social science disciplines such as political science, sociology, and economics. During this time, producers of policy information were likely to be university professors who specialized in teaching and research. Governments increasingly called on these individuals to provide practical advice on policymaking and government administration. Social scientists played an active role in the administrations of Woodrow Wilson and Herbert Hoover. The greatest influx of social scientists into government, however, came during the administration of Franklin D. Roosevelt.

World War II greatly expanded opportunities for policy analysts to demonstrate their value in solving practical problems. Following World War II, growth in policy analysis did not come from social scientists but from more technically oriented fields such as engineering, operations research, systems analysis, and applied mathematics. The primary orientation of these fields was technical, with the broader political, social, and administrative aspects of public policy going largely ignored.

By the 1970s, a number of organizations related to the social sciences became more involved in policy analysis. Organizations such as the Policy Studies

Organization (political science), the Society for the Study of Social Problems (sociology), and the Society for the Psychological Study of Social Issues (psychology) were established as academics became more engaged in practical policy concerns. By the 1980s, multidisciplinary professional associations were established. In Washington, as well as in state capitals, "policy analyst" became an official job description, and policy analysis became one of the growing knowledge-based industries of American postindustrial society.[9]

To summarize, the concept of rationality, as it applies to public policy, is rooted in the view that (1) problems can be identified, analyzed, and addressed; (2) policies can be adopted that are superior to alternatives; (3) policymakers will utilize analytical procedures; (4) policymakers will maximize some agreed upon value; (5) policymakers are nonbiased, adhering to objective principles of analysis.

In addition to rationality, the issue of power is also viewed as an important input into the policymaking process. The power framework, however, is more difficult to measure, as a result of hidden actors. From the power perspective, policy simply is the preferences of those who have the ability to force or entice others to follow their wishes.

Power

The distributions of power in society and its impact on policy have sparked debate in America and elsewhere. In the United States, controversy has ensued between three parties: those who believe that power is (1) concentrated in what has been termed a ruling class, (2) controlled by a power elite within organizations, or (3) distributed more widely in what has been termed pluralism. These perspectives are discussed here in an effort to more fully understand the relationship between power and public policy.

Briefly stated, the ruling class perspective identifies power in a social class structure, which usually reflects the economically dominant class. This class exerts control through political institutions. The concept of the power elite, on the other hand, associates power with high-ranking positions in organizational hierarchies. This concept was popularized by the sociologist C. Wright Mills, who claimed that America was ruled by officials in three hierarchies: the private sector corporations, the executive branch of the federal government, and the military.[10] Ruling class theory differs from the power elite view in that ruling class membership is defined in terms of social standing rather than positions in institutional hierarchies.[11]

In contrast to these perspectives, which see power as being highly concentrated in a relatively small number of individuals, pluralists emphasize political consensus, broad participation in the political process, and group activity. Pluralist theory contends that political resources (money, prestige, expertise, organizational ability) are widely dispersed. As a result of this dispersion, policies must follow a complex pattern of political negotiation, compromise, and shifting alliances. Policies are not viewed as simply following a mandate from an all-powerful elite. Pluralists acknowledge that political resources are not equally distributed; nevertheless they assert that resources are sufficiently divided for many interests to have a chance to affect the outcome of a policy decision.[12] The various conceptions on the distribution of power are described more fully below.

Ruling Class

Historically, many studies have identified ruling class relationships, in which a small group comes to dominate all others. Perhaps the most succinct statement of such a structure was offered by Gaetano Mosca, who stated that all societies break down according to two classes—those who rule and those who are ruled:

> In all societies—from societies that are very meagerly developed and have barely attained the dawning of civilization, down to the most advanced and powerful societies—two classes of people appear—a class that rules and a class that is ruled. The first class, always the less numerous, performs all political functions, monopolizes power and enjoys the advantages that power brings, whereas the second, the more numerous class, is directed and controlled by the first in a manner that is now more or less legal, now more or less arbitrary and violent, and supplies the first, in appearance at least, with material means of subsistence.[13]

Many studies have addressed the question of ruling class at the community level. Early studies of community power seemed to belie the ideal notion of democracy and claimed that a definitive class structure based upon income, education, and occupation existed. A statement from a classic study of Muncie, Indiana, provides an illustration of the degree of control elites seemed to exercise at the local level:

> If I'm out of work I go to the X plant; if I need money I go to the X bank, and if they don't like me I don't get it; my children go to the X college; when I get sick I go to the X hospital; I buy a building lot or house in an X subdivision; my wife goes downtown to buy clothes at the X department store; if my dog stays away he is put in the X pound; I buy X milk; I drink X beer, vote for X political parties, and get help from X charities; my boy goes to the X Y.M.C.A. and my girl to their Y.W.C.A.; I listen to the word of God in X-subsidized churches; if I'm a Mason I go to the X Masonic Temple; I read the news from the X morning newspaper, and if I am rich enough, I travel via the X airport.[14]

Evidence of concentration of power was also uncovered at the national level. During the Great Depression enormous concentrations of wealth were identified to be located in the hands of just sixty families. It was believed by some critics that such concentrations of wealth eroded the value of elections and undermined the concept of democracy.[15]

More recently, claims of a national ruling class have surfaced. This class is perceived as owning a disproportionate amount of the country's wealth, receiving a disproportionate amount of the country's income, and contributing a disproportionate amount of its members to the controlling institutions in the country. This "national ruling class" was said to comprise at most 0.5 to 1.0

percent of the population of the United States, with its core made up of wealthy business people and their descendants. These individuals provided leadership for top banks and corporations. They exerted influence through their positions on boards of directors of numerous companies (interlocking directorships) and through ownership of common stock. Consistent with this perspective, the ruling class supplies corporations with legal advice and also controls the limits of permissible debate. Members of the national upper class were believed to exercise influence over elite universities, the dominant firms in the mass media, the executive branch of the national government, regulatory agencies, the federal judiciary, the military, the CIA, and the FBI.[16]

The ruling class conception of power emphasizes social class distinctions. An alternative (power elite) view focuses upon the role of large organizations in American society. The power elite theory contends that important actors are corporate executives, political leaders, and military officials. These elites exercise power through decision making in their organizations.

Power Elite

Following World War II, concern with the concentration of power in American society and its impact on democracy led to the identification of a power elite. This group was believed to command the major institutional hierarchies and organizations of modern society: big corporations, government, and the military. In the power elite model, power is an attribute of organizational position. According to the major proponent of the power elite perspective, C. Wright Mills,

> power is not of a man. Wealth does not center in the person of the wealthy. Celebrity is not inherent in any personality. To be celebrated, to be wealthy, to have power, requires access to major institutions, for the institutional positions men occupy determine in large part their chances to have and to hold these valued experiences.[17]

The basic argument of power elite theorists posits that governance is dominated by a few top leaders, most of whom are outside the public sector. These leaders enjoy great advantages in wealth, status, or organizational position. Institutional elites maintain a consensus regarding fundamental American values such as the place of private enterprise, the virtue of limited government, and the value of due process. Disagreements are narrowly focused on means to reach specific ends rather than on a more fundamental disagreement over ends.[18]

The power elite theory stresses the role of organizations and managerial elites who can convert the public into a mass society of subordinate, passive individuals. This mass society is created through a breakdown of attachments to religious, ethnic, community, neighborhood, and class groupings. These attachments break down as individuals and families become socially isolated, atomized, and fragmented. The power elite theory asserts that this process of fragmentation and detachment is abetted by the mass media.[19] The power elite perspective has been rejected by many who propose that a much wider distribution of power exists in the United States. Such a distribution of power is consistent with the pluralist point of view.

Pluralism

In the 1950s and 1960s, scholars such as Robert Dahl and David Truman defended a model of politics that viewed democracy as a two-fold process involving competition among political elites and bargaining among interest groups. The underlying assumption of this pluralist doctrine was that political power is and ought to be wielded by a number of groups rather than by any single set of interests.[20] Pluralism has been defined as:

> A model of political decision making in which multiple and competing elites determine public policy through a process of bargaining and compromise. Pluralism posits that the best policy decisions emerge from clashes of interest groups in the political arena, where issues are freely and openly discussed, and where an overall balance of power is maintained.[21]

Pluralist theory concentrates upon the idea that power, or the ability to make decisions in American society, is diffuse and attained through a process of bargaining. Since power is believed to be fairly widely distributed, pluralists emphasize the role of groups and multiple sources of influence in public policy.[22] In the *Federalist Papers*, a series of newspaper articles defending the Constitution, James Madison, "father of the Constitution" and fourth president of the United States, discussed the distribution of power in America. In "Federalist 10," Madison claimed that the Constitution was designed to control the power of interest groups (which he called "factions") and that the Constitution could successfully prevent the concentration of power in the nation. Madison also believed that the Constitution would prevent tyranny of the majority (mob rule) through the concept of representation. Under this concept, the people would not govern directly but would instead govern indirectly through their elected representatives. Madison believed that the large size of the nation worked against domination by the few. He hypothesized that the larger and more diverse the nation, the less likely it was that an unjust group could dominate.[23]

Three features of the American political system were identified for their ability to disperse power:

1. The separation of power among the legislative, executive, and judicial branches,
2. The separation of the national government from state and local governments,
3. The widespread participation of individual citizens in voluntary associations.[24]

Pluralist theory shifted the focus of democratic government from the mass electorate to organized groups. Under the theory of pluralism, the criterion for democratic governance changed from responsiveness to mass public opinion to responsiveness to organized groups of citizens.[25] Pluralism, in general, relates closely to what has been termed group theory. This theory maintains that public policy is the product of continual struggle among groups since every man and woman is a product of life in groups, in which political attitudes, opinions, orientations, and preferences are formed.[26]

The pluralist view suggests that power is tamed through the existence of multiple centers of influence. This view is in sharp contrast with the power elite and ruling class perspectives, which see power as highly concentrated in the few who exercise authority through mechanisms such as interlocking directorates or control of institutions.

The third input into the policymaking described in Figure 2.1 views policy as a conflict of ideological values. This input contributes to our understanding of public policy in the sense that ideologies are idea-based, and ideas often lead to specific policy-related legislation or other policy-related activity.

Ideology

Ideology deals with belief systems that simplify complexity and shape views of how the world works. In the past, ideologies such as marxism, anarchism, socialism, capitalism, and totalitarianism have been associated with specific world views. In American society, concepts such as equity, fairness, freedom, opportunity, liberty, and justice are shaped by frames of references that can loosely be termed ideologies.

What Is Ideology?

Ideology is not a simple concept to grasp, and attempts to explain its meanings has produced an enormous quantity of literature. Various conceptions and definitions of ideology have been refined over time. Three important senses stand out: (1) to refer to very specific kinds of beliefs, (2) to refer to beliefs that are in some sense distorted or false, and (3) to refer to any set of beliefs, covering everything from scientific knowledge, to religion, to everyday beliefs about proper conduct, irrespective of whether such beliefs are true or false.[27]

Ideology represents a set of images and expectations, like a road map, for interpreting the complexity of the world. Because ideologies rest on deeply rooted values and unconscious assumptions, they provide an easy conceptual tool for interpreting the world. Ideologies usually contain the following characteristics:

1. They deal with questions about who will be the rulers, how rulers will be selected, and by what principles they will govern;
2. They constitute an argument, intended to persuade, and contradict, opposing views;
3. They affect major values of life;
4. They embrace a program for the defense, reform, or abolition of important societal institutions;
5. They are, in part, rationalizations of group interests; and
6. They are normative, ethical, or moral in tone and content.[28]

Ideologies may represent any reasonably coherent body of moral, economic, social, or cultural ideas that refer to political power, remain alive for a considerable period of time, have major advocates, and possess a respectable degree of institutionalization. Ideologies also represent values, or a belief system, that provide a picture of the world, both as it is and as it should be. Ideologies attempt to organize the tremendous complexity of the world into something fairly simple and understandable. Conceptions of how the world should be appear in terms of something better than the past or present. For example, Marxist visions, as well as other perspectives, claim to provide a map for a better society. Visions of these societies usually are expressed in materialistic terms and include a definite plan of action, as well as a sense of urgency.[29] Urgency may be noted in terms of economic deprivation or other injustices.

Ideologies do not exist solely as theoretical constructs but also perform practical functions. These practical functions include

1. Setting up standards of behavior,
2. Providing individual identity and a sense of belonging,
3. Achieving social solidarity and cohesion,
4. Engendering optimism, hope, or promise,
5. Supporting and maintaining a political regime,
6. Challenging a political regime,
7. Serving as instruments for the manipulation and control of the people.[30]

The concept of political ideology has also been viewed from the perspective of a system of ideas about a government that includes answers to a number of questions about who rules, whose interests prevail, and whose attitudes toward the role of government will predominate.

Ideologies also provide a means by which vested interests justify their actions. They can legitimize even the most heinous action, if such action is believed to be necessary for the attainment of the greater good. For example, Marxist ideology has been used to justify elimination of the aristocratic or the capitalist classes on grounds that they oppress the working classes. Nazi ideology attempted to justify eliminating whole races of people in order to to create a master race. Capitalist ideology has tried to justify massive differences in wealth since they create incentives for thrift and diligence. Traditionally, ideologies have served to reassure vested interests and to provide legitimacy for the status quo:

> The powerful have to reassure themselves, as well as convince others, of the rightness of their might: that power is a trust held for the common good rather than self-advantage. The powerless, on the other hand, need to believe either that they are not exploited or, if they nurture a grievance and desire political change, that right is on their side.[31]

Ideologies have often mobilized elements of the largely apathetic public. They accomplish this goal by defining a moral vehicle for change. Such vehicles have been used throughout history in order to bring about cataclysmic change. The French, Russian, and Iranian revolutions provide examples of such massive upheaval. Ideology can also play a role in providing a rationale for less drastic change. Specific public policy questions, such as whether tax levels are too high, whether the narrowly focused pursuit of profit is detrimental to society, whether crime prevention is feasible, whether choice in education should be pursued, or whether alternative lifestyles should be protected, are examples of concrete public policy choices faced by decision makers. Attitudes toward each of these choices usually depend upon deeply held philosophical perspectives.

Ideology and Public Policy

In this book, we contend that knowledge about ideology is helpful in explaining public policy. One should be able to make some predictions about policy change based upon the ideological predispositions of various actors. If a new mayor, governor, or president came into office advocating starkly different ideological positions from his or her predecessor's, one could anticipate change. The question of how ideology influences public policy can be asked at every level of government. Taxing and spending efforts of American cities have been linked with voting records of representatives elected from urban areas. Many large cities such as New York (where a majority of the U.S. representatives located in its congressional districts had liberal voting records) followed policies of relatively high per capita taxes, a progressive tax structure, relatively high per capita spending, and relatively high per capita spending for social services. Other cities possessing more conservative voting records of U.S. representatives from the area) were characterized by lower per capita taxes, more regressive taxes, lower per capita spending, and a higher priority to infrastructure.[32] These findings suggest that the prevailing sentiments or ideologies prevalent in a given area can successfully predict policies.

At the national level, the Reagan administration altered tax and defense spending policies according to a specific vision of the world. The economic policies of the Reagan administration lowered taxes in order to create incentives to investors, a policy consistent with what came to be known as "supply-side economics." This view contended that high tax rates inhibited risk taking, prioritized leisure over work, and reduced economic growth. In contrast, low taxes were believed to unleash entrepreneurial forces that would produce growth.

Policy preferences clearly differ between liberals and conservatives on economic, social, religious, and political dimensions.[33] In general, liberals are believed to (1) favor a more equal distribution of power, (2) accept more government intervention in the economy, (3) advance a more idealistic foreign policy, and (4) advocate greater economic equality. Conservatives are more accepting of natural inequalities, favor less government intervention in the economy, and advance a more self-interested foreign policy.

Today, both conservatives and liberals attempt to appeal to common American citizens. Historically, appeals to the common citizen were vigorously employed by liberal politicians such as William Jennings Bryan, Huey Long, and Jesse Jackson, all supporting the "little guy" against the abusive powers of some large entity such as "big businesses."

In recent years, conservatives have attempted to appeal to average Americans by decrying "big government." To conservatives, government elites are corrupting the morality of the country, undermining family authority, redistributing money to the undeserving, allowing American ideals to be subverted, taxing at exorbitant rates, permitting the transfer of American military might to international authorities, acting in a capricious manner, and, in general, not being responsive to the wishes of ordinary citizens. "Social conservatives" focused on the "moral agenda" of school prayer, abortion, gay marriages, and character. "Economic conservatives" focused on taxes, spending, and regulatory issues. Conservatives attempt to portray liberals as (1) "elitists" who think they know more about solving the problems of the country than the ordinary citizens of the nation, (2) "big spenders" who want to increase their already powerful position by taxing more of our hard-earned income, (3) "internationalists" who want Americans to die for poorly defined missions that are led by the United Nations, (4) "bleeding hearts" who want to redistribute our hard-earned money to people (welfare recipients) who should get jobs, and (5) "secular humanists" who want to erode the moral foundation of the nation. Variations on these themes have been used by a number of national Republican party leaders to generate enthusiasm and fervent support. Ronald Reagan successfully tapped conservative sentiments in 1980 and 1984 by assailing liberals with some of the criticisms mentioned above. The brief surge of interest in 1996 for presidential aspirant Pat Buchanan suggests that stridently conservative messages can still attract fairly large numbers of followers.

These views have been linked to the policy prescriptions emerging from conservative think tanks such as the Heritage Foundation and the Manhattan Institute. In regard to economic policy, reducing taxes and regulation is high among the policy prescriptions of conservatives. Traditional values such as the dignity of work, love for family, concern for neighborhood, faith in God, a belief in peace through strength, and a commitment to freedom as a unique legacy of America are also hallmarks of conservative ideals. In the 1980s, issues such as abortion, school prayer, tougher sentencing of criminals, affirmative action, pornography, and the Equal Rights Amendment became "hot button" political issues for conservative candidates wishing to tap into voter discontent.

The three inputs of rationality, power, and ideology (RPI) are believed to influence the creation of public policies individually as well as collectively. A description of each of these inputs is provided in Table 2.2. This table serves as a quick point of reference and definition of these inputs.

A description of the relationships between policy inputs, institutions, and public policy outputs has also been provided (Figure 2.1) in this chapter. The model presented here serves as a framework for analyzing public policy that is used throughout the book.

TABLE 2.2 Rationality, Power, and Ideology Inputs

Rationality
Problems can be identified, analyzed, and addressed.
Policies adopted are superior to alternatives on the basis of some criteria.
Policymakers will utilize some analytical procedure.
Policymakers will maximize some agreed on value.
Policymakers claim to be nonbiased and to adhere to "scientific" principles of analysis.

Power
Concentrated by social class (ruling class)
Concentrated by place in organizations (power elite)
Dispersed by competing interest groups (pluralist)

Ideology
A set of beliefs
A simplistic view of the world that orders thinking
A set of beliefs that shapes public policies according to prescribed visions

CONTEMPORARY POLICY CHOICES

Battles over policy are often intense, since winners and losers emerge from the process, with some individuals or groups advancing their agenda while others fall by the wayside. Policy choices impact both specific groups and the public at large. A brief look at some of the key policy choices that confront the nation's leaders today is instructive. Resolution of these and other policy challenges will to a large extent determine the future direction of the nation.

The model of policymaking described in this chapter provides insight for understanding public policymaking. In addition, this book reviews many of the contemporary policy issues that are of interest and importance to the nation. A primary contention is that policy is also shaped behind the scenes by the influences of rationality, power, and ideology as well as by the more readily observable actions of presidents, the members of the courts, congressional representatives, bureaucrats, and others.

Major choices exist in virtually every aspect of American life. Problems appear to be extensive and complex. Massive budget deficits provide one example of such problems. Scarcity of financial resources and resistance to raising taxes are key forces that shape the environment of budgetary decision making. Other problems also exist. The farm crisis of the 1980s and the consequent demographic shifts away from rural areas suggest a restructuring in this sector of the American economy. The issues of subsidies, the conflict between family farming and agribusiness, the efficiency of American food production, and the economic survival of rural America constitute key elements of this policy area. The extent to which the natural environment must be protected is another controversial issue. How far should government go in ensuring a sound environment for present and future generations? How much of a free hand should be given to the private sector, which may in turn endanger the environment? Survival of cities in America is another source of concern. The riots of Los Angeles suggest that deep cleavages between the "haves" and "have nots" in American society threaten stability. Can cities maintain their tax bases and reduce income disparities or will inequalities expand? "Intermestic" policy addresses matters that overlap into both domestic and foreign affairs, including issues of immigration and trade. These concerns are likely to attract great attention as American citizens look beyond domestic borders for solutions to problems.

Other issues also rank high on the nation's policy agenda. Education is salient for multiple reasons including future national prosperity, opportunity for individual citizens, and income equity. A mediocre educational system, as illustrated by graduates from American schools who cannot compete with graduates in other developed nations, does not bode well for future national prosperity. As societies become more sophisticated technologically, the quality of education becomes an even more important component of economic growth. In addition, an educational system that does not provide the entire population with opportunity may perpetuate income disparities.

The rapidly escalating cost of health care is another concern of American policymakers. New diseases, such as AIDS, combined with the needs of the rapidly growing number of elderly citizens, place great pressure on the ability of the health system to respond to the explosive growth in demand for services. The threat to society from crime and use of illicit drugs represents another policy challenge. Are drugs corrupting and weakening America's youth? Do the high rates of crime and incarceration in America suggest enduring pathologies within American society? Finally, controversies surrounding the family represent major issues on the contemporary policy agenda. Controversies over abortion, sex education, school prayer, and acceptance of alternative lifestyles exemplify the increased salience of social issues. Welfare remains a constant source of concern. The question of how far the government should go in providing welfare support to the nation's poor must be addressed as well as the question of whether monetary support creates a "welfare trap" that destroys incentives to succeed.

Decisions made regarding these policy issues will shape the future directions taken by the United States. As in other periods of its history, America faces great challenges to its economic and social well-being. A general understanding and discussion of public policy illuminates issues that will have a bearing on our lives and the future of American society.

The following case study illustrates how rationality, power, and ideology can broaden our understanding of contemporary issues.

Case Study

Capital Punishment

D AVID LAWSON died in the gas chamber in Raleigh, North Carolina, at 2:14 A.M., on June 16, 1994, dressed only in white boxer shorts, a diaper, and socks, as he was asphyxiated by cyanide gas that had been released into his execution chamber. For about five minutes, Lawson, strapped to a wooden chair, screamed muffled words through a leather mask, "I'm human! I'm human!" "Don't kill me." He heaved about twenty times, turned from bright red to pale white, and finally stopped moving.

In 1980, Lawson's victim, thirty-five-year-old Wayne Shinn, had been shot at point-blank range in the head, pleading for his life after he had caught Lawson breaking into his house. Shinn's father was also shot in the head but survived the attack. Lawson had gained Warholian temporary fame in the mass media, when it became widely known that he wanted to have his execution televised live on the *Donahue* show (the show's host opposes the death penalty). That request was rejected without comment by the U.S. Supreme Court on the day before his death. In his final statement before the execution, Lawson said: "I'm a human being, no more and no less than any other human being. It is no more right for the state of North Carolina to take my life than it was for me to kill Wayne Shinn. I'm sorry I killed Wayne Shinn. I hope North Carolina will one day be sorry that they killed me."[34]

David Lawson became the 244th person executed in the United States, and the ninth to die in the gas chamber, since the U.S. Supreme Court permitted states to resume capital punishment in its 1976 *Gregg v. Georgia* decision. In the case of capital punishment, the highest federal court had made an authoritative decision: that executions would resume in this country after a long hiatus. In the 1930s, an average of about 200 inmates each year were executed in the United States. Over the ensuing decades, the use of the death penalty became increasingly rare. By the mid-1960s, hardly any executions took place at all, and in 1972, in its *Furman v. Georgia* ruling, the Supreme Court held that the death penalty was random and arbitrary as it was then applied. This decision was far short of declaring capital punishment to be cruel and unusual, and hence unconstitutional under the Eighth Amendment to the U.S. Constitution. Instead, the *Gregg* decision indicated that death penalty statutes could be constitutional if they were made more sufficiently precise to apply the ultimate punishment more consistently. Since then, most states and, more recently, the federal government have implemented revised death penalty laws, and the states have accelerated the pace of executions.

On the day before his execution, David Lawson's final appeal on grounds that death in the gas chamber is cruel and unusual punishment was rejected by the Supreme Court, with dissent from only one justice, Harry Blackmun, who was soon to retire from the Court. The 1994 crime bill considered by Congress, and endorsed by the Clinton administration, expanded the death penalty to cover fifty-two federal offenses, including

(continued)

the attempted assassination of the president, as compared to only imposing the death penalty for murder in a drug-related crime as was the case in previous federal law.[35]

Rationality

How can we apply the frameworks that make up our model of public policymaking? We can follow each of the conceptual frameworks of rationality, power, and ideology. First, we can ask how rationality enters the public policy debate over the death penalty. In part, rationality provides inputs into that debate in the form of data supporting or refuting legal arguments over constitutional interpretations. As an example, consider the matter of whether members of some groups are executed at higher rates than members of other groups. Does this make the death penalty unconstitutional, or at least make it a suspect punishment?

Most research agrees that African-Americans and the poor are far more likely to be convicted of capital crimes and to be executed; whites and the wealthy are the least likely to suffer this fate. This kind of evidence has affected rational decision making in past Supreme Court rulings. In the case of *McCleskey v. Kemp*, the Court decided in 1986 that statistical evidence of racial disparities in death-penalty sentencing was inevitable in the criminal justice system and did not make the death penalty unconstitutional. This decision was rendered in spite of statistical evidence gathered from more than 2,000 Georgia murder cases showing that death sentences were imposed significantly more often on black alleged killers of white victims than on white alleged murderers of black victims. The Court held that such statistical evidence does not prove that race was a factor in death penalty cases.

Between the resumption of capital punishment in 1977 and the mid-1980s about 55 percent of all those sentenced to death were nonwhite. This was only slightly more than the proportion of all criminal homicides committed by nonwhites but far more than the nonwhite proportion of the national population. An ever more severe disparity existed regarding gender. Only about 1 percent of those sentenced to death were female, although about 23 percent of all murders were committed by women.[36]

In at least one area, however, the Supreme Court has decided that exceptions may be entertained to the general presumption that state death penalty decisions and procedures are applied fairly. In a June 26, 1986, ruling, in the case of *Ford v. Wainwright*, the Court held that the U.S. Constitution did not permit states to execute convicted killers who became insane during the often long years they spent on death row. In its 1988 *Thompson v. Oklahoma* ruling, the Supreme Court held that executing a defendant who was fifteen years old when the murder was committed was unconstitutional, as a violation of the prohibition against "cruel and unusual punishment" of the Eighth Amendment. However, two other rulings made in 1989 (*Stanford v. Kentucky* and *Wilkins v. Missouri*) upheld death sentences against sixteen- and seventeen-year-old defendants, based on state laws that permitted capital punishment for defendants aged sixteen or above. The Supreme Court never declared it unconstitutional to execute convicted murderers who were demonstrated to have substantially impaired levels of intelligence, although when a sentence was imposed authorities were required to consider the defendant's mental capacity as a possible mitigating factor.[37]

The logic underlying support for the death penalty, offered by an obvious critic of such logic, is summarized below:

I hazard the view that an awareness of the undeniably superior incapacitative effects of the death penalty, yoked to the illusion that retribution requires death for murder ("murderers forfeit their lives"), results in what passes for rational belief that society at present needs the death penalty. Add to this the further illusion that the more severe the threatened punishment the better a deterrent it is, and the nagging and annoying conviction that it costs the public treasury thousands of dollars each year to keep a convicted murderer in prison when the same money could be put to better social use, and you have the mind-set of the modern believer in capital punishment.[38]

Empirical evidence for the deterrent effect of the death penalty is mixed. A statistical analysis based on national data from 1933 to 1969 found that each execution saved seven or eight innocent lives by deterring murders that otherwise would have occurred.[39] A greater risk of execution was also found to be associated with lower homicide rates, when controlling for other factors. Subsequent reanalyses, however, generally refuted or strongly modified these claims, and most of the more recent research has tended to find that executions may actually provoke homicides, rather than deter them.[40]

Six main reasons offered in support of the death penalty include

1. The death penalty is a far less expensive method of punishment than the alternative of life imprisonment;
2. The death penalty is more effective in preventing crime than the alternative because it is a more effective deterrent;
3. The death penalty is superior to life imprisonment because it more effectively incapacitates the convicted felon;
4. The death penalty is required by justice;
5. There often is no feasible alternative punishment;
6. The death penalty vindicates the moral order and cannot be dispensed with as an essential symbol of public authority.[41]

A precise understanding of whether or to what extent the death penalty deters crime is elusive. Some analysts contend that the death penalty exercises no greater deterring effect on murder than long-term imprisonment:

In general, our knowledge about how penalties deter crimes and whether in fact they do—whom they deter, from which crimes, and under what conditions—is distressingly inexact. Most people nevertheless are convinced that punishments do deter, and that the more severe a punishment is the better it will deter. For half a century, social scientists have studied the questions whether the death penalty is a deterrent and . . . the deterrence achieved by the death penalty for murder is not measurably any greater than the deterrence achieved by long-term imprisonment. . . . [S]uch evidence as we have fails to show that the more severe penalty (death) is really a better deterrent than the less severe penalty (imprisonment) for such crimes as murder.[42]

Power

What role do power considerations play in decision making on the death penalty? For one thing, public opinion in recent years has become overwhelmingly supportive of capital punishment. For example, in a 1991 Gallup Poll, 76 percent of respondents agreed with the statement: "Are you in favor of the death penalty for persons convicted

(continued)

of murder?" In that same poll, just 18 percent responded no to the question, and 6 percent had no opinion.[43] One consequence of the pattern of public sentiment has been a tendency for most political candidates to run as supporters of the death penalty, because that is where the majority of voters are likely to be found. In the end, the realities of how elected policymakers are chosen makes it unlikely that many opponents of the death penalty will hold public office. However, some officeholders opposed to capital punishment are elected (and reelected), but they tend to downplay that policy preference when they run for office.

A majority of the population was found by Gallup to support the death penalty for people convicted of murder. Does this attitude hold true for different groups? The Gallup data show that 78 percent of whites, but just 59 percent of blacks (and 74 percent of all nonwhites), favor the death penalty for persons convicted of murder. When asked, "What do you think should be the penalty for murder—the death penalty or life imprisonment, with absolutely no possibility of parole?" racial differences in opinion become much more pronounced. Among whites, 56 percent favor the death penalty alternative, compared to just 26 percent among blacks. Also, when asked, "Do you feel that the death penalty acts as a deterrent to the commitment of murder—that it lowers the murder rate, or not?" 53 percent of white respondents said "yes," compared to 38 percent of blacks. A minority (41 percent) of whites agreed with the statement that "A black person is more likely than a white person to receive the death penalty for the same crime," but 73 percent of blacks agreed, and so did 64 percent of all nonwhite respondents.[44]

Several reasons for a racial divide on the death penalty can be surmised. From 1930 to 1967, 50 percent of all executions for murder and 89 percent of all executions for rape were carried out on blacks. Following the resumption of capital punishment in 1977, after a ten-year hiatus, 40 percent of those executed have been black and over 80 percent of those who were executed were convicted of killing whites.[45] It is important to note, too, that the incidence of executions in the United States has been disproportionately high in the southern states, characterized by sharper and more pervasive racial conflicts and by a generally more conservative culture than the rest of the United States. A total of 1,887 executions in the South occurred from 1935 to 1969, compared to 453 in the Northeast, 413 in the West, and just 298 in north central states.[46] This differential pattern of executions remained fairly constant over time, with Georgia, Texas, and North Carolina carrying out the greatest numbers of executions. A pattern of differential sentencing based upon race was also discovered. For example, in Ohio, between 1974 and 1977, the probability was about .254 that a black killing a white would receive a death sentence, versus probabilities of about .046 when a white killed a white, .017 when a black killed a black, and zero when a white killed a black.[47]

There are other differences in opinions about capital punishment that suggest that different groups in American society favor or oppose the death penalty and that the power of one group over another may be important. If one hypothesized that those in positions of power possessed higher income, as well as higher education, and that they wished to suppress those out of power, then one would assume that support for the death penalty would correlate positively with these traits—those with the highest income and education would be most inclined to support capital punishment. The evidence for this assertion, however, is mixed. Respondents to the 1991 Gallup survey with the lowest household incomes (under $20,000) had the lowest level of support for capital punishment, but support was greatest in the $20,000 to $30,000 household income range. These households certainly would not qualify as elites based on income.

The data concerning education and capital punishment were directly opposite predictions based upon the hypothesized relationship that those with higher levels of education would be less sympathetic toward groups that held little power. College graduates were most inclined (54 percent) to agree that blacks were more severely punished than whites for the same crime. Respondents who were never graduated from high school were least likely to agree with that view.[48]

A number of interest groups are active in the struggle over capital punishment. Those organized to oppose the death penalty include the National Association for the Advancement of Colored People (NAACP); the American Civil Liberties Union (ACLU); Amnesty International; a variety of religious groups (for example, the American Baptist Churches, the American Friends Service Committee, the Presbyterian Church of the United States, the Union of American Hebrew Congregations, the Southern Christian Leadership Conference, the Unitarian Universalist Association, and the United Methodist Church); medical groups such as the House of Delegates of the American Medical Association (which in 1980 resolved that physicians could not participate ethically in a legally sponsored execution), the American Psychiatric Association, and the American Nursing Association; many legal and professional groups (for example, the National Bar Association); and a large number of academic researchers. Of the organizations opposed to the death penalty, the most effective has been the Legal Defense Fund of the National Association for the Advancement of Colored People, which brought the original class-action lawsuits that stopped all executions between 1967 and 1977.

Two of the comparatively few national organizations favoring the death penalty are the National District Attorneys Association and the National Association of Attorneys General. National police organizations also favor capital punishment. That there is something of an elite-mass division on the question of abolishing the death penalty is clear from the facts that lay members of churches, as well as many of the clergy, do not support the pro-abolition views expressed by their national organizations or spokespersons, and the reality that strong majorities of the mass public regularly endorse at least limited application of the death penalty. Also, a 1985 poll conducted by the American Bar Association showed that 68 percent of the nation's lawyers favored carrying out the death sentences already imposed by the courts.[49]

Since 1964, when Oregon voters temporarily outlawed the death penalty, public referenda on capital punishment invariably have restored the death penalty. These include votes in California in 1972, and in Oregon in both 1978 and 1984. No legislature has abolished any death penalty statute since the 1960s. Since 1972, thirty-seven states have enacted one or more statutes carrying a death sentence, and in 1984 the U.S. Senate voted to restore the federal death penalty.[50]

Ideology

What role does ideology play in decision-making about capital punishment? It has been asserted in the literature that ideology is particularly relevant to emotional, "hot button" political issues such as capital punishment. For example, scholars note:

(continued)

It is preeminently a political and a moral question, not an empirical one. Some social policy issues may be settled simply by reference to empirical data and the inferences drawn from their analysis, but the issue of whether or not the death penalty should be prescribed by law for any crime is certainly not one of them. In facing that issue we confront not one but two fundamental moral questions: not merely whether we regard the idea of putting a person to death for a crime as morally acceptable, but also whether the state should be granted the power to terminate human life. . . . [T]he motivating force behind the abolitionist movement . . . has not . . . come from advances in the scientific assessment of the comparative deterrent effectiveness of different penalties. Rather, it has come from development in prevailing attitudes and beliefs regarding what is moral and just. . . . [W]hen executions cease in America it will not be because of the findings of deterrence research.[51]

Ideology plays another role in setting the limits of capital punishment debate. When supporters of the death penalty for murder were asked by a Gallup Poll why they held that point of view, the top choice was "revenge; an 'eye for an eye'" (50 percent), well ahead of other possibilities such as "acts as deterrent" (13 percent), "keeps them from killing again" (19 percent), "costly to keep them in prison" (13 percent), or "judicial system is too lenient" (3 percent).[52] At the execution of David Lawson, Jerry Shinn, brother of Lawson's victim, Wayne Shinn, and one of six family members to watch Lawson die, was quoted as stating: "I personally think lethal injection is too easy. I think they should have to suffer. He did have to suffer some."[53] Opponents of the death penalty held a vigil before the execution took place and prayed following the event.

Among those opposed to capital punishment, the dominant motivation revealed in Gallup surveys was that it is "wrong to take a life" (41 percent), followed far behind by "punishment should be left to God" (17 percent), "persons may be wrongly convicted" (11 percent), "does not deter crime" (7 percent), "possibility of rehabilitation" (6 percent), and "unfair application of penalty" (6 percent). The ideological nature of these beliefs is attested to further by responses to challenges to both the pro- and anti-death penalty points of view. Only 29 percent of supporters expressed a willingness to change their views if "new evidence showed that the death penalty does not act as a deterrent to murder—that it does not lower the murder rate." Likewise, just 25 percent of opponents said they would reverse their point of view if "new evidence showed that the death penalty acts as a deterrent to murder—that it lowers the murder rate." In other words, even in the presence of evidence to the contrary, only about a quarter of either the pro- or anti-capital punishment believers would be willing to shift positions. Such unwillingness to change is often associated with the emotional commitment of ideology.

Rational input into the capital punishment debate appears to be weaker than deeply held convictions. One analyst of the death penalty concluded the following about adherence to rational study:

One of the reasons people seem to support capital punishment is that they believe that although it is a very severe sanction it is necessary in order to protect the lives of innocent persons. Those who believe in the need for capital punishment for public protection make two specific claims that (1) executing those who have already killed is the only way to keep those who are contemplating murder from acting on their desires, and (2) executing those who have already killed is the only way to keep them from killing again. . . .

After years of research with different methodologies and statistical approaches, the empirical evidence seems to clearly suggest that capital punishment is not a superior general deterrent. [T]hose states that had capital punishment had no lower homicide rates than those without it.[54]

The policy debate over capital punishment always takes place with the knowledge that there is no way of rectifying a mistaken execution. In the United States during the twentieth century, at least twenty-three people have been executed when in fact they were innocent, and another forty-eight were released from death row when the evidence demonstrated their innocence before they were killed. Furthermore, the General Accounting Office has reported that blacks who kill whites were sentenced to death at a rate nearly twenty-two times as high as the rate of death sentences for blacks who kill blacks, and at over seven times the rate of whites who kill blacks.[55] Questions about the arbitrary nature of punishment by death, racial disparities, and the very real risk of killing an innocent person will continue to pervade the debate over capital punishment. This debate will continue to be tinged by ideology.

It is evident that rationality, power, and ideology, all in their own manner, exert influence in shaping policies that are related to capital punishment. This case study identified various empirical studies that were carried out in order to determine the deterring effects of capital punishment. Results of such studies were inconclusive and contradictory. These studies, in addition to others addressing the issue of racial disparities in sentencing, nevertheless attest to the perceived value of empirical studies. The power input in capital punishment policy is observed in interest group behavior. The hypothesis that individuals with greater power (identified through measures of income and education) will be more willing to accept capital punishment, however, was not supported by the data. Finally, the role of ideology in the emotional issue of capital punishment is most evident. Capital punishment is an issue that carries a great deal of ideological and moral baggage. The moral nature of the issue suggests that acceptance of one position or another is likely to be based upon deep-seated beliefs about fundamental concepts such as justice, retribution, and equality.

Case Study Questions

1. In your opinion, which perspective (rational, power, ideology) best explains the expanded use of the death penalty in the United States in recent years?
2. How would you explain differential racial sentencing in capital punishment cases?
3. How do you explain changes in public opinion over time toward capital punishment?
4. What do you believe to be the future direction of capital punishment? Explain why you believe this to be the case.
5. Is capital punishment really a moral question for religious leaders and philosophers to decide?

Suggested Readings

Baradat, Leon P. *Political Ideologies*. Englewood Cliffs, NJ: Prentice-Hall, 1979.

Dahl, Robert. *Who Governs? Democracy and Power in the American City*. New Haven: Yale University Press, 1961.

Domhoff, William G. *The Power Elite and the State: How Policy Is Made in America*. New York: Aldine DeGruyter, 1990.

Dunn, William. *Public Policy Analysis: An Introduction*, 2nd ed. Englewood Cliffs, NJ: Prentice-Hall, 1994.

Notes

1. Charles E. Lindblom, "The Science of Muddling Through," *Public Administration Review* 19 (Spring 1959), pp. 79–88.

2. Steven G. Koven, "Base Closings and the Politics-Administration Dichotomy Revisited," *Public Administration Review* 52 (5) (1992), pp. 526–531.

3. Graham Allison, *Essence of Decision* (Boston: Little, Brown, 1971), pp. 29–30.

4. William Dunn, *Public Policy Analysis: An Introduction,* 2nd ed. (Englewood Cliffs, NJ: Prentice-Hall, 1994), p. 274.

5. Michael T. Hayes, *Incrementalism and Public Policy* (New York: Longman, 1992), p. 14.

6. Thomas R. Dye, *Understanding Public Policy*, 8th ed. (Englewood Cliffs, NJ: Prentice-Hall, 1995), pp. 30–32.

7. Herbert Simon, *Administrative Behavior,* 3rd ed. (New York: Free Press, 1976), p. xxix.

8. Dunn, op. cit., p. 29.

9. Dunn, op. cit., p. 50.

10. C. Wright Mills, *The Power Elite* (New York: Oxford University Press, 1956).

11. Nicholas Abercrombie, Stephen Hill, and Bryan Turner, *Dictionary of Sociology*, 2nd ed. (London: Penguin Books, 1988), p. 211; G. William Domhoff, *Who Rules America Now?* (Englewood Cliffs, NJ: Prentice-Hall, 1983), p. 2.

12. James Q. Wilson, *American Government*, 5th ed. (Lexington, MA: Heath, 1992), p. 8.

13. Gaetano Mosca, *The Ruling Class*, ed. A. Livingston (New York: McGraw-Hill, 1965), p. 50.

14. Robert Lynd and Helen Lynd, "Middletown's 'X' Family: A Pattern of Business-Class Control," pp. 41–50 in *The Search for Community Power*, 2nd ed., W. Hawley and F. Wirt (Englewood Cliffs, NJ: Prentice-Hall, 1974), p. 42.

15. Ferdinand Lundberg, *America's Sixty Families* (New York: Vanguard Press, 1937).

16. William G. Domhoff, *Who Really Rules? New Haven and Community Power Reexamined* (New Brunswick, NJ: Transaction Books, 1978), pp. 153–160.

17. Mills, op. cit., pp. 10–11.

18. Thomas Dye, *Who's Running America?* (Englewood, Cliffs, NJ: Prentice-Hall, 1985).

19. Robert Alford and Roger Friedland, *Powers of Theory: Capitalism, the State, and Democracy* (Cambridge: Cambridge University Press, 1985), p. 198.

20. William A. Kelso, *American Democratic Theory: Pluralism and Its Critics* (Westport, CT: Greenwood Press, 1978), p. 3.

21. Ralph Chandler and Jack Plano, *The Public Administration Dictionary,* 2nd ed. (Santa Barbara, CA: ABC-CLIO, 1988), p. 93.

22. Robert Dahl, *Who Governs? Democracy and Power in the American City* (New Haven, CT: Yale University Press, 1961).

23. Alexander Hamilton, James Madison, and John Jay, *The Federalist Papers* (New York: New American Library, 1961), p. 322.

24. Chandler and Plano, op. cit., p. 94.

25. Kenneth Janda, Jeffrey Berry, and Jerry Goldman, *The Challenge of Democracy: Government in America,* 4th ed. (Boston: Houghton Mifflin, 1995), p. 42.

26. Charles Lindblom, *The Policy Making Process* (Englewood Cliffs, NJ: Prentice-Hall, 1968).

27. Nicholas Abercrombie, Stephen Hill, and Bryan Turner, *Dictionary of Sociology,* 2nd ed. (London: Penguin Books, 1988), p. 118.

28. Robert Lane, *Political Ideology: Why the American Common Man Believes What He Does* (New York: Free Press of Glencoe, 1962), pp. 14–15.

29. David Ingersoll, *Communism, Fascism, and Democracy* (Columbus, OH: Charles E. Merrill, 1971).

30. Mostafa Rejai, *Comparative Political Ideologies* (New York: St. Martin's Press, 1984), p. 11.

31. Robert Eccleshall, "Introduction: The World of Ideology," in *Political Ideologies*, ed. R. Eccleshall, V. Geoghegan, R. Jay, and R. Wilford (London: Hutchinson, 1984), p. 23.

32. Steven Koven, *Ideological Budgeting: The Influence of Political Philosophy on Public Policy* (New York: Praeger Publishers, 1988), p. 123.

33. Charles Dunn and David Woodward, *American Conservatism from Burke to Bush* (Lanham, MD: Madison Books, 1991), pp. 35–40.

34. "Killer's Screams Punctuate Execution," *Des Moines Register*, 16 June 1994, p. 5A.

35. Michael Kramer, "Frying Them Isn't the Answer," *Time*, 14 March 1994, p. 32.

36. Hugo Bedau, *Death Is Different: Studies in the Morality, Law, and Politics of Capital Punishment* (Boston: Northeastern University Press, 1987), p. 133.

37. Raymond Pasternoster, *Capital Punishment in America* (New York: Lexington, 1991).

38. Bedau, op. cit., p. 63.

39. Isaac Ehrlich, "The Deterrent Effect of Capital Punishment: A Question of Life and Death," *American Economic Review* 65 (1975), pp. 397–417.

40. William Bowers, *Legal Homicide: Death as Punishment in America, 1864–1982* (Boston: Northeastern University Press, 1984).

41. Bedau, op. cit., p. 238.

42. Ibid., pp. 33–34.

43. *The Gallup Poll, 1991* (Wilmington, DE: Scholarly Resources, 1992).

44. Ibid.

45. Pasternoster, op. cit.

46. Franklin Zimring and Gordon Hawkins, *Capital Punishment and the American Agenda* (Cambridge: Cambridge University Press, 1986).

47. William Bowers and Glenn Pierce, "Arbitrariness and Discrimination under post-*Furman* Capital Statutes," *Crime and Delinquency* 26 (1980), pp. 563–635.

48. *The Gallup Poll, 1991*, op. cit.

49. Lauren Reskin, "Law Poll: Majority of Lawyers Support Capital Punishment," *American Bar Association Journal* 71 (April 1985), p. 55.

50. Bedau, op. cit.

51. Zimring and Hawkins, op. cit., pp. 167–168.

52. *The Gallup Poll, 1991*, op. cit.; "Killer's Screams Punctuate Execution," op. cit.

53. "Killer's Screams Punctuate Execution," op. cit.

54. Pasternoster, op. cit., pp. 240–241.

55. Kramer, op. cit., p. 32.

3

Economic and Budget Policy

ORANGE COUNTY BANKRUPTCY

On December 5, 1994, only two days prior to the fifty-third anniversary of the attack on Pearl Harbor in 1941, Robert Citron, treasurer for Orange County, California, resigned in disgrace after falling victim to an attack of rising interest rates. The sixty-nine-year-old public servant had lost $1.5 billion of the county's money in a $20 billion investment pool of his design. The large loss of funds forced Orange County to file for bankruptcy under Chapter 9 (the public sector's equivalent to Chapter 11) of the Bankruptcy Code. Orange County had fallen victim to poor investment strategies of Treasurer Citron. Citron invested county funds in a manner that would have reaped significant returns if interest rates had continued the downward trend that prevailed between 1991 and 1993. Orange County's investments, however, declined precipitously in value after interest rates rose following a February 1994 meeting of the Federal Reserve Board.

Prior to this miscalculation, Citron had been a star of California's $120 billion municipal bond market. Citron was hailed for his earnings on investments. Contrary to many local treasurers, who saw their primary role as safeguarder of public funds, Citron was willing to take greater risks (with county funds) in an effort to earn substantial returns. Some perceived this strategy to be the entrepreneurial wave of the future and derided other treasurers for being behind the times or lacking an entrepreneurial spirit. Citron clearly did not suffer from such a lack of daring and hoped that his investments would both enhance his prestige as County Treasurer and ease the tax burden on Orange County's 2.5 million residents. His strategies worked well for a while, but in the end he could not protect the county from large losses.

The details of the Orange County fiasco are both complex and simple. The simpler story appears to be one of a dedicated public servant who in his zeal to assist the public good grossly mishandled county funds. The saga evolves over a period of time. In 1979, Citron participated in changing California law to make it easier for the state's counties to accumulate funds in arrangements called reverse repurchase agreements. Such agreements permitted California county treasurers to take out short-term loans and invest the proceeds of those loans in longer-term bonds that paid higher interest rates. Using such arrangements, Citron added $12.5 billion of borrowed bonds to the $7.7 billion of public funds that he supervised. This strategy worked well while interest rates were falling since not only did Citron's fund earn a higher return on long-term bonds than the borrowing costs of short-term bonds, but the market value of the long-term bonds also appreciated. Declines in interest rates increase the price of a security (such as a bond) that provides a fixed return. Throughout the 1980s, the Orange County fund earned returns of more than 9 percent a year, or nearly double the average earnings of other California investment pools. Citron's luck or good management (depending upon one's perspective) of the Orange County investment pool, however, began to run out in 1994 as interest rates rose and the market value of his investments fell.

The Orange County investment portfolio was highly sensitive to fluctuations of the bond market because of two factors: Citron had borrowed $12.5 billion in short-term loans and used the funds for long-term borrowing (this strategy is termed "leveraging"), and he invested $8.5 billion of trust funds in risky investments termed derivatives. These strategies accelerated the losses incurred by the Orange County trust fund as interest rates rose in 1994. Analysts claimed that either Citron was unwilling to believe that interest rates would continue to rise or that he was unable to bail out on his complex financial arrangements without a considerable loss to his personal prestige. Either way, December 5, 1994, marked the end of what was once considered to be a highly distinguished career in the public service.

Following the bankruptcy, recriminations abounded. A number of lawsuits were filed. Holders of Orange County municipal bonds sued county officials, as well as brokerage companies, claiming that securities firms had not properly notified government officials of the risk involved. A dozen cities and other public agencies filed a $50 million lawsuit against a major brokerage house, contending that the securities firm had defrauded them. The lawsuit accused Merrill Lynch & Company of breaching their fiduciary duty, as well as fraud, deceit, knowing receipt of stolen property, and violation of the California Unfair Business Practices Act. Cities and public agencies sought damages, maintaining that investments of a more conservative nature were mandated by California law. A spokesman for Merrill Lynch and Company stated that the lawsuit was absurd, had no legal merit, and represented an attempt to shift the blame to others.

Immediate fallout from the Orange County bankruptcy followed. Dozens of municipal projects were put on hold, from a new stadium for the Los Angeles

Rams (who later moved to St. Louis and became the St. Louis Rams) to a $1.5 million elementary school expansion in La Habra City. The city of Anaheim imposed a hiring freeze and halted capital improvement projects. The county also missed payment on some of its debt, which prompted Moody's Investment Service to downgrade its bonds. Standard & Poors had earlier downgraded Orange County's long-term credit rating from a blue chip AA to junk bond status of CCC. Citron, however, appeared to be defiant as he surrendered his $100,000 a year job, claiming that what he did was not irresponsible in any manner, shape, or form.

In the fallout from the Orange County affair, analysts asked how County Treasurer Robert Citron, described as a shy, bespectacled public servant, had managed to dig such a large hole for the county and how Orange County (perceived to be ultra-conservative) had allowed itself to get into such a position. Answers to these questions were not immediately forthcoming. It was clear, however, that citizen disillusionment with an already discredited public sector had grown. Citizen outrage even inspired ideas for new bumper stickers such as the catchy slogan: "It's 10 P.M. Do you know where your tax dollars are?"[1]

Rational, power, and ideological inputs play important roles in this story. First, from the rational perspective, it could be argued that Orange County Treasurer Robert Citron tried to utilize what he thought to be resourceful and innovative managerial practices in order to maximize governmental revenue. Citron relied on what he believed to be a well-conceived plan to optimize revenue for the county. The fact that Citron ultimately lost public funds does not in any way suggest that his strategy was not based upon a rational plan, utilizing a careful assessment of what he viewed as the best information and the most thoughtful judgment of the County Treasurer.

Orange County's actions can also be explained by the ideological perspective with two philosophies competing for influence. One philosophy of public service represents the view that government fiscal officers have a stewardship responsibility to the taxpayers to protect funds, even if revenues are not maximized. In this role, officials exercise a high degree of caution in investments. An alternative philosophy concerning the role of fiscal officers in the public sector contends that public officials have a responsibility to maximize the use of their revenue, which includes obtaining a high return on investments.

From the power perspective, some groups had a vested interest in which of the two broad philosophies would be accepted. Specifically, it is logical that brokerage houses who are in business to handle investments stand to benefit from public sector strategies that prioritize maximizing returns on investments. A philosophical acceptance in the public sector of such an investment strategy therefore will benefit private brokerage firms. Similarly, government officials may have a vested interest in changing the role of treasurer from steward to investor. It could be argued that if managers have considerable discretion in investments they may begin to command salaries comparable to those of mutual fund managers or investment bankers. Public officials (even those with control over large sums of money), however, are usually paid only a fraction of what private sector fund managers receive.

The three perspectives of rationality, power, and ideology appear to be especially relevant to budgetary policy. First, rationality is a part of the conception of budgeting, which is a process of maximizing the utility of scarce resources. Budget analysts follow various techniques, procedures, and routines to achieve efficiency. Second, power is related to budgeting in the sense that budgets reflect the pulling, hauling, negotiating, subtle bribing, and compromising that make up the political process. For example, it is not surprising that politicians are not willing to attack programs such as Social Security or that they are reluctant to cut off subsidies to powerful special interests. The ability of those with power to protect and expand their vested interests is a hallmark of the budgetary process. Third, ideology has always played a role in budget policy, since values provide a guidepost for conflict over outputs.

Interrelationships are also evident between ideology and power, since the enhanced popularity of certain values helps to increase the power of individuals or organizations that promote those values. Similarly, research that purports to be rational can bolster both ideological philosophies and special interests. This chapter will identify the role of the three inputs (rationality, power, ideology) in budget policy, provide an historical overview of budget policy in the United States, discuss the relevance of budget deficits, and profile through a case study the pressures that are ever present in the budgetary process.

THE RPI INPUTS TO ECONOMIC AND BUDGET POLICY

The Rationality Input

Budgeters have always sought to answer the classic question of, "On what basis shall it be decided to allocate X dollars to activity A instead of activity B?"[2] To answer the question of how scarce resources should be allocated, many scholars looked to rational procedures found in the discipline of economics. Over time, economists have developed a number of theories to guide behavior. The theory of marginal utility contends that when more money is spent on an activity, the marginal benefits (benefits from the last dollar) attributed to that activity will decline. Economists apply this theory in a process of maximizing returns on government spending. The logic of marginal utility is apparent when one compares the benefit attributed to building a 10,001th nuclear weapon compared to the benefit of the first atomic bomb. As more and more spending is heaped on a category (such as military preparedness), the value of additional spending declines. If the value of spending additional dollars in one category falls below the value of spending in another category, rationality mandates that money must be transferred to spending categories that provide a higher return. In theory, such a process of transfers would maximize social returns of public sector funds.

In contrast to ideological views of economic and budget policy that advance certain positions based on values (such as progressive or regressive taxes, larger or smaller government size, and social spending versus other types of spending), the rational perspective is grounded on assumptions of objectivity, neutrality, and scientific method. In line with such thinking is the view that costs, as well as benefits, of certain types of behavior can be measured and that decision makers can be unbiased. An explicit attempt to incorporate rationality into the budgetary process appears in techniques of budgeting, cost-benefit analysis, and forecasting. A budget technique that is heavily influenced by assumptions of rationality is Planning Programming Budgeting System (PPBS). PPBS was popularized by Secretary of Defense Robert McNamara in the early 1960s in an effort to get "more bang for the buck" and consists of the following:[3]

1. Analyze program goals in operational terms. For example, instead of saying that the goal of a program is to reduce crime, the operational goal would be to reduce the murder rate by X percent or to lower the rate of property crime by Y percent.
2. Analyze the total costs of programs over one and several years.
3. Analyze alternative ways of achieving the goals. In the above example, one could alternatively consider how much it would cost to place more patrol officers in the neighborhood compared to how much it would cost to create a neighborhood watch program.
4. Develop a systematic way of considering the costs and benefits of all government programs. For example, one would consider the cost of a death averted in the crime program versus the cost of averting death through health or education programs. One would also consider the total benefits of each approach.

Benefit-Cost Analysis and Forecasting

Benefit-cost analysis as well as forecasting techniques are examples of other rational techniques employed in economic and budgetary analysis. At the turn of the century, many American cities used rather simplistic benefit-cost analyses to describe investment in infrastructure. The Tennessee Valley Authority as well as the state of Oregon also employed such analysis to assess water and highway projects. During World War II, more sophisticated techniques of analysis were developed. Following World War II, the RAND Corporation continued to apply benefit-cost analysis techniques to issues in the public sector.[4]

Benefit-cost analysis in budgeting required a number of steps: (1) specifying objectives, (2) stipulating limitations, (3) quantifying relationships, and (4) calculating outcomes. Efforts were made to exclude personal values of the analyst and to maximizing the public good. Long-range forecasting models also as-sisted analysts in formulating public policy. Through forecasting, it was be-lieved, economic and budget policy analysts could do more than simply react to circumstances. Predictions of population, income, and employment trends were of great value to all levels of government. Local governments employed a variety of forecasting techniques, such as location quotient analysis, shift-share analysis, and fiscal impact analysis. Each of these techniques provided analysts with essential information relating to their jurisdiction's economic health.

Location quotients are based on a comparison of local employment with national employment. Shift-share analysis focuses upon changes in the com-position of local employment over time. Fiscal impact analysis tracks changes in population, income, and land use to predict revenue streams or expendi-ture needs.[5]

Medium-range forecasting techniques are also of value to policymakers. Such techniques include expert forecasts and deterministic techniques. Expert fore-casters often can generate an accurate "best guess" of what revenues will be in the following year. Deterministic techniques base forecasts on preestablished formulas. For example, an educational formula might predict spending levels based upon certain mandates. A locality operating under a mandate of no more than thirty students assigned to a single teacher would have to budget for five additional teachers if 150 additional students were anticipated. Deterministic techniques are straightforward calculations of costs based upon specific assump-tions. All of the rationalistic procedures are based on the fundamental assump-tion that neutral, objective analysis is possible. Skeptics, however, do not believe that this assertion is realistic and look for alternative explanations.

The Power Input

The power perspective holds that policy is made by those in positions of influ-ence, which depends upon such factors as wealth and the ability to mobilize voters. Wealth can interact with rationality since wealthy families can influence research conducted in foundations that were established through endowments. Groups such as the American Association of Retired People (AARP) may influ-ence policy through their ability to alter elections. Well-funded special interest lobbyists can influence policy through their access to policymakers and knowl-edge of the policymaking process. An investigation appears below of how spe-cial interest groups can influence policy.

The AARP

The AARP is an interest group with a great deal of power in the electoral process. From the power perspective, Social Security and other programs aimed at the elderly are favored by politicians who have learned to fear the electoral influence of the elderly. Ronald Reagan was challenged in 1981 when he attempted to reduce benefits to Social Security recipients. Efforts to reduce benefits opposed by this powerful interest group led to a political defeat, as senior citizens flooded the offices of Congress with letters, telegrams, and telephone calls in protest. After Reagan's Social Security plan died in Congress, the administration named a study commission, headed by former Council of Economic Advisers Chairman Alan Greenspan, to address the issue. The commission quickly produced a plan that increased payroll taxes for workers, made more workers subject to Social Security taxes, and took the Social Security program "off-budget" so that it would not be part of the annual budgetary deliberations. Over time, elected officials learned that Social Security beneficiaries could not be trifled with and that any notion of altering the Social Security program was political suicide.[6]

Sugar Price Supports

The power input also appears in lobbying behavior, such as the 1995 action in House and Senate committees to save sugar price supports. Sugar growers triumphed by striking alliances with influential members of Congress from several regions. Alliances between cane growing states (Florida, Louisiana, Texas, and Hawaii), midwestern corporate producers of corn sweeteners (such as Archer Daniels Midland Company), and small-scale sugar beet farmers (in Minnesota, North Dakota, and Idaho) were struck, which in turn defeated a campaign to eliminate subsidies by corporate sugar users such as Coca-Cola and Hershey Foods Corporation. The alliance between representatives of cane, corn, and sugar beet producing states has been effective at keeping American prices for sugar at roughly twice the world price. This has been achieved by limits on imports and domestic production.[7] Power also interacts with ideology since those pursuing material interests usually find a coherent philosophical perspective to support their activities.

The Ideological Input

From the ideological perspective, economic and budget policy can be viewed as a conflict between differing views of the world (ideologies), since ideological interests marshal their clients at critical points in the budgetary process.[8] In American economic and budget policy a number of basic modes of thought have competed for attention: primary among them are the *Keynesian* and *supply-side* views.

A vigorous debate between demand-side and supply-side economic theorists provides much of the theoretical underpinning for contemporary economic and budget policy. The demand-side focus traces its roots to the writings of British economist John Maynard Keynes.

Keynesian Economic Theory

In 1936, Keynes transformed the whole direction and emphasis of modern economics with the appearance of his book, *The General Theory of Employment, Interest and Money.* Keynes challenged classical theories of economics, maintaining that market equilibrium, or stable market conditions, might be established at less than full employment. According to Keynes, the Great Depression of the 1930s indicated that free-market economics did not ensure market equilibrium at satisfactory levels of employment. Furthermore, Keynes contended that cuts in production could produce a vicious downward cycle. In order to avoid such a spiral, he postulated that the public sector could prop up market demand. Such a demand-oriented focus had the effect of altering traditional economic thinking away from the idea of a self-correcting marketplace that automatically returned to levels of full employment.

Keynes proposed what were termed strategies of *fiscal* and *monetary* policy in order to control unemployment. Fiscal policy addressed public-sector taxing and spending, maintaining that when market demand exceeded supply the government should increase taxes (which would take money out of circulation) to reduce the likelihood of inflation. When demand was too low, Keynes advocated the opposite strategy of lowering taxes. Lower taxes in turn would allow citizens to keep more of their earnings for purchases. Government spending was another mechanism for stimulating the economy. Keynes believed that public sector spending in periods of economic stagnation would stimulate economic growth, while cuts in public sector expenditures would restrain growth. It was hypothesized that fiscal policy could "fine-tune" (smoothing out the up and down cycles) the economy and prevent sudden downturns.

Monetary policy was another tool of the government advanced by Keynes to manage the economy. Monetary policy operates through the Federal Reserve System, a banking system that expands (to stimulate growth) or tightens (to control inflation) the money supply. Methods for decreasing the supply of money include open-market operations such as selling bonds (taking money out of circulation and promising to repay over many years) and buying bonds (infusing money into circulation).

The Keynesian era dominated the post–World War II period, but by the late 1970s these beliefs were coming under attack. Stagflation of the 1970s (when unemployment and inflation rose together) could not be solved within the Keynesian framework.[9] Confidence in Keynesian views was further undermined by a faltering economy and concern over the creeping enlargement of the federal government. Unhappiness with the direction of the economy was fueled by knowledge that public sector expansion was financed by heavier debt and tax burdens.

Even more troubling than the growing debt and tax levels was an awareness of a sudden slowdown in productivity growth. After rising sharply in the postwar period, productivity flattened out in the late 1970s. A growing number of economists contended that government was responsible for these problems. Critics of Keynesian economics gained credibility, arguing that government action led to inadequate savings and investment, low growth in potential output, and high inflation.[10] A differing economic perspective emerged to fill the vacuum left by the 1970s attack on Keynes.

Supply-Side Economic Theory

In the late 1970s, the theory of *supply-side* economics emerged as a successor to the demand-oriented views of Keynes. Supply-side economics provided a modern-day rationale for the economic philosophies propounded by earlier *laissez-faire* enthusiasts of an "unfettered" marketplace. The supply-side doctrine contended that problems with the American economy could be traced to a punitive tax system that robbed people of the incentive to produce. Cutting taxes would increase incentives for savings and investment. Higher levels of savings, in turn, would lead to enhanced productivity, higher levels of economic growth, and greater employment. In addition, supply-siders contended that economic expansion could more than offset revenues lost in the tax cuts.

The supply-side doctrine was supported by Professor Arthur Laffer and his now-famous Laffer Curve. The Laffer Curve compared tax rates with tax revenues, noting that at some point an increase in tax rates would actually reduce tax revenue. This "backward bending" curve became a key part of tax reduction justifications presented by conservative economists. In theory, taxes would shrink the economy by deterring innovation, inhibiting risk-taking, and reducing productivity.[11]

Advocates of the supply-side perspective sought to change the distribution of tax burdens to influence the behavior of workers, employers, and others. They believed that proper incentives would increase savings, encourage work, and preserve the long-term health of the economy. With the election of Ronald Reagan in 1980, supply-side theories were put into practice. When Reagan left office, however, eight years after supply-side policies were introduced, there was little consensus in regard to what supply-side policies had actually accomplished.[12] Critics of the supply-side view (also labeled *trickle-down* economics) claimed that strategies favored the wealthy, represented nothing new, and were just a recycling of the same message that Andrew Mellon conveyed to Calvin Coolidge in the 1920s.[13]

Supply-side versus Keynesian philosophies appear in a host of contemporary economic and budget issues. In regard to the distribution of taxes, the supply-side view contends that benefits (tax breaks) must be given to those who are capable of increasing the supply of goods. Once benefits have been given to these interests, there should be a trickle down to others. The Keynesian view, as a demand-oriented philosophy, focuses on placing money in the hands of those who can purchase more goods. As demand increases supply will respond.

These rival views also differ on the size and scope of government. The Keynesian view of government is much more positive and proactive, asserting that it serves as a manager of the economy, ready to step in to stimulate economic activity when the private sector falters. In contrast, the supply-side vision of the public sector is more negative, believing that government spending leads to more taxes, which erode individual initiative and drive. Government spending also replaces the more productive private sector activity with less useful public sector behavior. The free market philosophy (advanced by supply-siders) is also less responsive to calls for redistribution. Attempts to enlarge the social safety net for the poor are likely to be viewed as debilitating to those who need assistance since such aid would reduce their incentive to work. In contrast, Keynesians justify their philosophy on the need for governmental action to ease the pain of economic downturns.

Application of RPI

Elements of rationality, power, and ideology can be found in different aspects of economic and budget policy. The case study on tax reform in this chapter illustrates how rationality, power, and ideology interrelate with each other to produce policy. The decision by the Clinton administration to press for deficit reductions appears to be based upon some objective determination that deficits have a negative impact on the long-term economic health of the nation. Impairment of the economy would also have negative impacts on the long-term electoral prospects of President Clinton.

Power intervenes in the political ability of the president and party leadership to exert pressure on representatives to enact policies. Such pressures stand out in the events surrounding Representative Margolies-Mezvinsky's vote for President Clinton's tax plan.

Finally, ideology makes its appearance in Clinton's efforts to make sure that the burden of taxation falls on those with greater abilities to pay. In a State of the Union address, Clinton assured the nation that tax increases will be targeted to the top 1.2 percent of Americans. Such "soak the rich" strategies have their roots in values/normative visions of what is fair or unfair for the majority of the population. Popular support in turn enhances the power of the elected leaders.

The Clinton tax reform case study illustrates the interrelationship that is present in RPI. It appears, however, that power and ideology exert more influence on economic and budget policy than rationality. Rational techniques that were advanced in efforts to improve budgeting proved to be ephemeral. Executive budgets (developed by the Office of Management and Budget) that did not enjoy political support were "dead on arrival" when they reached Congress. Power therefore appears to be a major input in economic and budget policy, aided and abetted by the ideological input. One can see that strong interests such as the elderly are protected at budget time. Weak interests such as the poor see their funding levels slashed in attempts to give them more incentive to work and pull themselves up by their bootstraps.

Ideology intersects with power by providing a rationale for leaders to advance certain policies. A "broken system" provided President Clinton and the Republican Congress with intellectual justification for changing welfare provisions. A call for a 15 percent tax cut (to spur economic growth) by 1996 presidential candidate Bob Dole was justified on the basis of the need to spur economic growth. Such a tax cut proposal served as a philosophical reflection of the supply-side rhetoric that dominated in the early 1980s.

When properly utilized, ideology can become a vehicle for electoral advertising campaigns. The outcomes of these campaigns can alter power relationships in government, as new leaders assume positions of influence and old leaders depart from the scene. The struggles between groups as well as the interplay of ideologies have influenced economic and budgetary policy in the past. A review of American economic and budget policy is therefore instructive in assessing the role of rationality, power, and ideology on public policy.

HISTORY OF ECONOMIC AND BUDGET POLICY IN THE UNITED STATES

Early Economic Policy and Budget Reform

During the formative years of the American republic, the government adhered to a "hands off" policy toward the economy, in keeping with the prevailing sentiments of the times. Throughout the 1800s, there was a view that government should be small in size, and the major revenue source of the federal government (customs duties) provided more than enough revenue for running the country. By the early 1900s, however, government spending was outpacing revenue collections. In response to this pressure, governmental units tried to instill greater efficiency in the budget process.

History of Legislative Budget Reform

Spurred by organizations such as the National Municipal League (founded in 1899) and the New York Bureau of Municipal Research (founded in 1906), local governments pushed to reform their budget systems. To a certain extent, these reforms could be viewed as an outcome of both ideological and group conflict. From the ideological perspective, conflict emerged between one value system that prioritized a system of patronage, padded contracts, and special favors and a contrary value system that sought to attain efficiency. The efficiency model was supported by urban property holders who wished to keep their tax rates down. The patronage model was supported by ethnic groups who benefited from a system of government that was based on personal relationships and rewards that were granted in return for favors. From the perspective of power, early budget reform reflected a struggle between business interests who demanded efficiency in government and other interests who wished to utilize government as an engine for personal advancement.

At the forefront of the budget reform movement was Dr. Frederick Cleveland, Director of New York City's Bureau of Municipal Research. Cleveland claimed that inefficiency in the public sector was rampant and that government had a responsibility to its citizens to improve performance.[14] Examples of public sector inefficiency were plentiful. A Finance Commission, appointed in 1907 by Boston Mayor John Fitzgerald, found that between 1895 and 1907 the population of Boston had increased by 22.7 percent, but that in the same period the number of clerks on the city payroll rose by a total of 75 percent. At the same time, clerical salaries for city workers were three times higher than salaries for those employed in similar work at the state level or in the private sector. These disparities were attributed to political pressure. The Finance Commission concluded in their study that because of political pressure, the city's payroll increased regardless of the amount of work to be done, the appropriations for the year, or the ultimate loss to the public.[15]

At the national level, reform interests also began to push for efficiency. In response to these pressures, a thorough review of the budgetary process began in 1911 with a commission appointed by President William Howard Taft. Recommendations of the Taft Commission focused upon the need for the president to develop a systematic and comprehensive budget that would be submitted to Congress at the beginning of each regular session.[16] President Taft, however, was defeated in the 1912 presidential election, and the recommendations of his commission were not enacted. Nevertheless, the idea of budget reform did not die. In 1916, both political parties incorporated planks in their platforms that supported budget reform. Such support accelerated with the increase in the national debt (from $1.2 billion in 1916 to $25.5 billion in 1919) that resulted from World War I.[17] Pressure from the debt contributed to congressional passage of the Budget and Accounting Act of 1921.

The basic philosophy of the Budget and Accounting Act revolved around the idea of increasing executive power. The budget was to be formulated by the president (an executive budget), but (as stipulated in the Constitution) formal responsibility would still rest with Congress. Specifically, the 1921 Act required that the president submit to Congress estimates of expenditures, appropriations, and receipts for the ensuing year. The Bureau of the Budget (which had responsibility for preparing the president's budget) as well as the General Accounting Office (to audit government activity) were created in the Act to assist in budget activities.[18]

The balance between executive and congressional influence in the budgetary process has shifted back and forth in the nation's history. The 1921 Act increased presidential power, but at various times Congress has moved to limit presidential authority. Perhaps the most notable reassertion of congressional power in the budgetary process occurred with the passage of the Congressional Budget and Impoundment Control Act of 1974. Next to the Budget and Accounting Act of 1921, the 1974 Act was the most important piece of budget legislation in the history of the country and, along with the War Powers Resolution, the most profound in the post–World War II era with respect to the balance of constitutional powers between the president and Congress.[19] The 1974 Act established new budgetary organizations such as Budget committees and a Congressional Budget Office to provide Congress with its own source of information. In addition, the 1974 Budget Act established a mechanism for asserting congressional influence over presidential impoundment, or executive seizure of funds that had been allocated to agencies from Congress.

Other budget reforms followed such as the Balanced Budget and Emergency Deficit Control Act of 1985 (commonly referred to as Gramm-Rudman-Hollings) and the 1990 Budget reform. The intent of Gramm-Rudman-Hollings was to reach a balanced budget. If deficit reduction guidelines were not met, automatic cuts in programs were to take effect.[20] The Budget Enforcement Act of 1990 required that increases in direct spending (so-called uncontrollable appropriations) had to be offset by decreases in other areas. The intent of this legislation as well as the 1985 Act was to control deficits.

History of Administrative Budget Reform

Over time, various administrative reforms were implemented. New procedures, in general, reflected a desire to increase rationality and efficiency in the governmental budget process. Procedures, however, were often tied to political leaders and disappeared with the coming of new administrations. The abandonment of old budget reforms and the embrace of new procedures is illustrative of how political influence altered procedures over time. Three major administrative reforms included performance budgeting, planning-programming-budgeting systems, and zero-base budgeting.[21]

Performance Budgeting

Beginning around 1940, efforts began to base budgets upon functions, activities, and projects rather than upon line items. These *performance budgets* included tangible measures of activities such as expected number of letters that could be processed by one Post Office employee. These measures were then applied to assess efficiency. New York State was in the forefront of performance budgeting, calculating unit cost figures for medical care (how many patients served), food service (how many meals provided), and laundry services (how many uniforms cleaned).[22]

The strengths of performance budgeting included a more comprehensive approach to decision making and a movement away from budgeting as control of line items to budgeting as a tool of effective management. Performance budgets allowed public sector managers to see what they received or did not receive for given levels of spending. Efforts to develop more sophisticated tools of rational budget analysis led to implementation of the planning-programming-budgeting systems in the early 1960s.

Planning-Programming-Budgeting Systems (PPBS)

In theory, PPBS presented policymakers with estimates of the effectiveness of various alternatives. Choices were then made based upon those estimates. This

Contemporary Controversy

Deficit Reduction

Growth of Deficits

The inability of legislators to keep spending in line with expenditures is a continuing source of great concern. Total federal debt, yearly deficits, and debt as a percentage of Gross Domestic Product (GDP) have increased since 1980. Table 3.1 describes these trends.

Table 3.1 shows that the total federal debt has grown from less than $1 trillion in 1980 to approximately $5 trillion. Total debt as a percentage of GDP also expanded from 34 percent in 1980 to 71 percent by 1995. The 71 percent figure represents the highest proportion of total debt as a proportion of GDP since 1955. Debt levels as a

process, which became known as "cost-effectiveness" analysis, involved a conscious search for the least costly means of accomplishing specific objectives. To be successful, PPBS required a rigorous and explicit definition of objectives, a wide consideration of alternatives, a careful analysis of the benefits and costs of each alternative, and the use of analysis in decision making. PPBS represented a major step toward developing a more rational decision-making process.[23] PPBS became associated with quantification, centralized control, and rigorous methodologies. These orientations provided PPBS with an aura of scientific certainty, rationality, objectivity, and precision. Workload measures, a longer time horizon, benefit-cost analysis, and arrangements for enforcing decisions all were part of the PPBS budget concept.

Strengths of PPBS included the fact that it tied expenditures to overall program goals. Critics of PPBS, however, maintained that it was too complex and as a result of its complexity, it turned out to be a sham that piled up meaningless data under vague categories.[24] Plagued by critics, PPBS lost its allure as a budgetary innovation, and with Richard Nixon's election as president in 1968 the public sector moved away from this orientation. Nixon replaced the Kennedy administration's budgetary reform of PPBS with an idea of his own, a management by objective (MBO) approach. This approach, however, was abandoned with the Carter administration and zero-base budgeting was adopted.

Zero-Base Budgeting

Zero-base budgeting (ZBB) gained national attention in 1976, when it became a prominent element of Jimmy Carter's campaign for the presidency. Follow-

percent of GDP were at the highest point during World War II, when the very survival of the nation was in question.

When yearly deficits and outlays as a percent of GDP were considered, a more stabilized situation is presented. Yearly deficits peaked in 1992 at $290 billion and receded from that point to $255 billion in 1993, $203 billion in 1994, and an estimate of $192 billion for 1995. Outlays as a percent of GDP were 22 percent in 1993–1995, a decrease from levels in the mid-1980s and early 1990s. Borrowing habits of the federal government compared to those of state and local governments appear in Table 3.2.

Table 3.2 indicates that growth of federal revenues has not kept pace with the growth of state and local revenues between 1980 and 1992. Federal expenditures as a share of all government spending, however, slipped only slightly during this time, from 64 percent to 61 percent. It is apparent that the federal government has been able to maintain spending levels by incurring more and more debt. Federal debt constituted 73 percent of all governmental debt in 1980, and 81 percent of such debt by 1992. The willingness of the federal government to borrow in order to maintain spending levels has generated a great deal of anxiety and debate.

(continued)

ing his election, President Carter directed federal agencies to implement the new reform. Agencies were directed to rank-order groups of activities and their costs at four hypothetical levels: (1) the minimum level, below which the enterprise would no longer be viable; (2) the maintenance level, or what was needed to continue existing levels of operation; (3) the intermediate level, some point between minimum and maintenance; and (4) the improvement level, requiring additional funds to expand operations. Perceived advantages of zero-base budgeting included its ability to eliminate or reduce low-priority programs, reward high-priority programs, improve general program effectiveness, and retard tax increases.

As with other budgetary reforms, however, in time zero-base budgeting was abandoned. Critics of zero-base budgeting claimed that the budget technique was a high-cost, low-payoff process that did little to save tax dollars or improve government programs. Zero-base budgeting fell out of favor in many agencies with the ending of the Carter administration.

Major changes in economic and budget policy occur periodically. Smaller administrative changes often coincide with electoral cycles. As new leaders assume public office, they discard older budgetary techniques and implement their own plans. Larger, more fundamental economic changes occur less frequently. These changes coincide with significant concerns about the economy, as well as leadership capable of setting a new direction. Franklin Roosevelt's New Deal plans were implemented in response to the Great Depression. Ronald Reagan's programs of cutting taxes were enacted after confidence in Keynesian economic philosophies eroded. A dominant economic policy issue of today is that of deficits.

TABLE 3.1 Deficit and Debt 1945–1995 (in billions of dollars)

Year	Total Federal Debt	Debt as Percent of GDP	Surplus or Deficit	Outlays as Percent of GDP
1945	$ 260	123%	$ (48)	44%
1950	257	97	(3)	16
1955	74	71	(3)	18
1960	290	58	.3	18
1965	322	48	(1)	18
1970	381	39	(3)	20
1975	542	36	(53)	22
1980	909	34	(74)	22
1985	1817	46	(212)	24
1990	3206	59	(221)	23
1991	3598	63	(270)	23
1992	4002	67	(290)	23
1993	4351	69	(255)	22
1994	4647	70	(203)	22
1995*	4962	71	(192)	22

*Estimate

Implications of Budget Deficit

Deficit Scenarios

There is no unanimity about the implications of budget deficits. Economists fall within one of three broad schools of thought: (1) deficits as a domesticated pussycat; (2) deficits as a wolf at the door; and (3) deficits as termites in the basement.[25] The domesticated pussycat school of thought contends that the deficit was greatly overrated as a problem, when inflation, state and local surpluses, and long-term investment in infrastructure are taken into account. The wolf at the door perspective forecasts imminent crisis, with investors losing confidence in the American economy, the value of the dollar dropping, interest rates rising, inflation accelerating, the stock market falling, and recession ensuing. A third group of economists view the impact of the deficit as equivalent to having termites in the basement. In this scenario, deficits work quietly, without notice for years and ultimately ruin the foundation of the nation's economy. Economic decline proceeds so gradually in this scenario that by the time the members of the next generation are old enough to ask who was responsible for their diminished circumstances, they will not even know what they have lost.[26]

Deficit Effects

Concerns about the deficit relate to the effect of deficits on inflation, investment, equity, intergenerational transfers, transfers to residents of other nations, and savings.[27] Econ-

TABLE 3.2 Federal Revenues, Expenditures, and Debt as a Percent of All
Government Revenues, Expenditures, and Debt 1980–1992 (in billions of dollars)

Year	Federal Revenue as Percent of All Government Revenue	Federal Expenditures as Percent of All Government Expenditures	Federal Debt as Percent of All Government Debt
1980	61	64	73
1990	56	63	79
1991	57	62	80
1992	47	61	81

Source: Statistical Abstract of the United States, 1995, p. 299.

omists contend that as deficits increase, governments may be tempted to engage in behavior termed "monetizing" the debt. This refers to the printing of large amounts of
money, which enables borrowers to pay off debts with a less valuable currency. From
the power perspective, lenders would lose and borrowers gain from such an outcome.
From the ideological perspective, protectors of sound and reliable "hard money" conflict with advocates of "easy" money. This was seen in American history through debates over gold or sound currency versus currency linked to silver.

Another commonly cited effect of deficits involves the concept of *crowding out*. This
is based on the premise that governmental borrowing will drive out (crowd out) private-
sector investment. Since lending to the national government is almost risk free (because
of the government's power to tax and print money), private borrowers may be unable
to obtain loans. A fall in private loans in turn may produce economic stagnation and a
fall in the overall standard of living for all Americans.

The budget deficit also has implications for the distribution of income. It was estimated that households with assets worth a half million dollars or more own about 20
percent of federal bonds, and that the average American family owns no government
bond directly. Therefore, it can be said that the government debt represents a net expense
for the lower three-quarters of the nation, and a net benefit for the upper one-quarter.[28]

Budget deficits also transfer the burden of repaying debt to future generations. This
burden might be quite onerous, especially if money was borrowed and spent without
making the necessary investments to ensure future prosperity. Future generations appear to be doubly burdened by the recent government practice of incurring long-term
debt to pay for short-term consumption. In assessing the impact of the budget deficits,
the distinction between internal and external debt is also important. A national debt is
considered to be internal if the people who are obligated to repay the debt live within
the same borders as their creditors. For example, the American deficit is considered internal if it is owed largely to American citizens who are subject to the American tax
structure and are likely to spend a significant proportion of their money in the United
States. To the extent that the American budget deficit is funded by external creditors,
the deficit, however, acts to drain funds from the national economy and to send interest payments from American taxes to residents of other countries.

(continued)

In addition to the drain on domestic revenue, external debt also may diminish economic sovereignty. This would occur if foreign lenders used the threat of withdrawing funds as leverage to alter domestic policies. In the extreme, heavy dependence on external sources of revenue could relinquish domestic control over economic policy to others. During most of American history the federal debt was held almost entirely by individuals and institutions within the United States. In the late 1960s, foreign holdings were less than 5 percent (just over $10 billion) of the total federal debt held by the public. Foreign holdings, however, began to grow in the 1970s and by the end of fiscal year 1994 totaled $635.9 billion or 19 percent of the total debt held by the public. In 1994 interest on debt paid to foreigners amounted to $44.5 billion, compared to $0.5 billion in 1965, $0.8 billion in 1970, and $11 billion in 1980.[29]

Case Study

Tax Reform through Profiles in Courage

I N HIS 1994 State of the Union Address, President Clinton claimed that his administration had raised income taxes on only the top 1.2 percent of Americans. With this statement, Clinton boasted indirectly that he had reversed the supply-side tax policies promoted by Ronald Reagan. Clinton accomplished this reversal of the Reagan tax cuts when his budget was passed by Congress on August 6, 1993, with no votes to spare in the House of Representatives and with Vice President Gore breaking a tie in the Senate. The budget promised a significant reduction in the deficit over a five-year period. Revenues would be increased by creating a new top income tax bracket of 36 percent on taxable income of more than $140,000 for couples and $115,000 for individuals; a surtax on income over $250,000; a tax hike on some Social Security benefits; a gas tax increase; and an increase in corporate taxes.

The aura of excitement, partisanship, and ideological struggle that characterized passage of President Clinton's version of tax reform presented in the Omnibus Budget Reconciliation Act of 1993 is described vividly in an account of the casting of the deciding vote on that fateful day on August 5, 1993. This account illustrates how cross-pressure to support party leaders, follow constituent desires, and work for the general good are inherent to the budgetary process:

President Clinton's entire deficit-reduction package rested for a few tense, tumultuous moments at the end of the vote on Aug. 5 in the hands of a wide-eyed, terrified-looking freshman Democrat named Marjorie Margolies-Mezvinsky. She had just gotten off the telephone with Clinton, who told her, in no uncertain terms, that he needed to have her vote. There was only one problem: her career.

The first Democrat in 76 years to be elected from her heavily Republican district along Philadelphia's wealthy Main Line, Margolies-Mezvinsky had pledged to her constituents during her campaign and as recently as the previous day that she would vote

Deficits are also related to savings. From 1972 to 1981, net national savings in the United States was about 7 percent of gross national product. This rate of savings, however, fell to about 2 to 3 percent of gross national product in the 1980s.[30] Economists contend that a lack of savings will hurt investment in plant, equipment, and other forms of capital, which in turn will lower productivity.

The deficit has exerted a tremendous amount of pressure on American politicians to do something about it. Ross Perot generated significant support in 1992 with a message that was focused on the deficit issue. George Bush raised taxes out of fear of the deficit. This strategy of raising taxes, as we can see in the case study below, was also followed by the Clinton administration.

against higher taxes. But Democratic leaders also thought they had extracted a promise from Margolies-Mezvinsky to support the deficit-reduction package if her vote proved necessary to pass it, according to lawmakers and a top leadership aide. . . . With the Democrats two votes short of a majority and no time left, a grim Margolies-Mezvinsky waded into the crowded well of the House accompanied by a supportive but insistent group of fellow Democrats. . . . Margolies-Mezvinsky had to vote for the conference report or it would go down. Rep. Sander M. Levin, D-Mich., held her arms with his hands and spoke to her for a few moments. "Just do what's right," he says he told her. Rep. Cardiss Collins, D-Ill., rubbed her back. Rep. Butler Derrick, D-S.C., gave her a green card. Hoping to spare her the burden of being the final vote, Rep. Pat Williams, D-Mont., says he told her, "we have to vote together." Williams then signed his card and handed it in, and, finally, agonizingly slowly, Margolies-Mezvinsky did the same. Cheers erupted. Republicans reportedly chanted, "Goodbye, Marjorie," and waved at her. A few Democrats waved defiantly back.[31]

Marjorie Margolies-Mezvinsky did indeed lose her race for the House of Representatives in 1994. It is a matter of speculation whether or not her vote on the budget bill directly caused her defeat. One could ask whether or not Margolies-Mezvinsky should have been more responsive to her constituents.

Was she providing a service to the nation by allowing the budget plan to go forward? Did she save Clinton's presidency? Did she kill her career? Was she suckered into defying her core of supporters?

Case Study Questions

1. If you were Marjorie Margolies-Mezvinsky, how would you have voted on the Clinton administration budget?
2. Is it best to vote what your broader conscience tells you is right or to vote in a manner that will satisfy constituents and ensure your reelection?
3. Did rationality, power, or ideology convince Margolies-Mezvinsky to vote as she did?
4. In retrospect, what do you think the congresswoman should have done?
5. Do leaders put too much pressure on new members of Congress to abide by their wishes?

Suggested Readings

Friedman, Benjamin. *Day of Reckoning.* New York: Random House, 1988.

Krugman, Paul. *The Age of Diminished Expectations.* Cambridge, MA: MIT Press, 1994.

Schick, Allen. *The Capacity to Budget.* Washington, DC: Urban Institute Press, 1990.

Shuman, Howard. *Politics and the Budget*, 2nd ed. Englewood Cliffs, NJ: Prentice-Hall, 1988.

Wildavsky, Aaron. *The New Politics of the Budgetary Process.* Glenview, IL: Scott, Foresman, 1988.

Notes

1. Jim Inpopo, "Trouble in Paradise," *U.S. News & World Report*, 19 December 1994, pp. 52–54; Marc Levinson, "A Big Bet Gone Bad," *Newsweek,* 12 December 1994, pp. 58–59; John Greenwald, "The California Wipeout," *Time*, 19 December 1994, pp. 55–56; Floyd Norris, "In Orange County, Strategies Sour," *New York Times,* 5 December 1994, pp. D1, D4; Sallie Hofmeister, "Fund Head Resigns in California," *New York Times,* 6 December 1994, pp. D1, D42; Sallie Hofmeister, "Orange County, Calif., Makes Bankruptcy Filing," *New York Times,* 7 December 1994, pp. A1, D5; Sallie Hofmeister, "A Default by Orange County," 9 December 1994, *New York Times,* pp. D1, D5; David Margolick, "Ill-Fated Fund's Manager: Mr. Main St., Not Wall St.," *New York Times,* 11 December 1994, pp. A1, A36.

2. V. O. Key, Jr., "The Lack of Budgetary Theory," *American Political Science Review* 34 (1940), p. 1138.

3. David Rosenbloom, *Public Administration: Understanding Management, Politics, and Law in the Public Sector,* 3rd ed. (New York: McGraw-Hill, 1993), p. 304.

4. Leonard Merewitz and Stephen H. Sosnick, *The Budget's New Clothes: A Critique of Planning-Programming-Budgeting and Benefit-Cost Analysis* (Chicago: Markham, 1971), p. 10.

5. Larry Schroeder, "Forecasting Local Revenues and Expenditures," in J. Richard Aronson and Eli Schwartz, eds., *Management Policies in Local Government Finance* (Washington, DC: International City Management Association, 1987), pp. 100–101.

6. Donald Kettl, *Deficit Politics: Public Budgeting in Its Institutional and Historical Context* (New York: Macmillan, 1992), p. 53.

7. Keith Bradsher, "Budget Ax Misses in Swing at Sugar-Crop Aid," *New York Times,* 29 September 1995, pp. A1, A26.

8. Key, op cit.

9. Aaron Wildavsky, *The New Politics of the Budgetary Process* (Glenview, IL: Scott, Foresman, 1988), p. 141.

10. Allen Schick, *The Capacity to Budget* (Washington, DC: Urban Institute Press, 1990), pp. 66–67.

11. George Gilder, *Wealth and Poverty* (New York: Basic Books, 1981), p. 59.

12. Schick, op. cit., p. 70.

13. Anthony Campagna, *U.S. National Economic Policy 1917–1985* (New York: Praeger, 1987), p. 486.

14. Frederick Cleveland, "Evolution of the Budget Idea in the United States," *Annals of the American Academy of Political and Social Science* 62 (1915), pp. 15–35.

15. Martin Schiesl, *The Politics of Efficiency: Municipal Administration and Reform in America, 1880–1920* (Berkeley: University of California Press, 1977), p. 103.

16. Frederick Mosher, ed., *Basic Documents of American Public Administration, 1776–1950* (New York: Holmes & Meier, 1976), p. 76.

17. Percival Flack Brundage, *The Bureau of the Budget* (New York: Praeger, 1970), p. 10.

18. Thomas Lynch, *Public Budgeting in America*, 4th ed. (Englewood Cliffs, NJ: Prentice-Hall, 1995), p. 41.

19. Howard Shuman, *Politics and the Budget*, 2nd ed. (Englewood Cliffs, NJ: Prentice-Hall, 1988), p. 185.

20. Don Cozzetto, Mary Kweit, and Robert Kweit, *Public Budgeting: Politics, Institution, and Process* (New York: Longman, 1995), p. 45.

21. Nicholas Henry, *Public Administration and Public Affairs*, 6th ed. (Englewood Cliffs, NJ: Prentice-Hall, 1995), p. 209.

22. Robert Lee and Ronald Johnson, *Public Budgeting Systems*, 3rd ed. (Baltimore: University Park Press, 1983), p. 72.

23. Robert Haveman, *The Economics of the Public Sector*, 2nd ed. (New York: Wiley, 1976), p. 172.

24. Aaron Wildavsky, "Rescuing Policy Analysis from PPBS," *Public Administration Review* 29, 1968, pp. 189–202.

25. Kettl, op. cit., p. 30.

26. Benjamin Friedman, *Day of Reckoning* (New York: Random House, 1988), p. 300.

27. Steven Koven, "Deficit Issues in American Politics and the Appeal of Ross Perot," in Philip Davies and Frederic Waldstein, eds., in *Political Issues in America Today: The 1990s Revisited* (Manchester: Manchester University Press, 1996), pp. 63–67; James D. Savage, *Balanced Budgets and American Politics* (Ithaca, NY: Cornell University Press, 1988).

28. Robert Heilbroner and Peter Bernstein, *The Debt and the Deficit* (New York: Norton, 1989), p. 50.

29. Executive Office of the President of the United States, *Budget of the United States Government, Fiscal Year 1996, Analytical Perspective* (Washington, DC: U.S. Government Printing Office, 1995), pp. 195–196.

30. Paul Krugman, *The Age of Diminished Expectations* (Cambridge, MA: MIT Press, 1994), p. 89.

31. David Cloud, "Big Risk for Margolies-Mezvinsky," *Congressional Quarterly Weekly Report* 51 (32) (1993), p. 2125.

4

The Environment

THE BUTTERFLY EFFECT AND THE GLOBAL ENVIRONMENT

One of the basic concepts of chaos theory[1] is that dramatic events may happen from something as simple as a butterfly in, say, Lawrence, Kansas, flapping its wings, and setting off a chain reaction of ever-greater magnitude until violent cyclones drown thousands of people in Bangladesh. The concept of the butterfly effect illustrates the linkages many students of environmental policy emphasize in their study of contemporary issues and problems. Ozone depletion and acid rain are two examples of environmental problems that involve complex linkages and are therefore widely understood to require the development of international policies. Public attitudes worldwide demonstrate both the breadth and depth of environmental policy concerns. The 1992 Health of the Planet Survey[2] found that environmental problems were rated among the three most serious problems in eleven of the twenty-two countries surveyed. Concerns were expressed regarding air pollution, water pollution, and loss of natural resources.

Environmental issues have reached the forefront of the policy agenda in the United States. Concern over environmental degradation, pollution, and industrial excesses also has become central to attitudes held by the mass publics in countries throughout the planet. Attitudes of Americans during the 1980s toward environmental policy efforts were predominantly pessimistic. A survey by Cambridge Reports[3] found that respondents believed the overall quality of the environment had worsened between 1983 and 1989. Pessimism about the environment increased sharply after 1987. In a 1989 Gallup survey, 66 percent of those interviewed were "extremely concerned" about the pollution of oceans and fresh water; 50 percent were "extremely concerned" about air pollution; and 41 percent were "extremely concerned" about the disposal of household garbage and trash.[4] A 1991 report on the complexities of contemporary public attitudes[5] revealed strongly increased public concern over environmental degradation but uncertainty over what society was willing to do to ensure protection of the environment.

The rational input operates in environmental policymaking. One measure of the global scope of environmental issues is that the United Nations (UN) has convened two highly visible international meetings on many aspects of the environment—the 1972 Conference on the Human Environment, in Stockholm, Sweden, and the 1992 "Earth Summit" Conference on Environment and Development, in Rio de Janeiro, Brazil. The global dimensions of contemporary environmental policy debates within the United States and in other countries were clear from reactions to the agenda the Earth Summit helped to stimulate. One analyst has summarized the policy milieu in this way:

> The Earth Summit refocused the need for environmental issues to be viewed globally, rather than locally. It also provided dramatic evidence of the need for international cooperation to solve the larger issues of global warming, transboundary pollution, biodiversity and the critical question of whether the industrialized world is willing to pay for environmental protection in developing countries. It also spotlighted the North/South split between industrialized and developing nations—a controversy not likely to be resolved by the end of this decade.[6]

Many of the aspects of environmental issues with which policymakers must come to grips are controversial among those who pursue environmental scientific research. Is global warming actually occurring, or is the probability greater of a new ice age? What would be the implications for the planet's inhabitants if either interpretation is correct? How essential is it to restrict carbon dioxide emissions? How is deforestation related to human utilization of the rain forests, and how, in turn, are possible trends in weather systems related to cutting down massive segments of the forest canopy? The public has come to associate radon with life-threatening danger, but how do political institutions come to grips with establishing a threshold above which speedy action must be taken? Acid rain has become both an interstate and international issue, particularly between the United States and Canada. Can the public policy process be expected to address these and other environmental problems? What does it take for governmental intervention to be successful?

The role played in environmental policy by the power input is illustrated by global events in the mid-1980s, when decision makers were forced to follow the lead of public opinion as expressed through organized group pressure. On December 3, 1984, fatal concentrations of methyl isocyanate gas were released from a Union Carbide pesticide plant in Bhopal, India. Over 4,000 residents of the shantytowns of the city died, and approximately 200,000 were injured. The claims for compensation filed by 60,000 people were litigated by the company until 1994, when the plant was sold and part of the proceeds from the sale were held in deposit subject to attachment by Indian courts. An identical plant operating at the same time in Institute, West Virginia, was shut down for several months to undergo inspections and safety checks. This climate made it easier to pass environmental legislation, including the Safe Drinking Water Act Amendments of 1986, which expanded provisions of the 1984 law, and the Federal Insecticide, Fungicide, and Rodenticide Act Amendments of 1988.

The ideological input also operates in the environmental policy context. For example, *The National Review*, a conservative newsmagazine, editorialized that United States participation in the 1992 Rio Earth Summit was tantamount to giving up control over the domestic and international economy, much as the United States was seen by conservatives as having relinquished control over Eastern Europe to the Soviet Union near the end of World War II at the Yalta Conference. The *Review* editorialized that Senate ratification of agreements related to the release of carbon dioxide and ozone-depleting chemicals into the atmosphere and to preserving the diversity of plant and animal species would lead inexorably to "green socialism—a suffocating regulation of American society enforced by federal agencies, the courts and environmental groups answerable not to the American voter but to international agencies acting on the authority of Rio."[7]

Throughout this chapter, we illustrate the many ways in which U.S. political institutions interact with (1) ideology, (2) the political power of organized environmental and antienvironmental interest groups, and (3) expert scientific information. Economic growth strategies, which are at the cutting edge of debates about environmental policy, "are profoundly affected by and, in turn, significantly affect economic and political interests and institutions."[8] Pursuit of economic self-interest often leads industrial, agricultural, and financial interests to oppose public policies that are designed to reduce environmental damage. Similarly, governmental agencies and officials responsible for stimulating economic expansion often oppose expanding the power of agencies and officials who implement environmental policy.

THE RPI INPUTS TO ENVIRONMENTAL POLICY

The Rationality Input

The role of technical expertise in environmental policymaking is determined largely by the receptiveness of decision makers to scientific evidence and success in integrating experts into the policy process. This goal is pursued in a number of ways. For example, there is a Section on Statistics and the Environment within the American Statistical Association, which has as one of its primary functions to educate the public and the professional community to the rigors and virtues of a scientific focus on environmental policy:

Environmental science is concerned with issues affecting our ability to survive in a physically limited, global environment. It involves a spectrum of crucial elements of global sustainability, among them: population distribution, marine and agricultural productivity, and energy requirements and resources. Uncertainties in all areas of environmental research stem from the limits of resolution of the information we can distill from observations of environmental systems, whether they are geophysical, chemical, biological, or social/political.[9]

The confusion that tends to characterize government's environmental policy-making makes it clear that the legislative branch rarely possesses such expertise. For example, political scientist Walter Rosenbaum notes that Congress is "an assembly of scientific amateurs enacting programs of great technical complexity to ameliorate scientifically complicated environmental ills most legislators but dimly understand."[10] The lack of expertise in environmental policy debates frequently leads to the subservience of policymakers to other interests.

In the case of some highly complex, technical issues, neither the agency nor environmentalist interests may be able to testify knowledgeably about how best to implement new legislation. A natural consequence is that rule making often depends heavily on the comments provided by the very industries that are meant to be the targets of the rules.[11] In rule-making areas where agency expertise is especially thin, such as airborne toxins, government bodies may be forced to hire outside, often industry-based, consultants to recommend preliminary rules.[12]

Recent policy debates regarding the environment have addressed a much broader set of issues than had been dealt with in earlier policymaking. One consequence of this diffusion of focus in protecting the environment was the emergence of counterpressures from business groups and their conservative supporters within the environmental policy network and in government and at least the partial "capture" of the issue arena by technical considerations:

> Environmental organizations were no longer able to monopolize the policy debate to serve their own interests. The range of environmental issues had become so extensive that organized environmental groups were unable to act effectively in all areas. Even more important, many issues had become matters not for public debate and legislative action but for administrative choice, an area in which politics was dominated by technical issues that placed a premium on the financial resources necessary to command expertise. This gave considerable political advantage to administrators and private corporate institutions that employed far more technical personnel than did environmentalists.[13]

A major problem for policymakers is how public opinion perceives impending or already-arrived environmental crises. Should policy decisions be driven by what the public thinks should be done, or rather by scientific and "objective" knowledge? Political scientist Jacqueline Switzer summarizes this dilemma:

> Critics point to sweeping government regulation enacted during the Reagan and Bush administrations to reduce concentrations of toxic compounds in water, air, and land even when there was little scientific evidence of risk to humans. Congress,

responding to highly publicized concerns about the dangers of asbestos, radon, and toxic waste dumps, quickly wrote legislation that has ended up costing both the government and business an estimated $140 billion a year. . . .

When the American economy was relatively healthy, few bothered to question the cost/benefit ratio for such expenditures. But with resources growing more and more scarce, and with the federal government placing a new emphasis on domestic problems like health care, education, and the urban infrastructure, this questioning of environmental priorities seems long overdue.[14]

A large part of the rational approach to environmental policy involves properly setting the agenda for debate. Environmental politics specialist Denise Scheberle has discussed environmental agenda-setting when public health is an issue, drawing her examples from scientific evidence of harm from exposure to asbestos and radon. Two points are relevant. First, she found that scientific and medical evidence are necessary, but not sufficient, conditions for agenda setting. In both cases, the scientific evidence alone that identified asbestos and radon as carcinogens failed to propel either problem onto the formal policymaking agenda. However, once those problems reached the agenda, scientific experts became central to shaping the policy debate. Second, Scheberle noted that the long latency periods associated with both carcinogens make it much more difficult to attain scientific consensus; consequently, it becomes more difficult to mobilize public response, while making it easier for policymakers to put off serious efforts to deal with the issue: "Radon offers no evidence, either to the homeowner who can't feel it, or to the researcher looking to attribute particular deaths to radon exposure but who has no similar mesothelioma marker. . . . If radon gas entering homes was blue, or malodorous, undoubtedly public interest would be stirred and the risk would seem more credible."[15]

To develop a more rational focus for environmental policy decisions about when environmental problems may be bad enough to justify governmental action, the area of risk analysis, based on economic arguments, has emerged dramatically in public debates. Efforts to emphasize environmental risk assessment, however, run up against realities of the power input, such as the "Delaney clause" that makes it difficult to establish a meaningful threshold for possible adverse effects on humans of environmental contaminants or the NIMBY (Not In My Back Yard) phenomenon that frequently leads communities to oppose landfills or waste dumps that carry the implicit risk of health and safety hazards. An example of legislative efforts to introduce rational economic motives into environmental policy is the provision of the Clean Air Act Amendments of 1990, which allows companies to trade "pollution credits" among themselves as long as total emissions of pollutants (particularly sulfur from electric power plants) do not increase.

Scheberle argues that participation in policy decisions is determined by public opinion, interest-group activity, and the preferences of new presidential administrations and the changing membership of Congress. Issues pass through a "policy window" of opportunity when the three streams converge: that is, when political conditions favor a solution, policy entrepreneurs devote appropriate resources to pursuit of the issue, and viable solutions are seen as being available:

For radon, a key focusing event, a dramatic spike of media attention, a lack of countervailing pressures by external groups, and the availability of EPA solutions resulted in rather palatable policymaking. For asbestos, multiple focusing events, sustained media presence, and relentless documentation of health risks by medical experts, subsequently legitimized by litigation, were necessary to prompt Congress to pry open an agenda-setting window that had remained shut for decades.[16]

Scheberle concluded that radon, as a naturally occurring substance and thus without ready-made culprits, did not lend itself well either to pinpointing villains or to generating opportunities for hidden agendas, and thus led to "underwhelming" policy responses with no dramatic steps taken to deal with what EPA had defined as the nation's leading health risk. In sharp contrast, villains both inside and out of government were rather easily identified with asbestos-related problems. Consequently, asbestos was placed on the nation's formal policy agenda for congressional action following activities by policy entrepreneurs, media attention, and legal proceedings.

One effort to establish a science-related rational basis for controlling environmental hazards has used provisions of the Superfund Amendments and Reauthorization Act (SARA) of 1986 contained in its Title III, which came to be known as The Emergency Planning and Community Right-to-Know Act. A reaction to the Bhopal disaster of 1984, Title III of SARA was designed to help communities prepare for similar chemical emergencies and to reduce the risks from such incidents. This was done by requiring every state to establish a system of Local Emergency Planning Committees, to identify potential sources of accidents involving hazardous materials, to develop integrated plans for responding to such emergencies, and to assimilate private industry information in developing their response plans. Rich, Conn, and Owens determined, however, that the "regulation-through-information" approach attempted by SARA Title III was not likely to succeed without stronger provisions for implementation of the Title's mandates. They call for the Local Emergency Planning Committees to "adopt the role of planning for and advocating active risk communication by other organizations."[17] Table 4.1 shows the scope of the hazardous waste problem confronting efforts taken under the Superfund legislation.

Policy theorist John Dryzek has proposed a framework for ecological rationality, based upon what he regards as the characteristics of ecology: complexity, nonreducibility, variability, uncertainty, and the pursuit of collective or public goods. Dryzek's analysis found that none of seven conventional mechanisms for social choice or policymaking (markets, administered systems, polyarchy, law, moral persuasion, armed conflict, and bargaining) is acceptable as a means to ecological rationality. Drawing from critical theory, Dryzek argued for the implementation of practical reason, communicative rationalization, and radical decentralization, to facilitate ecological and political interchange of ideas, to build consensus, and to stimulate collective action.[18] In a study of fish and wildlife conservation, Matthew McKinney concluded that "[w]hile many of these recent policy developments have been created by genuine ecological needs and are based on sound scientific information, their formulation and implementation have been fraught with conflict." The challenge

TABLE 4.1 Hazardous Waste Sites in the United States, 1995

State	Final	Proposed	State	Final	Proposed
Alabama	12	1	Montana	8	1
Alaska	8	0	Nebraska	9	1
Arizona	10	0	Nevada	1	0
Arkansas	12	0	New Hampshire	17	0
California	92	4	New Jersey	106	1
Colorado	16	2	New Mexico	10	1
Connecticut	15	0	New York	81	0
Delaware	19	0	North Carolina	23	0
District of Columbia	0	0	North Dakota	2	0
Florida	54	4	Ohio	34	4
Georgia	13	0	Oklahoma	10	1
Hawaii	4	0	Oregon	11	1
Idaho	8	2	Pennsylvania	100	2
Illinois	37	0	Rhode Island	12	0
Indiana	32	1	South Carolina	25	0
Iowa	18	1	South Dakota	3	1
Kansas	10	2	Tennessee	16	2
Kentucky	20	0	Texas	28	1
Louisiana	13	4	Utah	12	4
Maine	10	1	Vermont	8	0
Maryland	12	2	Virginia	24	0
Massachusetts	30	0	Washington	55	0
Michigan	75	2	West Virginia	6	0
Minnesota	39	0	Wisconsin	40	0
Mississippi	2	3	Wyoming	3	0
Missouri	19	3			
Totals	1,224	52			

Source: Environmental Protection Agency, *National Priorities List,* April 1995.

is to develop policy that, from a scientific and ecological input, will get the job done, and that, from a political perspective, is generally acceptable to all affected parties.[19]

The Power Input

Pro-environmental Groups

Contemporary environmental policy actors have evolved a complex array of groups active in diverse specific issues. Membership figures range from the 5.8 million enrolled in the National Wildlife Federation, 4 million worldwide in Greenpeace, roughly 500,000 each in the Sierra Club and the National

Audubon Society, 360,000 in the Wilderness Society, 200,000 in the National Parks and Conservation Association, 170,000 in the National Resources Defense Council, 150,000 in the Environmental Defense Fund, and about 50,000 each in the Izaak Walton League and Friends of the Earth.[20]

Points of access vary from presenting testimony before congressional committees and exerting pressure through mobilizing public opinion, to a more recent emphasis on legal action by groups such as the Environmental Defense Fund and the Natural Resources Defense Council. Provisions in most national environmental legislation since the Clear Air Act of 1970 have encouraged the growth of litigation by permitting any person to sue private parties for civil penalties and for noncompliance with injunctions to stop pollution-generating acts.[21] Successful lawsuits can provide litigating groups with very profitable payments from companies found guilty.

One of the more spectacular means of indirect lobbying is the publication by Environmental Action of "Dirty Dozen" lists of leading congressional opponents of environmental legislation. Similarly, the League of Conservation Voters publishes an annual report, the *National Environmental Scorecard*, that ranks the voting records of members of Congress on environmental issues, and publicizes a "Greenscam" list of antienvironmental members of Congress who masquerade as being in favor of environmental legislation.

More specialized environmental interest groups include Clean Water Action, which lobbies on issues pertaining to drinking water and groundwater, toxic chemicals, and hazardous waste sites. The Defenders of Wildlife act to protect wildlife habitats, and has thrown its 80,000-member organization into strengthening the Endangered Species Act and funding for wildlife refuges. The National Toxics Campaign, a 100,000-member group formed in 1984, is focused on preventing pollution derived from pesticides and on reducing toxic waste. Through its Consumer Pesticide Project, the National Toxics Campaign opposes the use of suspected carcinogens in food production and opposes selling pesticides which are banned in the United States to Third World countries. Its Citizens' Environmental Laboratory at Boston University provides low-cost tests for residents who may have been exposed to toxic contamination. Ducks Unlimited, founded in 1937, purchases land to help maintain wetlands. The Nature Conservancy, founded in 1951, with over 600,000 members, has preserved over five million acres scattered across all fifty states as well as ecological preserves to maintain endangered species across national boundaries.

More radical environmental groups include Earth First!, which has been active since 1980 and is at the cutting edge of the environmental movement. Its activities include inserting large metal spikes into trees so that they can't be harvested for timber, blocking logging roads, and threatening to sabotage utility power lines that run through forested areas. Members of Earth First! were arrested in 1989 for conspiring to sabotage western nuclear power facilities. The Sea Shepherd Conservation Society, founded in 1977 as an offshoot from Greenpeace, protects sea mammals and birds, with its members sometimes exposing themselves to physical harm in order to prevent the hunting of whales or seals.

Although the actions of radical groups may make it difficult for more mainstream environmental groups to form workable political coalitions with other societal interests, such coalitions are not rare. In 1946, the Natural Resources Council of America was established as an umbrella coalition of more than seventy groups; it is active in sharing information among member organizations and in conducting policy briefings and opinion surveys on energy and natural resources. Other examples of coalitions include a common lobbying effort in 1978 and 1979 directed at Forest Service plans for designating wilderness areas, and formation of the National Clean Air Coalition that came together to support the 1977 and 1990 Clean Air Act amendments. In 1981, a number of environmental groups, led by the National Wildlife Federation, pressured President Reagan to remove James Watt as Secretary of the Interior and to reverse his plans to open up public lands for commercial development. Informal coalitions also form from time to time, such as the Group of Ten that brings together many of the heavy-hitters of environmental lobbying.

Antienvironmental Groups

Organized opposition to the goals of environmental interest groups has become far more evident since the rise of activist conservationism in the 1960s. Much of this opposition arises from the shift in the environmental policy debate from Progressive-era prodevelopment arguments over the exploitation of natural resources to proposals that are seen as more threatening to established corporate interests. The "wise use" movement unites farmers, ranchers, industry, and elements of organized labor in a loose alliance directed toward blocking gains for environmentalism.[22]

Rural prodevelopment interests have reacted against expanded recreational uses of farm land and range land, raptor protection programs, regulation of agricultural land use practices (regarding pesticides, herbicides, soils, and irrigation, for example), oil pipelines, and utility transmission lines. Labor lobbyists, although frequently supportive of worker-protection aspects of environmental legislation, have opposed policies addressing pollution control, as well as implementation of the Endangered Species Act on the grounds that jobs were at stake.

The fiercest and most unyielding opposition to the environmentalist agenda, however, has come from the oil, natural gas, uranium, timber, and other extractive industries, as well as from electric utilities, textile manufacturers, and chemical companies. Industry positions have been described as "marked not by agreement of values but by tactics of containment, by a working philosophy of maximum feasible resistance and minimum feasible retreat."[23] Trade associations and nonprofit research groups, such as the American Forest Institute, created by the logging industry to justify increased timber production, were established to foster legislative goals of large corporations. To some segments of industry, particularly the oil sector, active opposition to environmental concerns represents justifiable self-defense against threats to profit.

Corporations counterattack against the environmentalist agenda in several ways: (1) public relations campaigns, to suggest that these "soulful" companies protect and clean up the environment; (2) retaining lobbyists at both national and state levels, and in-house policy experts, to intercede in the policymaking process before rules and/or legislation go into effect; and (3) influencing the scope and nature of policy implementation at lower levels of administrative rule making, particularly by proposing standards for assessing the risks associated with regulated substances and by refusing to release product or research data on grounds of trade secrecy or proprietary interests.[24]

More recently, affected industries have taken preemptive action by drafting their own legislation, rather than letting the policymaking process fall under the control of antagonists. This approach was evident in the Clear Air Act Amendments of 1990, when chemical industry representatives actively pursued their own legislative proposals, and when the utility industry's Clean Air Working Group joined with sympathetic members of Congress to introduce amendments that would reduce the costs of complying with legislative proposals that addressed the issue of acid rain.[25]

A shift in the arena of combat between environmentalist and corporate interests was evident by the late 1980s. Efforts by both sides to mobilize popular support through ballot initiatives and referenda became increasingly common. Eighteen environmental referenda measures had been approved by 1986, but at least seventeen such proposals were adopted in 1988 alone. California's proposed "Big Green" Proposition 128, which would have banned pesticides, prohibited new offshore drillings, stopped the cutting of virgin redwood forests, and required sharp reductions in emissions of carbon dioxide from utility plants, was defeated by about two to one, with the assistance of over $6 million from oil and chemical companies. Environmentalist ballot measures in other states have also lost recently, in the face of formidable opposition. A corporate counterattack solicited signatures for probusiness initiatives like the Global Warming and Clear-Cutting Reduction, Wildlife Protection and Reforestation Act of 1990 ("Big Stump"), and the Consumer Pesticide Enforcement Act ("Big Brown").

The concept of the "wise use" of natural resources arose from the 1988 Multiple Use Strategy Conference of 250 industrial groups that were brought together by the Center for Defense of Free Enterprise. The conference propounded twenty-five goals to be pursued for opening up national parks and wilderness areas to mineral exploration, expanding park visitor facilities and commercial operations, and restricting enforcement of the Endangered Species Act. Switzer notes:

> Today, the wise use movement is a loosely organized coalition of hundreds of groups led by three umbrella organizations: the Alliance for America, the National Inholders Association, and the Western States Public Lands Coalition. The groups share a deep antigovernment feeling and opposition to efforts by environmentalists to close off use of federal lands. Their efforts are supported by legal assistance from the Mountain States Legal Foundation, agricultural groups, and oil, timber, and mining companies. . . .
> In addition to cattlemen opposing higher grazing fees, the grass-roots efforts tap into gulf shrimpers opposing the use of turtle-excluding devices, Alaskans seeking oil

drilling, and private property owners from eastern states battling the National Park Service. What seems to bother environmentalists most is the fact the wise use movement's leaders are using the same tactics they themselves have used successfully for more than two decades. They appear to be well organized, well funded, and ready to even out the political seesaw that has characterized the policy process thus far.[26]

It has become common for industry opposition to environmental policy initiatives to remain latent during the adoption stage of the policy process, to project a better public image, and to exert maximum influence during decision-making about how to implement newly adopted policies. Prime targets have been the Environmental Protection Agency and other executive-branch agencies. One consequence of this strategy of pursuing industry advantage behind closed doors is to reduce the role that can be played by environmental interests, who profit from exposing industry's influence on public policy.

As an example, consider the rule-making process related to implementing key provisions of the 700-page Clean Air Act Amendments of 1990, which required over the span of two years 150 separate regulatory activities, 100 of which were adoptions of rules, compared to the much smaller number (fewer than ten per year) of major regulations promulgated annually by EPA. In this policymaking context, interest group action to counter industry pressures is complicated by the short time available to consider components of decisions required to implement the law. Thus, public input is likely to be discounted heavily by agencies that are forced to make up their collective minds on the spot about how to implement a vast array of rules.[27]

The sheer complexity of such a rule-making process is daunting. It wasn't until 1980 that EPA implemented initial rules under the less complex, though still far-reaching, Resource Conservation and Recovery Act of 1976. Even slower rule-making action by state governments waiting to receive funding for new federal mandates) gave more time for industry to resist or shape the resulting rules.[28]

It is difficult to balance inherently contradictory governmental goals:

> All governments . . . place highest priority on economic growth, even at the expense of the local and global environment.
>
> Powerful economic and political or bureaucratic interests present a formidable obstacle to the development of sustainable environmental strategies. . . . Industrial, commercial landowning, and other powerful economic interests oppose, often successfully, enactment of strict environmental laws and, if they are enacted, weaken their implementation. Government agencies and legal and political institutions often oppose environmental restrictions and even contribute to environmental degradation.[29]

The Ideological Input

Much of the philosophy of the modern environmental movement arose in the nineteenth century. The concept of national parks, for instance, was first proposed by George Catlin, in 1832. Henry David Thoreau's Walden Pond writings popularized the idea of an unspoiled countryside. Frederick Law Olmsted, one of the nation's first landscape architects and the "father of Central Park," toured the Yosemite valley in 1864. Olmsted was appointed a manager of Yosemite in 1865 and became active in the effort to preserve its rugged natural beauty. George Waring, who built the nation's first separate sewer system, in Lenox, Massachusetts, in 1876, became known as "the apostle of cleanliness" for his attempts to educate the public and policymakers about the public health consequences of garbage.

At the turn of the century, the environmental battlefront pitted a generally prodevelopment perspective against forces opposed to all uses of wilderness areas except for education and recreation. The struggle was personified by the clash of views between Gifford Pinchot, following European "technocratic utilitarianism"[30] or principles of forest management emphasizing sustainable development, and John Muir, who opposed the encroachment of commercial timber cutting and other exploitative interests.

The Progressive movement, and its emphasis on efficient use of natural resources, gave way in the Great Depression to direct government activity to foster job growth and resource conservation. The end of World War II greatly increased public demand for access to recreational opportunities in the national parks. By the 1960s, open ideological warfare broke out between supporters of unrestrained capitalist industrial growth and those wishing to limit environmental damage from pollution and resource depletion. The two primary dimensions of the debate involved environmental hazards[31] and overpopulation.[32]

An ideological focus to environmental policy conflicts was evident in reactions to the inaugural April 22, 1970, Earth Day, which was sponsored by Democratic Senator Gaylord Nelson of Wisconsin, coordinated by Denis Hayes, former student body president at Stanford University, and modeled on 1960s-style teach-ins opposing the Vietnam war. President Richard Nixon refused to issue an official proclamation supporting Earth Day.[33] Other conservatives argued that holding the first Earth Day on Lenin's birthday indicated its anticapitalist spirit. The Ford presidency generally continued its predecessor's policies toward environmentalist interests.

Energy problems, compounded by an Arab oil embargo, plus a severe recession late in President Carter's term, shifted the policy emphasis to economic growth and energy independence. Further signs of an antienvironmental backlash were clearly evident in the "Sagebrush Rebellion" that united agricultural, mining, timber, ranching, and other corporate interests, supported by conservative law firms and political action committees opposed to what they regarded as further governmental encroachments on free enterprise and unrestricted exploitation of natural resources, particularly in the mountain and far western states.

The ideological edge of environmental policy debates became much sharper during the Reagan administration, which pursued with great vigor its program of free-market deregulation, loosening governmental restrictions on resource exploitation, and keeping conservationist interest groups away from policy decisions. Environmental groups saw the Reagan administration, and particularly two of its leading energy and environmental policymakers—Secretary of the Interior James Watt, a product of the Sagebrush Rebellion, and Environmental Protection Agency Administrator Anne Burford—as fiercely antagonistic to conservationism. Watt had divided the public into two categories—liberals and Americans—and referred to the Audubon Society as "a chanting mob."[34] A major analysis of the state of environmental policy under Reagan's presidency found that Watt viewed supporters of environmental action as "dangerous and subversive, suggesting they sought to weaken America and to undermine freedom. He called them extremists and likened them to Nazis."[35] One result was a dramatic growth in the membership of leading environmental organizations, which saw the Reagan policy team as a mortal threat to their agendas. From 1980 to 1983, membership in the Wilderness Society shot up by 144 percent, by 90 percent in the Sierra Club, by 40 percent in the Defenders of Wildlife, and also by 40 percent in Friends of the Earth. By 1990, the combined ranks of the environmental lobbying groups numbered over 3 million.[36]

The Bush administration partly defused the anger that had developed during the Reagan years, particularly by reemphasizing professionalism within EPA. This was exemplified by the appointment of William Reilly as EPA administrator. Reilly, former environmental interest group activist and someone who clearly knew at least as much about the subject matter as about the politics of environmental policy, turned to science and risk assessment "to help the Agency put together a much more coherent agenda than has characterized the past twenty years."[37]

Conflicts over the relative virtues of centrally planned or free market economic ideology, as well as divisions within United States society over the proper role of governmental regulation within a mixed-capitalist base economic structure, shape the context within which environmental policy debates are carried to fruition or to frustration. As stated by Uday Desai:

> Dominant ideology, a set of assumptions and prescriptions about the world, both natural and social, defines the parameters within which problems, including ecological ones, are defined and discussed and solutions conceived and carried out. . . . [D]rastically different perspectives . . . limit the ways in which ecological problems are perceived, and influence the range of policy responses that are designed and implemented to deal with those problems.[38]

Robert Paehlke[39] argues that environmentalism may provide "the first original ideological input to develop since the middle of the nineteenth century," and hopes that it will align with the moderate left in western societies to form a new progressive coalition. Paehlke notes that developing this breadth of progressive ideology will require a major transformation and broadening of environmentalism from its origins as a limited and narrow movement, but hopes that signs of this greater breadth are present in the focus on sustainable development, environmental protection as a means to produce jobs, urban environmental needs, the greater impact of environmental degradation on the poor and on racial minorities, global consciousness regarding environment and resources, and the transition to post–Cold War thinking.

The ideological input into environmental policy should not be expected to work in isolation from the other two inputs. Research by Evan Ringquist, for example, has shown that varying mixes of political and ideological factors have been important for hazardous waste management, owing to the high visibility of hazardous materials and negative public opinion on that issue, whereas interest group influence was the most important input in water pollution control:

> First, there is little evidence that state governments are "captured" by pollution industries. The only evidence of capture in state pollution control regulation is the influence of the mining industry on state water pollution control programs. Second, wealth does not determine state policymaking in pollution control. Third, once we discount the capture thesis and the "economics determines politics" perspective, we find that states are fairly responsive in developing pollution control programs. All other things equal, states with more liberal citizens, more environmentally concerned political elites, stronger environmental groups, more professional legislatures, and greater threats to environmental quality enact stronger pollution control regulations. Finally, the influence of these factors and the responsiveness of the political system vary across policy areas, even when the policies are of the same general type.[40]

Application of RPI to Environmental Policy

An example of the technical complexity of environmental issues is provided by the impending deregulation of the electric utility industry, with likely consequences of cost-cutting (and hence service reduction), diversification, location of power plants for U.S. consumption in other countries, mergers of existing utilities into larger conglomerates, and the bankruptcy of those that cannot compete in the new framework.[41]

The decision in 1994 by the California Public Utilities Commission, consistent with the free-market policies of recent national and state administrations, to allow utilities to compete for customers across state borders and to transmit to those customers through any available power lines, set the pattern for far-reaching change with potentially important environmental consequences. In 1996, the Federal Energy Regulatory Commission (FERC) ordered 166 regulated electric utilities to open up their transmission systems to outside energy providers. Applying only to the distribution of wholesale power, the order enables lower-cost energy producers, particularly in the Midwest, to deliver electricity through a national network to higher-cost areas, such as the Northeast. States were given the right to determine the extent to which local power competition would be implemented, and some, particularly California and in the Northeast, moved to do so as early as 1997. Environmental interests, such as the Natural Resources Defense Council, noted that energy costs in the Northeast were higher because of more stringent environmental restrictions and feared that free market policies would result in customers' buying cheaper power from midwestern plants that burned air-polluting coal. A hint of possible energy and environmental policy issues to come was provided by blackouts that affected many western states through increasingly interconnected power grids.

One likely outcome of this reliance on "rational" market forces to drive down costs and enhance efficiency would be to reduce less profitable services, particularly assistance to low-income residential customers who lack the money, knowledge, expertise, or influence of the large corporations. Large corporations would be able to shop around for the lowest-cost energy supplier. Costs could increase for smaller business and residential consumers, if large corporations were left to get a better bargain elsewhere.

Worries among environmentalists focus on the prospects that market-driven efforts to rationalize the power industry will sidetrack research into more efficient ways to use existing energy resources, and delay or stop the development of alternative sources of energy from the sun, wind, or waste products. Ralph Cavanagh, director of the energy program of the Natural Resources Defense Council, worried that utilities would try to sell as much power as possible, to increase their revenues and profits, rather than stress conservation: "If utilities are going to live or die solely by how low they can drive the short-term commodity price of electricity, they will have every reason to resist investments to reduce pollution or to help customers save energy."[42]

HISTORY OF ENVIRONMENTAL POLICY

From Colonial Times to 1900

Environmental policy concerns within the United States predate the formation of a unified country out of the original colonies. In 1626, the Plymouth Colony of Massachusetts adopted regulations about cutting and selling timber from public lands. Various colonial governments placed limitations on deliberately set forest fires (perhaps an early version of Smokey the Bear's admonition that "Only you can prevent forest fires") and on the hunting of deer and other game; they also set aside land to grow new trees, for forest preservation, and for the protection of coastal water birds.

Economic and social developments during the nineteenth century led to concern over soil erosion and timber poaching (made more profitable by the Erie Canal, which opened in 1825 and made it easier to ship forest products eastward). Awareness of the nation's rugged natural beauty was enhanced by explorers such as Lewis and Clark (beginning in 1804) and John Wesley Powell (who explored the Colorado River in 1869). Popular publications, including *The American Sportsman* (which began in 1871) and *Forest and Stream* (starting in 1873) disseminated conservationist views. In 1870, the American Fisheries Society came into existence, followed in 1871 by the creation of the U.S. Fish Commission, the first federal agency established to conserve a specific natural resource.

The increasing concentration of rapidly growing urban populations, particularly in the northeast and midwest, was accompanied by increasingly severe problems of garbage disposal, industrial pollution, contamination of drinkable water sources, and sewage treatment. Federal government involvement in preserving ecosystems began in 1872, with the creation of Yellowstone National Park, followed fairly soon thereafter (in 1890) with Sequoia, Kings Canyon, and Yosemite National Parks, and in 1899 with Mount Rainier National Park. A further sign of expanding public consciousness of preservation and federal activism was the proclamation on April 10, 1872, of the first Arbor Day, due to the work of Nebraska activists including the editor of the state's first newspaper.[43] More broadly based environmental organizations are traceable to the Sierra Club, founded in 1892 by John Muir.

Conservationism in the United States laid down deep political—and thus also policy—taproots during the Progressive era at the end of the nineteenth century. Early organized efforts to conserve spring flood waters for use during the dry season, to foster "planned and efficient progress," helped to give rise to a much broader environmental consciousness.[44] A clear divergence arose, however, between those who believed that sustainable exploitation of resources was possible and those who favored restricting the use of wilderness areas to recreation and education only. The battle was won by those emphasizing coexistence of conservation with commercial exploitation and multiple uses of wilderness areas.[45]

Women's organizations were in the forefront of developing the national environmental policy agenda as it evolved from awareness of early urban environmental issues such as solid waste and water quality. By the end of the nineteenth century, worsening urban pollution associated with rapid industrialization gave rise to citizens' movements focused on alleviating environmental problems. These groups included the Ladies' Health Protective Association, founded in New York; the Civic Club of Philadelphia; Boston's Women's Municipal League; and the Women's Organization for Smoke Abatement, of St. Louis. Civic groups largely organized and led by women monitored the scope of pollution and proposed solutions to other problems such as garbage and sanitation. However, the struggle for women's suffrage took precedence until the late twentieth century, when groups associated with the ecofeminist movement became key players in both feminist and environmental policy arenas.[46]

From 1900 to World War II

Near the dawn of the twentieth century, the environmentalist movement in the United States split into sustainable development supporters and those favoring preservation of the pristine qualities of the natural wilderness. The conflict generally was resolved in favor of the sustainable developmentalists, largely because of the strategic resources brought to bear by Gifford Pinchot, who directed national policy away from preservationist alternatives. Trained in the French Forest School and later forester for George W. Vanderbilt's 7,000-acre North Carolina estate, Pinchot became in 1898 chief of the Division of Forestry (precursor of the U.S. Forest Service). A personal friend of President Theodore Roosevelt, he led national policy toward a system of setasides for future timber harvesting and the adoption of scientific forestry practices.

A concomitant of the urban middle-class Progressive movement in the early twentieth century was the formation of major environmental interest groups, many of which are still active today. The National Audubon Society was founded in 1905, the National Conservation Association in 1909, the National Parks Association in 1919, and the Izaak Walton League in 1922. Switzer summarizes these groups' interest in "good government": "The Progressive reforms were focused on the term *efficiency*. There was a sense that it was possible to make better use of natural resources. The reformers were not radicals in the traditional political sense, and for the most part, Progressive conservation posed only a modest threat to the existing distribution of power in the United States."[47]

The division of policy aims within the environmental movement between conservationists and preservationists came to a head during the 1930s, giving rise to a new set of interest-group actors. The Wilderness Society was established in 1935 by Aldo Leopold to protect public lands, and the National Wildlife Federation became active in 1936. The National Wildlife Federation focused on educating the public on threats to environmental preservation, through activities such as schools' National Wildlife Week. The emphasis on efficiency persisted largely because of active cooperation with environmental groups by various engineering societies, including the American Society of Civil Engineers, the American Society of Mechanical Engineers, the American Institute of Electrical Engineers, and the American Institute of Mining Engineers.

In May of 1908, hundreds of national leaders on the emerging environmental policy arena were brought together at a White House Conference on Resource Management. This convocation, under the direction of Gifford Pinchot, chief of the Department of Interior's Division of Forestry and a leading proponent of appropriate exploitation of America's natural resources, was among the first official agenda-setting efforts in that policy domain. One of its major recommendations resulted in the creation by President Theodore Roosevelt of the National Conservation Commission, chaired by Pinchot, with the goal of making an inventory of the country's natural resources. Parallel entities were established in forty-one states within a year.[48] Conservation congresses were held until 1917, discussing problems related to forests, soil, water, public control of railroads, foodstuff speculation and gambling, rural education, and coordination among governmental agencies.[49] In 1916, the National Park Service was created.

National consensus about the need for vigorous public-sector efforts to mitigate and reverse the catastrophic effects of the Great Depression brought about a greatly expanded role for the national government in environmental policy, as in many other aspects of society. This greater commitment to governmental activism in the environmental policy arena took the form of new federal agencies having specific resource responsibilities. In 1933, the Tennessee Valley Authority provided low-cost electrical and hydroelectric power to rural and low-income households in the southeast. In 1935, the Soil Conservative Service was created. Between 1933 and 1942, the Civilian Conservation Corps provided productive work for two million unemployed young men.

From World War II to the 1960s

New environmental interest groups arose after World War II. In 1947, the Defenders of Wildlife was founded, with the goal of improving and maintaining the diversity of wildlife and their habitats. In 1951, the Nature Conservancy began to acquire habitat areas to preserve endangered species. Growing affluence and increased population pressure changed environmental policy priorities (as new recreational needs arose from the prosperity, free time, and population growth of postwar society) to eclipse the previous commitment to efficient scientific management. By 1950, the national parks recorded 30 million visitors. Combined with lagging development of infrastructure, this growth led the National Park Service to develop its Mission '66 plan for a program of improvements that established a blueprint for evolution of the park system through the 1980s.

As the number of national park visitors grew in the following years (72 million by 1960), Congress enacted the Land and Water Conservation Fund to add new wilderness areas and national parks. The National Wilderness Act of 1964 and the Wild and Scenic Rivers and National Trails Acts of 1968 expanded recreational areas. The administration of Lyndon Johnson supported the creation of urban parks, and the First Lady, Lady Bird Johnson, fostered the 1965 Highway Beautification Act, limiting highway advertising and providing incentives to clean up litter along roadways.

During the 1960s, political efforts to protect the environment that in some cases had begun decades earlier came to fruition. Congress enacted the Clean Air Act in 1963, later amending it in the Air Quality Act of 1967, the Water Quality Act of 1965, the Endangered Species Conservation Act in 1966, and the National Environmental Policy Act (NEPA) in 1969. The crowning achievement of this 1960s legislative flurry was NEPA, which provided the policy foundation for much of the subsequent activity in the environmental policy arena. NEPA, however, did not become meaningful until federal courts granted environmental groups the right to sue to ensure the enforcement of environmental impact statements.

The emergence of a new generation of environmental interest groups and renewed congressional interest in the political complexities of overpopulation and environmental degradation led to a flurry of legislative activity during the 1960s. Among the salient developments of the decade were two offshore oil spills in 1969 near Santa Barbara, California, which produced sharp public reaction. Media images of oil-soaked birds and beaches heightened public awareness of environmental hazards and environmental depletion. Major new groups included the African Wildlife Foundation (1961), the World Wildlife Fund (1961), the Environmental Defense Fund (1967), and the Council on

Economic Priorities (1969). Membership in the Sierra Club increased tenfold from 1952 to 1969, and the roster of the Wilderness Society grew over four times between 1960 and 1970.

The 1970s

Yet another set of environmental interest groups arose in the early 1970s. These included the Center for Science in the Public Interest, Citizens for a Better Environment, Environmental Action, Friends of the Earth, the League of Conservation Voters, the Natural Resources Defense Council, Save the Bay, Greenpeace, and Ralph Nader's Public Citizen. The mobilization of business and industry interests opposing the proenvironmental, and often antidevelopment, thrust of these and other groups also gained momentum in the 1970s.

In 1970, President Nixon—overcoming his initial opposition to activist environmental legislation and taking the opportunity to upstage Congress by taking advantage of rising public concern over perceived environmental problems—created the Environmental Protection Agency (EPA) by executive order. A bidding war ensued between the two ends of Pennsylvania Avenue, with Congress adopting major new environmental legislation and refining previous laws. Among the accomplishments of the 1970s were the Marine Mammal Protection Act of 1972, the Federal Environmental Pesticide Control Act of 1972, the Federal Water Pollution Control Act Amendments of 1972, updating the original 1948 legislation, the Resource Conservation and Recovery Act of 1976, and the Toxic Substances Control Act of 1976.

Presidential involvement in environmental politics, until recently, was generally limited, apart from occasional bursts of activism such as those under Theodore Roosevelt early in the twentieth century. The Nixon administration started the contemporary presidential role in this arena, by initiating the Environmental Protection Agency (which originally was supposed to have been an independent pollution-control agency), a rather reluctant initiative since Nixon believed that the focus on environmental problems was "faddish."[50]

Under the inaugural direction of William Ruckelshaus, EPA emphasized air and water pollution, resulting in better compliance with then-current urban air quality standards and refocusing water-related issues from aesthetics to health implications. One consequence of the creation of EPA was to reduce the role of the Department of the Interior and its more traditional focus on recreational and developmentalist concerns regarding the environment.

The Ford administration faced a different environmental policy agenda, as the nation confronted the effects of the 1973 Arab oil embargo, which now outweighed fears of pollution by spreading concern that the costs to industry to comply with environmental legislation were harming economic growth and by lessening pressures from public opinion and environmental interest groups. During Ford's tenure, Congress expanded the EPA's authority with the Safe Drinking Water Act of 1974, the Toxic Substances Control Act of 1976, and the Resource Conservation and Recovery Act of 1976.

Jimmy Carter's 1976 presidential campaign appealed openly for support from environmental groups. Although he retained their support throughout his presidency and during his unsuccessful reelection campaign in 1980, Carter overrode the wishes of one of the political heroes of environmentalism, Maine Democratic Senator Edmund Muskie, by selecting Douglas Costle as EPA administrator. To the dismay of many in the environmental movement, Costle endeavored to redirect EPA's activities "to convince the public that EPA was first and foremost a public health agency, not a guardian of birds and bunnies."[51] One of the major developments of Carter's tenure, however, was the adoption in 1980 of Superfund legislation, setting up a $1.6 billion emergency account to be drawn on to clean up spilled or dumped toxic materials, and shifting the agency's emphasis away from conventional pollutants. This shift also helped the EPA budget to grow by about 25 percent.

In addition, the Carter administration claimed success with the Alaska Land Bill of 1980, bringing millions of acres of untouched wilderness under federal protection; a windfall profits tax on oil to fund research into solar energy; and stricter energy conservation measures. The tenor of Carter-administration environmental policy perhaps is summarized best in the statement by his secretary of the interior, Cecil Andrus: "I am part of the environmental movement and I intend to make the Interior Department responsive to the movement's needs."[52] The Carter record, however, did not include comprehensive planning; instead, Carter emphasized the "malaise" in public attitudes regarding energy policy.

The 1973 Arab embargo on oil exports to the United States, in retaliation for American support of Israel in the "Yom Kippur War," focused national attention on energy policy issues. In 1978, problems associated with toxic waste storage and disposal became salient to the public and to policymakers because of extensive media coverage of dumping by the Hooker Chemicals and Plastics Corporation at Love Canal, in Niagara Falls, New York. The dumping site was located near a school, in a residential area, and authorities detected abnormally high rates of birth defects, miscarriages, and related medical problems in the local population. The federal government bought 240 homes near the site, and spent over $30 million to relocate the dispossessed families.

The Reagan and Bush Administrations

Related toxic waste disposal problems in the following years focused public concern more firmly on policy approaches to hazardous materials. In 1979, thousands of drums of waste chemicals were discovered to be leaking in Kentucky. In 1983, high levels of dioxin were believed to have contaminated the entire town of Times Beach, Missouri. The Hudson River was contaminated by over one million pounds of polychlorinated byphrenyls. Carcinogenic carbon tetrachloride trichloroethylene was found in well water throughout the western states. The public outcry over these and other events in the U.S. and abroad led to the enactment in 1980 of the "Superfund" law, known officially as the Comprehensive

Environmental Response, Compensation, and Liability Act (reauthorized in 1986), and passage of the Hazardous and Solid Waste Amendments in 1984.

The overtly probusiness policies of the Reagan administration proved devastating to the cause of conservation and environmental protection, apart from occasional breakthroughs attained through congressional action. Emblematic of the dramatic turn in environmental policymaking by the executive branch were the actions of Secretary of the Interior James Watt. These actions included a moratorium on further National Park acquisitions (which was accomplished by refusing to spend the more than $1 billion in the Land and Water Conservation Fund and by failing to spend half of the funds appropriated by Congress for land acquisition,[53] opening federal lands to mining and logging, proposing to lease over 1 million offshore acres of California coastline for oil and gas exploration, and auctioning off more than a billion tons of coal in Montana and Wyoming. In reaction, leading environmental groups collected one million signatures on petitions asking that Watt be fired, and pressured the White House to take that action. Nonetheless, even under Watt's tenure at Interior, more than $1 billion was spent to upgrade the national parks system, and nearly two million acres were added to the wilderness system. Reagan fired Watt following a series of public embarrassments to the administration owing to Watt's insensitive statements about race and ethnicity; he was succeeded by two comparatively moderate secretaries of the interior: William Clark (1983–1985) and Donald Hodel (1985–1989).

Political problems at least as serious as those engendered by Watt's conduct were sparked by the activity of Anne Gorsuch (later Anne Burford) as Reagan's initial administrator of the EPA. Under her administration, morale at the agency plummeted; a series of contradictory reorganizations shook the agency's resolve; 20 percent of its employees were cut; the agency's budget was slashed; and external forces exerted control over EPA's actions. Furthermore, under Burford's leadership, the Office of Enforcement was dismantled; political appointees commonly overruled professional staff members; and there was rapid turnover among senior officials, who in a number of cases became the subjects of investigations.[54] Burford was brought down by an investigation by the House Committee on Energy and Commerce regarding abuses in the enforcement of Superfund legislation, and she was held in contempt of Congress. The incident behind her resignation in March 1983 was the criminal sentencing of Rita Lavelle, EPA's assistant administrator for hazardous waste, for perjury and obstructing a congressional investigation into mismanagement of a toxic chemical cleanup in Times Beach, Missouri, and the resulting sense that EPA was out of control.

Burford was succeeded in office by William Ruckelshaus, the original EPA administrator, to restore morale, reintroduce professionalism, and soothe the conflicts that had arisen between Congress and the agency. Serving until Reagan's reelection, when Lee Thomas was appointed to head EPA, Ruckelshaus revised the standards for lead content in gasoline and declared an emergency ban on a widely used pesticide, ethylene dibromide. Thomas redirected EPA's efforts toward domestic problems such as medical waste and garbage, and toward the global dimensions of ozone depletion and chlorofluorocarbons. Essentially, he returned the environment to the policy agenda[55] and restored the agency's reputation for policy enforcement. In particular, he achieved agreements with major corporations to bear much of the cost of environmental cleanup.

Throughout the 1980s, national environmental policy efforts were made against the opposition of the Reagan administration, whose policy agenda focused on reducing governmental regulation. The cumulative effects of Reagan's years in power were reduced budgets for environmental policy implementation, the choosing of key policymakers antagonistic to activist legislation, and the watering down of previous policies. George Bush campaigned successfully in the 1988 election as "the environmental president," although most of the policy momentum he inherited from the Reagan years (and to which he contributed as Reagan's vice president) was anything but friendly to conservationist interests. During the Bush administration, two major pieces of legislation were enacted. These were the Clean Air Act Amendments of 1990 and the Energy Policy Act of 1992.

In 1989, George Bush appointed William Reilly as EPA administrator. Reilly, who was formerly head of the United States branch of the World Wildlife Fund and a leader of the Conservation Foundation, brought renewed focus to pollution prevention and helped to establish a legislative breakthrough on the Clean Air Act amendments. However, more aggressive domestic and global environmentalist actions were thwarted by White House opposition, from Chief of Staff John Sununu, Budget Director Richard Darman, and Vice President Dan Quayle's Council on Competitiveness. Further complications for "the environmental president" were associated with actions of Secretary of the Interior Manuel Lujan, Jr., to open up the habitat of the endangered northern spotted owl to commercial logging and exempting thousands of acres of wetlands from federal protection.

The Clinton Administration and the Contemporary Scene

Environmental issues played an important role in the 1992 United States presidential election. The successful presidential and vice presidential candidates, Bill Clinton and Al Gore, capitalized on dissatisfaction with the Bush administration's seemingly halfhearted endorsement of serious efforts to contain damage to the environment and with its comparatively minimal allocations of government funds to environmental cleanup and prevention. In addition, Vice President Gore had already made a name for himself in the Senate as a proponent of reasoned environmentalism and in his book, *Earth in the Balance*[56] had expressed the desire of the incoming Clinton/Gore administration to balance business interests with care for environmental protection. The Clinton/Gore policy agenda attempted to bridge the gulf separating commerce's needs for growth and expanded output from environmental activists' commitment to conservation, preservation, and economic minimalism.

The election of the "New Democrats," Bill Clinton and Al Gore, to the White House in 1992 brought major change to the institutional leadership of the main agencies involved in environmental policymaking and implementation, and an expectation of rollbacks in the prodevelopment policies of the Reagan and Bush administrations that had opposed the goals of conservationist interests. Clinton promised to limit United States carbon dioxide emissions to 1990 levels by the year 2000; halt global warming, in a reversal of Bush's unwillingness to endorse that position at the Rio Earth Summit; create recycling and energy conservation incentives; set national water pollution runoff standards; support a fuel standard of 40 miles per gallon; restore funding to the United Nations Population Fund; and oppose drilling in the Arctic National Wildlife Refuge.[57]

The Clinton administration tried to shift the focus of national environmental initiatives from Congress to the White House, openly courted the leaders of major environmental organizations and their followers, and made environmental issues central to their policy process. Clinton eliminated the Council on Competitiveness and dismantled the Council on Environmental Quality, which was replaced by the White House office of Environmental Policy chaired by Kathleen McGinty and supported by Al Gore. Clinton also supported cabinet status for the EPA as a Department of the Environment.

Overall, Clinton's administration was not characterized by landmark environmental policy innovations. President Clinton waffled on the logging of timber on federal lands, earning the enmity of some environmentalist groups. The 103rd Congress expanded the National Park system to include about three million acres in the Mojave Desert of California. Following the midterm elections of 1994, much of the energy of the Clinton White House was devoted to stemming efforts by the Republican congressional majority to demolish the regulatory framework established in previous decades. One policy advance, however, was the 1996 law strengthening protections for infants and children against pesticide contamination.

The leading actors in making and implementing contemporary environmental policy in the United States today are summarized in Table 4.2. Within the White House, the Office of Environmental Policy is the chief locus of advice to the president and provides an overview of executive-branch environmental protection programs.

Until the creation of the Environmental Protection Agency in 1970, the national government had a comparatively minor commitment to federal environmental policy.[58] Apart from a scattering of agencies with partial responsibility for such matters, the most important federal effort to coordinate environmental policy prior to 1970 was the creation by Congress of the Department of the Interior, in 1849. The secretary of the interior is nominated by the president and must be confirmed in office by the Senate; the same is true of the directors of agencies subsumed under Interior. Many of the original functions of the department (such as supervising the General Land Office) were either abolished or transferred to other agencies, and over time it absorbed previously separate agencies devoted to the management of land, mineral rights, and other public resources.

TABLE 4.2 Current Major Actors in Environmental Policy

White House
  Office of Environmental Policy
Department of Agriculture
  Agriculture Stabilization and
    Conservation Service
  Soil Conservation Service
Department of Commerce
  National Bureau of Standards
  National Oceanic and Atmospheric
    Administration
Department of Defense
  Army Corps of Engineers
Department of Energy
  Federal Energy Regulatory Commission
  Office of Conservation and Renewable
    Energy
Department of Health and Human Services
  Food and Drug Administration
  National Institute for Occupational
    Safety and Health
Department of Labor
  Mine Safety and Health Administration
Department of Transportation
  Federal Aviation Administration
  Federal Highway Administration

Material Transportation Bureau
National Transportation Safety Board
Coast Guard
Department of the Interior
  Bureau of Indian Affairs
  Bureau of Land Management
  Bureau of Mines
  Bureau of Reclamation
  Minerals Management Service
  National Park Service
  Office of Surface Mining Reclamation
    and Enforcement
  Geological Survey
  Fish and Wildlife Service
Environmental Protection Agency
Regulatory agencies and
  commissions
  Consumer Product Safety
    Commission
  Federal Maritime Commission
  Federal Trade Commission
  Nuclear Regulatory Commission
Congress
Federal courts
State and local governments

EPA is an independent agency operated by an administrator, a deputy administrator, and nine assistant administrators, all of whom must be nominated by the president and confirmed by the Senate. In large part, the EPA serves as a regulatory agency in issuing permits, establishing and overseeing environmental standards, and enforcing relevant federal statutes and rules.

Congress often has been the major focus of environmental policymaking but recently has been unable to develop an overall national environmental policy,[59] particularly owing to the "gridlock" or lack of progress in the national legislature generally.[60] Switzer presents four reasons for this lack of congressional leadership in setting the environmental policy agenda: (1) a fragmented committee system, (2) diverse pressures from both proenvironmental and probusiness interests, (3) inadequate time and expertise, and (4) the "all politics is local" limitation on developing the national perspective needed for comprehensive policymaking.[61] Eleven Senate and fourteen House committees have some jurisdiction over environmental legislation, and rivalries among those committees arise over "hot" issues, providing multiple points of access for pressure groups on all sides of environmental controversies. These impediments to long-range planning are compounded by the inability

Contemporary Controversy

Is Environmentalism for Everyone?

A 1990 SURVEY, conducted in conjunction with Earth Day, found that about 20 percent of adult citizens in the United States described themselves as strong environmentalists and felt that drastic action, possibly at the cost of reduced economic growth, may be necessary to avoid major societal disruptions that could be brought on by environmental crises.[80] This figure, however, may substantially overstate the breadth of activist strength. An earlier study by Resources for the Future showed that only 8 percent of respondents reported belonging to an environmental group. Furthermore, membership in an environmental group was more than six times more likely among those with incomes of $30,000 or more than for lower-income respondents, and the college-educated similarly were much more likely to be active participants in the environmental arena.[81] Comparable findings show up in other surveys, which also tend to emphasize the disproportionately western (and specifically California-based) orientation of environmental groups.[82]

As is true of most predominantly middle-class movements in the United States, participation by people of color has been comparatively lower than the level of involvement among whites. According to research by Joyce Baugh, this situation reflects the gener-

of congressional members and staff to address the complexities of environmental legislation expertly and by the bargaining that goes on among competing constituency interests.

Before the adoption of the National Environmental Policy Act (NEPA), the role of the federal courts had been limited to adjudicating disputes between citizens and industries accused of pollution, with penalties generally limited to orders to cease and desist and occasional monetary fines. New vistas of judicial capacity to intervene in environmental policy were opened up by (1) NEPA's requirement that agencies comply with provisions of the legislation, (2) the need for administrative orders to implement legislative intent and the consequent need for judicial interpretation, and (3) the lack of clear congressional intent. Judicial intervention in implementing environmental legislation and agency rules has followed public support for environmental initiatives, strict enforcement of procedural requirements provided for in the legislation, and a tightening up of courts' review of agency decisions.[62]

At first, the "standing" of parties to introduce legal issues related to the environment was limited only to actions by citizens who had been affected directly by alleged pollution through loss of property or personal injury. The tendency of the courts not to see environmental harm as personal injury initially made it difficult for environmental activist groups to engage in such litigation.[63] Over time, however, it became easier for representatives of environ-

ally stronger concern among nonwhite communities with social welfare and jobs-related issues, as well as physical survival, than with environmental preservation. Conventional wisdom has attributed the previously low rate of participation by African-Americans in environmental causes to less concern for the environment by African-Americans relative to other issues, lack of attention by mainstream environmentalists to issues that affect the quality of life for African-Americans, and racism within environmental organizations. It is clear that environmental hazards have not been distributed equitably in American society, with African-Americans bearing a disproportionate burden of environmental contamination.[83]

The "environmental justice" movement, however, has emerged recently from already-existing social action groups, focusing on problems such as the perception that hazardous waste materials are more likely to be dumped near low-income and minority neighborhoods. Baugh concluded that "there now is increasing activism by African-Americans in environmental issues,"[84] and noted that African-American grassroots organizations were forced to emerge because the mainstream environmental movement "fails to recognize how these problems both differently and disproportionately affect them."[85] In October 1991, the First National People of Color Environmental Leadership Summit was held to endeavor to forge an environmental alliance across racial lines.[86]

Recent research conducted by Robert Paehlke and Pauline Vaillancourt Rosenau has addressed general questions regarding how the environmentalist movement may expand its scope to be more inclusive of racial minority, lower-income, labor, feminist, and other groupings outside of the societal mainstream. Paehlke and Rosenau focus on

(continued)

mental groups to sue in defense of the public interest against the effects of environmental damage. The breakthrough came in the 1971 case of *Scenic Hudson Preservation Conference v. Federal Power Commission*,[64] in which a local conservation group challenged New York Edison's application to construct a power plant and was granted standing under the Federal Power Act, which compels the Federal Power Commission to take the impact of proposed projects into consideration.[65]

This opening of access points within the federal judiciary led to much more frequent lawsuits against both industries and government agencies failing to comply with environmental legislation and rules. However, much of this legal activity is not by environmental interests, but rather by industry, since it provides a convenient means by which to delay rule implementation, to avoid the negative publicity that might come from more overt opposition to new rules and laws, and to try to win a more proindustry ruling than might have been obtained through legislative and executive policymaking processes, which are often visibly dominated by interest groups.[66]

Environmental policy activities at the state and local levels have been fragmented, sporadic, and of limited impact.[67] By 1950, most states had established agencies to manage natural resources, particularly related to forests and mines, but there was little environmental protection. Responsibilities to combat emerging pollution problems were not consolidated within a single type of state

the need to resolve the "perception of tension between societal equity objectives and the environmental agenda"[87] by redirecting the discussion of proposed solutions to the chief environmentalist concerns of wilderness and habitat protection, human health, and economic sustainability toward broader societal concerns for jobs, the universality of health issues (rather than aesthetics), and the need to protect people who are targeted by corporations for environmental exploitation.

Divisions among the ranks of organized labor regarding the virtues and disadvantages of environmentalism have emerged in recent decades. Many rank-and-file union members and labor leaders worry that jobs and incomes might be lost from overzealous implementation of environmental protections. However, efforts to improve workplace safety and workers' conditions of employment are one area of clear overlap between labor and environmental activists, especially when obvious hazards are involved in exposure to toxic substances or to airborne particulates. One of the strongest supporters of clean air legislation has been the United Steelworkers of America, who are sensitive to the responsibility of their industry for contributing to air pollution and to the immediate threat posed by pollution to their workers and their families.[88]

Whatever may be the tendencies toward coordination of interests and activities among the disparate elements of the environmental movement, it is clear that what Switzer has called a "great schism" tends to dissipate their efforts:

> Where the national organizations like the Sierra Club and the National Wildlife Federation pay their executive officers high salaries and run massive fund-raising operations,

or local agency. Local health departments gained authority over air quality monitoring because of the obvious health implications of air pollution, but responsibility for response to water pollution lay more commonly with separate agencies rather than with public health authorities.[68]

During the late 1960s and early 1970s, federal mandates regarding the environment resulted in the formation of specialized state agencies to implement the new provisions, and Congress provided funds to plan, monitor, manage, and conduct technical studies regarding particular problems. Some states opted to create "little EPAs"—superagencies designed to provide more efficient delivery of mandated services over a variety of environmental concerns (for example, New York and Washington), or for political acceptability (for example, Minnesota). Part-time citizens' boards are often associated with these consolidated agencies, but their members seldom have expert knowledge of the subject areas. Other states (Illinois, for example) established an entirely separate environmental agency devoted to controlling pollution, occasionally with more substantial research capabilities and more functional citizen boards.[69]

Corporate interests felt threatened by the heightened competence of state environmental agencies, and thus attempted to use the federal government to preempt state regulatory authority and to provide relief from what they regarded as a dual burden of federal and state requirements. State environmental officials consequently tried to improve their lobbying efforts by working in consort to

most groups are strictly volunteer based and funded on minimal membership dues. A deeper conflict among the groups may be the substance of their interests. The Association of Sierra Club Members for Environmental Ethics, founded by dissident members in 1991, has accused the Sierra Club of compromising its principles in order to get legislation through Congress. Others have criticized groups like the National Audubon Society for bringing officials from industry onto their boards of directors. While the disputes may not be enough to cause a real rift among groups, they are symptomatic of the fragmentation in the environmental movement that keeps it from speaking as one voice in the political arena.[89]

The more radical and activist strains of environmentalism in the United States are motivated by what has been identified as *deep ecology*: "a form of ecological consciousness founded on the idea [that] man is no more important than any other species."[90] Deep ecology is based on the goals of self-realization and ecocentrism, that is, the need for taking decisive measures to make one's policy point and for placing humans in a nonantagonistic relationship with nature.[91]

It remains to be seen whether the environmentalist movement in the United States can adjust to its internal ideological strains and to the societal cleavages that divide the country along lines of race, income, and region. Whatever the outcome of efforts to resolve those contradictions, there is no doubt that environmental policy and related energy policy problems will continue to occupy a large share of the future policy process in the United States.

form groups such as the Northeast States for Coordinated Air Use Management (NESCAUM), which worked vigorously to reauthorize the Clean Air Act in 1987. In that effort, states, rather than the federal government, operated as the policy initiators, assisted by groups such as NESCAUM with proposed legislation, technical support, and expert documentation.[70]

State government responses to environmental issues vary with the severity of pollution and urbanized population concentration, the state's fiscal resource base, partisan control of the state legislature (with Democratic-controlled legislatures more likely to foster environmental protection), and the prevalence of professional legislators and administrators.[71] States with more serious hazardous waste problems have imposed stronger regulatory programs.[72] States have not regulated large-scale producers of hazardous waste aggressively because those industries have forced the public to bear the costs of regulation, and because environmental interest groups have been only marginally influential in state regulation of hazardous waste.[73] State efforts in air and water pollution control are determined by the amount of discretion and support provided by the federal government, levels of state wealth, and the relative level of pollution in a state.[74] Stronger pollution control legislation emanates from states having more liberal public opinion, political elites who are more concerned with environmentalism, stronger environmental interest groups, more highly professionalized members of state legislatures, and more serious threats to environmental quality.[75] The aggressiveness with which states have

Case Study

Natural Resources, Energy, and Land Use

CONFLICTS OVER land use are nothing new in the history of American politics and public policy. William L. Graf has identified four principal conflicts between western and eastern interests over the use of western public land resources: (1) irrigation, in the late 1800s; (2) forest reserves, immediately before and after the turn of the twentieth century; (3) grazing districts, in the 1930s and 1940s; and (4) designating public lands as protected wilderness areas, principally from the 1960s to the present.[92] Even earlier, before the American west extended much beyond the Allegheny Mountains, the national government sold millions of acres to private owners, starting with the Ordinance of 1785 allowing parcels of land to be sold to the highest bidder (above a minimum of $1 per acre, and for a minimum of 640 acres).[93]

Currently, responsibility for the more than 650 million acres of public lands is split among five agencies—the Bureau of Land Management (270 million acres), the Forest Service (191 million acres), the Fish and Wildlife Service (92 million acres), the National Park Service (80 million acres), and the Department of Defense (25 million acres)—with frequently competing clienteles and agendas induced in part by the provision of lands for multiple use. Switzer explains the multifaceted complexities of the debate over the use and ownership of public lands:

> Angry environmentalists believe western lands are being exploited by ranchers who graze their cattle on subsidized federal land (and a reaction by ranchers during the late 1970s called the Sagebrush Rebellion). Another battle pits timber companies and their workers against those who feel agencies like the U.S. Forest Service are no longer protecting either trees or the public interest; the National Park System has come under fire by

pursued recycling is related positively to their environmental bureaucratic strength, the degree of innovativeness in environmental policy, and their level of commitment to environmental protection.[76]

Leslie Alm's study of regional differences in policymaking regarding acid rain found that the level of a state's commitment to environmental protection is the strongest predictor of the level of activity in environmental legislation across all regions and when controlling for differences in the natural resource base. He concludes: "Despite the recent trend toward the 'nationalization' of states, there remains a distinct regional flavor to American environmental policymaking. As long as large differentials in natural resource reserves between the regions remain, questions of equity will continue to pervade the search for national solutions. The framework of regional debate has changed, and considerations of energy, equity, and environment will continue to remain at the forefront of regional confrontations."[77]

organizations who believe the program has expanded unnecessarily, and by those who feel the parks' infrastructure and staffing levels are deteriorating because of overuse and budget cuts. Among the most controversial of the environmental protection issues is preservation of wetlands. . . . In the 1980s and early 1990s, state and local governments began to play a more important role in land management as urban sprawl and population growth threatens the quality of life for many Americans. As a result, public officials are being forced to make difficult (and often unpopular) decisions about the siting of facilities like sanitary landfills, electric utility substations, and transmission lines. Those decisions are resulting in a new wave of citizen participation in land-use decision making, . . . and enhancing the role of the courts in an attempt to determine how the land is best used.[94]

Much of the western land area of the United States is rich in mineral deposits and the natural resources that are essential for the nation to have a steady supply of fossil-based fuels. Nearly one-half of the land area of the western states currently is held by the national government. Consequently, decisions over how that land will be used—exploited or conserved—are central to the policy decisions regarding the environment, decisions that are being made now and that will continue to be made in the future by the federal and state governments. The impact of the outcome of this debate within the broader context of national environmental policy is not difficult to understand: More than 400 million acres of public land are open to commercial mining. In contrast to the virtually cost-free operation of western mining companies, operators of logging and livestock interests pay regulated fees and confront a considerable array of environmental regulations.

The route to large-scale exploitation of those resources was opened in 1872, when President Grant signed legislation giving primacy to the search for gold, silver, and copper over other uses of the western federal lands for the very low price of $5 an acre. Under this legislation—intended as a temporary extension of the Homestead Act to buttress the role of small farmers, merchants, and prospectors—if minerals are found, even in national forests, and if a mine operator can prove that they can be extracted commercially, then the national government is required to sell, or patent, the land at

(continued)

Local governments have played generally minor roles in implementing environmental legislation and rules, except where there are strong environmentalist groups (particularly in western states)[78] that pressure local officials to impose regulations that are stricter than what is required by the state or federal governments. Jacqueline Switzer has summarized the difficulties confronting local governments interested in environmental protection:

Since political values are often based on a specific place where citizens live, work, or play, it is not surprising that local governments are beginning to play a larger role in policy formation. Local initiatives may be the result of a smoke plume from a local factory or of an attempt to make the town more aesthetically pleasing to residents or tourists. But local officials must also balance those concerns with the historic tradition and prevailing mood of business toward development and growth, combined with a steadily decreasing revenue base that precludes many otherwise desirable environmental projects from being funded.[79]

the price set in 1872. Over 3.2 million acres have passed from public to private commercial control in this manner since the original act was signed.

More recently, foreign-owned corporations have taken advantage of this provision of United States law to mine gold from public lands without paying anything to the national treasury in royalties[95] after buying land for as little as $2.50 per acre. That foreign ownership should accelerate is not surprising, since most countries charge far higher rates for commercial use of public lands. For example, in Canada, some provinces charge indigenous companies royalties of up to 12 percent on extracted minerals. The Mineral Policy Center, a private research group that monitors the mining industry, estimated that in 1994 alone such corporate interests were seeking to gain control of over $34 billion worth of minerals available on cheaply purchased public lands.

In contrast to the efforts of environmentalist groups like the Mineral Policy Center, senators from western states are aligned with corporate interests to preserve a mining industry that they contend brings high-salary jobs to the scattered smaller rural communities that are characteristic of the region. Mining interests have benefited in the policymaking process from key resources, including steady support from western-state senators, the historical role played by the industry in settlement of the region during the nineteenth century, and a track record of success in beating off attempts to make mineral extraction companies pay a larger share of royalties. "Green" interests emphasize the absence in the 1872 legislation of any requirements that mining firms clean up or reclaim land from which they have conducted their extraction. An estimated 10,000 miles of streams in the West are ecologically dead, largely from waste generated by mining activities.[96] One explanation for the strong opposition to environmentalist encroachment on the mining industry (and also ranching and other rural interests in the West that were instrumental in supporting the Sagebrush Rebellion) came from Wyoming Republican Senator Alan K. Simpson: "This is not about money. We are defending our Western heritage. These people should have the guts to come out and say what they're really after. They don't like cows because they poop too much. And they don't like mines because they mar the scenery. They would like to get rid of them all."[97]

In 1993, the House of Representatives passed a bill that, if it had become law, would have established an 8 percent royalty on the value of minerals taken from the public lands, stopped the practice of selling western land cheaply, and imposed environmental standards for cleaning up the damage done by mineral extraction. The legislation was supported by President Clinton's secretary of the interior, Bruce Babbitt, who was quoted as saying of mining company officials: "They are ripping off the American people fair and square."[98]

Many senators and governors from the West argue, in contrast, that overly drastic changes from the 1872 legislation effectively would kill off their golden goose, by providing disincentives for mining companies, discouraging exploration of the massive public land holdings, and thwarting the new gold rush that has made the United States second to South Africa in world gold production. Supporters of the status quo assert that their exploration often fails, that profits are not guaranteed, and that risks are more readily computed for other extractive industries, such as oil, gas, and coal.

The leadership role of mineral extraction among western jobs-producing industries has been diminished substantially, compared to the past glories of the economic growth engine provided by mining ventures, but supporters of mining assert that many smaller communities exist due to benefits from the relatively high-wage jobs that long have been available from mineral extraction. However, although mining industry wages are considerably higher than wages for other blue-collar jobs in the West, those positions are not likely to last beyond the average of 10 years, the predicted life expectancy of a newly opened mine.

Unlike gold, copper, silver, and uranium mining, which pay no royalties for the development of natural resources on federal lands, other aspects of mineral extraction have been profitable for the federal treasury. Oil, natural gas, and surface coal mining companies have long paid the federal government at a rate of 12.5 percent of the value of the raw materials; underground coal carries an 8 percent payment; sulfur and phosphate, 5 percent; and sodium and potash, 2 percent. Since 1970, oil companies have paid a total of about $100 billion in lease fees and royalties.

After the easily extracted surface gold was exhausted, corporations replaced small-scale independent operators as the mainstay of the mining industry, introducing mechanized production systems that minimized the needed work force and concentrating output under the control of a handful of firms. When demand for gold, silver, and copper slumped, the closed mines left behind an estimated 500,000 abandoned sites and 50 billion tons of waste.[99] New technologies, particularly the use of cyanide to leach out microscopic gold particles from the surrounding rock, led to the reopening and intense automation of old mines, resulting in a 1,000 percent explosion in United States gold output, at the same time that the number of people employed in hard-rock mining fell by nearly one-half.

The operative principle behind the prodevelopment perspective on public land use is economic liberalism, which holds that "the public interest would be best served by transferring the public lands to the private sector."[100] Modern developments consistent with this policy outlook include the Sagebrush Rebellion, the movement to privatize public assets, and the "wise use" movement. As Klyza suggests, the most contemporary manifestation of this philosophy, the "wise use" movement, smacks more of state capitalism, with its emphasis on "government management designed to aid private commercial interests," rather than of classic free enterprise and its attendant risks. In sharp contrast to the "wise use" approach to the use of public lands is the "deep ecology" argument that preserving and enhancing the environment ranks above making use of resources to foster human needs.

Case Study Questions

1. Do you feel that national government policy on mineral extraction is correct? Why or why not?
2. How would you suggest that a reasonable pricing policy might be worked out for the use of western lands? Should those lands be available for sale at all?
3. Fossil fuel producers currently pay much higher royalties than do miners of many other minerals. What would be some of the advantages, and what would be some of the drawbacks, of equalizing the prices paid by all those who extract minerals from the public lands? Should an equal price be set higher, or lower, than the current royalties rate (12.5 percent) paid for oil, surface coal, and natural gas?
4. If the United States confronts another energy crisis (say, an embargo on oil shipments from the Middle East), would you favor opening up the western lands to immediate exploration? Why or why not?

Suggested Readings

American Environmentalism: The U.S. Environmental Movement, 1970–1990, ed. Riley Dunlap and Angela G. Mertig. Washington, DC: Taylor & Francis, 1992.

Devall, Bill, and George Sessions. *Deep Ecology*. Salt Lake City: Gibbs Smith, 1985.

Environmental Policy in the 1990s, ed. Norman J. Vig and Michael E. Kraft. Washington, DC: Congressional Quarterly Press, 1994.

Pepper, David. *The Roots of Modern Environmentalism*. London: Croom Helm, 1984.

Switzer, Jacqueline Vaughn. *Environmental Politics: Domestic and Global Dimensions*. New York: St. Martin's Press, 1994.

Notes

1. James Gleick, *Chaos: Making a New Science* (New York: Viking, 1987).

2. Riley E. Dunlap, George H. Gallup, Jr., and Alec M. Gallup, *The Health of the Planet Survey* (Washington, DC: Gallup International Institute, 1992).

3. David Rapp, "Special Report," *Congressional Quarterly Weekly Report* (January 20, 1990), p. 138.

4. "Household Waste Threatening Environment; Recycling Helps Ease Disposal Problem," *Gallup Report 280* (January 1990), pp. 30–34.

5. Riley E. Dunlap, "Public Opinion in the 1980s: Clear Consensus, Ambiguous Commitment," *Environment* 33 (8) (1991), pp. 9–15, 32–37.

6. Jacqueline Vaughn Switzer, *Environmental Politics: Domestic and Global Dimensions* (New York: St. Martin's Press, 1994), pp. 18–19.

7. "Yalta in Rio," *National Review* (July 6, 1992), pp. 14–16.

8. Uday Desai, Introduction [to a Symposium on Comparative Environmental Policy], *Policy Studies Journal* 20 (4) (1992), p. 622.

9. H. Jean Thiebaux, "Educating 'Environmental Statisticians' for the Twenty-first Century," *Amstat News* 212 (August-September 1994), pp. 26–27.

10. Walter A. Rosenbaum, *Environmental Politics and Policy*, 2nd ed. (Washington, DC: Congressional Quarterly Press, 1991), p. 83.

11. Marc K. Landy, Marc J. Roberts, and Stephen R. Thomas, *The EPA: Asking the Wrong Questions* (New York: Oxford University Press, 1990).

12. Switzer, op. cit., p. 55.

13. Switzer, op. cit., p. 15.

14. Switzer, op. cit., p. 19.

15. Denise Scheberle, "Radon and Asbestos: A Study of Agenda Setting and Causal Stories," *Policy Studies Journal* 22 (1) (1994), p. 84.

16. Scheberle, op. cit., p. 83.

17. Richard C. Rich, W. David Conn, and William L. Owens, "'Indirect Regulation' of Environmental Hazards Through the Provision of Information to the Public: The Case of SARA, Title III," *Policy Studies Journal* 21 (1), (1993), p. 31.

18. John S. Dryzek, *Rational Ecology: Environment and Political Economy* (Oxford: Basil Blackwell, 1987).

19. Matthew J. McKinney, "Water for Wildlife: Integrating Science and Politics in Wildlife Conservation," *Policy Studies Journal* 19 (3–4) (1991), p. 534.

20. John Seredich, *Your Resource Guide to Environmental Organizations* (Irvine, CA: Smiling Dolphins Press, 1991).

21. Michael S. Greve, "Private Enforcement, Private Rewards: How Environmental Suits Became an Entitlement Program," in *Environmental Politics: Public Costs, Private Rewards,* ed. Michael S. Greve and Fred L. Smith, Jr. (New York: Praeger, 1992), pp. 105–109).

22. Switzer, op. cit., p. 31.

23. Samuel P. Hays, *Beauty, Health and Permanence: Environmental Politics in the United States 1955–1985* (Cambridge: Cambridge University Press, 1987), p. 308.

24. Switzer, op. cit., pp. 31–34.

25. D. Kirk Davidson, "Straws in the Wind: The Nature of Corporate Commitment to Environmental Issues," in *The Corporation, Ethics and the Environment,* ed. W. Michael Hoffman, Robert Frederick, and Edward S. Petry, Jr. (New York: Quorum Books, 1990), pp. 57–66.

26. Switzer, op. cit., p. 35.

27. Henry V. Nickel, "Now, the Rush to Regulate," *The Environmental Forum* 8 (1) (1991), p. 19.

28. See Joseph Petulla, *Environmental Protection in the United States* (San Francisco: San Francisco Study Center, 1987), pp. 98–99.

29. Desai, op. cit., p. 626.

30. Christopher McGrory Klyza, "Framing the Debate in Public Lands Politics," *Policy Studies Journal* 19 (3–4) (1991), pp. 577–585.

31. Rachel Carson, *Silent Spring* (Greenwich, CT: Fawcett, 1962).

32. Paul Ehrlich, *The Population Bomb* (New York: Ballantine, 1968).

33. Switzer, , op. cit., p. 15.

34. Lou Cannon, *President Reagan: The Role of a Lifetime* (New York: Simon & Schuster, 1991), p. 531.

35. Jonathan Lash, Katherine Gillman, and David Sheridan, *A Season of Spoils: The Reagan Administration's Attack on the Environment* (New York: Pantheon Books, 1984), p. 231.

36. Robert Cameron Mitchell, Angela G. Mertig, and Riley E. Dunlap, "Twenty Years of Environmental Mobilization: Trends Among National Environmental Organizations," in *American Environmentalism: The U.S. Environmental Movement, 1970–1990,* ed. Riley E. Dunlap and Angela G. Mertig (Washington, DC: Taylor & Francis, 1992), p. 15; Robert Cameron Mitchell, "Public Opinion and the Green Lobby: Poised for the 1990s?," in *Environmental Policy in the 1990s: Toward a New Agenda,* ed. Norman J. Vig and Michael E. Kraft (Washington, DC: Congressional Quarterly Press, 1990), pp. 90–91.

37. "A Vision for EPA's Future: An Interview with William K. Reilly," *EPA Journal* 16 (5) (1990), p. 5.

38. Uday Desai, op. cit., p. 622.

39. Robert C Paehlke, *Environmentalism and the Future of Progressive Politics* (New Haven: Yale University Press, 1989). See also Michael E. Kraft, "Ecology and Political Theory: Broadening the Scope of Environmental Politics," *Policy Studies Journal* 20 (4) (1992), p. 716.

40. Evan J. Ringquist, "Policy Influence and Policy Responsiveness in State Pollution Control," *Policy Studies Journal* 22 (1), pp. 39–40.

41. Agis Salpukas, "Electric Utilities Brace for End of Regulation and Monopolies," *New York Times*, 8 August 1994, pp. A1, C5.

42. Quoted in Salpukas, op. cit., p. C5.

43. Switzer, op. cit., p. 6.

44. Samuel P. Hays, *Conservation and the Gospel of Efficiency* (Cambridge, MA: Harvard University Press, 1959), p. 5.

45. Switzer, op. cit., p. 7.

46. Switzer, op. cit., p. 4.

47. Switzer, op. cit., p. 8.

48. Hays, 1959, op. cit., p. 132.

49. Grant McConnell, "The Conservation Movement—Past and Present," *Western Political Quarterly* 7 (3) (1954), pp. 463–478.

50. Alfred A. Marcus, *Promise and Performance: Choosing and Implementing an Environmental Policy* (Westport, CT: Greenwood Press, 1980), p. 87.

51. Marc K. Landy, Marc J. Roberts, and Stephen R. Thomas, *The EPA: Asking the Wrong Questions* (New York: Oxford University Press, 1990), p. 41.

52. Ron Arnold, *At the Eye of the Storm: James Watt and the Environmentalists* (Chicago: Regency Gateway, 1982), p. 94.

53. Lash, Gillman, and Sheridan, op. cit.

54. Haynes Johnson, *Sleepwalking through History: America in the Reagan Years* (New York: Norton, 1991).

55. Landy, Roberts, and Thomas, op. cit., p. 256.

56. Al Gore, *Earth in the Balance: Ecology and the Human Spirit* (Boston: Houghton Mifflin, 1992).

57. Switzer, op. cit., pp. 63–64.

58. Thomas R. Dye, *Politics in States and Communities,* 7th ed. (Englewood Cliffs, NJ: Prentice Hall, 1991), p. 19.

59. Richard A. Cooley and Geoffrey Wandesforde-Smith, *Congress and the Environment* (Seattle: University of Washington Press, 1970).

60. Michael E. Kraft, "Environmental Gridlock: Searching for Consensus in Congress," in *Environmental Policy in the 1990s,* ed. Norman J. Vig and Michael E. Kraft (Washington, DC: Congressional Quarterly Press, 1990).

61. Switzer, op. cit., pp. 64–65.

62. Frederick R. Anderson, *NEPA in the Courts* (Baltimore: Johns Hopkins University Press, 1973), p. 17.

63. Werner F. Grunbaum, *Judicial Policymaking: The Supreme Court and Environmental Quality* (Morristown, NJ: General Learning Press, 1976).

64. 453 F.2d 463.

65. Switzer, op. cit., p. 71.

66. Lettie M. Wenner, *The Environmental Decade in Court* (Bloomington: Indiana University Press, 1982).

67. Barry G. Rabe, *Fragmentation and Integration in State Environmental Management* (Washington, DC: Conservation Foundation, 1986), p. 17.

68. J. Clarence Davies, *The Politics of Pollution* (New York: Pegasus, 1970), p. 128.

69. Elizabeth Haskell, *Managing the Environment: Nine States Look for New Answers* (Washington, DC: Author, 1971).

70. Edward Laverty, "Legacy of the 1980s in State Environmental Administration," in *Regulatory Federalism, Natural Resources, and Environmental Management*, ed. Michael S. Hamilton (Washington, DC: American Society for Public Administration, 1990).

71. James P. Lester, "A New Federalism?" in *Environmental Policy in the 1990s*, ed. Norman J. Vig and Michael E. Kraft (Washington, DC: Congressional Quarterly Press, 1990), pp. 70–76.

72. James P. Lester, J. Franke, A. O'M. Bowman, and K. Kramer, "Hazardous Wastes, Politics, and Public Policy: A Comparative State Analysis," *Western Political Quarterly* 36 (1983), pp. 257–281.

73. B. Williams and A. Matheny, "Testing Theories of Social Regulation: Hazardous Waste Regulations in the American States," *Journal of Politics* 46 (1984), pp. 428–459.

74. William Lowry, *Dimensions of Federalism: State Governments and Pollution Control Policies* (Durham, NC: Duke University Press, 1992).

75. Ringquist, op. cit., pp. 39–40.

76. Renu Khator, "Recycling: A Policy Dilemma for American States?," *Policy Studies Journal* 21 (2) (1993), p. 219.

77. Leslie R. Alm, "Regional Influences and Environmental Policymaking: A Study of Acid Rain," *Policy Studies Journal* 21 (4) (1993), pp. 647–648.

78. Samuel P. Hays, "The New Environmental West," *Journal of Policy History* 3 (3) (1991), pp. 223–248; Continental Group, *Toward Responsible Growth: Economic and Environmental Concern in the Balance* (Stamford, CT: Author, 1982); Deborah Hitchcock Jessup, *Guide to State Environmental Programs* (Washington, DC: Bureau of National Affairs, 1990); Switzer, op. cit., p. 68.

79. Switzer, op. cit., p. 69.

80. George Gallup, Jr., and Dr. Frank Newport, "Americans Strongly in Tune with the Purpose of Earth Day 1990," *Gallup Poll Monthly* 295 (April 1990), pp. 5–14.

81. Robert Cameron Mitchell, "The Public Speaks Again: A New Environmental Survey," *Resources* 60 (September–November 1978) p. 4.

82. Craig R. Humphrey and Frederick H. Buttel, *Environment, Energy, and Society* (Belmont, CA: Wadsworth, 1982); Stephen Fox, *The American Conservation Movement* (Madison: University of Wisconsin Press, 1985).

83. Joyce A. Baugh, "African-Americans and the Environment," *Policy Studies Journal,* 19 (2) (1991), pp. 182–191.

84. Ibid., p. 182.

85. Ibid., p. 190.

86. John M. Ostheimer and Leonard G. Ritt, *Environment, Energy, and Black Americans* (Beverly Hills, CA: Sage, 1976).

87. Robert Paehlke and Pauline Vaillancourt Rosenau, "Environment/Equity: Tensions in North American Politics," *Policy Studies Journal* 21 (4) (1993), p. 672.

88. United Steelworkers of America., *Poison in Our Air* (Washington, DC: United Steelworkers of America, 1969).

89. Switzer, op. cit., p. 31.

90. Ibid., p. 29.

91. Bill Devall and George Sessions, *Deep Ecology* (Salt Lake City: Gibbs Smith, 1985).

92. William L. Graf, *Wilderness Preservation and the Sagebrush Rebellion* (Savage, MD: Rowman & Littlefield, 1990).

93. Switzer, op. cit., p. 75.

94. Ibid., pp. 97–98.

95. Timothy Egan, "New Gold Rush Stirs Fears of Exploitation," *New York Times*, 14 August 1994, p. 1.

96. Ibid., p. 11.

97. Ibid., p. 11.

98. Ibid., p. 11.

99. Ibid., p. 11.

100. Christopher McGrory Klyza, "Framing the Debate in Public Lands Politics," *Policy Studies Journal* 19 (3–4) (1991), p. 581.

5

Rural, Agricultural, and Small-Town Policy

A POLICY OF HOPE

Shortly after his election in the fall of 1992, President-elect Clinton convened a "grand teach-in" on the economy and the government's role in it. The President learned quickly that the sluggish economy, the nation's trade deficit, the increasing federal debt and deficit, and the globalization of capital and production would compel him to prepare the nation for dramatic transformations. The president, the top policymaker and chief executive officer of the federal government, identified a set of problems and potential consequences. Among the broad spectrum of opinions advocating what should be done, one representative of the Iowa Farmers Union said:

> During your campaign you spoke frequently of a place called Hope, using your home town in Arkansas as a metaphor for restoring the confidence of the American people that things can change for the better. Many people identified with that, but I especially did because, for the last 40 years, I've worked a 400-acre farm in the heart of the heartland, near a place called Chelsea, Iowa.
>
> In Iowa, it's been said that agriculture creates somewhere between 60 and 70 percent of all of our jobs, and we were reminded rather painfully during the decade of the '80s that agriculture is indeed much more than the farms that dotted our countryside. We have approximately 96,000 farmers in Iowa, but only an estimated 3,000 under the age of 32. It is estimated that in the next five years nearly one-third of those 96,000 Iowa farmers will be retirement age, and somewhere between 12 and 15 percent of the Iowa farmers may face foreclosure in the next few months, while they have produced the best crops they have ever produced in their lifetime. And I say that because a tremendous change is about to take place, not only in our system of agriculture, but also in the economic and social infrastructure that surrounds us.

For two days now, we have heard the words and the infinite wisdom of some of our nation's most brilliant minds and most brilliant thinkers, and it's clear that the message and the challenge is to increase the productivity of our nation's industry and our nation's workers in all sectors of our economy, yet, no industry has increased its efficiency and productivity even close to that of American agriculture. But, it hasn't stabilized our farms, our rural communities; it hasn't created more well-paid jobs for our people; it hasn't lessened the pressure on our land and water resources; in fact, just the opposite—it's torn the literal heart out of our family farm system of food production in our rural communities. It's the very same system that has been the model and the envy of the world for decades, and it's the very same system that, today, Russia and other CIS Republics are trying to move toward.

Mr. Clinton, give us a rural policy that includes a long-vision farm policy, yes, that creates safety nets, but a rural policy that addresses the needs of all of rural America, all that's there and all that it encompasses. A policy that addresses not only hunger in this country, but hunger globally, as well. A rural policy not separate from urban or inner-city policy within our national agenda, but a rural policy that complements our inner-city policy within that same national agenda. Continuing to pursue public policy that encourages or economically forces human resources off of our farms and rural communities into the cities not only has a negative impact on rural America, it undoubtedly contributes to the growing unemployment, homelessness, hunger, crime and drug problems within our inner cities as well.

Give us a rural policy, Mr. Clinton, that may be the key connection between reforming and changing government and real economic growth. Our nation, the state of Iowa, or my farm, can neither tax nor borrow its way to prosperity. We must earn our way. Give us a rural policy that will allocate the research dollars to create value-added products, both edible and non-edible, like soy ink, soy diesel, ethanol, which would clean up our environment, reduce our dependency on foreign oil, and stimulate our rural communities. The potential is endless. That value-added agriculture products will, in turn, create more jobs and more revenue and contribute to a growing broad-based economic recovery, both in urban and rural America.

Give us a rural policy that does not focus on the weaknesses and vulnerabilities of rural America, but, rather, on our assets and our strengths. Give us a rural policy that recognizes our nation's most precious and valuable resources—our land and our water—must not be utilized—or, must be utilized for the good of many, not exploited for the greed of a few.

And, last, but not least, Mr. Clinton, give us a rural policy so those of us whose heritage and roots run deep in the American soil may once again dare to hope and dream that some day, if they so desire, our sons and daughters can return with their families to the Hope, Arkansas, and to the Chelsea, Iowa. It is absolutely essential that a new public policy for agriculture and rural America must be part of the national agenda in your administration.[1]

In 1996, in the middle of his reelection campaign, Bill Clinton returned to some of the themes (and scenes) of his 1992 rural policy initiatives. A major national conference was convened on the campus of Iowa State University, in Ames, Iowa, one of the nation's leading land-grant agricultural and rural policy research institutions. The location was particularly fitting, since many of the issues raised by the Chelsea, Iowa, farmer in 1992 remained unresolved or only partially addressed by the end of the 1996 presidential campaign and election.

This chapter will examine many of the leading contemporary topics in United States rural, agricultural, and small-town policy. Our themes include the different ways in which these policy issues have been approached, and the extent to which they are being—or have been—addressed with varying degrees of success.

THE RPI INPUTS TO RURAL, AGRICULTURAL, AND SMALL-TOWN POLICY

The complexities of the process of rural, agricultural, and small town policy have been characterized as being nearly impossible for the uninitiated to understand: "Farm politics in Washington has much in common with Br'er Rabbit's briar patch. Outsiders see only complicated arcane issues that elude understanding, but insiders—farm lobbyists and their allies in Congress—scamper through this thicket year after year, occasionally yelping about the pain of it all. Even as they bemoan their problems, which are significant, farm lobbyists also have managed to protect a multi-billion-dollar array of farm programs that is unlike anything provided for other industries."[2] Over the years, the balance of power has shifted away from the cohesive farm bloc to ideological rifts between and among farm and nonfarm interests. On the one hand, this generally has ensured an incremental approach to change, and on the other, it has dampened the forces of rational, coherent, comprehensive agricultural policy for the past six decades. Two related aspects of agricultural and rural policy will be addressed here. The first is why commodity price supports and farm income have received such favorable federal assistance. The second is why rural small towns and non-farm populations have received so little attention.[3]

The Rationality Input

There is virtually no evidence that a rational-comprehensive approach has been used either to formulate governmental intervention into agricultural policy in the 1930s, or to justify its withdrawal in favor of a market economy since the 1960s. Numerous reports by Congress have periodically attempted to anticipate future farm policy.[4] A comparative study of agricultural policy in the European Community and the United States has asserted that rational models do not explain farm policy adequately: "The rational actor would probably have eliminated commodity price and income support policies to reduce the burgeoning surpluses, allowing the market to clear. The financial resources saved could undoubtedly be more productively employed elsewhere."[5]

The alternative of bargaining between different self-interests and divergent perceptions seems to be a more applicable explanation of governmental action. The known limits of human cognitive capacities to comprehend have stimulated policymakers to seek "satisficing," or minimally satisfactory choices, rather than optimal choices. The tinkering that is evident with the various shifts in farm policy since the end of World War II reflect the gradualist maneuvers that were made at different times. These maneuvers kept the federal government heavily involved in the farm economy despite numerous efforts since the 1960s to move farm policy away from government support and toward the vagaries of the marketplace. Organizational perquisites and bureaucratic politics provide important insights into why efforts to reform agricultural policy have been unsuccessful, as past policies tend to persist until a consensus for change occurs. Agricultural policy has become so complicated, compartmentalized, and formulated in isolation from other policies that political participants with the greatest expertise and the strongest commitment tend to introduce inertia into the process and thereby encourage policy paralysis.[6]

The Power Input

The pluralistic model of an organized electorate asserting influence through competitive interest or pressure groups throughout the political process has been the prevailing power theory that has been used to account for agriculture policy.[7] Pluralists have focused upon the influence of the "farm bloc" of rural congressional districts that comprised the largest single plurality of seats in the House of Representatives—181 members—as late as 1966. However, shortly after the Supreme Court's approval of "reapportionment" based on the principle of "one man, one vote," there was a net loss of fifty-one rural districts to the advantage of suburban representation.[8] By 1995, there were only fifty members of Congress whose constituents derived more than 10 percent of their income from agriculture. Rural representation in the United States Senate also declined dramatically, from eighteen states that had a majority rural population in 1950 to only four such states by 1990. The enduring bipartisan coalition of rural Republicans who supported price supports, and urban Democrats who supported food stamps and nutrition programs came under tremendous challenge during the balanced budget debate of the mid 1990s. Members of Congress from rural districts, however, continued to be represented strategically on the key congressional committees that write the major farm legislation.

Some analysts of the power perspective have argued that pluralistic governments have a problem with government economic planning, since planning generally has required a balance among law, choice, priorities, and moralities, whereas pluralism replaces planning with bargaining among competing interest groups. For example, Theodore Lowi has contended that nowhere have the consequences of pluralistic principles been more clearly evident than in agricultural policy, where the distinction between public and private has come closest to being completely eliminated: "This has been accomplished not by public expropriation of private domain—as would be true of the nationalization that Americans fear—but by private expropriating of public authority."[9]

One key feature of pluralism is the concept of specialization by those attempting to influence specific agenda items in separate spheres, or policy domains. The "new politics of agriculture" represents an expanded agenda of consumer issues, such as resource conservation, water pollution, food safety, nutrition, occupational safety, research, and unionization of farm workers. The "new politics" has also brought about an expansion in the number and variety of participating groups. This has meant an irreversible decline in the dominant influence of groups such as the American Farm Bureau, which had exercised substantial "hegemony" in the group representation of farm interests for three decades, from the early 1920s to the 1950s. Ever since the 1950s, there has been an expansion of diverse players attempting to influence agricultural policy. As a result, policymakers have reported that lobbying in agriculture has often been "uneven, biased, inconsistent, hit-or-miss, inattentive to detail, unconcerned with major issues, and too incremental."[10] Some proponents of the pluralist, interest group-centered view of American politics have used network analysis to affirm a "hollow core" of policymaking in America.[11] The agriculture policy domain has been well settled politically among the private groups and their public-sector protectors, suggesting a pattern characterized as an "iron triangle." While President Carter perceived members of the iron triangle as his foes, Hugh Heclo referred to policy actors as being members of issue networks with varying degrees of mutual commitment or dependence on others, publicly debating rather than settling issues in secret.[12]

By contrast, those who believed that the country was ruled by an economic power elite viewed the "farm bloc" of the New Deal as a most successful lobby. C. Wright Mills, for example, argued that beliefs such as the Jeffersonian ideal that farming is a superior way of life had prevailed in the United States until after the Civil War. Shortly thereafter, however, independent proprietors and farmers gave way to industry and concentrated economic units.[13]

More recent concentrations of agribusiness have stimulated some analysts to characterize the food system of the United States as being much like an hour glass, with many producers and millions of consumers, but with just a handful of firms in the middle controlling agriculture from "seed to shelf." To achieve their public policy objectives, these firms were perceived to be working closely with top political leaders. A notable example of this process is Archer Daniels Midland's chief executive officer, Wayne Andreas, who has gained the reputation of being a "prince of political philanthropy" for some fifty years. He supported a large number of both Democrats and Republicans in Congress, including both liberals and conservatives, focusing only upon whether they could help his businesses. In 1992, he contributed to the campaigns of both President Bush ($1.1 million) and his leading challenger, Bill Clinton ($306,500), both of whom expressed support for ADM's ethanol business and the corn farmers from whose crops ethanol is derived. While there was little evidence that Andreas's generosity has been repaid directly, it is widely believed that he does benefit from "long-term personal friendships with politicians that evolve into attentive trust."[14] ADM gained from nearly every corporate benefit that national policymakers can bestow, including tax breaks, protective tariffs, import quotas, regulatory mandates, raw material subsidies, and loan guarantees. One observer, Ronald Henkoff, of *Fortune* magazine, has suggested that "Agriculture is the most manipulated industry on the planet. After Mother Nature, it is politicians—not farmers, traders, or processors—who hold the most sway over which crops are planted, where they will be sold, and what prices they will fetch."[15] Henkoff noted that, as the "industrialized countries pour $245 billion into price supports, import quotas, acreage set-asides, export subsidies, and other arcane "agripolicies," it becomes a necessity for agribusiness to communicate with the people who make the big decisions."[16]

While the question of "Who governs?" has not been settled, it appears that elites have played an important role in imposing and sustaining federal commodity price supports. In the past, "peak" interest group associations, such as the Farm Bureau and a variety of farm commodity organizations, exercised an inordinate degree of power within the agricultural policy domain.[17] The nature of the more recent omnibus farm bill, however, contains features that have drawn numerous interests, ranging from exporters and farmers with traditional concerns for commodity price supports to consumers, advocates of the poor, and the environmentalists. Two hundred organized private interests helped shape the 1985 farm bill.[18] It is difficult to determine who the players are in agriculture and what issues and interests are actually being represented. The general growth over time in the number of registered lobbyists and their organizations raises a number of relevant questions: "What sets of interests have observable impacts upon farm policy?" "How often are they likely to influence policy, and under what circumstances?" "Who represents what?" "Have coalitions of interest groups become essential to effect change?" "What is the relationship between policy activists and private interests?" Interest group theory provides a cogent, precise explanation of the dynamics of constant change and of the ways in which responding organizational efforts are nurtured by the entrepreneurial leadership of a few individuals who depend on the support and goodwill of their patrons, as they define and create acceptable policy alternatives.

Under these circumstances, congressional representatives have become distrustful of taking policy "cues" from national agricultural groups and have begun to rely on politically relevant "confidants" and on other individual, grassroots constituents for reliable information about public opinion.[19] This partially explains the increasing, but still insufficient, attention that is being paid now to rural community development and nutrition programs. Given the expanded scope of the omnibus national farm bills, one should expect politics not only to change public policy but also to change the organizations that determine these policies.[20] The trend in the number of persons working in farm occupations from 1850 to 1993 is summarized in Table 5.1. When first counted separately in the 1920 census, the farm population was defined as people living on farms, regardless of their occupation or source of income. Many people who live on farms today have no one in the household who is employed primarily in agriculture, and those employed in agriculture often do not live on farms. An

TABLE 5.1 Persons in Farm Occupations, 1850–1993 (in thousands)

Year	Total Workers	Number in Farm Occupations	Percent of All Workers
1850	7,697	4,902	63.7
1870	12,925	6,850	53.0
1900	29,030	10,888	37.5
1920	42,206	11,390	27.0
1930	48,686	10,321	21.2
1940	51,742	8,995	17.4
1950	59,230	6,858	11.6
1960	67,990	4,132	6.1
1970	79,802	2,881	3.6
1980	104,058	2,818	2.7
1985	106,214	2,949	2.8
1990	117,491	2,864	2.4
1991	116,000	2,848	2.5
1992	116,442	2,936	2.5
1993	117,238	2,988	2.5

Note: Total workers for 1985 to 1993 are employed workers ages fifteen years and older. Total workers for 1970 and 1980 are members of the experienced civilian labor force ages sixteen years and older. Total workers for 1900 to 1960 are members of the experienced civilian labor force ages fourteen years and older. Total workers for 1850 to 1890 are gainfully employed workers ages ten years and older.

Source: U.S. Department of Agriculture, Economic Research Service.

estimated 35 percent of persons living in farm operator or farm manager households do not live on a farm, and nearly 40 percent of farm residents are members of households in which no one operates or manages a farm or receives farm self-employment income. As a consequence, the federal government has discontinued the use of the conventional definition of farm residence. In 1993, about five million people lived in households associated with the operation of farms, as indicated by a household member's occupation or source of income. This farm population definition now is identified as the farm entrepreneurial population. The largest proportion of that population (47 percent) is found in the Midwest.

As the rural population of the United States declines and as their proportional degree of representational power in Congress correspondingly diminishes, there appear to be fewer rural interest groups competing with farm groups for success in the policy arena. Among rural and farm interests that interact and at least occasionally come into conflict with each other within the agricultural policy domain, it is important to identify the multiplicity of obstacles that have prevented a more forceful promotion of the nation's rural nonfarm interests: (1) their diverse socioeconomic conditions and values, (2) the basic weaknesses and lack of capacity of rural governments, (3) the public's misconceptions about the nature and needs of the rural component of American society, with farm interest groups having preempted the rural political turf, and (4) the interdependence of nonmetropolitan and metropolitan markets, as well as global markets.[21] These and other reasons have made the creation of a coherent vision of rural policy more difficult and more complex than would be necessary if there were a clearer commonality between narrower farm and broader rural interests. In a sense, rural policy is in search of a constituency that has yet to articulate the current and future needs of rural small towns.[22]

Who, then, governs rural, small town America? The predominant pattern of the distribution of power in smaller towns tends to be in the form of concentrated hierarchies, with informal rather than public officials carrying out important political functions.[23] Informal leaders do so without well developed institutions and organizations, relying principally upon nonofficial networks that include politicians as part of a loose coalition. Politicians develop a sense that they are expected to represent the public interest. There is thus a low probability that community conflict will occur, except when the town undergoes a dramatic change.

It is important to notice that the distribution and use of political power alone cannot explain policy outputs. The importance of the political ideologies that predominate among the most powerful cannot be understated, but often is not emphasized sufficiently in studies of public policy. One school of thought contends, for example, that not only do the powerful dominate, but they do so to benefit and protect their "ruling class" position.[24] Proponents of the pluralist perspective, reluctant to measure benefits and more interested in the competitive bargaining of the political process, tend to explain the pragmatic use of political resources and to downplay the ideological basis of policymaking. Periodic manifestation of protests and demonstrations by farmers reflects the deep-seated ideological base of agricultural and rural policy. Ideological predispositions have been identified by Daniel Elazar as falling into three prevalent political cultures that operate within the United States at both regional and community levels: traditionalistic, individualistic, and moralistic.[25] The rise of the radical right and left, as well as distinctions within the conservative doctrines—orthodox, Jeffersonian, and progressive—was articulated by Agger, Goldrich, and Swanson to explain different policy outputs.[26]

The Ideological Input

For some six decades, agricultural policy in the United States has been driven by a set of prevailing but changing values, ideologies, images, myths, and catchy slogans about farmers, foods, and rural communities. The core American values of survival, justice, economy, self-fulfillment, and self-respect have been undergoing a great transformation. The country has been moving away from the traditional "Lockean ideology" of individualism, property rights, competition driven by consumer desire, a limited state, and scientific specification toward the values of equality, consensus, rights, entitlements, collective and community needs, planning, coordination, and holism. Agriculture not only set the stage for the acceptance and utility of the Lockean ideology, but was among the most powerful forces in its transformation to the new values.[27] The impact of this transformation has been more dramatic for rural than for urban or suburban residents. Governmental intervention in the farm economy has brought about a fundamental change over the control of the land, the prices and income from food production, and environmental regulation over the use of the most advanced technologies.

While there has been a wide range of ideological perspectives about what should be the country's rural and farm policy, the salient ones can be best expressed by debate over the role of government. The dominance of liberals during the New Deal promoted an expansion of the scope of government. More recently, the ascendancy of conservatives has attempted to limit this role and to return farming to the marketplace. Neither has succeeded in displacing the other, nor in resolving the issue to their satisfaction. Both condemn the impact of federal agricultural policy upon farmers and other rural Americans. Liberals see federal farm policy as a necessary intervention in defense of the family farm, describing the farm crisis as essentially financial, a product of misplaced values, both economic and cultural. For example, liberal analysts condemned the myth that "big is better" for having all but eliminated the cherished tradition of the family farm.[28] In sharp contrast, conservatives contended that federal farm policy was a fiasco that trampled on individual rights, sacrificed the poor to the rich, and contradicted the marketplace.[29] Political commentators from both the left and the right seem to agree that agricultural policy has lost its relevance as technology, markets, and the political economy have changed the entire structure of agriculture, with farmers under attack today from subsidized foreign competition and unsympathetic domestic consumers.

The sphere of influence of most small town residents, including their leaders, tends to be limited in scope. These inhabitants tend to believe in a limited, minimalist government that matches their scarce public resources. Public officials are reluctant to join intergovernmental cooperative arrangements, except for mutual aid agreements to help other small towns when they are in need. Their constituents consistently oppose joining in centralized, consolidation reforms. Officials have been slow to reach out for state and federal grants for community development projects; they vigorously oppose the imposition of external mandates, fail to plan, and are slow to recognize the desire for collective bargaining rights of their public employees. Very often, local officials simply ignore state and federal mandates, such as the need to follow a comprehensive plan. One town in Florida filed its comprehensive plan with the state, then put it in a sealed envelope and placed the envelope in an unused storage cabinet.

By and large, citizens of rural towns prefer consensus over rancorous conflicts. When conflicts do occur, however, they generally involve major disagreements over challenges to the community's values and norms. Despite the sense of homogeneity, differences over values can disrupt community harmony. A classic study of small-town America, for example, found that the dominant ideologies of the upstate New York community "Springdale" supported equality, industriousness, improvement, and optimism. The study also found, however, that certain persons within the community held diverse views based upon their socioeconomic status. Prosperous farmers preferred investments; merchants preferred savings, professionals preferred work and consumption, and "shack people" were consumption-oriented.[30] Issues may split communities. One community may divide sharply over the introduction of liquor by the drink, another over the fluoridation of the water supply, while still another over development projects such as the introduction of a large shopping mall that competes with main street business.

Application of RPI to Rural, Agricultural, and Small-Town Policy

There is little evidence concerning the salience of rational-comprehensive analysis in formulating agricultural or rural policy. Patterns of ideological dissonance concerning the role of government in farm policy appear throughout American history. The Lockean ideology of rugged individualism was manifested early in American history in, for example, Thomas Jefferson's praise for the yeoman farmer as the demographic bedrock of postrevolutionary society. This bucolic ideal gave way, at least in part, to the emphasis in post-Depression policy on government intervention as the best way to ensure the survival of private ownership of the land and of agricultural products. However, the inability of more market-oriented presidents, such as Ronald Reagan, to reverse completely this interventionist policy, despite vigorous efforts to reduce federal payments for agricultural programs, suggests that political power rather than ideology drives agricultural and rural policy.

The role of the power perspective in explaining rural, agricultural, and small-town policy perhaps is manifested most clearly in the well-documented historical overrepresentation of rural interests in state legislatures and in Congress. The gross inequities in state legislative representation were often based on awarding state House and/or Senate seats to political subdivisions (usually counties) based more on geography than on population. In many states, this resulted in legislators from rural counties representing far fewer voters than were represented by most urban and suburban legislators. One obvious consequence of these vast demographic differences was that a person's vote in a heavily populated urban or suburban district was diluted relative to the vote cast by a resident of a more sparsely populated rural district.

The inequities inherent in this system of malapportionment created a major systemic problem in American politics with the rapid expansion of urban, and even more so of suburban, populations by the middle of the twentieth century, leading to landmark Supreme Court decisions in the early 1960s mandating that states must provide more equitable representation to citizens of nonrural counties. The 1962 Supreme Court ruling in the Tennessee case of *Baker v.*

Carr (369 U.S. 186) invoked the Fourteenth Amendment principle that no state could deny to any person "the equal protection of the laws." Two years later, this principle was applied in *Reynolds v. Sims* (377 U.S. 533) to conclude that both chambers of state legislatures must be apportioned with very nearly equal populations in each district.

Also in 1964, the Supreme Court decided in *Wesberry v. Sanders* (376 U.S. 1) that this one-man, one-vote principle also applied to the apportionment of districts for the U.S. House of Representatives. As it happened, the resulting re-allocation of political power away from rural areas provided only a relatively brief era of strength for urban residents, because the rapid suburbanization of the nation following the 1960s and population shifts to the Sunbelt states of the Southeast and West resulted in major gains in legislative power for suburban and more conservative areas of the country whose interests often conflict with those of urban residents. Supreme Court rulings about reapportionment, however, have not affected the representational base of the U.S. Senate, since the U.S. Constitution awards two senators to each state regardless of differences in populations among the states. Consequently, rural interests have enjoyed favorable representation in the Senate where rural states with small populations, such as Idaho and Wyoming, have the same number of senators (two) as states such as California or Texas with much larger populations.

The relative decline in the numbers of people associated with farming, however, does not bode well for the future of farm-related policy. From the power perspective, one would expect that the ability of farm interests to dictate policy would diminish as nonrural suburban and urban populations have grown relative to the rural citizenry. This appears to be the case today. Whether or not rural and agricultural interests will be successful in forestalling future cuts in subsidies and other programs will likely depend on their ability to forge coalitions with others and their ability to maintain political representation. The history of food stamp policy provides an example of how rural interests have succeeded in making common cause with urban residents. Legislative votes on food stamp expenditures and eligibility have been determined largely by a coalition of rural legislators (who see food stamps as a way of supporting agricultural production by putting more food in the mouths of people who otherwise might not be able to afford it) and urban legislators (who have large populations of constituents in need of the nutrition and income support provided by food stamps).

HISTORY OF RURAL, AGRICULTURAL, AND SMALL-TOWN POLICY IN THE UNITED STATES

The major developments and changes that have occurred in rural policies have been associated primarily with the changes that happen when new presidential administrations come to power. Franklin Roosevelt's New Deal expanded the scope of the federal government into agriculture in a dramatic way. Despite efforts by conservative presidents such as Richard Nixon and Ronald Reagan and moderate presidents like John Kennedy, Lyndon Johnson, Jimmy Carter, George Bush, and Bill Clinton to eliminate or modify federal involvement in rural and agricultural policy, most such efforts appear to have only "tinkered" with the earlier policy frameworks established during the New Deal of the 1930s.

National Initiatives

From the New Deal to the Great Society

The New Deal and Parity Commodity Prices

It was not until the New Deal and the very real threat of a collapse of farm prices and income that Congress intervened to pass the Agricultural Adjustment Act (AAA) of 1933. Secretary of Agriculture Henry A. Wallace (in office from 1933 to 1940, and a progressive Democratic candidate for president in 1948) viewed this act of controlling the supply of food as a temporary measure to deal with the emergency at that time. Initially, the AAA provided voluntary acreage agreements and established commodity price supports at varying percentages of a given target price level. Price guarantees were provided on a few politically favored farm commodities, such as wheat, cotton, field corn, hogs, rice, tobacco, and milk and dairy products. The revised 1936 AAA pegged price supports to the purchasing power of farmers who lived during the "golden age" of agriculture (1910 to 1914) and promoted soil conservation. The U.S. Supreme Court, however, struck down key features of the act, stimulating Congress to pass in 1938 a stronger AAA that established the "evernormal granary," including mandatory loans provided at flexible support rates to cooperating producers of farm products. During World War II, the nation's policy shifted from restraining production to encouraging it with higher price guarantees, to stimulate wartime provision of foodstuffs for both domestic consumption and foreign shipment.

The Fair Deal and Flexible Price Supports

Following World War II, the United States aggressively played the "food card" to compete with the Soviet Union's "hunger card" for dominance in the political, military, and economic struggle to restore a war-ravaged world. The Marshall Plan nearly depleted America's increasing stocks of surplus farm output, which in turn sent commodity prices soaring. The continuation of price supports was debated heatedly between proponents of the policy (primarily congressional Democrats from the South and the Plains states, supported by organized labor and government economists) and its opponents (Republicans, the Farm Bureau, private-sector economists, and the then-emerging agribusiness firms that later came to dominate the rural economy and its rapidly expanding international offshoots). The Republican-controlled 80th Congress (1947–1948) formulated a compromise by allowing one more year of price supports at 90 percent of parity. Flexible price supports set at 75 percent of parity were established to serve as a self-regulating mechanism to maintain the health of the rural economy by raising supports in times of scarcity and reducing them in periods of surplus.

With the return of Democratic control of Congress in 1949, price supports were restored to 90 percent of parity, thereby dealing a blow to the proponents of market-oriented agriculture. President Harry Truman's second secretary of agriculture, Charles F. Brannan (appointed in 1948), attempted unsuccessfully to replace the parity standard of 1910–1914 and to shift to a system of payments based on production levels or farm income, with limits determined by the size of the typical family farm.

Eisenhower's Soil Bank and Food for Peace

Eisenhower's secretary of agriculture, Ezra Taft Benson, believed that government intervention in the economy was wrong, both morally and economically. Facing costly increased farm surpluses due to increased productivity, Congress authorized flexible price supports in 1954 and temporarily developed the concept of the "soil bank." The two principal components of the "soil bank" concept—the Acreage Reduction Program and the Conservation Reserve Program—took out of production nearly 30 million acres. The administration also established the Food for Peace program (P. L. 480), to export the nation's growing agricultural surpluses abroad and increase U.S. political leverage around the globe. This greatly expanded the total worldwide demand for American farm products. Large surpluses were created through these programs because farmers tended to select relatively high levels of price supports with few or no production controls. The result was a massive increase in farm commodity stockpiles. For example, two billion bushels of corn were stockpiled by 1960 at a tremendous cost to the federal government.

Food Stamps, Exports, and Johnson's Great Society

Two television programs—*Hunger in America* and *Harvest of Shame*—called attention to the problems of poverty amidst the general wealth of the United States, as well as the severe problems confronting migrant laborers who moved around the countryside from one seasonal crop to another, living in deplorable conditions. This heightened awareness of the problems associated with rural poverty created an environment for action. President Kennedy's secretary of agriculture, Orville Freeman (who also continued in that position throughout Lyndon Johnson's administration), believed that the cost to the government to support agricultural commodities could be reduced and that farm prices could increase as a consequence of meeting the nutritional needs of those in poverty. The resulting food stamp program would serve to increase farm prices, lower the amount of food that needed to be stored, and help to feed the poor. Secretary Freeman also supported an expanded farm commodity export program. His administration unsuccessfully proposed to set up a system of acreage controls and to transfer from Congress to the Secretary of Agriculture the authority to set acreage allocations and price supports. Instead, Congress turned to voluntary land-retirement programs for feed grains, as farmers rejected strict wheat production controls in a 1963 referendum.

The general direction of farm policy changed little between the Kennedy and Johnson administrations, except for the overall strategy for dealing with poverty in America. While many of the Great Society's antipoverty programs were designed to address urban America, President Johnson also commissioned a study of rural poverty in 1968. That study found that 40 percent of the nation's poor lived in rural areas, particularly in the declining small towns that were located off the superhighways and generally out of sight. The traditional techniques of community development—self-study, self-help, and voluntary action—gave way to more aggressive strategies. Federal funds for economic development, housing, and infrastructure were made available to these communities, which long had been considered a national symbol of independence and self-reliance. The United States Department of Agriculture (USDA) and the nation's land-grant colleges, together with other technical specialists, resented this diversion of federal funds away from their traditional agricultural mission of commodity supports.

From Richard Nixon to the Present

Nixon's Set-Aside Program and Consumer Protection

After a considerable legislative struggle over whether to move toward a market-oriented farm policy, the Republican Nixon administration gave farmers greater freedom to plant when they desired. These directives would be based on their assessment of market conditions. While crop and price controls were continued, 1970 amendments to the AAA added a "set-aside" program that allowed farmers compensation for taking part of their land out of production and growing whatever they wanted on it. The 1973 amendments to the AAA replaced price supports on the major commodities with lower "target prices" that would reimburse farmers only in the event that there was a sharp drop in market prices.

Urban legislators, resentful of the large subsidy payments made to some individual farmers, secured limitations on the total amount that could be given to any farmer ($55,000 per commodity per producer). Huge sales of grain at bargain rates to the Soviet Union in 1972, which came to be known as "the great grain robbery," depleted the nation's grain bins and raised prices sharply. This development coincided with the adoption of the concept of a "target price" that would reimburse farmers only if market prices were to drop precipitously. Farmers responded by planting "fence-row to fence-row," raising record amounts of crops, bringing prices down, and increasing production in succeeding years. Nixon's secretary of state, Henry Kissinger (appointed to that post in 1973, and continuing in that position until the end of the Ford administration in 1977), proposed a system of nationally held but internationally coordinated grain reserves, but American farmers opposed that strategy out of fear that governments might be tempted to "dump" their stocks in times of rising prices, thereby causing prices and farmers' income to drop.

Jimmy Carter's Grain Embargo and Crop Insurance

The 1976 presidential election was characterized in part by the major candidates outbidding each other in regard to what they claimed that they could do for farmers. The winner, Jimmy Carter, a Georgia peanut farmer before entering politics, displeased the farm community by his approach to agricultural policy. Contradicting his political campaign promise "never" to use an embargo to settle international disputes, President Carter, without involving the USDA, placed an embargo upon the Soviet Union for its 1979 military intervention in Afghanistan. Carter allowed eight million tons to be exempt from the embargo, but canceled another seventeen million tons of prospective grain shipments. This became the largest embargo in the nation's history, and in theory simply would have had the consequence of dumping grain on the market, thereby forcing prices down and placing in jeopardy the most heavily indebted farmers who were just barely hanging on. However, to cover the impending crisis, the federal government assumed ownership of most of the canceled wheat and corn and locked those commodities away in storage for years. In the meantime, grain exporters in Europe, Australia, and Canada took advantage of the situation and replaced American exports.

Carter's administration ended direct payment to farmers whose crops had been damaged by natural disasters and offered them a greatly expanded federal crop insurance program. Carter rarely chose to use his standby authority to curb surplus production by paying farmers not to grow crops. He also encouraged the establishment of nutritional guidelines to cut down on the consumption of saturated fats, cholesterol, sugar, and salt. Secretary of Agriculture Robert Bergland endorsed a move to organic, or nonchemical, farming. Furthermore, the Carter administration stepped up enforcement of migrant labor laws and attempted to restrict the size of the farms that benefited from federal irrigation projects. These conditions incited farmers to organize the American Agriculture Movement (AAM), which conducted a "tractorcade march" upon Washington.

Reagan's Attempt to End Interventionist Federal Farm Policy

Despite candidate Reagan's acknowledgment that he did not know what "parity" meant, he received overwhelming support from farmers and rural voters in his successful 1980 campaign against Carter. But the good will dissipated quickly when David Stockman, Reagan's director of the Office of Management and Budget (OMB) believed that what was required was "severing the umbilical cords of dependency that ran from Washington to every nook and cranny of the nation."[31] Stockman viewed farm subsidies as "organized larceny" and wished to seize the opportunity for "the liberation of American agriculture from the whole rot of USDA subsidies and price supports. . . . [This] would free the labor and capital trapped in inefficient, surplus farm output for redeployment to productive, profitable uses elsewhere in the national economy."[32] He compared Carter's $30 billion outlays for farm support with Reagan's proposed crop support of $10 billion over five years. Despite the political rhetoric, the 1981 amendments to the AAA, which passed the House of Representatives narrowly—by only two votes—maintained price supports and even added a new support program for sugar. The projected estimate of $11 billion over four years turned out to be $54.6 billion for the same four years and $88.6 billion over five years.

The farm crisis that was associated with the recession of the early 1980s, together with drought, contracting export markets, the boom-and-bust cycle of farmland prices, increasing commodity surpluses, and falling farm commodity prices, began to hit even large and wealthy farmers, who faced total ruin. The growing integration of global capital and commodity markets, and the anti-inflationary efforts of the Federal Reserve reduced the value of farmland, drove down export demand, and held farmers hostage to foreign exchange rates, as well as to domestic interest rates, as never before. The Reagan administration turned to the Payment in Kind (PIK) program, which paid farmers more not to grow crops and enabled them to take half their cropland out of production. OMB hoped to keep farm program payments "off budget" by paying for land retirements with surplus crops already owned by USDA. However, a series of miscalculations and misjudgments cost the federal government some $28 to $30 billion in 1983.

The Reagan administration made another attempt to return agriculture to the marketplace with the omnibus agricultural bill of 1985. However, it was pronounced "dead on arrival." A severe drought and an "ill-conceived" acreage diversion program combined to make the Reagan agricultural policy the most "interventionist" in American history.[33]

The Bush Administration: Normal Crop Acreage, Flexibility Base, and GATT

Following the restoration of American agriculture under the generous support of the Reagan administration, the Bush administration proposed a "pragmatic package" of farm policy that stressed "flexibility" for farmers. Negotiations on the federal budget (resulting in the Gramm-Rudman-Hollings deficit reduction targets), the environment (leading to the Wetlands Reserve Program and the Water Quality Incentive Program), and the Uruguay Round of the General Agreement on Tariffs and Trade (GATT) all occupied greater attention in this administration. The 1985 omnibus farm bill established a five-year cycle for future legislation. The administration needed to cut over $13 billion of farm subsidies and proposed the Normal Crop Acreage scheme, which established a single-payment system based on a farmer's crop history, thereby providing a "flexible base." The Integrated Farm Management program allowed farmers to respond to environmental concerns while enhancing productivity and profits. The loss of farm state Republican senators resulted in a Democratic-controlled Congress that gave the secretary of agriculture authority to waive cost-reduction efforts and to raise export subsidies in the event that the GATT negotiations failed.

Reinventing Government and the Empowerment Initiative of Clinton/Gore

The Clinton presidency quickly gained the reputation of taking initiative and action, of being intensely personal and political, and also of being discontinuous and episodic, but as a leader Clinton appeared to be ambiguous ideologically: "In answer to the question, 'Who am I?' Clinton's response has been to say that he is an amalgam. He is a Democrat, but a new kind of Democrat. He is for government programs, but only if they work."[34] During its first two years, the administration ensured the passage of both the North American Free Trade Agreement (NAFTA) and the Uruguay Round of GATT. It also engaged in strenuous efforts to "reinvent" the government, both to make it work more effectively and to reduce the annual federal deficit. The administration planned to reduce the number of USDA agencies by a third, eliminate 13,000 departmental jobs, close down 1,100 field offices, and reduce spending by some $4 billion.

Clinton included three rural areas in his Empowerment Zones Enterprise Communities—the Kentucky Highlands, South Texas, and Mid-Delta Mississippi—which received $40 million each. The Mid-Delta project involved eight counties of 28,457 residents, half of whom lived in poverty, two-thirds of whom were black, a quarter of whom received public assistance, and 15 percent of whom were unemployed. The goals of the project were to improve race relations, develop job training centers, create trade zones, eliminate substandard housing, boost homeownership by 15 percent, reduce the numbers of illegitimate births and teenage mothers, end the waiting list for admission of preschool children to Head Start programs, and promote producer/consumer cooperatives.

State and Local Initiatives to Rural Communities and Small Towns

The fifty states are not involved in price supports, and instead focus upon ways to foster farming and to nurture small, rural communities. Most states have separate departments of agriculture that are expected to respond to and support the special needs and preferences of farmers. Traditionally, states have long provided "farm to market" roadways, supported land grant colleges to improve agricultural practices, and generally assisted farmers with property tax breaks. In fact, rural domination of state legislatures was commonplace until the U.S. Supreme Court's approval of the "one man, one vote" principle to reapportion the representative base of legislative bodies. Even in states with a single big city—New York, Illinois, Georgia, Missouri, and Massachusetts—

urbanites failed to gain ascendancy. Reapportionment was expected to foster urban domination of the states, but that seldom occurred as suburban districts became more influential at the expense of rural areas.

More recently, small towns within metropolitan areas have become popular with many Americans. Newcomers to these towns expect and demand good services. Land developers, seeking available and cheaper land in metropolitan areas, aggressively used farmland to enhance their projects. The efforts of private developers to build shopping malls have threatened downtown businesses and the environment. Rural interests have secured property tax breaks from localities to remain economically viable and have become recalcitrant to public planners who attempt to manage urban growth. In Florida, for example, growth management laws require that public infrastructure investments be provided to ensure little or no degradation in the quality of life. Florida laws also impose conservation measures on developers to protect endangered and threatened wildlife. Other states, however, that are not experiencing growth feel that they cannot afford to place such constraints on development.

As the twentieth century comes to a conclusion, we find that there are some 3,000 county governments that long have provided and likely will continue to provide the main political and public functions for the rural countryside, such as roads, law enforcement, and human services. In most cases, counties have vigorously retained their rural orientation even when most of their constituents sought to expand and improve upon services such as fire protection, public utilities, and parks and recreation. Only recently have county governments gradually begun to provide functions for those living in unincorporated areas. County governments collaborate with land grant colleges, state agencies, and the USDA to support and operate the system of county extension agents that fosters the interest of farmers.

In addition, a variety of decision-making arrangements at the local level range from small municipalities and towns, to special districts, and to villages without formal governments. These small communities, especially those located in nonmetropolitan areas, have experienced population decline and stagnant economies. Many small towns have been caught in farm cycles of boom and "crunch," as not many people who leave rural small communities ever come back. There also are regional differences. For example, in the eastern Midwest running from Ohio westward through Iowa, many small farm towns already either have died or have survived as bedroom communities for nearby cities. In the western Great Plains, however, many small towns have survived because farmers need a place to shop, bank, and secure services.

Many small communities have begun to "prowl" for state and federal grants to revitalize their economy, with some becoming potential sites for business firms searching for a competitive advantage. Other towns are located in areas that are favorable to tourism and to urbanites with second homes. The notion that telecommunications has reduced the need to live in the major metropolitan areas does not seem to have worked out in practice. Former Secretary of Agriculture Robert Bergland says that the nation will never engage in triage, but triage (being cannibalized by the marketplace) is happening anyway, with or without planning. The number of farms and their average acreage in 1994 are presented in Table 5.2.

Many towns survive less from farm subsidies than because of Social Security payments. In 1990, about 6 percent of the 69 million rural Americans lived on farms, and less than a quarter of them relied directly on agriculture for their living, with many commuting to nearby jobs. Many economists believed that the problems confronting American agriculture were not what ailed the rural parts of the country. Instead, the failure of the nonfarming sector of the rural economy was cited as the cause of economic hardship for so many residents of small towns.

The reputation of rural local governments has been one of inadequate policymaking, lack of professionalism among its administrators, and low levels of funding. Reduced federal aid has placed considerable strain upon these

TABLE 5.2 Number of Farms and Acreage, by State, 1994

State	Number of Farms (000)	Acreage per Farm	State	Number of Farms (000)	Acreage per Farm
United States	2,065	471	Montana	23	2,653
Alabama	46	222	Nebraska	55	856
Alaska	1	1,786	Nevada	2	3,667
Arizona	7	4,784	New Hampshire	2	183
Arkansas	44	343	New Jersey	9	97
California	79	378	New Mexico	14	3,274
Colorado	25	1,292	New York	36	219
Connecticut	4	103	North Carolina	58	160
Delaware	3	228	North Dakota	32	1,263
Florida	39	264	Ohio	75	203
Georgia	45	269	Oklahoma	70	486
Hawaii	5	331	Oregon	38	461
Idaho	21	659	Pennsylvania	51	153
Illinois	77	365	Rhode Island	1	90
Indiana	63	254	South Carolina	23	222
Iowa	101	329	South Dakota	34	1,300
Kansas	65	735	Tennessee	83	145
Kentucky	89	158	Texas	200	645
Louisiana	28	300	Utah	13	854
Maine	8	179	Vermont	6	226
Maryland	15	152	Virginia	46	187
Massachusetts	6	100	Washington	36	439
Michigan	52	206	West Virginia	20	185
Minnesota	85	349	Wisconsin	79	214
Mississippi	39	328	Wyoming	9	3,761
Missouri	105	287			

Source: National Agricultural Statistics Service, U.S. Department of Agriculture.

governments. Many rural towns experienced chronic recessions that were un-related to the farm crisis. Rural poverty persists, especially among African-Americans.[35] Looking to the future of small towns, some analysts call for the development of a "pool of visionary leaders" who are capable of approaching local concerns from a generalized orientation.[36]

More relevant is the relative inattention given the plight of small rural com-munities by national policymakers[37] and the lack of intense rural interest and clout by the local leadership.[38] Political coalitions that address the problems of both farmers and nonfarm populations living in small rural towns not only are difficult to organize, but have yet to find a coherent focus for common problems.

The Contemporary Situation

Agricultural Policy

The quandary for President Clinton in 1993 was whether to continue the $63 billion in federal outlays spent in fiscal year 1993 for agricultural purposes or to prepare the nation to respond better to the dynamic globalization issues that were confronting rural America. Immediately following World War II, na-tional policy had been concerned with maintaining the family farm, farm in-comes, and the capacity of a very rich rural resource base. By the 1970s, that policy arena also included foreign policy and the far more complex issues of nu-trition, safety, quality, and poverty. By the 1980s, the issues of rural economic and community development had drawn the attention of policymakers and of the public. The approval of two significant international trade agreements in 1994 (NAFTA and GATT) as a preliminary to the creation of the World Trade Organization to regulate and enforce international trade agreements was con-sidered a major step in positioning America favorably in world trade. The two agreements were expected to have a major impact upon the agricultural poli-cies of both developed and developing nations that were entangled in contra-dictory policy statements adopted by governments around the world. Policies were said to have "one foot on the accelerator and one foot on the brake—simultaneously encouraging and discouraging increased farm production."[39] The agreements reflect the transition from traditional agrarian issues of land reform, surplus farm labor, and the protection of the "family farm" toward such globalization issues as commodity overproduction, the uneven availability of food between and within nations, and protection of the environment.

Once considered the food basket to the world, by the 1980s the United States was no longer the dominant producer of the world's market share of farm products. By the 1990s, it produced two-thirds of the corn and soybeans, a third of the wheat, and less than a quarter of the cotton and rice. Only a third of the total value of food prices was associated with the cost of its production, and only 12 percent of that was generated from the farm, with the remainder in-volving middlemen associated with the distribution, marketing, and regulation of farm products. A sketch of the food system resembled an hourglass, with many producers and millions of consumers.[40] In the middle, however, a handful of firms control the processing of food. These firms therefore were in a position to control the food industry. For example, five firms (ConAgra, Cargill, Archer Daniels Midland, Budge, and International Beef Processors) controlled the slaughter of 72 percent of all the beef, 70 percent of sheep, 45 percent of pork, and 44 percent of young chickens, as well as 71 percent of flour milling and 76 percent of soybean processing (it was believed that when a few firms controlled 40 percent or more of a market, they no longer behaved competitively).

American farmers have been highly vulnerable to the vagaries of the "boom and bust" business cycles (national and international) and the cyclical unpredictability of weather. They have been unwilling to accept these risks, and periodically they have joined populist movements such as Shays' Rebellion (1786) and the Granger movement in the 1870s. The New Deal established the Agricultural Adjustment Act (AAA) of 1933 to correct the devastating impact of the Great Depression. Designed to reduce the vulnerability of agriculture, especially the vulnerability of smaller family farms, the AAA massively expanded the scope of the federal government. Some sixty years of dealing with agricultural issues and a trillion dollars of spending later, a sharp reduction in the number of farms and farmers still transpired. Farm numbers have dwindled from six million farms in 1950 to just two million in 1990. The number of farms with sales of $100,000 or more, which produce more than 80 percent of the nation's agricultural production, declined to a mere 360,000. In addition, there was a growing recognition that modern corporate farming had been transformed, not only from its national base to a new and expanded multinational scope, but more recently to a transnational philosophy respecting no national boundary.[41]

Toward the end of the twentieth century, federal commodity price supports grew to a point where general agreement arose that something must be done. By 1986, the total value of such transfer payments amounted to $88 billion, of which $59.4 billion came from taxpayers and $29.6 billion came from consumers. As a result of the high costs of these subsidies, national policymakers since the 1960s have attempted to make American agriculture more market-oriented. These efforts, however, have been at best incremental and halting. Persistent efforts to eliminate or reduce the federal deficit have developed ideological battle lines between "fiscalism" and "radicalism" in the 104th Congress.[42] The former focused upon the goal of deficit reduction, achieving it by such means as across-the-board freezes, payment-formula adjustments, benefit-payment delays, and accounting "gimmicks." This would avoid substantial structural changes. The latter effort proposed reducing the scope of government by eliminating or privatizing federal programs. The total value of government agricultural payments for each state is shown in Table 5.3. In 1994, nearly $8 billion was spent on cash payments and payments-in-kind; of this total, nearly $1.5 billion was for feed grains, about $1.156 billion was spent for wheat, almost $340 million for rice, nearly $827 million for cotton, over $200 million for wool, nearly $2 billion for conservation, and nearly $2 billion more for a variety of miscellaneous programs related to rural water supplies, forests, dairy programs, commodity storage, livestock emergency assistance, disaster support, loan deficiency, and interest payments.

Rural Policy

The prevailing set of values that guided rural policy well into the twentieth century was the "agrarian creed" of Jeffersonian democracy and the classic economics of Adam Smith. Don Paarlberg[43] has characterized this creed as including the following elements: (1) farmers are good citizens, and a high per-

TABLE 5.3 Government Agricultural Payments by State, 1994 (in thousands of dollars)

State	Total Payments	State	Total Payments
United States	$7,881,036	Montana	$256,151
Alabama	89,386	Nebraska	348,333
Alaska	1,348	Nevada	4,785
Arizona	72,073	New Hampshire	1,475
Arkansas	302,752	New Jersey	7,596
California	272,781	New Mexico	61,092
Colorado	177,109	New York	42,443
Connecticut	2,368	North Carolina	77,646
Delaware	5,590	North Dakota	457,346
Florida	58,637	Ohio	117,097
Georgia	139,825	Oklahoma	207,036
Hawaii	2,911	Oregon	74,426
Idaho	127,289	Pennsylvania	32,686
Illinois	303,159	Rhode Island	451
Indiana	137,020	South Carolina	60,196
Iowa	732,567	South Dakota	289,214
Kansas	467,710	Tennessee	95,610
Kentucky	54,894	Texas	863,213
Louisiana	181,575	Utah	32,051
Maine	14,101	Vermont	4,234
Maryland	15,634	Virginia	34,254
Massachusetts	4,694	Washington	152,854
Michigan	102,092	West Virginia	5,513
Minnesota	622,325	Wisconsin	236,484
Mississippi	225,483	Wyoming	38,128
Missouri	267,397		

Notes: Total includes both cash payments and payments-in-kind. Conservation component of total includes amount paid under agriculture and conservation programs (Conservation Reserve, Agriculture Conservation, Emergency Conservation, and Great Plains Program). Miscellaneous component of total includes Rural Clean Water, Forestry Incentive Long Term, Water Bank Practice Cost Share, Dairy Indemnity, Dairy Termination, Extended Warehouse Storage, Extended Farm Storage, Colorado River Salinity, Livestock Emergency Assistance, Interest Payments, Disaster, Loan Directory, Market Gains, Naval Stores Conservation, Milk Marketing Fee, Options Plot, Milk Diversion, Emergency Feed, Rice Marketing, 90 Day Rule, Payment Limitation Refund, Additional Interest, Arkansas Beaver Lake, and Wetlands Reserve.

Source: Economic Research Service, U.S. Department of Agriculture.

centage of our population should be on farms, (2) farming is not only a business but also a complete way of life, (3) farming should be a family enterprise, (4) land should be owned by those who cultivate it, (5) it is good to "make two blades of grass grow where only one grew before," (6) anyone who wants to be engaged in agriculture should be free to do so, and (7) farmers should be their own bosses.

Rural America comprises more than the production of agricultural products. These areas face many, if not most, of the same problems that confront the nation as a whole, except that the problems of rural areas seldom reach the intensity or visibility of the urban sector of the nation. Compared to urbanites, rural residents have larger average household size, slightly higher birth and death rates, greater proportions of elderly, a higher ratio of males to females, lower educational attainment, lower income, more families in poverty, and lower levels of services. Prospects for the twenty-first century indicate that rural life will continue to be affected by global, national, and regional trends, face growth and encroachment of suburbs and shopping malls, confront the migratory patterns of newcomers, witness decreasing rural/urban gaps in jobs and income, garner more nonfarm family income, encounter persistent income differentials between whites and minorities, see further concentration of agricultural production, and behold a continued impact of public regulations.

Former Secretary of Agriculture Robert Bergland contended that at the end of the twentieth century the nation had reached "a monumental watershed," which may determine the survival of rural America, as well as the rest of the country. He and others contend that rurality is more than a place and people, but rather a state of mind that was on the verge of vanishing. There was a sense that a death spiral had gripped many rural areas, first through experiencing a loss of population, then through the closing of public schools and community hospitals, and eventually through the pressure to cut local taxes that only made matters worse by reducing the rural resource base even further. To preserve what remains of the depressed and shrinking rural sector of the economy will take more than private investment and/or federal government price supports for agriculture. It will involve instead a rural development program that mobilizes a wide range of relevant participants.

The dominant paradigm for rural communities held that the fundamental structure of family farming was contrary to the massive size and economies that characterized agribusiness. By implication, the social class structure of rural America was the primary, if not the main, factor in determining the life of small towns and their inhabitants.[44] The small-farm communities supported local businesses, newspapers, public facilities, and community organizations. In contrast, massive farms would not support these organizations and structures since fewer people would be required for production. More recent studies suggest that the viability and character of the nonfarm economy had the greatest influence on community well-being. Luloff and Swanson claimed that at the end of the twentieth century, "a rural person is more likely to be employed as a wage laborer in a factory or the service sector than on the farm."[45]

Contemporary Controversy

How to Prepare Rural America for Globalization

IN THE past, American agriculture was very competitive in world markets. Recent trade agreements (NAFTA and GATT), however, have exposed the agricultural sector as never before to the full impact of international competition. Agriculture has become detached significantly from the industrial economy; the rate of improvement in productivity has shrunk; and rural areas have become less competitive because of the declining availability of investment capital. These trends in the past have threatened, and will continue to threaten, small family farms, already challenged by large-scale agribusiness. Small rural communities will face stagnation, if not elimination, and rural poverty may persist and even worsen. The implications are clear as rural workers are likely to be hired in factories and service jobs.[46] However, agricultural policy has not lost its relevance.[47]

Technology, markets, and the political economy have changed the entire rural economic structure of the United States, as farmers have felt that they are under attack by subsidized foreign competition as well as by unsympathetic domestic consumers. The trend in United States agricultural exports and imports from 1974 to 1994 is summarized in Table 5.4, and a breakdown of agricultural commodity exports and imports is provided in Table 5.5.

The USDA has addressed a comprehensive array of programs involving agricultural research, international trade, resource management and conservation, nutrition and food assistance, food safety, rural development, farm credit, and commodity programs. Table 5.6 provides comparative data on the growth of federal food assistance programs from 1985 to 1994. The Clinton administration vowed that the principal goal of any new farm bill should be to "do no harm." Clinton would have changed the name of the USDA to the Department of Food and Agriculture, to reflect its mission to both producers and consumers. He proposed (1) investing in rural economies, (2) targeting areas of greatest need, (3) improving the information infrastructure, (4) improving housing, (5) improving water quality, and (6) developing business activity.

Budget constraints driving the 1995 omnibus farm bill, however, began to force national policymakers to move toward a reduced role for government over commodity supports. Senator Richard Lugar (R-Indiana) proposed to save $15 billion by eliminating export subsidies and to reduce target prices for crops by 3 percent a year for the next five years.

The inability of policymakers (presidents, legislators, and various interest groups) to reform American agricultural policy has persisted for some four decades. Despite the strenuous unsuccessful efforts of the conservative Reagan administration, starting in 1981, to cancel nearly every farm subsidy, eight years later the administration had spent as much or more than all spending in agriculture for the previous forty-eight years. David Stockman explained this "failure" as being the result of disagreements within the agricultural coalition: "One faction wanted to subsidize less and regulate domestic production even more, the other faction wanted to regulate less and subsidize

TABLE 5.4 Value of United States Agricultural Exports and Imports, 1974–1994
(in billions of dollars, except for percentages)

Year	Trade Balance	Exports	Percent of All Exports	Imports	Percent of All Imports
1974	$11.8	$22.0	23%	$10.2	10%
1975	12.6	21.9	21	9.3	10
1976	12.0	23.0	20	11.0	9
1977	10.2	23.6	20	13.4	9
1978	14.6	29.4	21	14.8	9
1979	18.0	34.7	19	16.7	8
1980	23.9	41.2	19	17.4	7
1981	26.6	43.3	18	16.8	6
1982	21.2	36.6	17	15.4	6
1983	19.5	36.1	18	16.6	6
1984	18.5	37.8	17	19.3	6
1985	9.1	29.0	13	20.0	6
1986	4.8	26.2	13	21.5	6
1987	8.3	28.7	12	20.4	5
1988	16.1	37.1	12	21.0	5
1989	18.2	39.9	11	21.7	5
1990	16.6	39.4	10	22.8	5
1991	16.5	39.2	10	22.7	5
1992	18.3	42.9	10	24.6	5
1993	17.6	42.6	10	25.0	4
1994	18.9	45.7	10	25.8	4

Source: Economic Research Service, U.S. Department of Agriculture.

foreign markets. Neither approach would work, and a hybrid of the two would be a fiscal nightmare."[48] The result was a five-year farm bill that provided everything— production controls, price supports, subsidy payments, and export financing.

Advocates of market-oriented public policies proclaimed that the past six decades of commodity price supports have produced a "fiasco"[49] and a farm "welfare" program for agribusiness.[50] They proposed that American farmers should be prepared to compete in GATT and that most governmental intervention should be withdrawn from agricultural markets. The mood was "for farmers to produce whatever commodities they feel will profit them best and sell them freely at home and abroad; for traders to move goods in expectation of profits, without fear of repression; for consumers to buy foods at the lowest prices, from foreign or domestic sources; and for taxpayers to keep their hard-earned income safe from plunder from farm welfare programs."[51] It was maintained that these policies would "redefine" government's role in agriculture, increase efficiency nationally, and create a smoothly functioning world trade system.

(continued)

TABLE 5.5 United States Exports and Imports of Agricultural Commodities, by Principal Commodity Groupings, 1994 (in millions of dollars, not seasonally adjusted, current dollar basis)

Agricultural Commodity	Exports	Imports	Agricultural Commodity	Exports	Imports
Total	44,957	25,935	Meat and		
Animal feeds	3,353	433	preparations	5,195	2,627
Bulbs	112	238	Oils/fats, animal	586	21
Cereal flour	1,159	970	Oils/fats, vegetable	963	1,051
Cocoa	34	696	Plants	117	106
Coffee	53	2,270	Rice	1,009	130
Corn	4,197	65	Seeds	315	152
Cotton, raw and			Soybeans	4,355	46
linters	2,641	21	Sugar	5	552
Dairy products,			Tobacco,		
eggs	717	583	unmanufactured	1,304	697
Fur skins, raw	131	78	Vegetables and		
Grains, unmilled	696	181	fruit	6,757	6,075
Hides and skins	1,391	126	Wheat	4,055	291
Live animals	587	1,392	Other agricultural	5,225	7,134

Source: Office of Trade and Economic Analysis, U.S. Department of Commerce.

Advocates for continued governmental intervention have sharpened their focus upon what they perceive as a fundamental conflict between agribusiness and family farming. Agribusinesses may be defined as firms operating in the rural economy that are (1) industrially organized and management centered, (2) financed for growth and capital intensive, (3) large-scale, concentrated, and standardized in their production processes, (4) specialized to take advantage of controlled markets, and (5) resource consumptive. In contrast, family farming may be defined as being (1) owner-operated, (2) entrepreneurial, (3) dispersed, (4) diversified, (5) at equal advantage in open markets, (6) family-centered, (7) technologically progressive, (8) striving for production processes in harmony with nature, (9) resource conserving, and (10) a way of life.[52] The precepts of corporate agribusiness have begun to displace the nostalgic notions of the family farmer.

Most policy analysts agree that America has not developed a "coherent" rural policy.[53] For example, Willard Cochrane and C. Ford Runge, who believe that current farm policy is dysfunctional, have offered four rational criteria to assess rural policy. The first is fairness, which involves correcting the present situation in which the lion's share of the benefits go to the relatively few large commercial farmers, which in turn skews the distribution of farm income, encourages the enlargement of farms through the cannibalization of smaller farmers, and provides almost no help to part-time operators and nonfarm rural people. The second is efficiency, to correct the manifest distortions and

TABLE 5.6 Federal Food Assistance Programs, 1985–1994[1] (in millions of dollars)

Program	1985	1994
Food stamps[2]	11,703	24,492
Puerto Rico nutrition assistance[3]	825	1,079
National school lunch[4]	3,380	4,964
School breakfast[5]	379	959
Women, Infants, and Children (WIC) program[6]	1,489	3,169
Summer food service[4]	112	231
Child/adult care[4]	452	1,358
Special milk	16	18
Nutrition for the elderly[4]	134	153
Food distribution to Indian reservations	60	65
Commodity supplementary food program[4,7]	48	107
Food distribution-charitable institutions[8]	170	101
Emergency food assistance	1,026	201
Soup kitchens/food banks	0	40
Other costs[9]	56	116
Total[10]	19,850	37,053

Source: Food and Nutrition Service, U.S. Department of Agriculture.

[1]Data are for fiscal (not calendar) years.
[2]Includes the federal share of state administrative expenses and other federal costs.
[3]Puerto Rico participated in the Food Stamp Program from fiscal year 1975 until July 1982, when it initiated a separate grant program.
[4]Includes the value of commodities (entitlement, bonus, and cash in lieu).
[5]Excludes startup costs.
[6]Includes program studies and WIC Farmers' Market Nutrition Program.
[7]Includes elderly feeding projects.
[8]Includes summer camps.
[9]Includes child nutrition state administration expenses, nutrition studies, nutrition education and training, Northern Marianas nutrition assistance grant, and commodity disaster relief.
[10]Excludes food program administration costs.

contradictions that prevent the achievement of policy goals. Agriculture has become a leading candidate to be considered the most serious "government failure," as farmers are accused of "farming the government" because farm policy encourages farmers to plant crops whether or not they are in demand. The third addresses the serious negative environmental impacts of agriculture, which require policymakers and administrators aggressively to improve water quality, reduce soil erosion, expand greenbelts and wilderness areas, protect wildlife, and enhance the quality of food. The final criterion is continued competitiveness, not to turn commercial producers loose to fend for themselves in an open market but instead to utilize governmental intervention as: an income stabilization program; a commodity stabilization program that purchases, stores, sells, and donates surplus production; an expanded crop insurance plan; and a government purchasing program for perishable commodities when market gluts occur.

Case Study

The Freedom to Farm Act

THE REPUBLICAN-CONTROLLED 104th Congress was determined to move agriculture away from commodity subsidies programs run by the federal government and toward reliance on the dictates of the marketplace. Ideological lines were drawn, as the Republicans' appetite, especially in the House of Representatives, for a conservative "radicalism" (by reducing the government), as distinct from conservative "fiscalism" (by reducing the budget), was tested in the 1995 farm bill. That legislation represented an ideal opportunity to implement long-term changes in the direction of national farm and rural policy because, like all farm bills, it would be in effect for five years and its consequences were expected to set the tone for policy far into the future.

There was far from unanimous agreement among interest groups as to how best to implement the new realities. For example, there was conflict within the sugar segment of the farm commodity policy arena. The Sweetener Users Association, representing soft drink producers, chocolatiers, bakers, and ice cream companies, favored the radical approach to revising farm legislation because the existing sugar program restricted imports and regulated domestic supplies and thereby raised the price of sugar. On the other hand, the American Sugar Alliance, representing sugar growers and other beneficiaries of higher sugar price levels, supported the fiscal approach because this method would reduce the federal deficit across the board, save their subsidies, and impede free-market competition.

As the congressional session began, the smart money was placed on the fiscalism option that would cut costs by downsizing the federal government's agriculture bureaucracy through closing about 1,000 underutilized offices and by reducing the U.S. Department of Agriculture (USDA) staff by some 75,000. This option, however, would not fundamentally alter the role of government in supporting commodity prices. The seventy-three Republican freshmen members newly elected to the House, half of whom represented rural areas, however, were considered generally to favor radical change as they asked why it was necessary to take five years to reform agriculture when they intended to reform welfare in only two years. The power of the Republican Congress and the Gingrich "revolutionaries" within the House threatened the government's traditional role in agriculture of providing support for farm commodity price levels. The power shift created an atmosphere of "unpredictability" regarding the outcome of farm bills that customarily had been changed rather little in successive rounds of legislation.[54]

Efforts to eliminate or substantially reduce federal programs for peanuts, milk, sugar, tobacco, and other special agricultural projects placed some freshmen from agricultural districts under severe cross-pressure to protect the agricultural interests of their districts. For example, Congressman George Nethercutt (R-Washington), who had defeated Speaker of the House Tom Foley (D-Washington) in 1994, fiercely defended wheat subsidies and research conducted at Washington State University, which is located in his district. He believed that it was more important to maintain farm programs rather than public supports for welfare recipients: "The difference between the safety net for farmers and the safety net for other entitlements is that agricultural products benefit our economy."[55]

In the Senate, in an attempt to conduct a rational "bottom-up review," much like that conducted by the Department of Defense, the Chair of the Agriculture Committee, Richard Lugar (R-Indiana) posed fifty-three questions related to the 1995 comprehensive farm bill. These questions related to commodity programs, conservation, exports, nutrition, and rural development programs. For example, regarding commodity programs, Lugar asked for (1) methods to enhance American competitiveness in world markets, (2) an evaluation of which agricultural agencies should be streamlined and/or privatized, (3) fiscal justification supporting acreage reduction plans, (4) failure and exit rates of family farmers, (5) the level of gross income needed to constitute full-time employment, (6) evaluation of who really benefits from price supports, (7) analysis of risks to the abundant food supply, (8) evaluation of what impact there might be on land values if commodity support programs were abolished, (9) rationale for subsidizing some crops and not others, (10) explanation of why crop insurance and disaster relief programs were appropriate for agriculture and not for other sectors of the economy, (11) study of the impact there might be on smoking if tobacco programs were ended, and (12) analysis of whether consumer prices have risen on cotton, rice, peanuts, milk, and sugar as a result of public policies and whether one commodity benefited indirectly from subsidies conferred on another community.

Senator Lugar then proposed to reduce target prices for crops by 3 percent per year for five years, which he believed would put prices just above likely future market prices. This not only would terminate the New Deal farm support system, but it also would eliminate the Export Enhancement Program that essentially had been used to benefit the nation's largest grain merchants. The new House majority leader, Richard Armey (R-Texas) and conservative "think tanks" such as the Heritage Foundation believed that the time was right to end the sixty-year-old program of commodity subsidies. Opponents of this radical approach, however, pleaded for moderation, arguing that Congress had cut farm subsidies from $26 billion a year to $10 billion during the past decade while leaving many other programs untouched. Some broad-based agricultural organizations, such as the Farm Bureau, contended that such deep cuts would depress land values and create chaos in rural America.

The Clinton administration proposed reducing USDA spending by $2.5 billion, compared to a much larger reduction of nearly $6.5 billion proposed by the House of Representatives and more than $5 billion proposed by the Senate for fiscal year 1995–1996. The administration was prepared to reduce crop supports to large growers, but still to provide a "safety net" for small farmers, proclaiming to "do no harm" to rural America. Pat Roberts (R-Kansas), Chair of the House Agriculture Committee, proposed what came to be known as the "Freedom to Farm Act," which would turn subsidies into capped entitlements; guarantee fixed but declining payments for seven years; continue the lucrative marketing loan programs, capped at 1995 levels; give all

(continued)

participating farmers broad planting flexibility on 85 percent of their acreage; and cut price supports.

This effort to revamp substantially the six-decade-old farm programs was rejected stunningly on September 20 in the House Agriculture Committee when four Republicans joined all the Democratic members in opposing the plan. Speaker Gingrich considered punishing the disloyal members of his party by either moving them from the Agriculture Committee or stripping them of their existing or prospective chairmanships of other committees. Furthermore, Speaker Gingrich, majority leader Armey, and House whip Tom DeLay (R-Texas) warned that if the bill was defeated, they would bring the bill to the floor under an open rule that would protect it from hostile floor amendments. They also threatened to replace the committee's legislation with "true reforms" and even voiced doubts about whether the Agriculture Committee itself would be permitted to continue as a standing committee of the House.

Roberts, a potential candidate for the U.S. Senate to fill the vacancy caused by the impending retirement of Nancy Landon Kassebaum (R-Kansas), argued that his bill still provided $43.2 billion in agriculture expenditures over seven years, and that this was the best outcome that farmers could hope to attain. He then proceeded to negotiate compromises between regional interests. Midwest wheat and soybean farmers favored the proposed planting flexibility, while southern rice and cotton growers wanted to maintain marketing loans in the event that prices fell. The supporters of environmental conservation disapproved of the proposal's provision that would direct subsidies to farmers who had received subsidies in the past rather than to new planters. Strenuous efforts were made to save existing subsidies for dairy products, peanuts, and sugar, and a commission was proposed to examine future directions for farm policy.

In December 1995, the USDA estimated that the nation's grain reserves, some 31.2 million metric tons, were at their lowest level in a quarter of a century. Nearing an uncomfortably low level might inflate food prices and depress livestock producers, and possibly could reduce U.S. farm commodity exports. The "freedom to farm" bill also proposed to put more land into production. Eventually a bill was passed in Congress. Fifteen prominent agricultural economists who had served presidents since John Kennedy urged President Clinton to accept the essential elements of the Republican proposal.

President Clinton's veto of the bill (HR 2491) on December 6 raised serious questions about whether any farm proposal would become law, thereby possibly forcing Congress to move quickly to reauthorize existing farm programs for one additional year. Pressure grew on policymakers to resolve their differences in time for the spring planting season. Senate Democrats were split and unable to respond fast enough to the compromise proposed by Republican Senate leader Bob Dole (R-Kansas) on February 1, after the Democrats had blocked consideration of an earlier version of the bill. Both Senators Dole and Lugar, who were also presidential candidates, were anxious to have an agreement, even if it meant retreating from the original goal of phasing out subsidies in seven years. They both wanted something before the spring recess and the intense politicking associated with the Iowa presidential caucuses. Fourteen Republican senators denounced Dole's compromise, which was then withdrawn. On February 6, eleven Democrats joined Senator Leahy's (D-Vermont) alternative, which retained fixed, declining payments, but added funding for nutrition, conservation, and dairy programs in the Northeast.

By March, the House and Senate had moved closer as their separate and distinct bills headed for conference committee where attempts would be made to resolve differences between the two chambers' perspectives on the future of agricultural policy.[56] The dairy program, which in fact was a bundle of thirty-three regional programs, had pitted agricultural interests in California against those in Florida, processors versus consumers, and even one dairy cooperative against another. It had now been pulled from the House version while the Senate had no dairy provision at all. The strategy pursued by the House conferees was to wait until the last minute before trying to put together a dairy agreement.

Republicans, facing a threatened presidential veto, mollified Democrats by providing new farm conservation programs and by blocking attempts to scale back wetlands regulations. About 480 of the 500 differences between the Senate and House versions were disposed of in a single package. Knotty disagreements still surrounded the food stamp program (which was reauthorized for two years) and the dairy programs. The fundamental farm law that was established in 1938 and 1949 was retained, but a Commission on Twenty-first Century Agriculture Production was created.

On March 28, the Senate passed the agriculture bill by the margin of 74 to 26, despite fierce opposition by those who feared that it would cause the government's safety net to unravel. Only a few hours later, the House passed the measure, by a vote of 318 to 89. President Clinton signed the Freedom to Farm bill into law on April 4. If the balance of political power shifts again in the nation's capital, it is likely that there will be numerous and strenuous efforts to revisit and revise this historic change.

Case Study Questions

1. Why does the United States lack a rational comprehensive rural policy?
2. What has impeded the movement toward the market-oriented policies that have been advocated since the 1960s, and why did Congress take a major step toward doing so in the 104th Congress?
3. What set of political ideologies in the United States have prevailed over the past six decades to enable the federal government to intervene in favor of rural America, which constitutes only a very small proportion of the nation's population and whose representation in Congress has declined over time?
4. What interests have prevailed in setting agricultural policy, and how were they able to succeed?
5. What changes, if any, do you believe will be made to the Freedom to Farm Act? Do you think that these are changes that should be made?
6. Should farmers be required to compete in the marketplace without any government involvement? In what ways is the business of farming different from other business operations? Do these differences justify public support for farming?
7. Should family farms receive government support to continue a traditional way of life? How does this type of support differ from government payments to entitlement programs like Social Security or unemployment compensation?

Suggested Readings

Bonanno, Alessandro, et al., eds. *From Columbus to ConAgra: The Globalization of Agriculture and Food.* Lawrence: University Press of Kansas, 1994.

Browne, William P., Jerry R. Skees, Louis E. Swanson, Paul B. Thompson, and Laurian J. Unnevehr. *Sacred Cows and Hot Potatoes: Agrarian Myths in Agricultural Policy.* Boulder: Westview Press, 1992.

Browne, William P. *Cultivating Congress: Constituents, Issues, and Interests in Agricultural Policymaking.* Lawrence: University Press of Kansas, 1995.

Luloff, A. E., and Louis E. Swanson, eds. *American Rural Communities.* Boulder: Westview Press, 1990.

Strange, Marty. *Family Farming: A New Economic Vision.* Lincoln: University of Nebraska Press, 1988.

Notes

1. CNN Live Report, transcript #91-15, December 14, 1992.

2. Willard W. Cochrane and C. Ford Runge, *Reforming Farm Policy: Toward a National Agenda* (Ames: Iowa State University Press, 1992), p. 260.

3. Congressional Quarterly, *Farm Policy: The Politics of Soil, Surpluses, and Subsidies* (Washington, DC: Congressional Quarterly Press, 1984).

4. Joint Economic Committee, Congress of the United States. *Toward the Next Generation of Farm Policy* (Washington, DC: U.S. Government Printing Office, 1984); Joint Economic Committee, U.S. Congress, *New Dimensions in Rural Policy* (Washington, DC: U.S. Government Printing Office, 1986); Joint Economic Committee, U.S. Congress, *Towards Rural Development Policy for the 1990s: Enhancing Income and Employment Opportunities: A Symposium* (Washington, DC: U.S. Government Printing Office, 1989).

5. H. Wayne Moyer and Timothy E. Josling, *Agricultural Policy Reform Politics and Process in the EC and the USA* (Ames: Iowa State University Press, 1990), p. 4.

6. Moyer and Josling, op. cit., p. 204.

7. Robert Alan Dahl, *Pluralist Democracy in the United States: Conflict and Consent* (Chicago: Rand McNally, 1967).

8. Congressional Quarterly, "Suburbs: Potential but Unrealized House Influence," *Congressional Quarterly Weekly Report* (April 6, 1974), p. 78.

9. Theodore J. Lowi, *The End of Liberalism: The Second Republic of the United States,* 2nd ed. (New York: Norton, 1969), p. 67.

10. William P. Browne, *Private Interests, Public Policy, and American Agriculture* (Lawrence: University Press of Kansas, 1988), p. 24.

11. John Heinz, Edward O. Laumann, Robert L. Nelson, and Robert H. Salisbury, *The Hollow Core: Private Interests in National Policy Making* (Cambridge, MA: Harvard University Press, 1993).

12. Hugh Heclo, "Issue Networks and the Executive Establishment," in *The New American Political System,* ed. Anthony King (Washington, DC: American Enterprise Institute for Public Policy Research, 1990) pp. 87–124.

13. C. Wright Mills, *The Power Elite* (New York: Oxford University Press, 1956), p. 261.

14. Frank Greve, "He Gives, He Gets—You Pay," *Charlotte Observer,* 23 January 1995, p. 9.

15. Ronald Henkoff, "Oh, How the Money Grows at ADM," *Fortune* (Oct. 8, 1990), p. 105.

16. Ibid.

17. Raymond A. Bauer, Ithiel de Sola Pool, and Lewis Anthony Dexter, *American Business and Public Policy: The Politics of Foreign Trade* (New York: Atherton Press, 1963).

18. Browne, op. cit.

19. Ibid.

20. Stephen Skowronek, *Building a New American State: The Expansion of National Administrative Capacities, 1877–1920* (New York: Cambridge University Press, 1992).

21. James T. Bonnen, "Why Is There No Coherent U.S. Rural Policy?" *Policy Studies Journal* 20 (2) (1992), pp. 190–201.

22. J. William Nagel, "Federal Organization for Rural Policy," in Joint Economic Committee, U.S. Congress, *Towards Rural Development Policy for the 1990s: Enhancing Income and Employment Opportunities: A Symposium* (Washington, DC: U.S. Government Printing Office, 1989).

23. Bert E. Swanson, Richard A. Cohen, and Edith P. Swanson, *Small Towns and Small Towners: A Framework for Survival and Growth* (Beverly Hills, CA: Sage, 1979).

24. G. William Domhoff, *Who Rules America Now?* (Prospect Heights, IL: Waveland Press, Inc., 1997), p. 209.

25. Daniel Judah Elazar, *Cities of the Prairie: The Metropolitan Frontier and American Politics* (New York: Basic Books, 1970); Daniel Judah Elazar, *American Federalism: A View from the States,* 2nd ed. (New York: Crowell, 1972).

26. Robert E. Agger, Daniel Goldrich, and Bert E. Swanson, *The Rulers and the Ruled* (New York: Wiley, 1964).

27. George C. Lodge, *The New American Ideology: How the Ideological Basis of Legitimate Authority in America Is Being Radically Transformed: The Profound Implications for Our Society in General and the Great Corporations in Particular* (New York: Knopf, 1975), pp. 14–32.

28. Marty Strange, *Family Farming* (Lincoln: University of Nebraska Press, 1988).

29. Bovard, op. cit.

30. Swanson, Cohen, and Swanson, op. cit., p. 88.

31. David A. Stockman, *The Triumph of Politics: Why the Reagan Revolution Failed* (New York: Harper & Row, 1986). p. 11.

32. Ibid., p. 53.

33. John L. Palmer and Isabel V. Sawhill, eds., *The Reagan Record: An Assessment of America's Changing Domestic Priorities* (Cambridge, MA: Ballinger, 1984), p. 174.

34. Stanley A. Renson, "A Preliminary Assessment of the Clinton Presidency," *Political Psychology* 15 (2) (1994), p. 386.

35. Theodore J. Davis, Jr., "Income Inequities Between Black and White Populations in Southern Nonmetropolitan Counties," *Review of Black Political Economy* 22 (1994), pp. 145–158.

36. Lionel J. Beaulieu and Vernon D. Ryan, "Hierarchical Influence Structures in Rural Communities: A Case Study," *Rural Sociology* 49 (1984), pp. 106–116.

37. William P. Browne, *Cultivating Congress: Constituents, Issues, and Interests in Agricultural Policymaking* (Lawrence: University Press of Kansas, 1995).

38. Bonnen, op. cit., pp. 190–201.

39. Odin Knudsen and John Nash, *Redefining the Role of Government in Agriculture for the 1990s* (Washington, DC: World Bank, 1990), p. 1.

40. William Heffernan, *Houston Post,* 12 December 1994, p. 6

41. Alessandro Bonanno et al., eds., *From Columbus to ConAgra: The Globalization of Agriculture and Food* (Lawrence: University Press of Kansas, 1994), p. 6.

42. Jonathan Rauch, "Plowing a New Field," *National Journal* 27(4) (1995), p. 212.

43. Don Paarlberg, *American Farm Policy: A Case Study of Centralized Decision-making* (New York: Wiley, 1964), p. 3.

44. Walter Rochs Goldschmidt, *As You Sow: Three Studies in the Social Consequences of Agribusiness* (Montclair, NJ: Allanheld, Osmun, 1978).

45. A. E. Luloff and Louis E. Swanson (eds.), *American Rural Communities* (Boulder, CO: Westview Press, 1990).

46. William A. Galston, *A Tough Row to Hoe: The 1985 Farm Bill and Beyond* (Lanham, MD: Hamilton Press, 1992), p. 306.

47. William P. Browne, Jerry R. Skees, Louis E. Swanson, Paul B. Thompson, and Laurian J. Unnevehr, *Sacred Cows and Hot Potatoes: Agrarian Myths in Agricultural Policy* (Boulder, CO: Westview Press, 1992).

48. Stockman, op. cit., p. 153.

49. James Bovard, *The Farm Fiasco* (San Francisco: ICS Press, 1989).

50. Clifton B. Luttrell, *The High Cost of Farm Welfare* (Washington, DC: Cato Institute, 1989).

51. Knudsen & Nash, op. cit., p. iii.

52. Strange, op. cit., pp. 32–39.

53. Bonnen, op. cit.

54. Jonathan Rauch, op. cit., p. 212.

55. David Hosansky, "Freshman Republicans Attempt to Fence Off Farm Subsidies," *Congressional Quarterly Weekly Report,* 17 June 1995, pp. 1732–1734.

56. For detailed highlights of the two versions, see David Hosansky, "Senate Passes Agriculture Bill at Odds with House," *Congressional Quarterly Weekly Report,* 9 March 1996, pp. 653–660.

6

Urban Policy

CHICAGO SCHOOLS: A CRUMBLING FOUNDATION?

As global society enters the information era, with its requisite demand for higher education, sophisticated knowledge, advanced job skills, and mental competence, there is evidence that large urban school systems are falling short of the mark in their responsibility to train citizens for the economy of the future. It also appears that they are not just missing the mark, but that they are not even coming close to providing the educational foundation that is increasingly essential as the United States moves into the postindustrial, "knowledge"-based era. An investigation of the situation in the Chicago public school system is instructive in conceptualizing the extent of the challenge facing urban schools.

Chicago's Mayor Richard Daley has been at the forefront in restructuring a public school system that has been characterized as a total failure. In June of 1996, the release of Iowa Tests of Basic Skills scores, since a 1995 restructuring of the public schools, revealed some improvement in elementary school performance, but the already low levels of performance at the high school level declined even further. These mixed test results provided an indication of both the distance that Chicago schools needed to go as well as the daunting nature of their task.

It is interesting to note that in grades three through eleven the vast majority of Chicago public school students scored below national average scores on reading and math. In reading, roughly one-third (33.5 percent) of Chicago's eighth-graders read at the eighth-grade level or higher; two-thirds of these students did not read at their level. Scores for other grades reflected poorer performances. In math scores, third-graders recorded the best performance in the city, but even so only 36.7 percent performed at their grade level. The following table (Table 6.1) describes the percentage of third- to eleventh-graders in the Chicago public school system that performed at their grade level in reading and math.

While performance at grade level for only about one-fifth to one-third of public school students could be viewed with great dismay, Chicago public school officials found some silver linings in the 1996 data. Paul Vallas, the Chicago public school system's chief executive officer, declared that toughening standards in the elementary schools, changes in personnel, the threat of mandatory summer schools for eighth-graders, and local reform efforts were responsible for the improvements at the elementary school level. Education officials, however, admitted that things did not seem to be working out well for the city's seventy-five

TABLE 6.1 Iowa Test Score Results, June 1996

	Percent at level 1995	Percent at level 1996	Percent change
Reading			
Elementary			
Grade 3	21.6%	22.6%	+1.0%
Grade 4	25.1	26.9	+1.8
Grade 5	25.6	31.1	+5.5
Grade 6	25.5	32.0	+6.5
Grade 7	31.6	29.0	−2.6
Grade 8	29.7	33.5	+3.8
High School			
Grade 9	21.2	18.2	−3.0
Grade 11	28.1	24.6	−3.5
Mathematics			
Elementary			
Grade 3	34.9	36.7	+1.8
Grade 4	30.2	30.7	+.5
Grade 5	28.6	30.8	+2.2
Grade 6	34.4	34.4	0
Grade 7	26.9	26.2	−.7
Grade 8	24.6	27.4	+2.8
High School			
Grade 9	22.8	19.7	−3.1
Grade 11	30.0	25.4	−4.6

Source: *Chicago Tribune* (North Edition), June 4, 1996, p. 10, Sec. 1.

public high schools. One education officer qualified the declining performance with the view that "throughout urban America, high schools are having the same problem."[1] A multitude of reasons were cited for the failure of Chicago's high schools: large size, social promotion, an exodus of better students to private or suburban schools after the eighth grade, watered-down classes, absenteeism, and a lack of parental involvement. The loss of slightly better students to other schools (following the eighth grade) was documented. Eighth-graders leaving the public school system in 1994 possessed an eighth-grade reading level while remaining eighth-graders had an average reading score of 7.4.

Some officials discussed the "improvements" that had been achieved since Mayor Daley's reorganization in 1995, but problems remained and were concentrated in certain schools. In October 1996, Chicago's school board placed 109 of the city's 557 public schools on academic probation. A school was placed on probation if fewer than 15 percent of its students performed at grade level on national standardized reading tests.

The action to place the schools on probation was announced by the president of the Chicago School Board of Trustees. This official stated, "[W]e have no choice but to act and to act now, so more young lives aren't wasted."[2] It was reported that at eight of the thirty-eight high schools on probation fewer than 4 percent of the students were reading at grade level. At one school, 2.5 percent were at grade level. At Martin Luther King High School, a state basketball power, only 3.5 percent of the students were reading at their grade level.

No time limits were mandated for improvement, but the new board of trustees for the Chicago public schools system noted that principals could be removed from a school and sent to a desk job at the central office if they did not show results. After a four-year contract, principals then could be fired following a disciplinary hearing. As a last resort, a school on probation that did not improve could be closed.

The impact of Chicago's schools can also be viewed in human terms. Such an impact, no doubt one case among thousands, appears in the experience of Karen and Sharon Franklin, twins who graduated with honors from Chicago's Orr High School. The twins recounted in 1995 how they had earned As and Bs in their high school and faithfully did whatever homework (not much was required) that was assigned to them. They responded with "shock" and "horror" two years after they graduated from Orr High School when they learned that they had failed the entrance exam for Malcolm X College, one of the seven City Colleges of Chicago known for lenient admissions requirements.The Franklin sisters were told that they could not read beyond a sixth-grade level.

This situation of low reading scores was by no means unique in the city of Chicago. William Rice, director of research and student assessment for Chicago schools, reported in 1995 that a disturbing number of graduates from the city's schools did not master basic skills. The twins were referred to Malcolm X's remedial reading and math programs, which have been recognized for success in boosting the skills of public school graduates, some of whom could not read at all.[3]

This vignette is useful in assessing some of the problems that cities face. Declining institutions such as schools, however, do not represent the full range of problems confronting urban areas: drugs, crime, unemployment, lack of opportunity, declining tax bases, welfare dependency, single-female-headed households, and a sense of hopelessness.

The three underlying factors of rationality, power, and ideology should assist in understanding federal urban policy. The few attempts to formulate a rational-comprehensive approach to urban affairs have been thwarted. While power analysts differ as to who governs or who rules America (pluralist analysts versus power elitists), the interests and resources of political elites (public and private) are believed to be critical in determining who gets what, when, and how in the nation's urban areas. In addition, it is important to discern prevailing beliefs of the leaders at the national, state, and local levels.

THE RPI INPUTS TO URBAN POLICY

The Rationality Input

Over the years, national leaders usually have responded only incrementally to pleas for assistance from cities to cope with economic recessions, develop thresholds of support for households, and generate neighborhood revitalization efforts. One exception to this rule of incremental behavior occurred in the administration of President Jimmy Carter.

President Carter made a couple of attempts to formulate a coherent federal urban policy involving targeting, leveraging, and reorganizing. His Urban and Regional Policy Group (URPG) instructed federal departments to review policies and programs including expenditures for training, employment, transfer payments, taxes, regulations, safety, and affirmative action.[4] Carter's *Commission for a National Agenda for the Eighties* (1980) concluded that both people and places suffered with a changing economy. The Commission suggested that past policy successes were too few, given dwindling public resources, and that the primary responsibility of the federal government should be assisting communities to adjust to trends, in the recognition that many trends could not be reversed.

Much earlier in an effort to foster a comprehensive urban policy, New York City undertook the Mobilization for Youth (MFY) project, a multidisciplinary social agency demonstration, research, and social action project. A forerunner of the federal Economic Opportunity Act of 1965 and its War on Poverty, this project utilized a sociological approach (poverty is due to a lack of opportunity in society) rather than a psychological approach (poverty is due to individualistic deficiencies). In dealing with the causes of impoverishment, the MFY focused upon the need to reform societal institutions rather than the need to change people to make them fit with institutions. The project involved street-level bureaucrats and academics who attacked juvenile delinquency through casework, community organization, legal aid, and other techniques. The Mobilization for Youth program further established the principle that public institutions should be held accountable to their clients.

Over the years, academics as well as government agencies have employed various "objective" methods for studying cities. The United States Census Bureau, for instance, compiles extensive data on urban areas. Researchers use these data to uncover underlying trends, find out more about existing characteristics of cities, and propose remedial initiatives to address concerns. Prior to data collection, however, it is necessary to agree upon fixed labels for given geographical locations. A review of the designations of the Bureau of the Census suggests that some confusion exists in the terminology used in urban research.

The Bureau of the Census defines urban populations as all persons in places of 2,500 inhabitants or more that are incorporated as cities, villages, boroughs, or towns. The term urbanized area refers to a city of 50,000 or more inhabitants plus the surrounding suburbs. A metropolitan statistical area (MSA) refers to areas that have a large urban nucleus (a city of 250,000) and surrounding communities that are closely linked to it through economic and social activities. A consolidated metropolitan statistical area (CMSA) refers to large metropolitan areas that have more than one large core area, such as Dallas–Fort Worth.[5] While definitions can be confusing, they at least serve as a starting point for data collection, empirical analysis, and comparisons.

Urban places also have been identified on the basis of such characteristics as a densely settled area where manufacturing, commerce, administration, and a variety of specialized services are available. These characteristics contrast with features of rural locales—low density and economies focused upon agriculture, forestry, or exploitation of resources.[6] Historical changes such as the change from a mercantile (trading) to an industrial economic system, as well as technological transformations are also linked to urbanism. Urban areas also display social stratification, segregation, and high rates of mobility.[7]

Urban data are often collected on indicators of a city's health or infirmity. Some of the most famous urban studies did not rely upon large amounts of data but on personal interviews. Such methodologies, however, can still be considered rational attempts to study cities. Two differing methods of assessing the influence of leaders on policymaking are identified in the reputational approach and the decisional approach.

In the 1950s, sociologist Floyd Hunter set out to discover the "real" leaders and policymakers of Atlanta. He began his "reputational" approach with a list of people who held positions of power in Atlanta. The list was submitted to fourteen local informants who then selected ten persons that they felt were the most powerful. This produced a list of forty reputational leaders who were subsequently interviewed. Interviewers then asked these leaders to choose ten individuals on the list who could make decisions that nearly everyone would accept. The forty reputational leaders named twelve individuals consistently enough to convince Hunter that they represented the top echelon of the community power structure of Atlanta.

In contrast to Hunter's approach, the "decisional" method employed by Robert Dahl in his study of New Haven, Connecticut, analyzed policy decisions made in three areas: public education, political nominations, and urban renewal. Dahl contended that viewing the actors in actual policy decisions was a superior strategy for studying power and urban policymaking. Using the decisional approach, Dahl found a much more dispersed, pluralistic distribution of power in New Haven than Hunter found in Atlanta using the reputational approach.[8]

The Power Input

The central question of politics is who has the authority and power to determine who gets what, when, and how. It is important therefore to understand which competing institutions and organized groups are most influential in setting the agenda, as well as formulating and implementing national, state, and local urban policies. One view of power explains acceptance of an attitude of "benign neglect" toward urban problems as a result of political forces (declining power of the Democratic party) and the growth of Republican suburban voters. The relative share of urban congressional districts, about one-quarter of the total House of Representatives, was retained following the reapportionment of 1970. Over time, urban representation was expected to increase at the expense of rural representation.[9] Instead, suburban representation grew, with these districts increasing by 39 percent from 1966 to 1993. Gains came at the expense of both urban and rural areas. The balance of power also shifted from the Snowbelt north to the Sunbelt south. As the population in big northeastern and midwestern cities peaked in the 1950s, urban representation in federal and state legislative bodies began to decline. In 1970, cities had a 148 to 144 seat advantage over suburbs in the U.S. House of Representatives. By the 1980s, suburban representatives became more numerous, 228 compared to seventy-nine urban and 128 rural congressional districts. The decline of rural power was aided and abetted by the law. The Supreme Court's support of the "one-man, one-vote" principle (representation must be allocated according to population) also imposed reapportionment on state legislatures and local legislative bodies. Representation from the half-dozen biggest cities (New York, Los Angeles, Chicago, Houston, Philadelphia, and Detroit) diminished within their respective states.

The proportion of big city residents actually voting also declined sharply, weakening the relative influence of urban areas in national and state policymaking. New York City, for example, dropped from nearly half (47.9 percent) of the state's vote in 1952 to less than a third (30.9 percent) by 1988.[10] The Republican party's southern strategy also altered the political balance, shifting power away from the declining Snowbelt to the rising Sunbelt cities. This consequentially shifted resources away from big cities of the north to Sunbelt and suburban constituencies.

While most urban centers have been traditional Democratic strongholds, supported by white ethnics, blacks, and Hispanics, Republicans have begun to challenge this arrangement and have won the mayoralty in New York City and Los Angeles. The political landscape changed as a result of population migrations and business firm relocations. Half of the biggest cities in the nation not only lost population, but also increased their proportion of "new urban migrants" (African-Americans, Latinos, and Asians) who participated in politics at lower rates. By the 1990s, only a quarter of the nation's white population lived in central cities.

Pluralists expected national urban policy to evolve incrementally, marginally changing, or "muddling through."[11] More comprehensive or sweeping innovations (such as those experienced during the Great Society) were believed to be possible only if significant shifts occurred in the relative influence and ideological perspectives of the politically attentive interest groups. Pluralism, the prevailing theory held by political scientists, proposed that power was highly diffused and involved a multiplicity of checkpoints with an extraordinary variety of opportunities for an organized minority to block, modify, or delay policy. Similarly, pluralists saw vast networks of local governments existing with considerable autonomy and serving as a means of "denationalizing" many conflicts, thereby reducing the strain on national political institutions. The civil rights movement, however, revealed the limitation of this process, and showed how some issues could reach the national agenda.[12]

According to elite theory, public policy reflects the values and preferences of a small socioeconomic group that holds and exercises power. The majority, or the masses, are ruled by the powerful and acquiesce in the decisions of the wielders of power. Domhoff maintained that a "ruling class" of less than 1 percent of the population owned most of the country's wealth, received a disproportionate amount of its yearly income, and controlled the major banks, corporations, and large law firms. This elite provides the basic leadership for the top banks and corporations, as well as dominating the philanthropic foundations, prestigious universities, the media, and influential opinion-shaping associations. This ruling class was also believed to dominate powerful administrative and regulatory agencies through a variety of policy-planning organizations. In the case of the New Haven leadership, Domhoff found that local elites were a part of the "national ruling class," which formed an "urban policy-planning network" to revitalize the community.[13]

While power analysis has been used sparingly to explain national policy-making, especially urban policy, there have been even fewer power studies at the state level. An exception was a study of corporate power in the state of Delaware that reported on the external domination of state governments by economic elites. The DuPont Corporation, a powerful force, largely ignored the City of Wilmington until it decided to protect its sizable investment in the central business district by boxing in the downtown area with a network of interstate highways and connectors.[14]

The most extensive study of power, its distribution, and impact upon public policy has occurred at the community level. Here the proponents of the two distinct and opposing schools of thought (the elite and pluralist schools) have conducted the most empirical research and continue to debate their differences. In an analysis of some ninety community studies, it was found that pluralistic power systems were more effective in mobilizing local resources to match funding for federal programs such as urban renewal, model cities, and public housing.[15]

The Ideological Input

Definitions of urban problems and their potential solutions are often discussed in practical terms, but underlying ideological currents guide policy. These currents range from traditional liberal and conservative doctrines, to moderate and radical perspectives regarding the appropriate scope of government. Liberals would not only expand the scope of government, but also promote concerns for equity. Conservatives prefer to reduce the scope of government in urban affairs and to rely upon an unfettered marketplace and individual choice to promote efficiency and effectiveness. Those who consider themselves neither conservative nor liberal, but "moderate," tend to emphasize decision-making processes rather than substantive issues, while those who consider themselves "radicals" of the left appear to be more concerned about the substantive ends or results of public policy. The ideological left focuses upon socioeconomic class in their analysis and upon who controls the means of production, whereas the ideological right seriously questions the rationale for government interfering with the pursuit of individual endeavors.

As examples of liberal and conservative regimes, President Johnson's Great Society spawned hundreds of government programs to address virtually every urban problem, while President Reagan unsuccessfully attempted to severely reduce or abolish existing urban programs. The Democratic-controlled Congress prevented the conservative Reagan administration from destroying the "social safety net" for the very poor in society.[16] Fourteen years later, in 1995, the 104th Republican Congress intended to finish the work Reagan set out to achieve as they challenged a whole array of federal programs that fostered entitlements, regulations, and (according to many of the newly elected Republicans) wasteful spending. Entitlement spending, however, continued to grow.

Conservative commentators not only disagreed with the definition and magnitude of the liberal diagnosis of urban problems, but prophesied that problems of the cities would disappear or dwindle into relative unimportance. In general, conservatives did not believe that urban problems could be "solved" by government programs but that such programs would prolong problems or make them worse.[17] During the Nixon administration, advisors such as Daniel Patrick Moynihan recommended "benign neglect" toward race. Moynihan believed that the reaction of the 1960s to the civil disorders was overstated, as was the insistence upon the need for a national approach to conditions of American cities.[18]

Urban commentators on the left of the political spectrum contended that politicians manipulated issues for their own purposes and that the War on Poverty should have spent considerably more money.[19] Others viewed the expanded intervention of the federal government as reminiscent of the traditional big city political machines. Such an expansion of federal interest undercut both the Republican-dominated state legislatures and the Democratic big city mayors. Radicals criticized increases in federal aid since if the aid truly helped the poor it would diminish their affinities toward disruptive behavior—behavior that was perceived to be necessary to bring about fundamental change in the structure of society.[20]

Radicals of the left and right have often opposed government poverty programs. Goldwater, for example, challenged the official definition of poverty as he believed it was a statistical artifact and thus mathematically impossible to abolish poverty. There would always be inequality for there is no way to eliminate the lowest one-fifth of income earners in the nation. Those on the left also were opposed to the existing welfare system. They believed that only if indigents overloaded the welfare system and provoked a political crisis would they see significant change in the political system.[21] Thirty years and a half dozen presidents later, the debate continues over the causes and consequences of poverty. Liberal and conservative policymakers and commentators have put forth very different interpretations about what has happened during this time; they also disagree in regard to what should be done. For example, they differ dramatically on the amount of money that should be spent. In general, conservatives contend that much too much money has been expended, while liberals claim that more money is needed to address the issue.[22]

In a study of city finances, four types of political cultures were identified in urban areas. *New Deal Democrats* were liberal on both fiscal and social issues, and they aggressively used government programs to solve public problems. *New Deal Republicans* were conservative on both issues and believed that the private market was more efficient than the public sector. *Ethnic Politicians* were defined as liberal on fiscal issues, but conservative on social issues. They stressed ethnicity and group solidarity as the basis of decision making rather than relying on public policies. Finally, *New Fiscal Populists* tended to emphasize fiscal conservatism, but were liberal on social issues such as race. Each culture preferred different urban policies, especially in regard to revenue and spending packages.[23]

Application of RPI

Facing cutbacks of federal monies, taxpayer revolts, increased citizen dissatisfaction, and declining citizen participation, urban officials and political activists have searched for new ways not only to survive, but to improve the quality of life for urban residents. While it appears less fashionable to discuss "urban" policies today, problems that are identified with cities (such as race, welfare, and crime) have dominated the policy agenda in the Clinton administration. Clinton's pledges to end welfare as we know it and to place 100,000 police officers on the nation's streets indirectly addressed underlying concerns of cities.

It appears that ideology and power have both played a major role in the evolution of urban policies while the contribution of the rational input has been marginal at best. From the ideological perspective, the environment of the Great Society was conducive to an expansion of the government in order to address urban problems. Aid to cities grew significantly during the 1960s and early 1970s. Between 1965 and 1977 per capita aid to all big cities increased from approximately $50 to $244.[24] These funding increases were generally supported in the popular sentiment of citizens in the country. According to a leading scholar of urban policy, however, funding levels to cities declined sharply with changes in the ideological predispositions, or "mood," of the nation's citizens:

> In the mid-1970s the mood changed. . . . New York became a symbol of urban profligacy that, along with a new conservatism and burgeoning federal deficits, would undermine pro-urban forces in Congress. National aid to big cities fell from $9.3 billion in 1977 to $4.5 billion in 1990. Per capita aid fell from $244 to $109. . . .[25]

More important than the partisan shifting of funds to one part of the country or another are the tides of ideology about the proper role to be played by the federal government in addressing the country's social problems. The enormous increments in federal dollars that came to the cities during the 1960s and early 1970s were rooted in the belief in cooperative federalism. Public officials were committed to the principle that all governments, working together, could ameliorate the country's social ills. In more recent years expectations that government could solve social problems have been sharply dampened. As a result, federal aid to states and localities has been cut back to levels not much higher—as a percent of GNP—than those prevailing when Dwight Eisenhower held the presidency.[26]

Urban policies usually have been piecemeal, ad hoc arrangements depending upon which sets of socioeconomic elites are in power, what vision they have for urban America, and what their views are concerning the role of government. Policy responses are screened by national institutions (executive, legislative, judicial), interest groups (big city, suburban, rural), and economic elites. Changes are generally assumed to be evolutionary, incremental, minimalist, following the practice of "muddling through" with piecemeal, ad hoc remedies for specific problems and solutions. As political power continues to shift away from big cities toward suburban constituencies, the most that can be expected for cities will be a set of "nonurban national urban policies." These policies address the equity needs of those who reside in urban America with generic reforms on taxes, welfare, and training. The lack of an explicit rational-comprehensive urban policy at the national, state, and local level does not mean policymakers are without theories, conceptual frameworks, models, or insights to guide decision making. What is suggested is that rational influences are often ignored and that other influences are more salient.

HISTORY OF URBAN POLICY: A PRESIDENTIAL PERSPECTIVE

Roosevelt to Nixon

With the New Deal, the federal government became directly involved in solving urban problems. Ever since the New Deal, some presidents have attempted to expand, while others have tried to maintain or limit the scope of the federal government in resolving urban problems. The results are reflected in alternating goals, objectives, policies, and programs. Most policies were formulated by specialists in substantive areas of transportation, housing, education, economic and community development, and environmental protection. These specialists pursued quite separate and distinct solutions that may or may not have taken into account the interdependent nature of urban problems. Policies often responded to the prevailing special interests of advocacy groups that supported federal involvement in urban problem solving. Furthermore, the full impact of federal policies was highly dependent upon varying interpretations of federalism, which seldom took into account the broad range of local readiness, willingness, and capacity to respond to problems.

National attention to urban issues seemed to ebb and flow during presidential eras, from the pragmatic, makeshift expansion of Roosevelt's New Deal to Johnson's Great Society, which sought to ensure equal opportunities. President Nixon attempted to transform many specific "categorical" grant programs to "block" grants that would include all local governments without regard to need. Categorical grants provide funds for specific federal program purposes; block grants provide lump sums or federal allocations to places. The contributions of each administration added to, subtracted from, or modified existing policies, agencies, and programs. In this evolutionary process, new constituencies and bureaucrats were created.

Roosevelt's New Deal and Truman's Fair Deal, 1933–1952

Even though the nation had lost its rural flavor by the beginning of the twentieth century, it was not until President Roosevelt's New Deal that the federal government showed much interest in urban America. The attempt to "prime the pump" of the nation's economy involved assisting localities with agencies such as the Works Progress Administration (WPA). The Housing Act of 1937 also helped individuals to obtain and maintain homes, as well as assisted cities in slum clearance and public housing. Roosevelt's primary purpose, to provide temporary assistance to individuals and communities, became an enduring legacy of government involvement in housing and other areas.

Truman's Fair Deal adopted the Housing Act of 1949, which declared that there would be a minimum standard of "decent, safe, and sanitary" housing for all Americans. The Housing Act provided direct financial assistance to local governments, which often contributed their own funds to housing efforts.

New York City, for example, applied a penny cigarette tax as seed money to finance the clearance of slums, and also used federal funding to house some 12 percent of its population. The urban poor, long dependent on charitable and religious organizations, were encouraged to turn to public assistance to meet their needs. Advocates of housing programs inculcated the principle that government had a responsibility to provide citizens with minimum needs, such as decent housing. Public housing was intended to serve as a "way station" for the working poor, who eventually would purchase private homes. Public housing was not envisioned as a permanent solution.

Eisenhower's Public-Private "Partnerships," 1953–1960

While the real estate industry opposed public housing as a subtle form of socialism, some leaders began to explore ways of rebuilding American cities, which had been neglected during the Great Depression and World War II. The Rockefeller Brothers Fund study estimated that hundreds of billions of dollars would be required to accomplish this task, identifying transportation, schools, parks, improvement of urban blight, health services, welfare, fire, and police protection as services in need of attention.[27] President Eisenhower established the Urban Renewal Agency (URA) to address these problems through a "partnership" of public and private contributions. Cities were required to apply for categorical grants (narrowly focused federal grants) to renew "blighted" areas and clear slums where low-income families were living in crowded, unsanitary, and crime-ridden conditions. While local government could have eliminated slums through strict enforcement of housing codes and the demolition of dwellings subject to fire and health hazards, this was not feasible politically, given the power of the real estate industry. Instead, local leaders cleared lower-income sections of the city. These areas had a higher cost in terms of demand for services than they had benefits in terms of revenue generation. Ultimately, through the use of the police powers of local government, urban renewal programs removed housing in areas where costs of services were high and transferred land ownership to private developers who were interested in utilizing the land for uses that would generate profits.

Kennedy's "New Frontier" and Johnson's "Great Society," 1961–1968

The New Frontier of President Kennedy continued existing federal programs but did little to lift discrimination against blacks with the promised "stroke of the pen." It did claim credit for some accomplishments, however, such as assisting in the revitalization of New Haven, Connecticut.[28] Even these efforts nevertheless were criticized for representing more rhetorical than substantive action.[29]

Revitalization of urban programs coincided with the administration of Lyndon Johnson. President Johnson's Great Society expanded the number of federal programs from forty-four in 1960 to over five hundred by 1968. Johnson's ambitious objectives were enunciated by the Department of Health,

Education, and Welfare (HEW), which specified the following goals to be accomplished within a decade:

1. Eliminate illiteracy and poverty, and empty state mental hospitals;
2. Reduce infant and maternal mortality by half, and approximately double the number of physicians;
3. Improve the education of preschoolers, high schoolers, and college graduates;
4. Double the income of the lowest quintile of the population;
5. Increase the participation of voters to 80 percent.[30]

While previous administrations generally assisted localities with infrastructure construction projects, the Great Society also sought to expand government provision of social services. The purpose of Johnson's War on Poverty focused upon eliminating the causes of poverty rather than simply treating the consequences of low income. Huge sums of money were spent on urban programs. In addition to spending programs, Johnson's creation of Community Action Programs (CAP) of the Office of Economic Opportunity (OEO) had profound political implications as the program attempted to "empower" the underclass and provide for "maximum feasible participation" of the poor.[31]

The Department of Housing and Urban Development (HUD) was created in 1966 (a year after riots in Watts racked Los Angeles) to coordinate most federal urban programs. Six million publicly assisted subsidized housing units, the outlawing of discrimination in the sale and rental of housing, and the Model Cities Program (designed to rebuild blighted neighborhoods in a few cities) were all legacies of Johnson's Great Society and activities of the Department of Housing and Urban Development.

Nixon and Ford's "New Federalism": The Shift Toward the Sunbelt and Suburbia, 1969–1976

President Nixon's "New Federalism" shifted federal spending from the federal government to the states, and from categorical to block grants. For example, the categorical approach of the Urban Renewal Agency (URA) was eliminated and consolidated into the Community Development Block Grant (CDBG). This action combined seven grant programs into a single grant. In addition, a general revenue-sharing program was enacted, allocating $2.5 billion to all local governments (urban, suburban, and small cities). This program intended to curb, if not eliminate, the domination of the federal bureaucracies, as well as to shift money from the perceived liberal thinking in Washington to state and local leaders, who were believed to be more conservative.

The crowning blow to big cities came in 1975 under the presidency of Gerald Ford, when New York City asked for a federally guaranteed loan to avoid an impending bankruptcy (much as the federal government had approved for Lockheed Aircraft and Chrysler Corporation). President Ford's answer was interpreted by those sympathetic with the plight of cities as telling the largest city in the nation to "Drop Dead!" This city was seen by many as a "big spender" that needed to curb its appetite, cut taxes, and return to the verities of the marketplace.

Carter to Clinton

President Carter attempted to consolidate federal involvement and articulate a coherent urban vision in order to maximize the effectiveness and efficiency of hundreds of disparate federal programs. President Reagan launched a dramatic contraction of urban policies through his version of New Federalism. President Clinton failed in his initial attempt to once again expand the involvement of the federal government in urban "reinvestment," forcing his administration to address urban problems through general programs of crime prevention, income tax credits, youth service, and enterprise zones.

Carter's Search for Coherent Federal Urban Policies, 1977–1980

President Carter came to office with the announced goal of improving inter-governmental relations by (1) targeting federal aid to needy cities, (2) using public money to attract private investment, and (3) attacking the tangle of red tape that reduced efficiency in governmental operations. Carter's cabinet-level Urban and Regional Policy Group (URPG) reviewed the impact of transfer payments to state and local governments. The URPG attempted to produce a coherent federal urban policy without spending additional monies. As part of their rational approach to urban problems, dozens of agencies were required to submit urban impact statements. No policy proposals were rejected outright on the basis of impact statements, but some proposals were modified to miti-gate the damaging effects of proposed programs. The requirements for impact statements ultimately had the effect of heightening the federal bureaucracy's sensitivity to urban concerns. Impact statements, however, were not embraced by local political interests who wished to operate without constraint.

The Carter administration also utilized Urban Development Action Grants (UDAG) to stimulate private investment in the central cities. The UDAG pro-gram disbursed some $4 billion to over 2,200 cities, which in turn attracted some $30 billion in private money and produced over half a million jobs. Urban legislators and liberals, however, felt deserted by President Carter, as he refused to spend more money to solve mounting urban problems. By the conclusion of the Carter presidency, it was clear that the end of large-scale federal financial assistance had arrived. During Carter's presidency, a shift in urban strategy from one based on bringing jobs to people to a strategy of bringing people to jobs was advanced. Instead of supporting programs that stimulate business activities in declining cities, the new strategy endorsed helping people move to places where the marketplace was already growing. Urban advocates viewed this recommendation as a death knell for distressed cities of the Rustbelt.[32]

The "Nonurban Policy" of Reagan/Bush and Their Attempt to Eliminate Federal Involvement in Urban America, 1981–1992

President Reagan intended to terminate the Great Society, not just stop its continued expansion. Office of Management and Budget (OMB) Director David Stockman unsuccessfully attempted to reduce expenditures from $33 billion to zero for all local education, health, welfare, and employment services.[33] The Democratic Congress refused to go along with this goal and was able to maintain a "social safety net" for the poor. President Reagan not only intended to limit federal spending, but to return initiative, responsibility, and authority for addressing social problems to state and local governments, as well as to the private and voluntary sectors. The Reagan administration referred to the adage, "If you want to do something, do it on your own."

The aim of the Reagan administration was to shift attention and priorities from cities to counties, suburbs, and rural districts. Direct financial aid to cities fell from 28 percent of all urban spending in 1978 to 17 percent by 1988. At the same time, federal funds to nonurban areas nearly doubled, from $69 billion to $114 billion. The conservative Reagan administration also encouraged cities and states to exercise greater independence, and stimulated them to adopt regressive taxes (such as users' fees and sales taxes) that placed higher burdens on lower-income groups. This strategy disappointed liberals, who maintained that it violated principles of equity and that underlying urban problems such as poverty, social disorganization, crime, poor schools, and economic disinvestment were not being addressed.[34]

President Bush found it difficult to continue Reagan's strategy of holding the line on federal spending since he promised both "no new taxes" and a "kinder and gentler" administration. Bush, less ideological than Reagan on domestic policy, appointed an interagency task force that refused to propose new strategies for cities, telling city leaders to "just make things work better."[35] While the administration passively allowed federal spending on urban programs to increase, the protracted business recession enlarged the number of Americans falling below the poverty line; concomitantly those receiving food stamps rose by a third, and those receiving AFDC rose by a quarter. Secretary of Housing and Urban Development (HUD) Jack Kemp was unable to gain support from either the White House or Congress for his concept of "enterprise zones" (a program of tax incentives for businesses choosing to locate in highly distressed urban areas). Kemp's enterprise zone plans were consistent with the "supply-side" view of stimulating growth through tax breaks to producers, such as owners of factories or service industries. In theory, the most depressed sections of inner cities would be revitalized through policies of relaxing government regulation and lowering taxes. This would lead to the creation of many new jobs as small entrepreneurs rushed to take advantage of their new opportunities.[36]

Kemp's other initiatives such as empowerment and vouchers (to give choices to the poor) were also stymied. Eventually, the Reagan/Bush administrations eliminated a number of pro-city federal programs such as General Revenue Sharing (GRS), Urban Development Action Grants (UDAG), the Economic

Contemporary Controversy

What to Do About Urban Problems?

THE URBAN condition has most often been referred to negatively by policy analysts as being "unheavenly," a "predicament," or in "crisis."[38] The older big cities are "ungovernable" or "contested."[39] Various perspectives explaining the decline of urban areas in America include

1. A lack of political will,
2. A lack of money and unwillingness to discuss behavioral problems,
3. An absence of the sense that healthy cities are essential to the survival of the social body,
4. Foreign entanglements such as the Persian Gulf War,
5. Discouragement and lack of incentive,
6. Physical and cultural isolation,
7. A captivating and violent drug culture,

Development Administration (EDA), and the Comprehensive Employment and Training Act (CETA). The Reagan and Bush administrations, however, were unable to enact all the cuts that they sought.

The 1992 Los Angeles riot, the most serious in the nation's history, did not seem to produce a great alteration in urban policy. Black conservatives, who had disdain for the "poverty industry," distanced themselves from the rioters, whom they believed were in need of personal discipline. Others simply re-adopted their attitude of neglect. By the end of the 1992 presidential campaign (only six months following the riot), the plight of the cities was again placed on the nation's back burner. The *Los Angeles Times* reported that for a few fleeting moments, it was as if a window had flown wide open after being frozen shut for years, yet except for a flurry of local efforts, nothing much happened.[37] The Bush administration proposed funding for various programs that emphasized aid to individuals instead of assistance targeted to specific locations. The nation's mayors were bitterly disappointed by the federal response.

Clinton's Empowerment Zones/Enterprise Communities, 1993

President Clinton's initial urban strategy was to increase public investment in both people and places. As a Democrat, Clinton perceived government to be a catalyst for growth. The size of the federal deficit and cost of the national debt, however, made it difficult for him to secure large sums of money for new investments in urban areas. The Democratic-controlled Congress was finally

8. Poor educational and employment opportunities,
9. A welfare system that supports a culture of poverty,
10. A system that does not empower the poor but makes them dependent.[40]

Efforts to formulate a comprehensive national urban policy have been relatively limited. The lack of major achievements and inadequate coherence in urban policy has been attributed to factors such as

1. Analytical flaws (lack of an adequate theory of the causes and consequences of urban problems),
2. Institutional problems (budgetary constraints, incoherence in roles and missions of organizations, and the lack of local competence to initiate and implement effective policies),
3. Political deficiencies (urban places losing their clout in the nation as a whole to others, losing influence to suburban areas within metropolitan areas, and witnessing more affluent communities losing their desire to help needy cities). Central city representation in federal and state legislatures has decreased.

Proposed policies are formulated more often according to the perspectives of individuals or groups with influence, either in the public or private sector. These individuals or groups are prepared to mobilize their political resources to protect and promote their

(continued)

able to pass, without a single Republican vote, a reduced economic stimulus package.

Clinton turned to a "bottom-up" process in which distressed cities submitted plans of action to a Community Enterprise Board made up of fifteen federal agencies. This Board would allocate $2.5 billion in federal tax incentives and $1.33 billion in flexible grant assistance. The Board also designated six urban "Enterprise Zones" (EZs), which each received $100 million dollars. Sixty-five cities were designated "Enterprise Communities" (EC), which allowed them to receive tax-exempt bond financing, easier access to federal grants, employer wage credits, and tax-exempt investments. Some states, such as Florida, started their own enterprise zones to stimulate investment in deteriorated areas.

In general, enterprise zones were characterized by pervasive poverty and high unemployment. What was notable about the enterprise zone approach was that it reflected a shift in federal involvement from treating a single problem in isolation from others, to the notion that public problems come in "clusters," requiring treatment of the underlying dynamic. Joblessness, crime, and a breakdown in family life were believed to be interrelated, and enterprise zones would address these problems. The enterprise zone approach also recognized that distressed communities required both private and public investment. Each enterprise zone community was chosen partly on the basis of commitments of the private sector to invest and operate within the targeted zones. In some regards, enterprise zones represented a boon to business (tax and regulatory concessions) as well as a benefit to the depressed community, since jobs and economic activity would be located in the depressed area.

interests. In theory, interests of the masses may be represented as leaders consider public opinion when they make their decisions. In reality, however, the wishes of the masses may not receive a great deal of attention compared to the desires of those knowledgeable in the use of power.

A variety of perspectives have been adopted to resolve complex urban problems.[42] Ever since the impositions of the federal government during the New Deal and the proliferation of federal initiatives during the Great Society, there have been conflicting ideas and competing strategies about what should be done to resolve urban problems and improve the quality of life in urban America. These conflicts have been protracted, and little consensus has emerged. No one controversy best exemplifies the urban predicament, since a large number of interrelated proposals have been identified.

Liberals initiated the expansion of government in urban affairs. In general, liberals sought federal involvement to ensure the following:

1. Equal protection (voter rights, desegregated public facilities, and programs for the disabled),
2. Environmental protection over land uses (air and water pollution, wildlife habitat, and historic resources),
3. Redistributive programs to those in need (public welfare, food stamps, job training, and health care),
4. Efforts to share an imagined "peace dividend" by converting the Department of Defense's spending to domestic initiatives.[43]

Conservatives preferred regulatory authority to remain at the state and local level and successfully worked to set limits upon federal "unfunded mandates." Conservatives also opposed the use of the "police power" of government to condemn and seriously modify private property for slum clearance. They also contended that many of the environmental regulations were unnecessary. Some conservatives favored "benign neglect," since they believed that urban and racial matters eventually would correct themselves.[44] Some extreme conservatives even took the position that the federal government should be eliminated entirely in favor of state and local government. A review of these positions is summarized in the following:

1. Limit unfunded mandates, and limit federal regulatory powers;
2. Limit power of the federal government to modify property rights, and limit environmental regulations;
3. Ignore the problems of cities;
4. Drastically cut the power of the federal government or even eliminate it in favor of state and local entities.

Since the 1960s, numerous urban strategies have been adopted. The immediate response of the Johnson administration to urban riots was the War on Poverty, as part of their vision of the Great Society involving hundreds of pro-city programs and projects. Following the Johnson administration, prescriptions of Nixon advisor Daniel Patrick Moynihan encouraged the Nixon administration to engage in "benign neglect" toward the race issue and urban areas in general. Unlike the nation's vital interest in foreign affairs, no consistent doctrine for urban policy was enunciated, with each administration developing its own judgment about the appropriate role of the federal government in local affairs. More recent interest in urban centers has focused upon the themes of economic development, growth management, urban revitalization, and fiscal reform.

The Los Angeles riot of 1992 forced political leaders to begin a dialogue about what went wrong and what to do about the problems of American cities. There was a great deal of finger pointing about who was to blame, however, and a paucity of concrete proposals. President Bush and his spokesmen blamed the Great Society of President Johnson; Bill Clinton cited the "benign neglect" of Presidents Reagan and Bush. In general, Republicans believed that federal programs created the conditions that led to riots, while Democrats believed that aid was insufficient. Conservatives contended that government spending only exacerbated urban problems.[45] Liberals asserted that not enough money was spent. From their perspective, instead of a "war" on poverty, there had been a "piddling battle," which did not achieve the national objective of "eliminating" poverty.[46]

Perhaps one reason for the lack of consensus in regard to urban policy is that policymakers have been burned in the past as policies that were adopted with the best intentions had unintended consequences. Policies were blamed subsequently for worsening the plight of those in need of assistance. These unanticipated consequences include

1. Urban renewal programs that bulldozed neighborhoods in anticipation of newer development that never came,
2. Tax breaks that encouraged suburban housing, accelerating the outflow of people from the inner cities,
3. Programs for the jobless that encouraged them to move away from declining areas to areas where opportunities were more plentiful,
4. Tensions resulting from constitutional and political quarrels over distributions of grants and the imposition of mandates,
5. A political backlash from the white middle class,
6. The convergence of social pathologies in neighborhoods with public housing,
7. The perceived erosion of incentives to work due to welfare dependency,
8. The flight of whites from city schools as a result of busing,
9. The displacement of established residents from neighborhoods as a result of government's efforts to attract middle-income occupants to declining neighborhoods,
10. The inability of people to get to jobs in the suburbs because of poor transportation.

The readiness and willingness, as well as the ability and efforts, of local, state, and national leaders to tackle urban problems and the recurring sense of crisis depend upon who has the authority, power, and influence to determine urban policies. The opinions, attitudes, beliefs, and ideologies of leaders, organized interests, and active constituents play an important role in determining the agendas and policy alternatives that are adopted. The ability of urban analysts to formulate a comprehensive understanding of the dynamics of urban America has not been well developed. Furthermore, urban analysts have not been effective in persuading policymakers to heed their advice. It may be that urban leaders have little confidence in the recommendations of urban scholars, or perhaps they simply prefer to operate upon their own intuition or sense of what is politically feasible. In any event, the issue of "what to do" about urban problems remains largely unanswered.

Attention from policymakers to this issue may ebb and flow over time as events such as the Los Angeles riot of 1992 periodically focus the nation's attention. While attention to urban matters may not be great and may be redirected to other policy concerns, the pathologies emanating from urban areas cannot be ignored permanently without the nation suffering severe consequences.

Case Study

Responses to Urban Civil Disorders

THE CIVIL Rights Act of 1964, President Johnson's Great Society, and the establishment of HUD in 1966 all demonstrated a national purpose to address tough urban problems. The Watts riots of 1965 in Los Angeles focused the nation's attention on urban blight and racial injustice. In 1968, additional riots in many other cities led to the deployment of state National Guard units; in the case of Detroit, federal troops were needed to quell the civil disorders. Following the riots, there was a general sense that the root causes of the explosion of American big cities should be addressed.[47]

A large number of federal programs were formulated to focus upon problems of both people and places. The War on Poverty spent billions, and cities such as Detroit received hundreds of millions of dollars in state and federal assistance. Yet, an ominous and awesome sense of deep-seated urban problems persisted. Had national and local public efforts to improve the quality of life of urban dwellers failed, had they ameliorated the problems, or were community-oriented programs simply "cooling" the growing anger and alienation of inner-city residents?

The nation received another wake-up call on April 29, 1992, when a suburban jury acquitted four Los Angeles police officers accused of beating motorist Rodney King. The officers were acquitted despite a videotape showing Los Angeles police taking as many as fifty-six baton swings at King. A dramatic outburst following the trial of the police officers became the largest riot in the country's history, involving 58 deaths, 2,383 injuries, 17,000 arrests, 10,000 fire calls, and a billion dollars of property damages. This compared with 220 dead, over 8,300 injured, and more than 53,000 arrests in the riots which occurred in 48 American cities from 1964 to 1968.[48]

Urban analysts became more profoundly aware of the smoldering embers of urban deprivation, schools and families under pressure, increased racial discord and violence, and the loss of trust in leaders and institutions. Nevertheless, they were surprised and stunned by the fury of the outbursts. The socioeconomic status of the residents of the area had not improved much since 1965; unemployment and welfare dependency actually had increased.

New immigrants (Hispanics and Asians) increased ethnic conflicts as groups competed for the same slice of the American pie. The political optimism following the civil rights movement, which stimulated better political representation, eroded as whites migrated to the suburbs.

Deficiencies were discovered in the delivery of urban services to minorities. A member of the California McCone Commission studying the 1965 Watts riot claimed that the fundamental causes of the two riots were "resonant" thirty years later. In the early 1990s, a new Commission investigated the behavior and performance of the Los Angeles police department, noting the following glaring faults:

1. a group of police officers who used excessive force;
2. a debilitating breakdown of discipline among officers;
3. an unwritten "code of silence" not to turn against each other.

Social scientists identified various "theories" to explain civil disorders. Those on the right of the political spectrum tended to characterize rioters as "riff-raff" who engage in riots mainly for "fun and profit." In contrast, some on the left of the political spectrum believed the riots were class-based over "bread." Students of race and ethnic relations tended to view the disturbances as racial protests or "multi-ethnic conflict" based on real grievances. The "bladerunner syndrome" heralded the final breakdown of a civil society plagued by the underclass, drugs, and the criminal element. A scenario was portrayed where public cynicism grows; whites, money, and power flee to the suburbs; black mayors are sell-outs to downtown business interests; and the process of electoral politics is irrelevant to the problems of the poor.[49] Twenty years after the issuance of the widely read Kerner Commission Report in 1968, two of the Commission members offered the following assessment of urban conditions:

> There are "quiet riots" in all of America's central cities: unemployment, poverty, social disorganization, segregation, family disintegration, housing and school deterioration, and crime are worse now. These "quiet riots" are not as alarming as the violent riots of twenty years ago, or as noticeable to outsiders. But they are even more destructive of human life. National security requires renewed human investment. . . . We have the means. We must summon the will.[50]

In 1992, other Kerner Commission members were asked to comment about the Los Angeles riot and identify what changes had occurred since their report. They expressed sadness, but little surprise. Former Mayor Lindsay of New York City noted that federal funds to the city had been cut by $20 billion during the 1980s. He blamed lack of national leadership and commitment to address the underlying conditions of systematic poverty and segregation.

In the midst of the 1992 presidential campaign, mayors and top national officials were quick to lay blame for the riot. President Bush's press secretary blamed the federal programs of the Great Society. Vice President Quayle blamed the disintegration of traditional family values. Mayor Dinkins of New York City contended that President Bush's response to the LA riots and the problems of cities in general had been "woefully inadequate." Mayor Riley of Charleston complained that this most urban nation in the world had no national urban policy. Senator Sarbanes (D-Maryland) explained that budget constraints had stifled debate on national priorities. Felix Rohatyn, an investment banker, challenged prevailing views that the government was (1) impotent to solve society's problems, (2) incompetent and simply unable to get things right, and (3) broke, without any resources to deal with such matters. Rohatyn contended that the nation had not invested adequately in research, human capital (education and training), and public facilities. He called for a national recovery program that would maintain America's global position, ensure economic security, and enhance social cohesion.

Three days after rioting began, Mayor Bradley appointed Peter Ueberroth, former Olympics czar, to head Rebuild LA (RLA) to focus on "long-term sustainable change." Their goal was to bring jobs (75,000 to 94,000) and capital ($6 billion) to the area of neglect. At the end of the first year, however, Ueberroth resigned amid mixed reports of progress. RLA blamed government for insufficient support, while minority groups complained that their voices were not heeded. Shortly after the riots, the public displayed a great deal of pessimism toward improvements: (1) two-thirds of the public expected more violence, (2) 85 percent felt things in the community were going badly, and (3) public perception of "racism" rose from 2 percent the year before to 15 percent.[51]

(continued)

Los Angeles applied for an enterprise designation from the Clinton administration, but did not receive it. The administration claimed that Los Angeles's leadership did not demonstrate that they could formulate a strategic plan that would effectively use "grassroots" initiatives and broad-based partnership to manage its urban affairs. Los Angeles Mayor Bradley's coalition (composed of Jewish and African-American members) began to falter.

One immediate consequence of the 1992 riot was the turnover of public officials. Four-term Mayor Bradley chose not to run for reelection and was replaced by a moderate-to-conservative Republican who was well connected to business interests. Police Chief Gates eventually was replaced by an African-American from Philadelphia. The district attorney was defeated in a reelection bid. The school district not only changed its superintendent, but initiated a move to decentralize into smaller districts.

Case Study Questions

1. Do you think federal "urban" and "nonurban" policies since the Watts riots of 1965 increased, decreased, or had nothing to do with the problems that contributed to the 1992 riot in Los Angeles? Identify federal policies that may have contributed to resolving urban problems. Were policies influenced more by rational analysis, ideology, or power?

Suggested Readings

Edward Banfield. *The Unheavenly City.* Boston: Little Brown, 1970.

Terry Clark and Lorna Ferguson. *City Money.* New York: Columbia University Press, 1981.

John Harrigan. *Political Change in the Metropolis.* New York: HarperCollins, 1993.

Dennis Judd and Todd Swanstrom. *City Politics.* New York: HarperCollins, 1994.

Marshall Kaplan and Franklin James, eds. *The Future of National Urban Policy.* Durham, NC: Duke University Press, 1990.

John Mollenkopf. *The Contested City.* Princeton: Princeton University Press, 1983.

Douglas Yates. *The Ungovernable City.* Cambridge, MA: MIT Press, 1977.

Notes

1. Michael Martinez and Janita Poe, "Chicago Grade Schools Pull Off Test Turnaround," *Chicago Tribune,* 4 June 1996, p. 1, sec. 1.

2. Don Terry, "One Fifth of Schools Put on Probation in Chicago," *New York Times,* 1 October 1996, p. A14.

3. Jacquelyn Heard, "College Program Goes Back to Basics," *Chicago Tribune* (Southwest), 6 September 1995, p. 7, sec. 2; Jacquelyn Heard, "Reformers' Biggest Hurdle," *Chicago Tribune* (Evening), pp. 1–2, sec. 2.

2. What should be the responsibilities of the public sector (federal, state, and local), compared to the private sector (business, civic, neighborhood), in addressing the problems that appear in urban areas? How do ideological views about the scope of government affect American urban policy?

3. What institution, if any, has the authority, and which group(s), if any, have the informal influence to prevent future civil disorders? What philosophy does or should guide their actions toward reducing "quiet riots?"

4. What have we learned from recurring riots that might be applied to formulate a national urban policy? Should there be a comprehensive, approach, or should each state formulate its own policies?

5. What should the federal government do to help residents of poor, deteriorating, and crime-infested neighborhoods in the innercity? Whose responsibility do you think it is to help such citizens: the citizens themselves, the government, or some combination of both? Can private interests take the lead in providing assistance to inner-city residents?

6. What type of behavior should inner city citizens pursue in order to improve their lives? What type of public sector action would best help such citizens?

7. Why do you think problems of the inner cities persist? Which of these problems are the most serious? Are certain ideological preferences more amenable to efforts to solve the problems of cities?

4. Roger Vaughn, Anthony Pascal, and Mary Vaiana, *The Urban Impacts of Federal Policies* (Santa Monica, CA: Rand, 1980).

5. William Kornblum and Joseph Julian, Social Problems, 7th ed. (Englewood Cliffs, NJ: Prentice-Hall, 1992), p. 427.

6. Donald Bogue, *Principles of Demography* (New York: Wiley, 1969), p. 465.

7. Dennis Judd, *The Politics of American Cities: Private Power and Public Policy,* 3rd ed. (Glenview, IL: Scott, Foresman, 1988), p. 18.

8. Larry Lyon, *The Community in Urban Society* (Lexington, MA: Lexington Books, 1989), pp. 184–187.

9. "Suburbs: Potential But Unrealized House Influence," *Congressional Quarterly Weekly Report,* 32 (14) (1974), pp. 878–880.

10. Dennis Judd and Todd Swanstrom, *City Politics* (New York: HarperCollins, 1994), p. 253.

11. David Braybrooke and Charles Lindblom, *A Strategy for Decision* (New York: Free Press, 1963).

12. Robert Dahl, *Pluralist Democracy in the United States* (Chicago: Rand McNally, 1967), p. 182.

13. William Domhoff, *Who Really Rules?* (Santa Monica, CA: Goodyear, 1978).

14. James Phelan and Robert Posen, *The Company State* (New York: Grossman, 1973).

15. Michael Aiken, "The Distribution of Community Power," in *The Structure of Community Power,* ed. M. Aiken and P. Mott (New York: Random House, 1970).

16. Martha Burt and Karen Pittman, *Testing the Social Safety Net* (Washington, DC: Urban Institute Press, 1985).

17. Charles Murray, *Losing Ground: American Social Policy, 1950–1980* (New York: Basic Books, 1984).

18. Daniel P. Moynihan, "The City in Chassis," in *Toward a National Urban Policy* (New York: Basic Books, 1970), pp. 313–337.

19. Michael Harrington, *The New American Poverty* (New York: Penguin Books, 1984).

20. Frances Piven and Richard Cloward, *Regulating the Poor* (New York: Vintage Books, 1971).

21. Piven and Cloward, op. cit.

22. Harrington, op. cit., p. 21; William A. Rusher, "Forward, March! Instead of Lamenting the Lost Reagan Era," *National Review* 45 (3), (15 February 1993), pp. 37–42.

23. Terry Clark and Lorna Ferguson, *City Money* (New York: Columbia University Press, 1981).

24. Paul Peterson, *The Price of Federalism* (Washington, DC: Brookings Institution, 1995), p. 167.

25. Ibid., p. 166.

26. Ibid., p. 174.

27. Rockefeller Brothers Fund, *Prospect for America* (New York: Doubleday, 1958).

28. Fred Powledge, *Model City* (New York: Simon and Schuster, 1970).

29. Clarence Stone and Heywood Sanders, "Reexamining a Classic Case of Development Politics," in *The Politics of Urban Development,* ed. C. Stone and H. Sanders (Lawrence: University of Kansas Press, 1987), pp. 159–181.

30. Wilbur Cohen, *Toward a Social Report* (Ann Arbor: University of Michigan Press, 1969), pp. ix–x.

31. Daniel Patrick Moynihan, *Maximum Feasible Misunderstanding* (New York: Free Press, 1969).

32. Presidential Commission for a National Agenda for the Eighties, *Urban America in the Eighties* (Englewood Cliffs, NJ: Prentice-Hall, 1981).

33. William Grieder, *The Education of David Stockman* (New York: Dutton, 1981).

34. John Harrigan, *Political Change in the Metropolis* (New York: HarperCollins, 1993).

35. Yvonne Scruggs, "HUD's Stewardship of National Urban Policy," *Cityscape* 1 (3) (September 1995), pp. 33–68.

36. Stuart Butler, *Enterprise Zones* (New York: Universe Books, 1981), p. 5.

37. Jonathan Peterson, "Plight of Cities Again on Back Burner," *Los Angeles Times,* 26 October 1992, pp. A1, A24.

38. Edward Banfield, *The Unheavenly City* (Boston: Little, Brown, 1970); William Gorham and Nathan Glazer, eds. *The Urban Predicament* (Washington, DC: Urban Institute, 1976); Peter Steinberger, *Ideology and the Urban Crisis* (Albany: State University of New York Press, 1985).

39. Douglas Yates, *The Ungovernable City* (Cambridge, MA: MIT Press, 1977); John Mollenkopf, *The Contested City* (Princeton: Princeton University Press, 1983).

40. Jason DeParle, "Suffering in the Cities Persists as U.S. Fights Other Battles," *New York Times,* 27 January 1991, pp. A1, A27; Peter Applebome, "As Urban Blight Worsens, Victims Find Their Isolation Is Deepening," *New York Times,* 28 January 1991, pp. A1, A20; Peter Applebome, "Ideas to Help Poor Abound, But a Consensus Is Wanting," *New York Times,* 29 January 1991, pp. A1, A18.

41. Marshall Kaplan and Franklin James, eds., *The Future of National Urban Policy* (Durham, N.C.: Duke University Press, 1990), pp. 4–5.

42. David Judge, Gerry Stoker, and Harold Wolman, eds., *Theories of Urban Politics* (Thousand Oaks, CA: Sage Publications, 1995).

43. Norton Long, "A Marshall Plan for Cities?," in *Towards a National Urban Policy,* House Committee on the City, 95th Congress, 1st Session, September 28, 1977, pp. 43–51.

44. Moynihan, op. cit.

45. Rusher, op. cit., p. 37.

46. Harrington, op. cit.

47. Kerner Commission Report, *National Advisory Commission on Civic Disorder* (New York: New York Times, 1968).

48. Brian Downes, "A Critical Reexamination of the Social and Political Characteristics of Riot Cities," *Social Science Quarterly* 51 (2) (September 1970), pp. 349–360.

49. David Sears, "Urban Rioting in Los Angeles," in *The Los Angeles Riots,* ed. M. Baldassare (Boulder, CO: Westview Press, 1994), p. 250.

50. Fred Harris and Roger Wilkens, *Quiet Riots: Race and Poverty in the United States* (New York: Pantheon Books, 1988), p. xiii.

51. Frank Clifford and Penelope McMillan, "Most in L.A. Expect New Riots But Feel Safe," *Los Angeles Times,* 14 May 1992, pp. A1, A20; Bob Sipchen, "More Musings on the Causes of L.A.'s Riots," *Los Angeles Times,* 14 May 1992, pp. E1, E7; Los Angeles Times Staff, "Understanding the Riots, Part 4, Seeing Ourselves," 14 May 1992, pp. T1–T8; Los Angeles Times Staff, "Understanding the Riots, Part 5, the Path to Recovery," 15 May 1992, pp. T1–T10.

Education Policy

IS THE NATION STILL AT RISK OF EDUCATION FAILURE?

On August 26, 1981, Ronald Reagan's secretary of education, H. Terrel Bell, created the National Commission on Excellence in Education. Its charge was to examine the quality of education in the United States and to make practical recommendations for improving the nation's education system, particularly regarding students in high school. Advertised as an "open letter to the American people," the report declared:

> Our Nation is at risk. Our once unchallenged preeminence in commerce, industry, science, and technological innovation is being overtaken by competitors throughout the world. . . . [W]hile we can take justifiable pride in what our schools and colleges have historically accomplished and contributed to the United States and the well-being of its people, the educational foundations of our society are being eroded by a rising tide of mediocrity that threatens our very future as a Nation and a people.[1]

Likening this challenge to "an act of war" committed by "an unfriendly foreign power," the report placed blame for the dire condition of American education on policy decisions that had "squandered the gains in student achievement made in the wake of the *Sputnik* challenge" in the 1950s, which had mobilized national resources behind an earlier round of soul-searching and efforts to shore up the education framework. *A Nation at Risk* found that the country had "dismantled essential support systems" that had enabled previous successes in education policy reform, and concluded: "We have, in effect, been committing an act of unthinking, unilateral educational disarmament."[2] The chief consequence of this lapse was that the nation's "educational institutions seem to have lost sight of the basic purposes of schooling, and of the high expectations and disciplined effort needed to attain them."[3]

Indicators of the perceived crisis included several shocking findings. American students fared poorly compared to students in other countries; 23 million adults were functionally illiterate; about 13 percent of seventeen-year-olds and 40 percent of minority youth were functionally illiterate; standardized test scores were lower on average than at the dawn of the Space Age; "higher-order" intellectual skills were lacking in nearly 40 percent of seventeen-year-olds; science and mathematics skills had deteriorated; and remedial course work was increasingly necessary.

The motivation behind *A Nation at Risk* could be seen as part of a drive toward a more elite-focused education structure that would be better able to sustain a society capable of competing in a global economy that places a premium on advanced technical education and specialization:

> If only to keep and improve on the slim competitive edge we still retain in world markets, we must dedicate ourselves to the reform of our education system for the benefit of all—old and young alike, affluent and poor, majority and minority. Learning is the indispensable investment required for success in the "information age" we are entering. . . .
>
> Part of what is at risk is the promise first made on this continent: All regardless of race or class or economic status, are entitled to a fair chance and to the tools for developing their individual powers of mind and spirit to the utmost. This promise means that all children by virtue of their own efforts, competently guided, can hope to attain the mature and informed judgment needed to secure gainful employment and to manage their own lives, thereby serving not only their own interests but also the progress of society itself.[4]

Proposed solutions were public commitment to excellence in individual performance, institutional and societal support for that achievement, education reform, equitable treatment of a diverse population, parental support and pressure, and commitment to life-long learning. The ultimate goal was to create and sustain a "Learning Society," characterized by "commitment to a set of values and to a system of education that affords all members the opportunity to stretch their minds to full capacity, from early childhood through adulthood, learning more as the world itself changes."[5] The prime requirement for meaningful reform of American education was effective leadership to mobilize resources to the task.

This was to be accomplished by implementing five recommendations: (a) strengthened high school graduation requirements, including four years of English, three years of mathematics, three years of science, three years of social studies, and half a year of computer science, with two years of a foreign language recommended for college-bound students; (b) higher admission standards for colleges and universities, combined with more rigorous measurable standards and higher expectations for academic performance and student conduct; (c) longer school days or an expanded school year; (d) better teacher-preparation programs, higher and performance-based teacher salaries, eleven-month teacher contracts, teacher career ladders capped by master-teacher designation for the most out-standing, filling shortages of teachers in science and mathematics, financial in-centives for new teachers, and active participation by the most gifted teachers in designing teacher-preparation programs and in supervising probationary teachers; and (e) citizen surveillance of elected officials' leadership and finan-cial commitment to education reform.

In a ten-year follow-up to the original study, H. Terrel Bell, former U.S. secre-tary of education, concluded that the intervening decade had been "a splendid misery for American education." Despite frustration with a slow pace of change, there still was the opportunity "to shape education into the super-efficient en-terprise that it must become if America is to keep its proud place of leader-ship in the marvelous Information Age of this decade and beyond."[6] Corporate interests, concerned about what they regarded as the continuing inadequacy of American education, commissioned their own ten-year retrospective on *A Nation at Risk*. That report, *Ten Years After "A Nation at Risk,"* focused on the poor returns to the increased investment in education, which amounted to tripling per-pupil expenditures in public schools in constant dollars from the early 1950s to the mid-1980s. Summary statistics for the changing scope of American education are presented in Table 7.1.

TABLE 7.1 Historical Summary of Public Elementary and Secondary Schools

	1939–1940	1949–1950	1959–1960	1969–1970	1979–1980	1989–1990
Percent population 5–17 years of age	23%	20.3%	24.5%	25.8%	21.4%	18.2%
Enrollment (000s)						
Elementary	18,833	19,387	27,602	32,513	28,034	29,152
Secondary	6,601	5,725	8,485	13,037	13,616	11,390
High school graduates (000s)	1,143	1,063	1,627	2,589	2,748	2,320
Nonsupervisory instructional staff (000s)	875	920	1,393	2,195	2,300	2,860
Total revenue ($ million)	$2,261	$5,437	$14,747	$40,267	$96,881	$207,573
Total expenditures ($ million)	$2,344	$5,838	$15,613	$40,683	$95,962	$212,100
Current expenditure per pupil average daily attendance ($)	$88	$210	$375	$816	$2,272	$4,962

Source: National Center for Education Statistics, U.S. Department of Education.

Corporations, the update report stated, "have a large stake in the return on these dollars, and many feel that they are not getting their money's worth. In the workplace, they face the mounting costs of retraining, elaborate recruitment for entry-level positions, on-the-job errors, and other costs of poorly prepared workers."[7] The report noted the absence of consensus on precisely what direction should be taken by American education, and lamented the "strong differences between business people and educators on the role of business, and on the legacy of leadership it has begun."[8] Echoing conclusions arrived at earlier by the Business Roundtable,[9] the Conference Board report called for inculcating into corporate culture a sense of commitment to educational change by both the companies and their employees: "Institutionalizing the company commitment is the key to continued and meaningful involvement."[10]

By 1994, President Clinton's secretary of education, Richard W. Riley, announced (in the biennial National Assessment of Educational Progress report) that by 1992 students had gained almost a full grade level in science proficiency since the 1983 report called attention to the need for upgrading science education. Some gains were also made in mathematics, and students were taking more complicated science courses and were doing more homework. The improvement in mathematics and science performance, in the words of Assistant Secretary of Education Madeleine Kunin, showed that the previous decade's efforts were "starting to pay off" with "the first positive trend" apparent in twenty years.[11]

However, no perceptible progress was reported in enhancing reading and writing skills, and overall achievement levels were far below the goals set by national policymakers. In addition, a substantial gap in achievement levels persisted between white and nonwhite students. Previous progress by minority students, partially closing the gap in the early 1980s, did not carry over into the 1990s. In contrast to earlier generations, Secretary Riley said: "Holding our own in the information age is simply not good enough. It just doesn't cut it anymore."[12] The 1994 report revealed in the past decade that one-third of seventeen-year-old respondents did not do daily homework in all school subjects, that the amount of time spent viewing television had increased, and that the availability of reading materials at home had decreased. Reading proficiency levels for nine- and thirteen-year-old students declined, even though they were reading more. Fewer than 10 percent of seventeen-year-olds could do "rigorous" academic work in basic subjects, and only 2 percent of eleventh-graders wrote well enough to meet national goals.

Overall, the Department of Education concluded that home environments had become less conducive to learning. Decreases were recorded in the number of books, magazines, encyclopedias, and newspapers at home. In 1971, 39 percent of all nine-year-olds had responded that their families had all four types of reading material at home, but in 1992, this was true for only 30 percent of students. Thirty-seven percent of homes had two or fewer of these four types of reading matter, compared to 28 percent in 1971. Officials of the Department of Education blamed the comparatively low status afforded education in the United States for this state of affairs.

Secretary of Education Riley argued that more than money would be needed to rectify this situation and urged parents, teachers, and students to foster an environment rewarding academic accomplishments, rather than athletics and other extracurricular activities, social events, and work pursuits. Secretary Riley called for greater attention to be paid to basic reading and writing skills. Only about 50 percent of the eleventh- and eighth-grade students could write adequate brief reports; barely 2 percent of eleventh-graders and 1 percent of eighth-graders could write more sophisticated informative or argumentative reports.

THE RPI INPUTS TO EDUCATION POLICY

The Rationality Input

Unlike many other aspects of societal activity, such as medicine or engineering, about which most citizens do not pretend to be "experts," nearly all people feel that they are at least potential experts on matters of education.[13] This attitude is apparent particularly when one's own children are caught up in education policymaking. It is widely felt that the American education system fails to serve either students' or their parents' interests adequately. In contrast, others note that more students are graduating today from that educational process, with higher levels of knowledge than ever before.[14] Rational policymaking becomes nearly impossible when competing demands are made on education to redress society's ills and provide a better future:

> Many citizens want a return to the basics, but they also want art, music, computers, sex education, foreign language, athletics, vocational education, and a dozen other topics taught. Multiple constituencies need to be served, each wanting education to fulfill its version of the American dream. While education continues to be the hope for America's ills, it also serves as a focal point for public debate and criticism.[15]

A number of studies have attempted to assess objectively the state of education in the United States. One analysis reported that 30 percent of adolescents and young adults in the United States lacked basic literacy skills (as determined by the National Assessment of Educational Progress),[16] thereby impairing the chances in the labor market of a large component of the population. American students also were found to perform more poorly than students in most other industrialized countries on comparable tests of mathematics and science knowledge. This disparity in performance has been attributed more to socioeconomic circumstances, such as the percentage of families living below the poverty line and the percentage of students living in female-headed families, than to school practices, such as the amount of time devoted to mathematics instruction and the time that students spend on homework.[17] On average, African-American and Latino students score lower than white students, and children whose parents went to college score higher than children whose parents did not. Some researchers have concluded that improving the socioeconomic conditions of disadvantaged children and providing all students with challenging curricula may be the keys to improving the education of American children.[18]

Attempts to achieve educational reform have pursued different lines of attack. The National Council of Teachers of Mathematics took eight years to produce curriculum and evaluation standards for school mathematics, and similar developments of standards in other disciplines are under way. New assessment standards have been adopted or studied in many states, some of which have chosen to follow the privately funded New Standards Project, which has as its goal to develop assessments based on national standards that will increase expectations about what students should learn and encourage teachers to introduce school-based reforms.[19]

Corporate-supported organizations have addressed the need to increase students' incentives to work harder in school and to take more difficult courses. The Bush administration proposed that high school seniors take voluntary achievement tests in five core subjects, and encouraged employers and colleges to use the results in making their employment and admission decisions.[20] An alternative is to provide "situated learning" experiences for students to integrate academic material with occupational preparation.[21] Models for situated learning include the career academy (adopted extensively in California) for disadvantaged youth which combines strong support with incentives for students to learn and achieve,[22] and technical preparatory programs combining the final two years of high school with two years of community college leading to an associate's degree.[23] Too little research has been conducted to provide scientifically valid evaluations of the success of these alternative school-to-work transition programs.[24]

Debates have arisen over what performance indicators to use in assessing the adequacy of competing proposals for education reform. One of the most severe barriers to rational approaches to such assessments is the confounding effect of family background. Differences in student achievement measures across or within school districts may appear because some schools improve their mean performance ratings by barring low-achieving students or students from disadvantaged families, or just by getting them to stay home on the day that standardized tests are administered. Teachers may improve their own ratings of instructional effectiveness by working only in schools that already benefit from enrolling children of higher-income and better-educated parents and therefore can afford better salaries, equipment, and working conditions. One partial solution to this uncertainty over valid evaluation criteria may be to define improvement as the degree of progress toward achieving targets.[25]

Demonstrating how best to stimulate schools and school districts that need to upgrade their performance also confronts those who desire rational approaches to education policy. Schools may perform below par due to inadequate funding, bad hiring decisions, poor training of teachers, corrupt officials, or intractable societal problems. Proper solutions cannot be adopted and implemented rationally without first diagnosing problems correctly. As one example of concrete steps toward rational diagnosis and resolution, Kentucky has specified, in its Education Reform Act of 1990, that schools experiencing a decline of more than 5 percent in successful students are considered to be in a state of crisis, must develop an improvement plan, and become eligible for supplemental funds. This carrot-and-stick approach to improving deteriorating education environments also assigns an established education expert from another school district with the power to transfer or dismiss employees, and permits students to transfer to a more successful school.[26] Related efforts have been undertaken by other states.[27]

The most generally used and most widely accepted way to evaluate program success is to apply standardized tests to students across schools and school districts. The results of standardized testing are critical for teachers and administrators. Poor test findings can lead to firing academic officials and teachers, lower salaries, and possibly loss of control to outside authorities. Signs of such stress are evident in many states and localities. Beginning in 1997, Kentucky teachers' retention and salary bonuses are determined by their students' test scores, and all students must be tested as a requirement for graduation. The superintendent of the Minneapolis school system is paid according to attainment of performance objectives for students in the entire district and for students from minority groups. Sixteen other states and six districts, as of 1994, took part in the New Standards Project, cosponsored by the Learning Research and Development Center at the University of Pittsburgh and by the National Center on Education and the Economy, in Rochester, New York. This project assesses all students according to high standards and certifies scores only if schools can prove that every child was tested.

There is a serious threat to the validity of using standardized tests as a measure of progress in educational effectiveness over time: regression toward the mean. When a student scores below an acceptable level—that is, flunks a standardized test for moving on to the next higher grade and thus is held back at the lower grade level—that student is likely to score better by virtue of having the opportunity to restudy the same material that will appear on the next test. One solution to this problem is to adjust the scores of students who have failed such examinations previously. It also would help to replace multiple-choice tests with authentic assessment or performance-based tests that more closely resemble classroom learning. Performance-based tests include different types of writing, research projects, or portfolios of the students' work, and generally are seen as providing better evaluations of analytical skills. At least part of student assessments in twenty states are based on performance-based tests. The Goals 2000 legislation supports the development by states of voluntary standards and new testing instruments. State and local education leaders worry that national testing may lead to federal officials ranking state or district performance with noncomparable measures.

Scientific evidence regarding the efficacy of higher levels of per student expenditures has been mixed. Differences in student achievement across school districts do not correlate strongly with level of resources provided, even after controlling for socioeconomic differences.[28] The conclusion of this research—that increasing inputs into the educational process does not lead directly to better student performance—has been used to justify positions taken by conservative opponents of higher education expenditures. From this perspective, it is misguided to try to equalize educational outcomes across school districts.

Some researchers contend that the problems confronting American society also plague the nation's schools, and that those problems are tied integrally to inequalities of income and life chances. One-fifth of children in the United States live in families with poverty-level incomes and bring to their schools the consequences of physical and mental problems at home. Learning is thus hindered, particularly among children whose families have experienced racial, social, or economic discrimination. Liberals contend that students are disadvantaged because children from such backgrounds are likely to attend schools that lack the resources to alleviate the negative consequences of their histories.[29] One concrete manifestation of these compounded inequities is the fact that young adult black males who attended urban high schools earn about 9 percent less than comparable black males who attended suburban high schools.[30]

The Power Input

Education policymaking proceeds from decentralized authority over that arena. The federal role is largely one of providing limited financial support and general guidelines to state and local authorities who administer the education system. Washington, DC, supplies only about 6 percent of the roughly $200 billion annual budget for the nation's elementary, intermediate, and high schools. Although it is more important at the college level, even there the federal fiscal role encompasses only about 25 percent of the $50 billion annual higher education expenditures.[31]

Lacking a cohesive or coherent locus for national education policy, there are innumerable opportunities for interest groups and government officials to have an input in the outcomes of a convoluted process. Louann Bierlein, a leading education policy specialist, traces this condition to the provisions of the United States Constitution that grant to the federal government only limited implied powers to regulate the system of education.[32] The possibility of a national approach to education would require that greater power reside with federal authorities, and less with the states. Such innovations as a national curriculum or uniform student testing and evaluation have been supported by conservative proponents of education reform and are likely to be received well by Republican congressional majorities.

Balancing the power given, both expressly and implicitly, to federal education authorities is the Tenth Amendment to the United States Constitution, which reserves to the states any governmental powers that are not within the federal sphere. Largely as a consequence of the Tenth Amendment, education has become a responsibility of the states. State constitutions obligate their governments to support a system of free public education. State legislatures have enacted extensive legislation to provide resources for public education and to uphold standards. On average, one-half of precollegiate public education is funded through state revenues; thus, oversight of the education infrastructure and of its administration is a major objective of state legislative bodies. One or two committees within each state legislature emphasize education issues, from kindergarten to graduate school. Considerable influence over education policy is wielded by the chairs and staff of these committees.

The scope of the U.S. education system guarantees that education policy affects huge numbers of Americans and a very large component of the national economy and work force. In 1990, nearly 50 million students were enrolled in the primary and secondary schools (from kindergarten to twelfth grade); of these, 88 percent attended public schools and the remaining 12 percent went to private schools, most of which had a religious affiliation. Almost 3 million teachers were employed by elementary and secondary schools, and another 2.5 million employees provided professional, administrative, and support functions. Over $200 billion was spent annually on primary and secondary education.[33]

The complexity of education policymaking in the United States is compounded by the multitude of influences at work. What Bierlein characterizes as numerous constituencies within "the tangled lines of authority and power"[34] include government entities—Congress, the U.S. Department of Education, the U.S. Supreme Court and lower federal courts, governors, state legislators, state boards of education, state departments of education, state courts, school boards, and school administrators—and nongovernmental groups, such as teachers' unions, parent-teacher associations, student organizations, businesses, public interest groups, private foundations, testing and textbook companies, taxpayers' groups, or civil rights and civil liberties organizations. These multiple layers and entities involved in education policymaking result largely because the United States effectively has no national system of education, with most authority vested in state and local government.

The Boston, Massachusetts, school system illustrates the issues that confront education policymaking at the local level. Typical of many urban school systems, the Boston public schools have a racially diverse student body of 60,000 students in 117 schools. Recent problems and issues included debates between superintendents and school board members about governance; low test scores and high dropout rates; little to show from frequent program innovations; poverty, racial tension, and other social concerns; and severe budgetary constraints. A 1989 blue ribbon study expressed the consensus that the schools were not fulfilling their mission, but there was much less agreement on the nature of the problem. Ultimately, the problems that received the most attention included weak governance, inadequate school programs, and limited finances, because these issues were highly visible, had strong political sponsorship, and viable solutions existed.[35]

Despite constant criticism of the expense of education and persistent efforts by conservative groups to limit public expenditures generally, U.S. investment in education as a percentage of gross domestic product is lower than that of many other industrial countries—notably, Japan, France, and the United Kingdom.[36] Extended school days, year-round education, enhanced preschool opportunities, and more effective training for a high-technology workplace and the challenge of global economic competition—all require political commitment and citizen support for the funding that is essential to make any reformed or "reinvented" education system function as it must in the future.

Public support for education reform varies over time with changing perceptions of how well public education provides what is expected of it. Almost by definition, because there are drastically different beliefs about what education should do for American society, the process of education policymaking will always be evolving to meet new demands and expectations. In 1994, the Public Agenda Foundation conducted a survey of public attitudes regarding the accomplishments and shortcomings of education in the United States.[37] The survey revealed declining support for education reform, which the public believes has failed to come to grips successfully with school violence, discipline, and basic skills development. Forty-one percent of respondents believed that too many teachers emphasized their popularity with students over instilling respect and discipline, 88 percent agreed that students should not be allowed to graduate from high school until they can demonstrate basic writing and spoken English skills, and 81 percent felt that students should be passed on to a higher grade only after demonstrating that they had learned what they were expected to learn, rather than gaining "social promotion" for having made an honest effort.

In general, these responses are not consistent with the contemporary education reform agenda. However, other public attitudes are more consistent with popular reforms in American education goals and practices. For example, in the Public Agenda survey, 61 percent responded that schools should teach "respect for people who are homosexual," and 80 percent agreed that schools should convey the message that "girls can succeed at anything boys can." Teaching the biology of sex and human reproduction was supported by 95 percent of respondents, although 14 percent felt that schools spent too much time on sex education.

There is an important duality in public opinion regarding the performance of American education. A 1991 Gallup poll[38] showed that only 21 percent of respondents gave public schools nationally a grade of "A" or "B," but 42 percent gave those grades to schools in their own communities. In addition, 72 percent gave "A" or "B" grades to the school attended by their oldest children. Thus, Bierlein concludes: "The debate on restructuring schooling is driven by both the perception of American parents that education is satisfactory in their own backyard and by the need to please a very large constituency."[39]

Accountability of efforts at school reform are imperative because of pressures from both elites and citizens to ensure that increased spending improves the quality of the education system. Outcome-based accountability, in which performance is evaluated regularly and remedial actions are undertaken to enhance performance when it has not met expectations, has emerged as the favorite tool for assessing the consequences of reforming education.[40] To avoid the problem that teachers may merely instruct students to perform well on standardized tests, and thus make the instructors or the school system look like top performers even though other aspects of education go unfulfilled, alternative measurement systems are needed to ensure accountability. Among these are the South Carolina approach of collecting multiple performance indicators, including student attendance and dropout rates, in addition to measures of student skills,[41] and the suggestion by the Carnegie Corporation[42] that parents, teachers, and principals negotiate mutually agreed-upon performance goals with local school boards.

Most teachers belong to unions that are active in bargaining over issues such as wages, hours, and working conditions. Those unions are often militant in pressing their demands through strikes, demonstrations, and exercising political pressure. The National Education Association (NEA) has more than 2,000,000 members, accounting for about two-thirds of all public school teachers, and the American Federation of Teachers has another 500,000 members. The combined strength of these two unions has been regarded as one of the strongest political forces in the United States.[43] The NEA maintains a major political action committee and has mainly supported Democratic candidates. This support led to a major success in the creation of the United States Department of Education following Jimmy Carter's 1976 victory over Gerald Ford.[44] With a strong organizational infrastructure and ample funding, the NEA and AFT also wield substantial influence at the state and local levels. Their backing is essential for the successful implementation of major education reforms.

Other public groups exercising varying degrees of control over education policy include the Parent Teachers Association, the American Association of School Administrators, the National Association of Secondary School Principals, the Council of Chief State School Officers, the Education Commission of the States, the National Council of State Legislators, and the American Educational Research Association. Private organizations, such as companies that distribute tests or publish textbooks, also actively influence the outcomes of education policymaking. Bierlein concludes: "In reality, the legal and informal authority of these various groups is not clearly defined; no one entity has primary control over the educational system. Instead, educational governance involves multiple players trying to implement multiple missions" (i.e., a pluralistic environment).[45]

The elections of 1996, in which Democratic candidates generally did well against Republican opponents, provide an important perspective on the role played by, and the limits of, the power perspective on education policy. Postelection assessments led Republicans to reconsider the vehemence with which they had attacked public education with great success from about 1980 to 1994 and less successfully in 1996. Following their failure in 1996 to defeat President Clinton, many members of the GOP leadership urged a reconsideration of the party's threats to dismantle the U.S. Department of Education, believing that stance had cost votes, especially among women. A postelection survey sponsored by the Republican National Committee showed that Clinton received 59 percent of the vote among women, and Dole only 35 percent, although Dole carried the male vote by 49 percent to Clinton's 39 percent. The same survey led to the conclusion that Republican problems with women voters were due largely to perceptions that the party was hostile toward public education without offering new resources or autonomy to improve local schools. Senator Spencer Abraham (R-MI) concluded: "Instead of talking about abolishing the Department of Education, we should be talking about sending more money back to mothers and fathers. Closing the Department of Education translated into less benefits for your children."[46]

The Ideological Input

Bierlein has summarized the philosophical evolution of U.S. education from other developments within American society:

> While our forefathers did not set out to design a system in which only a certain number of students would succeed, the structure of American schooling was driven by the goal to educate the masses, including an ever-growing number of immigrants. It gathered input from scientific management principles during the 1930s, the same strategies used to sharpen industrial processes in factories during that time. It was also driven by an American public that expected schools not only to educate their children, but also to solve all of society's ills. Finally, to minimize the threat of centralized control, a very decentralized state, rather than national, system was created. It was not one master plot, but instead a strategy that evolved to educate a burgeoning population, using teachers who resemble blue-collar laborers more than professionals. Much like American industries, schools are now being forced to change toward a high-tech model.[47]

Two leading public policy scholars—Rita Mae Kelly and Dennis Palumbo—have noted: "Controversy is the norm rather than the exception in education. That is because the system has tried simultaneously to fulfill the conflicting goals of equity, efficiency, choice and excellence."[48] Such controversy is rooted in the integral relationship between education and democratic political systems, in which access to education plays a major role in equalizing economic and social class distinctions, sustaining economic growth and national security, and providing opportunities for future generations. Precisely because of its intimate connection with most families' most precious possessions—their children—education policy strikes a sensitive chord with American citizens.

Education policy inherently involves clashes of different perceptions of what is right and wrong about American society: "Education is the principal instrument through which societies pass on values and norms to future generations of citizens"[49] regarding equity, efficiency, liberty, and excellence. Debates over education policy largely revolve around the contradiction between conservatives' emphasis on an education system with little or no government control that maximizes individual choice, and liberals' preference for strong government oversight to provide equal access for all students. Conservatives support the rights of parents to choose whether to send their children to private or public schools, oppose bilingual instruction, support the inculcation of patriotic values, and promote confining education to academic pursuits. In contrast, liberal perspectives on education include using education to foster social equality, mitigate the negative effects of a free-enterprise market economy, open students to new ways of thinking, prepare students for a secular pluralist society, and provide bilingual instruction and programs for vocational training and self-awareness. Conflicts over goals and the means to attain those goals are inherent in education policy.

One of the most contentious education policy issues is the conservative attempt to turn public education over to private businesses. Support for privatization usually comes from more conservative elements in the policymaking debate; the liberal position is to support public control of the education process through existing political institutions and public employees. Jersey City, New Jersey, illustrates the political difficulty inherent in such efforts. In 1994, Mayor Bret Schandler and the state's Republican governor, Christine Todd Whitman, backed a school voucher plan, as did the president of the American Federation of State, County, and Municipal Employees union Local 2262, to partly reimburse parents who send their children to private or parochial schools. The blue-collar members of his local voted him out of office. Their reaction was understandable, because members of his union feared that mass layoffs inevitably would result from the voucher plan.[50]

In 1992, Education Alternatives Inc. (EAI), a Minneapolis corporation specializing in privatizing schools, was given a five-year contract worth $140 million to operate eight schools in Baltimore, Maryland. On October 18, 1994, however, the superintendent of the Baltimore schools reversed an earlier public announcement by stating that test scores at the EAI-run schools had dropped dramatically at the same time that test scores for the other Baltimore schools had improved. EAI's claims of cost efficiency were offset by the reality that the Baltimore school board had allotted an additional $600 in spending per pupil in the EAI-run schools, which led to angry complaints by the parents of children attending other institutions. At least six city council members called for the immediate termination of EAI. The city council president stated: "This system cannot afford to squander its credibility and resources on a pilot project to the detriment of the schoolchildren." Another city council member who originally supported the EAI project concluded, "I have to believe that this experiment has run its course. It's time to pull the plug on EAI."[51]

In October 1994, the Board of Education of Hartford, Connecticut, the state's-second-largest school district, with 24,000 students, voted, by six to three, to hire EAI to manage its thirty-two public schools. This was the first time an entire public school system was placed under private management. The system had received over $100 million annually in state aid, allowing it to spend annually about $8,450 per pupil, more than many wealthy suburbs could afford. However, Hartford schools had the lowest average standardized test scores in the state, and student performance was declining. Nearly two-thirds of the students were on welfare, and most came from homes in which English was not spoken.

EAI would repair and maintain school buildings, purchase all supplies, re-train teachers, and assist each school in adopting new curricula. The school board retained final decision-making authority, and the company was required to report to the school superintendent. One-half of any savings remaining after expenses were to be given to the company as profit. The other half was to go to the education board, which agreed to return most of it to the city to demon-strate to taxpayers the benefits of private education management.[52]

Chicago's Mayor Richard Daley has supported school privatization efforts, commenting that the city's public schools were "no longer a sacred cow" and that they were a waste of money.[53] He justified full privatization of the city's schools on grounds that their poor condition had driven middle-class white families out of the city, eroding the tax base. His privatization drive was sup-ported by Sharon Grant, president of the Chicago Board of Education, who had pursued actively the privatization of janitorial, food, and other school serv-ices. Opposition arose from other members of the Board of Education, the Chicago Teachers Union, and groups representing African-Americans and Latinos, among others.

While Daley criticized the quality of public schools in Chicago, as chair of the Chicago Public Building Commission—the bonding agency that funds school construction and repair—he had failed to release over $250 million raised through bond issues to finance badly needed school capital improve-ments. In 1988, Chicago had begun a program of radical decentralization of public schools, giving greater authority to locally elected school boards and to parents' groups. However, funding to implement new ideas that had emerged from that reform effort had been stymied by a severe financial crisis that re-quired teachers to use their own salaries to buy necessities like toilet paper for public school students.

One of the major private-sector programs designed to apply entrepreneurial skills to administering public schools is the Edison Project, financed by Chris Whittle, and planned for widespread implementation in 1995. Originally con-ceived as a national chain of private schools educating two million students by 2010, the scaled-down goal of the project was to take over a handful of public schools based on an academy system relying on team-teaching small groups that remain together over several school years. The emphasis was on recogniz-ing individual student differences in rates of learning, combined with high tech-nology, a longer school day, and an extended school year. The first school to sign on with the Edison Project was a new elementary school in Mt. Clemens, Michigan. The large Charleston County, South Carolina, school district, with 46,000 students, pulled out of a previous agreement due to concerns about how adequately the project would be funded by venture capitalists. The Project's early record of spending $40 million for research and development, market studies, travel expenses, and high salaries for its officials was not promising to many prospective investors. Academic luster was added to the project by the participation of Benno Schmidt, former president of Yale University.[54]

Another education policy debate, over bilingual education, provides a particularly sharp conflict between competing conservative and liberal values. Conservatives tend to regard students with limited English proficiency as being handicapped culturally and needing remedial assistance to overcome their language deficiency. More extreme versions of this viewpoint regard the United States as a monolingual, English-speaking society and offer assimilation as the best way to bring students with limited English proficiency into the mainstream. Many liberals see the primary language of the student as a national resource for a multilingual society dominated by English speakers. Proponents of the liberal view conclude that non-English-speaking students must be trained in the common American language, but want to enrich the educational environment for every student by including other languages in the curriculum.[55]

Nationally, about two million (5 percent) of the nation's school-age children are classified as limited in English ability,[56] including over 18 percent of the student population of New Mexico, and more than 16 percent of children attending school in California. Proponents of instructing students in both English and their native language believe that bilingual instruction will better foster nonnative-English-speaking students' integration into the educational process, and hence into American society more broadly. An additional assumed benefit of bilingual education is sensitizing English-speaking students (and their parents) to other cultures. In October 1994, a New York City Board of Education study concluded that the city's efforts to educate 154,000 students in their native languages were flawed (at an annual cost in excess of $300 million in 1993–1994). The study revealed that students taking most of their classes in English performed better academically than did students in bilingual programs who received less exposure to English-based instruction. The study questioned the benefit of the city's bilingual programs taught in Spanish, Chinese, Haitian Creole, Russian, Korean, Vietnamese, French, Greek, Arabic, and Bengali.[57]

During the Reagan and Bush administrations, education policymakers who favored the "English only" solution to students with limited English proficiency gained greater credibility. U.S. English, an interest group that emerged from the Federation for American Immigration Reform, argued that American society is held together by a common language and that its stability is threatened by drift toward bilingualism. Combined with movements to restrict immigration, groups favoring English-only curricula fostered state legislation or initiatives to control education policy and sponsored a constitutional amendment to declare English the official language of the United States.

The proposed use of tax-funded vouchers to allow parents to buy access to education at any public or private school has been another key element of the conservative policy agenda.[58] This extends conservative arguments favoring the efficiency of free market competition over the equity-driven concerns of the public sector. Voucher supporters believe that private schools are inherently better vehicles than public school systems to raise student performance because they see public schools as being too constrained by bureaucratic regulations to use resources efficiently.[59] The opposing view is that potential gains from vouchers are minimal and that voucher plans will exacerbate inequalities in educational access and quality.[60] Opponents point out that only minimal differences exist between mean achievement scores for private- and public-school children, despite the advantage of private-school students coming from better-educated families. National data show, for example, that among high school seniors 55 percent of those in public schools had not mastered reasoning and problem-solving involving fractions, decimals, percentages, elementary geometry, and simple algebra, compared to 46 percent of Catholic-school students and 49 percent of students attending other private schools. About half of the students who attend each type of school graduate from high school lacking strong basic mathematical skills.[61]

To opponents of voucher programs, these findings suggest that "[s]imply increasing the number of students attending private schools would do little to improve mathematics achievement."[62] The advantage on average in private-school student performance over public-school student performance is small compared to variation in performance indicators among all public schools or among all private schools.[63] Such findings may lead to policy prescriptions to make a larger number of public schools work more effectively, rather than to redirect national resources and attention away from public institutions to private ones. Although public-school proponents may concede that some practices, such as teacher hiring, are in need of revamping, they are less likely to agree that expenditures for compensatory education, bilingual education, and learning-disabled children should be reduced or eliminated because they see such programs as making schools more responsive to students' needs.[64] Ultimately, arguments over public versus private education must accommodate those who have little market power, such as children from low-income families and students with disabilities. Previous initiatives such as voucher plans and compensating more heavily families with lower incomes or other special needs, have failed to attract volunteers to the experiment.[65] The effects of other proposed innovations—magnet schools, alternative schools, or open enrollment—are modest compared to what might be gained from improving the curriculum.

A strongly market-based approach to education reform such as vouchers is supported by conservative proponents of education policy changes, who argue that the only way to redress perceived inadequacies of the education system is "to start thinking systematically about education as a market in which producers are driven by financial incentives."[66] The market proponents argue that inflation-adjusted costs of public education more than doubled from 1970 to 1990, with no corresponding improvement in test scores from reduced class sizes, hiring teachers with advanced degrees, wage increases outpacing productivity, mandates to educate handicapped children, and bureaucratic growth.[67]

Economists such as Eric Hanushek note that the solution is to construct incentive structures linking rewards to outcomes of the education process, which can be attained, they argue, by decentralizing education policymaking so that each school and teacher enjoys more latitude for experimentation. Critics of that approach see this as tantamount to a shift toward "market socialism" and away from the current "regulated monopoly," because they believe that this amounts to trying to simulate competitive markets where they do not or should not exist. Critics also complain that it is unrealistic to believe that correct incentives can be identified and implemented, because teachers naturally would train students to perform well on standardized tests rather than emphasizing less readily quantified skills or goals, and because decentralized control might be achieved at the cost of reduced teacher professionalism.[68]

The 1996 presidential election brought into sharp focus differences in philosophies regarding education policy. Republican candidate Bob Dole's campaign emphasized state tuition vouchers to break the power of government and teachers' unions on public education. He also favored tax-deductible interest on student loans, tax-sheltered family college education investment accounts, tax breaks for employers who pay workers' education costs, and abolishing the U.S. Department of Education. In contrast, the Democrats' campaign featured $5 billion to reduce interest costs for school construction bonds, increased funding for Head Start, support for technology education, $1,000 merit scholarships for the top 5 percent of high school graduates, and a "Hope Scholarship Tax Cut" that would provide to all high school graduates a $1,500 tax credit (or cash for families with limited tax liability) for the first year of college tuition and further credits for students maintaining a B average and not convicted of a drug felony.[69]

Application of RPI to Education Policy: Performance Evaluations and Resegregation

The interplay among the rational, power, and ideology perspectives on education policy is clear in contemporary efforts to evaluate the performance of education in the United States. Much of this evaluation is predicated on the rational viewpoint of policymaking, but the ideological input and to a somewhat lesser extent the power approach also play a major role.

The rational framework for understanding education policy is represented by recent empirical studies designed to evaluate how well the country as a whole is approaching the attainment of policy goals and to compare the degree of education reform among the states. For example, a 1996 study supported by the Pew Charitable Trusts gave no state consistently high grades for progress in education policy on seventy-five measures in six major areas: standards for student achievement; quality of teaching; school climate measured in terms of safety, class size, and building condition; spending per pupil; allocation of money to classroom and other activities; and the degree of equity with which funding was apportioned between wealthy and poor districts.[70] Among the top-ranking states were West Virginia, Kentucky, Vermont, Georgia, Indiana, and Maine; the lowest-ranked states included Arizona, Mississippi, Louisiana, Idaho, and

Nebraska. The report found that states whose students performed best on the National Assessment of Educational Progress (N.A.E.P.) did so because of relatively homogeneous populations and the absence of distressed urban areas rather than because of aggressive implementation of education policy.

A related opinion survey of educators showed that 96 percent of superintendents and 93 percent of teachers agreed that "rigorous content standards" were critical for building effective public schools. The poorest performances were found in Louisiana, where 85 percent of that state's fourth-graders read below the standard, and Mississippi, where 94 percent of eighth-graders scored below the level establishing reading proficiency. Although Maine had the highest N.A.E.P. scores for fourth-grade reading, 59 percent of fourth-graders in that state were unable to meet the goal for the year 2000 of being able to read at grade level. Similarly, Iowa students scored highest on N.A.E.P. mathematics, but 69 percent of Iowa eighth-graders could not perform proficiently.

The rationality perspective is also evident in the annual appraisals published by the National Education Goals Panel's evaluation of progress toward fulfilling the mission of the Goals 2000 agenda. The 1995 report, for example, found evidence of better national performance in improved health of infants, an increased proportion of preschoolers who are regularly read to and told stories at home, increased mathematics achievement at grades four and eight, more female students receiving degrees in mathematics and science, and declining threats and injuries to students at school. However, significant deterioration was found in seven areas: decreasing reading achievement at grade twelve, a decreased percentage of secondary school teachers holding a degree in their main teaching assignment, an increased gap in adult education participation between those with and without postsecondary education, increased student drug use, increased sale of drugs at school, increased threats and injuries to public school teachers, and increased reports of disruptions in classrooms that interfere with teaching. Finally, no discernible progress was reported toward reducing the gap in preschool participation between rich and poor districts, improving the high school completion rate, increasing reading achievement at grades four and eight, increasing mathematics achievement at grade twelve, increasing the number of degrees in mathematics and science awarded to minorities, reducing the gap in college enrollment and completion rates between white and minority students, reducing the percentage of students who reported using alcohol, and reducing student reports of classroom disruptions that interfere with learning.[71]

The ideological component of contemporary education policy is illustrated by the thinking shown in a study of curriculum reform conducted by the Office of Educational Research and Improvement of the U.S. Department of Education. The barriers to change emphasized in that report attest to the need to change the thinking of those involved most intimately in the educational system. The barriers to reform were said to include the beliefs and values of everyone involved in education; lack of teacher preparation to teach constructively; the need to reeducate students to their role in learning constructively;

the need for new instructional, curricular, and assessment materials to support changes in teaching and learning; and tensions associated with instituting the new educational system while operating within the old system.[72] The report emphasized: "Of critical importance to the reforms are changed values and beliefs about the goals of instruction and the means of fostering this learning. To reform education in the full sense demands more than the acquisition of new teaching strategies and techniques."[73]

The role of ideology in education policy today also is demonstrated by the debate over goals. Should excellence and quality of education lead to the sacrifice of wider societal goals of equality and racial balance? A Harvard University study released in 1997 concluded that the nation's schools are becoming resegregated at the fastest rate since the 1954 Supreme Court decision in *Brown v. Board of Education of Topeka* (347 U.S. 483), which struck down "separate but equal" education facilities for school children of different races. Instead, recent court decisions making it easier to dismantle desegregation plans have isolated Hispanic students even more than African-American students in predominantly poor and minority school districts.

Between 1991 and 1994, the percentage of minority students enrolled in schools with substantial white enrollments declined substantially, particularly in suburbs and in the South. In 1972, following the 1971 Supreme Court decision mandating school busing (*Swann v. Charlotte-Mecklenburg Board of Education* [402 U.S. 1]), 63.6 percent of African-American students attended schools in which less than half of the student body was white. Currently, that proportion has risen to 67.1 percent, and nearly 75 percent of Hispanic students attend predominantly minority schools. In 1980, the typical African-American student attended a school that was 36.2 percent white, versus 33.9 percent in 1997; the typical Hispanic student attended a school that was 35.5 percent white, compared to 30.6 percent white in 1997. At the same time, from 1968 to 1994, the number of Hispanic students in public schools increased 178 percent, and the number of African-American students expanded by 14 percent, compared to a decline of 9 percent in the number of public school white students.[74] This may reflect diminished commitment to liberal goals such as attaining racial balance. The author of the 1997 Harvard University report, Gary Orfield, argues that racially segregated schools are inadequate because they do not help minority students overcome previous disadvantages and do not prepare white students to exist in a more integrated society.

The role of the power perspective in education policy is clear from the manner in which education issues are decided. Actions are taken through an elective process, including the selection of school boards, state legislatures, Congress, governors, and the presidency. In addition, as is clear from the discussion above, many of the key policy actions affecting education come through court decisions, which are influenced not just by scholarly and judicial interpretations of the law but also by interest group demands and by political trends and societal pressures.

HISTORY OF EDUCATION POLICY

From Colonial Times to World War II

The first law passed in the future United States affecting education policy was the "Old Deluder Satan Act" of 1647 that required every Massachusetts town of fifty or more families to hire a teacher, thus establishing the principle that public responsibility for education would be vested in the local community. Elementary school instruction, however, was minimal, limited in many cases to basic literacy training so that children could read the Bible, and attendance at secondary schools was limited to upper-class males prepared for the ministry or political careers. Prior to and during the American Revolution, education policy disagreement revolved around whether a democratic polity was served best by national or localized control. A major issue was whether religious schools should receive public funding, contrary to the widely held preference for separating church and state. The emerging synthesis, persisting until the mid-nineteenth century, was a system of locally controlled and locally funded nonsectarian public schools, with students generally required to attend for only a few years. The values underlying this education structure were exemplified by Thomas Jefferson, who argued for minimal schooling for all and additional education only for an elite, as the surest way to ensure political stability.

Stimulated by the advocacy of reformers such as Horace Mann, by the 1830s the United States had moved toward a publicly financed elementary level of mass "common school" education. Mann viewed an educated citizenry as improving standards of living for everyone and equalizing conditions among people from varying social strata. By 1860, over one-half of school-age children in the United States were attending school. Property taxes came to be the main source by which local communities, given authority and responsibility by the states to operate public schools, financed this expanded access to education. Higher education also expanded substantially, partly to satisfy the growing demand for trained teachers, often in the form of state-supported teacher-training "normal schools."

A rapidly growing immigrant community, needing both work training and acculturation to a new country, along with the rising demand by an industrializing economy for more comprehensive education contributed to the emergence of mass-based secondary education by the mid-nineteenth century. Debates over secondary-school curriculum arose regarding whether vocational or academic preparation should be emphasized. By 1918, Congress attempted to resolve this curricular tension by providing federal support for vocational education programs, to help meet the demands of industry and to direct the futures of immigrant sons and daughters. This approach was enshrined in "The Cardinal Principles of Secondary Education," propounded by a group of leading educators. These principles held that the secondary-school curriculum should emphasize "health, worthy home membership, vocation, citizenship, worthy use of leisure time, and ethical character."[75] Most high schools adopted a highly utilitarian character for the majority of students, with only a small elite tracked into higher education preparatory programs. Systems of sorting and tracking students into those destined for more menial or more challenging types of employment were adopted early in the twentieth century to deal with the rapidly expanding ranks of high school students.

The need for public education grew during the Great Depression (1929–1941), which ended only with the nation's reindustrialization during World War II. The lack of jobs during the Depression, coupled with the belief that education was a road to future employment opportunities, resulted in rapidly growing secondary school enrollments. Between 1930 and 1941, the number of high school students grew from 5 million to over 6.5 million; secondary school graduation rates exceeded 50 percent for the first time in 1941. John Dewey's "progressive education" ideas gained currency, emphasizing learning "by doing" and critical thinking. Comprehensive public high schools, providing academic, practical, and workplace skills, emerged as curricula were rewritten to focus on "real life" and egalitarian concerns.

From World War II to the 1960s

Post–World War II society had a still greater need for education to provide practical skills and life training for an exploding population and for increasingly complex jobs. Nonacademic programs expanded, and a reaction developed among proponents of a greater commitment to academic excellence in public education.[76]

As the optimism of the immediate postwar era melted into the complacency of the 1950s' "happy days," American education was forced to contend on several fronts with developments that accentuated conflicts between equity and excellence. The Supreme Court's 1954 ruling in *Brown v. Board of Education of Topeka* found that segregated schools were inherently unequal, and focused attention on the dire need for federal assistance to minority and other low-income segments of the population. The emerging emphasis on equity was reinforced by the Civil Rights Act of 1964.

In 1957, the Soviet Union launched *Sputnik*, the world's first artificial satellite. This development gave greater urgency to the national defense basis for federal aid to public education, to avoid Cold War defeat by producing future generations who were better trained in technical subjects. Congress responded in that year with the National Defense Education Act, which provided millions of federal dollars for education in mathematics, science, and foreign languages. New curricula were constructed, large numbers of new teachers were trained, and the focus of education shifted dramatically to the pursuit of excellence through academic rigor. This focus faded, however, when the perceived threat from Soviet scientific successes had subsided.

The 1960s and 1970s

The emphasis on equity persisted as perhaps the dominant theme of American national education policy throughout the 1960s and 1970s, which were punctuated by student demonstrations against the war in Vietnam, for civil rights and free speech, and by governmental efforts to remedy past societal inequities. An important part of President Lyndon Johnson's Great Society was the $1.5 billion Elementary and Secondary Education Act of 1965, which funded remedial course work and other efforts to strengthen equal opportunity. The consequence of those decades was to ease graduation requirements and to maximize elective choices for students, as well as to encourage team-taught courses, open classrooms, and federal and state laws protecting access to education for racial and ethnic minorities, the handicapped, those with limited proficiency in English, and women.

A reaction against what frequently was dismissed as "permissive" education grew in the late 1970s. The emphasis of this revisionism was on academic rigor, opposition to civil rights and antipoverty efforts, and "back to the basics." Minimal skill levels for students were established, and pressure built to raise falling standardized national test scores and other performance indicators as visible evidence that the nation could compete in the global economy. Financing the higher level of educational performance, however, became a major problem, as tax limits were adopted in seventeen states between 1976 and 1980,[77] in reaction to dissatisfaction with public schools and with the failings of government more generally.

The role, if any, to be played by religion in public education remains a volatile component of education policymaking in the United States. About 12 percent of all school-age children from kindergarten to high school attend private schools, and 85 percent of all private schools are affiliated with a religious denomination. Probably the most visible aspect of this element of education policy is the debate surrounding school prayer. In 1962, in the case of *Engel v. Vitale* (370 U.S. 421), the U.S. Supreme Court reviewed the suggestion by the New York State Board of Regents that a prayer be spoken aloud in the public schools at the start of each school day. The parents of several students affected by the Regents' prayer challenged the action as a violation of the "no establishment" clause of the First Amendment to the U.S. Constitution, which states that "Congress shall make no law respecting an establishment of religion."

Although the parents lost initially when this issue came to trial, that result was overturned by the U.S. Supreme Court's ruling that "the constitutional prohibition against laws respecting an establishment of a religion must at least mean that in this country it is no part of the business of government to compose official prayers for any group of the American people to recite as part of a religious program carried on by any government." In part, the Court's reasoning in *Engel v. Vitale* was based on the "historical fact that governmentally established religions and religious persecutions go hand in hand." Furthering these principles, in its 1963 case of *Abington School District v. Schempp* (374

U.S. 203), the Supreme Court banned daily readings of the Bible and recitation of the Lord's Prayer in public schools.

Religious pressure groups have lobbied state legislatures to ban the teaching of Darwin's theory of evolution in public schools. The attempt by Arkansas to enforce such a law was overturned by the U.S. Supreme Court in its 1968 *Epperson v. Arkansas* decision (393 U.S. 97) because the legislation violated the separation of church and state by imposing religious beliefs on students. The Arkansas legislature responded by passing a law that required teaching the biblical version of creation as an alternative to evolution. In 1982, that effort also was ruled unconstitutional by the Supreme Court.

Limits have been imposed on public support for many other aspects of private education. In 1971, in *Lemon v. Kurtzman* (403 U.S. 602), the Court ruled that direct state aid could not subsidize religious instruction. It declared unconstitutional a Pennsylvania law using state resources to pay private schools for the cost of teachers' salaries in nonreligious courses because it provided direct benefits to parochial schools and their sponsoring churches. Government aid to religious schools can be constitutional when the purpose of the aid is secular and must not have the primary effect of either advancing or inhibiting religion, and the government must avoid "excessive entanglement with religion." Any legislation arising under the First Amendment's "no establishment" clause is subject to this three-part test. This has led, for example, to refusal by the Supreme Court to sanction state reimbursement to religious schools for students' field trips and for developing achievement tests.

The inequities inherent in financing school district expenditures based primarily on property taxes were challenged in court during the late 1960s with the argument that children in property-poor school districts were denied the Fourteenth Amendment's guarantee of equal protection under the laws and were thus subjected to unconstitutional discrimination. This approach was unsuccessful until the 1971 California Supreme Court ruling in *Serrano v. Priest* (487 P.2d 1241), which held that unequal distribution of funds for education violated the constitutions of both the United States and California. However, a 1973 U.S. Supreme Court ruling, *San Antonio Independent School District v. Rodriguez* (411 U.S. 1) reversed this decision, holding that the Fourteenth Amendment was not violated by the disparate allocation of state tax resources. Consequently, recent rulings regarding school financing have been based on provisions of state constitutions; because these are not uniform, there have been inconsistent court decisions on this element of education equity.

In reaction to successful or threatened lawsuits, many states have passed new or revised equalization statutes providing additional state funding to districts with lower levels of property wealth and have initiated programs for special education and for students with limited ability in English. However, considerable disparities persisted because in most cases higher-income districts did not impose spending ceilings.

The 1980s

In the early 1980s, support had grown for innovations such as vouchers that would give parents a choice of tax-supported private education if they were dissatisfied with available public school alternatives. Graduation requirements were increased; teachers' salaries were tied to performance; and standards for teacher certification were enhanced. Most notable among the commissions that attacked the education status quo was the National Commission on Excellence in Education, which in 1983 released its report, *A Nation at Risk: The Imperative for Educational Reform*, which called upon the country to react vigorously to a crisis in education quality. In the next three years, thirty-five states adopted legislation reforming education processes and structures.

With at best mixed evidence of success in these efforts and rising dissatisfaction with the incompleteness of the early-1980s innovations, renewed momentum for new approaches appeared in the late 1980s. Emphasis was placed on "reinventing" education through an emphasis on equality of performance (rather than access), restructuring school administration, decentralizing decision making, stricter accountability, and making schools more attuned to market needs. Such efforts have been undertaken by groups such as the National Alliance of Business, the Committee for Economic Development, the Business Roundtable, and the National Governors Association. Their work was predicated on the idea that great improvements would occur by running education like a business. Initiatives such as increased parental choice and training students to meet market needs were emphasized. Whether this is seen as desirable and effective depends largely on accepting the premise that private-sector approaches are appropriate to public education. Barriers exist to implementing the business perspective popularized in the 1980s and early 1990s, because some national reform leaders

> either do not understand or refuse to accept the differences between education and business. Policymakers seeking to reform education, as well as those analyzing educational public policies, need to understand the organizational and legal constraints on public education in order to minimize conflicts and maximize the probability of success.[78]

President Reagan initiated and accentuated policy debates on a number of matters dealing with education. William Bennett, Reagan's secretary of education, advocated tuition tax credits and actively opposed bilingual education. The Reagan administration fostered a "New Federalism" approach to education policy, by which responsibility and funding for many policies would devolve to the states. A similar thrust was pursued by Bush's secretary of education, Lamar Alexander, as exemplified by the America 2000 program that stressed enhancing the nation's education system to meet new competitive challenges.

Beginning in the late 1980s, funding equity cases emphasized state constitution provisions regarding education, rather than the equal protection clause of the Fourteenth Amendment. The language of state constitutions was fairly standard: to maintain "an efficient system of common schools" (Kentucky), "an efficient system of public free schools" (Texas), or "such laws as shall provide for the establishment and maintenance of a general and uniform public school system" (Arizona).[79] This approach was successful in lawsuits brought in Montana, Kentucky, and Texas (1989), New Jersey (1990), and Tennessee (1991).[80] A dramatic change in the tenor of rulings came in the 1989 Kentucky decision, which declared the entire statewide system of public schools to be unconstitutional, rather than just the system of school financing that had been the subject of previous court actions. This landmark case established the premise that financial equity was as important as quality in guiding state court decisions on education funding.

In 1985, another Supreme Court ruling in the case of *Wallace v. Jafree* (472 U.S. 38) overturned an Alabama law that authorized a minute of silent reflection in all public schools for prayer or meditation. The Court's majority opinion held that the law specifically endorsed prayer, and thus appeared to support religion. However, despite the firmness of Supreme Court rulings on state-sponsored religious practices in public schools, state governments have attempted to enact contrary legislation. Opposition to the Court's actions has been strongest in the South. In 1983, the Tennessee legislature adopted a law requiring public school classes to start each day with a minute of silence, following several years' effort by that state's legislature to bring "meditation, prayer, or silent reflection into school." A similar law was enacted in Alabama.

The Contemporary Case

Recent efforts at reforming education necessitate common action by federal, state, and local governments, in combination with teachers' organizations, courts, and public and private interest groups. These include the New Standards project, coordinating seventeen states' development of performance-based assessments of student achievement, and activities of the National Board for Professional Teaching Standards, working with states to develop assessments of teachers' skills. The federal role in such efforts largely amounts to providing funding and facilitating these and related movements.

The need for clearer direction from the federal government to coordinate national-level activities influencing elementary and secondary education is evident from the fact that many overlapping, redundant, and often contradictory institutions are shaping federal education policy. For example, sixteen federal agencies and eight congressional subcommittees address issues associated with mathematics and science education. This fragmentation and overlapping of largely uncoordinated policymaking bodies arises from fear that local schools might be dictated to by a strong national government.[81] Federally assisted efforts to coordinate other interests may reduce the often conflicting messages that federal policies send to school districts and help to make federal programs to improve education in the United States more effective.[82]

Funding

State courts have contended that the predominantly local property tax basis of funding for public education in the United States has further accentuated disparities between school districts. The most obvious consequence of this pattern of unequal educational financing is that the relative degrees of wealth among adults living in different school districts tend to perpetuate for the children their parents' and other adults' more privileged or disadvantaged social positions. The ancient dream that education might serve as a "great leveler" is therefore turned into myth. Sharp disparities are to be found in per-pupil expenditures across different districts. The general pattern is for school districts having large per-pupil tax bases also to have higher spending per student and relatively low property tax rates, and for school districts with smaller per-pupil tax bases and low per-pupil spending to have comparatively higher tax rates. Starting in the late 1960s a number of state supreme courts declared the then-existing state system of school financing (that depended heavily on property tax revenues) unconstitutional. Where this has happened, the pattern commonly has been for state funds to replace or supplement local revenues, particularly in formerly underfunded districts with smaller property tax bases. The result was to even out disparities in local property tax rates, but not by enough to bring per pupil expenditures to a point of rough equality.[83]

Until the late 1970s, the primary source of funding for most school districts was local property taxes. The major consequence has been to create severe disparities within states (and between them) in per-pupil funding in different school districts. Absent mitigating forces, students living in high-property-value localities are guaranteed better education financing than are students from less-well-off areas. A series of court rulings and legislation beginning in the late 1960s addressed these inequitable conditions.

The U.S. Department of Education is one of the leading actors in the fiscal federalism that underlies the national government's role in the predominantly state and local process of education policymaking. Among other programs, the department administers vocational and adult education, compensatory education for the disadvantaged, bilingual education, education for the handicapped, Indian education, and school improvement programs. Other components of the executive branch administer such major education programs as child nutrition, Head Start for preschool children, Job Corps, and related training programs.

Although federal financial support encompasses only about 6 percent of the total annual cost of precollegiate education in the United States, the money (over $20 billion per year) comes with regulations on the behavior of state and local education officials. The result of these restrictions is continued friction between state and local officials, who want greater autonomy, and federal officials, who attempt to smooth out the inequities that otherwise would become more severe if state and local authorities had a freer hand. Federal assistance generally is tied to programs designed to introduce greater equity into the education process.

Expanding enrollments and deteriorating physical facilities in aging school structures are giving rise to the need to better finance the nation's education system in an era of fiscal limits. Schools currently spend about $5 billion a year to repair and expand buildings, but the General Accounting Office has estimated $112 billion in urgent construction needs. Clinton's secretary of education, Richard W. Riley, estimated in 1996 that the 80,000 existing schools would need to expand by the construction of 6,000 new schools over the next ten years, at an average price of $10 million per new school. The U.S. Department of Education also estimated that by 2006, space would have to be found for another 3 million children, for a total of 54.6 million students, owing to the "baby boomlet" from the children of baby boomers (born from the mid-1940s to the early 1960s) entering school age years, as well as higher African-American and Hispanic birth rates, greater immigration, increased percentages of young children entering prekindergarten and kindergarten, and reduced high school dropout rates.[84]

Disadvantaged Students

The U.S. Congress has played its principal role in education as the source of funding and rules that facilitate and regulate certain aspects of an otherwise locally or state-controlled policy process. A focus of federal efforts has been to improve education opportunities for disadvantaged students and their families, as manifested particularly in Title 1 of the Elementary and Secondary Education Act of 1965. Subsequently renamed Chapter 1, this funding supported services for 5 million children in over 50,000 schools, at a cost of $6.1 billion.[85] Bowing to political pressures, in 1988 Congress reauthorized Chapter 1 with a number of changes. In particular, schools in which at least 75 percent of its students were eligible for Chapter 1 assistance were permitted to spend the funds on programs that would improve the entire school rather than on just the children targeted for support. Accountability criteria for individual schools were established, and schools that did not meet achievement state standards were targeted for improvement. However, because gains in student achievement were measured only at the end of the first grade, support for kindergarten and first-grade students was discouraged because it was advantageous not to have initial test scores elevated. For similar reasons, it was beneficial for schools to hold students back from advancing to higher grades.[86]

Measuring Progress

Some schools were able to demonstrate extraordinary increases in their test scores by giving standardized tests selectively to only a limited number of students.[87] Even marginal changes in student performance can make the difference between a school's benefiting from its students' apparent performance level and being placed on probation and possibly taken over by the state. To avoid such outcomes, there is a strong incentive, particularly for administrators of marginal schools, to exclude low-scoring students by holding them back in lower grades, placing such children in remedial work, or by assigning them to special education or bilingual classes.

Meeting the needs of severely disabled children living in poverty is an especially difficult component of contemporary education policy. In 1990, the Supreme Court ruled that too many children who needed assistance were being denied Supplemental Security Income (SSI) payments averaging about $400 a month. The result was rapid growth in the number of recipients (from about 300,000 in 1990 to 800,000 in 1994) and in expenditures (from $1.2 billion to $4.5 billion). These changes were a consequence partly of the Court's order that the Social Security Administration advertise the new eligibility regulations and make retroactive payments. Local governments also benefited from this arrangement because the Aid to Families with Dependent Children program required local governments to match funds while the SSI program did not require a local government match.[88]

Affirmative Action

On October 27, 1994, the United States Court of Appeals for the Fourth Circuit, in Richmond, Virginia, ruled in the decision of *Kirwin v. Podberesky* (38 F.2d 147) that the University of Maryland could not continue its Benjamin Banneker scholarship program, which was limited each year to thirty African-American students. Justified as compensation for previous discrimination against African-Americans, the lawsuit that ended the program had been brought by a white Hispanic student who was rejected for a Banneker scholarship. The court decreed that such scholarships should be available to members of other minority groups.

The future of other financial assistance programs for specified groups was left in doubt, including programs such as those for students with particular family names (such as at North Carolina State University or Harvard University), for Native American freshmen or transfer students talented in the visual or performing arts (at the University of Wisconsin-Eau Claire), for left-handed students (at Juniata College), for children of disabled firefighters and peace officers (at the University of Houston at Victoria), for dependents of a full-time Lutheran church worker (at Valparaiso University), for students pursuing a career in food crop production who are United States citizens and New Mexico residents (at New Mexico State University), for young women who were Girl Scouts for at least three years (at Reed College), or for an Eagle Scout who received the religious award (at Brown University).[89] When the University of California system ended its affirmative action program under pressure from Governor Pete Wilson, the future of such programs nationally also was jeopardized.

Limiting School Autonomy

In addition to actions taken by their legislatures, states also exercise control through elected or appointed state boards of education and chief school officers such as a superintendent of public instruction or a commissioner of education. The chief school officer oversees a state department of education and executes policies adopted by the legislature or by the state board of education. The state departments of education are responsible for distributing federal funds and for ensuring that the state complies with federal laws and regulations. States commonly also have regional or county school officials (operating agencies located between state and municipal-level officials) that provide varying combinations of control over, or support services for, local school districts. For state undergraduate and graduate institutions, education policy is commonly made through a board of regents, which tends to be sensitive to changes in the political climate.

Elected local school boards control the activities and operations of school districts. These boards often establish tax rates, generate the revenue needed to offer education services, hire and fire personnel, and set salary levels. Although nominally autonomous, school boards can be subject to pressures from parents, teachers, taxpayers, or other groups. Also, their autonomy has decayed over time, as federal and state authorities have come to exercise increased influence over education policy. States that have mandated funding equalization across school districts or that have restricted local school boards' latitude in granting parental choice over their children's schooling have reduced the autonomy of local school boards. Consolidations have reduced the number of local school districts nationally from 120,000 in 1938 to 15,000 in the early 1990s, thereby limiting the number of elected school officials. Some states, such as Kentucky and Illinois, have moved recently to implement radically decentralized school-site management that removes some personnel decisions from school board control. Other states, such as Arizona, have considered removing nearly all powers from the local boards.

Since the early 1980s, state governors have taken a more active and more visible role in education policy. Rising public discontent with achievements of the contemporary education system and with the financing of that system has forced state leaders to recognize the political advantages in giving education reform a prominent place in their policy agendas. It has become popular to link enhanced education systems with economic development and tax relief. Many governors have increased their visibility in education policy by hiring specialists and developing comprehensive plans for reform. Bill Clinton of Arkansas, Lamar Alexander of Tennessee, John Ashcroft of Missouri, and Richard Riley of South Carolina are examples of governors or former governors who became recognized as leaders in education reform.

Moment of Silence and School Prayer

Recently, at least six states—Georgia, Virginia, Maryland, Mississippi, Tennessee, and Alabama—have enacted legislation mandating a moment of silent reflection as a means of circumventing U.S. Supreme Court rulings banning mandatory prayer, and other states have considered similar actions. At least one Georgia teacher was suspended, and later fired, for telling his social studies students that he regarded the law as unconstitutional. The lower federal courts have issued conflicting rulings about whether students may lead prayers at school events such as pep rallies or football games.

The movement to establish a moment of silence for meditation, and possibly for prayer, in public schools has gained momentum partly because of strong public support. This support has come from otherwise unlikely alliances of African-American urban leaders, clergy, and liberal supporters of civil liberties. It has become common to interpret silent reflection as a weapon in the war against crime and violence. For example, Georgia state Senator David Scott, a liberal legislator favoring gun control and public school sex education, has argued: "We have young people drifting into heinous crimes. Girls joining gangs and having illicit sex with every gang member. No matter how many midnight basketball games you start, there is a missing ingredient. Young people need to communicate with their inner compass."[90] Washington, DC, mayoral candidate Marion Barry, in his successful comeback primary bid in 1994 following imprisonment, argued for school prayer in a city suffering from the nation's highest murder rate.

Nonetheless, the main pressure for reintroducing school prayer has come from conservative Christian groups whose agenda has much more to do with inculcating their values in school children than in preventing violence. Jay Sekulow, chief counsel for the American Center for Law and Justice, a "think tank" affiliated with Pat Robertson's Christian Coalition, argues: "This is coming from the soul of America. We need a moral guidepost for our children. Opponents are treating 'pray' like it's a four-letter word."[91]

Various programs of parental and student choice among available schools have been implemented by state governments. Wisconsin was the first state to incorporate private schools in a statewide education choice program, initially to about 600 low-income students attending nonsectarian private schools. The level of Wisconsin state funding, of about $2,700 per public school student, covers less than half of the total private school annual cost of about $6,500 per student. In contrast, the school choice program implemented in Minnesota does not involve private schools. Instead, public school districts compete among themselves for students on differences in curriculum offerings and extracurricular activities.

Charter Schools

One of the innovations currently spreading among the states is the notion of "charter schools," which operate autonomously under a state charter rather than under the control of a local school district. Proponents of charter schools maintain that their movement is an attempt to extend choice over public school education opportunities to a wider array of families, and a means by which parents who are committed to public education can expand their choices within that structure. However, the legal, financial, and physical requirements for starting a new charter school generally are significant. Charter schools are established under specific mission statements and goals for student learning, and can lose their charters if they fail to attain the goals under which they were set up. Such alternative schooling arrangements generally are pushed by parents and educators displeased with the range and quality of the choices in standard public school systems. Like public schools, charter schools are open to all children, are accountable to taxpayers because of their public funding base, and are subject to state and federal laws regarding health, safety, civil rights laws, and provisions in the law for the desegregation of their facilities. The first charter law was adopted in Minnesota in 1991, followed by at least ten other states. By 1994, a total of about 100 charter schools existed nationwide, with Colorado having the largest number per capita.

Among the questions concerning the future of charter schools are the following: (1) Would the charter be granted by the local school district or by the state, and how many charters may be granted? (2) What will need to be done to facilitate start-ups of charter schools, and what will be done to make it easier for low-income and minority communities to participate in the process successfully? (3) What role, if any, will religious instruction play? (4) Which children may enroll, and who will make the decisions about admission?[92]

Opposition to the charter school movement comes particularly from teachers' unions, administrators of school districts, and leaders of minority groups, who argue that charter schools drain away money and parental support from other public schools that are already hard-pressed to maintain their financial and parental bases of support. Opponents also claim that favoring charter schools is elitist, since it attempts to establish what are in effect very selective schools within the framework of public education. In addition to the charter school alternative, citizens concerned about the quality of public education also advocate the use of vouchers, or payments from governments that permit parents to choose to send their children to private schools with tax funds; the privatization of education systems; and home schooling, under which parents educate their children at home.

Recent education policy developments in Michigan demonstrate how the state adoption of charter schools legislation may be tied to other issues, particularly school finance. By 1993, school districts relied on local property taxes for 70 percent of public school funding. This led to vast disparities in per-student spending across school districts, stimulating Michigan to adopt charter schools legislation following extended debate and many failed efforts to enact statewide school taxes. From 1972 to 1993, Michigan voters rejected twelve of thirteen property tax proposals. Advocacy coalitions of groups and individuals interested in education reform combined with policy entrepreneurs to provide a resolution to this impasse. In the summer of 1993, the state legislature and its governor abolished the local property tax as a source of school funding, and the resulting climate of uncertainty about future school finance provided an opportunity for school reform advocates to gain approval of legislation approving charter schools.[93]

Workforce Training

The need for more effective education and training of the workforce is an increasingly important dimension of contemporary education policy. This is a function of demographics. In 1960, at the height of the baby boom, the 59 million children in the United States under age sixteen almost equaled the 69 million members of the workforce. New workers aged eighteen and over expanded the workforce by about 5 percent per year, so that average labor skills could be enhanced rather quickly by new entrants into the labor market. In the 1990s, the number of children under age sixteen is roughly what it was in 1960, but the workforce has grown to about 125 million. Adult education for job training therefore holds as much promise as traditional schooling for raising skill levels among those already employed.[94] This is a looming political issue, because of the growing disparity in salaries between workers who possess only high school degrees and those with college educations. On average, college-educated workers in 1979 earned 47 percent more than the average high school graduate; by 1993, the difference had grown to 82 percent.[95]

The federal role in job training is modest, mirroring the situation for primary and secondary education. Federal efforts have emphasized programs, such as the Job Training and Partnership Act, to assist low-income workers. However, unlike their dominant role in primary and secondary education, state and local governments have played only a limited role in job training, by supporting economic development activities and community colleges for vocational and technical training. Some experts argue for a stronger federal presence by facilitating the formation of consortia or associations among employers, and by training disadvantaged workers,[96] while others argue against focusing the debate too narrowly on the job-training aspects of education, at the expense of overlooking questions that are related more closely to pedagogy, institutional considerations, and politics. David Paris concludes: "How we respond to questions about critical thinking, general and vocational education, and equal opportunity has profound policy implications for our schools, as does our weighing of the civic, cultural, and economic goals of education. Thus, it is important that the current (and somewhat misguided) consensus about the relationship of education to the economy not foreclose critical exploration of these issues."[97]

Contemporary Controversy

Goals 2000 and Control of Education Reform

ON MARCH 31, 1994, President Clinton signed into law the Goals 2000: Educate America Act (PL 103-227). The act lays out eight national education goals to be obtained by the year 2000:

1. All children in America will start school ready to learn.
2. The high school graduation rate will increase to at least 90 percent. (Actual state graduation rates are shown in Table 7.2.)
3. All students will leave grades four, eight, and twelve having demonstrated competency in challenging subject matter, including English, mathematics, science, foreign languages, civics and government, economics, arts, history, and geography; and every school in America will ensure that all students learn to use their minds well, so they may be prepared for responsible citizenship, further learning, and productive employment in our nation's modern economy.
4. United States students will be first in the world in mathematics and science achievement.
5. Every adult American will be literate and will possess the knowledge and skills necessary to compete in a global economy and exercise the rights and responsibilities of citizenship.
6. Every school in the United States will be free of drugs, violence, and the unauthorized presence of firearms and alcohol and will offer a disciplined environment conducive to learning.
7. The nation's teaching force will have access to programs for the continued improvement of their professional skills and the opportunity to acquire the knowledge and skills needed to instruct and prepare all American students for the next century.
8. Every school will promote partnerships that will increase parental involvement and participation in promoting the social, emotional, and academic growth of children.[98]

Under the Goals 2000 legislation, a substantial number of federally supported and federally funded programs were continued or initiated. A partial listing of these initiatives is presented in Table 7.3. The main point to note from the table is the extensive array of social and economic needs that Congress has attempted to address under the broad rubric of education policy. In reality, what is labeled "education policy" entails policies related to multicultural awareness, combating disabilities and prejudice, and supporting research, among many other goals, as much as it has to do directly with what and how students learn in the nation's schools and colleges.

The debate over Goals 2000 illuminates much of the contemporary process of education "reforms," which properly also might be thought of as radical restructuring, or even as attempts to reinvent structures and processes that are regarded by many critics

TABLE 7.2 Public High School Graduation Rates, 1992–1993 (percent of fall 1989 ninth-grade enrollment)

State	Graduation Rate (percent)	State	Graduation Rate (percent)
Alabama	61.7%	Montana	86.7%
Alaska	73.4	Nebraska	86.9
Arizona	72.0	Nevada	69.6
Arkansas	78.4	New Hampshire	78.4
California	67.9	New Jersey	85.8
Colorado	75.3	New Mexico	68.2
Connecticut	80.8	New York	65.4
Delaware	70.2	North Carolina	67.6
District of Columbia	64.6	North Dakota	85.8
Florida	61.4	Ohio	75.0
Georgia	61.6	Oklahoma	75.9
Hawaii	74.9	Oregon	72.6
Idaho	82.3	Pennsylvania	80.6
Illinois	78.0	Rhode Island	75.5
Indiana	75.1	South Carolina	59.2
Iowa	87.5	South Dakota	89.1
Kansas	80.3	Tennessee	67.4
Kentucky	72.7	Texas	59.4
Louisiana	56.3	Utah	80.7
Maine	74.3	Vermont	82.0
Maryland	75.6	Virginia	74.2
Massachusetts	78.1	Washington	75.6
Michigan	69.9	West Virginia	77.9
Minnesota	89.1	Wisconsin	83.5
Mississippi	63.5	Wyoming	86.9
Missouri	72.8	**United States**	**71.1**

Source: National Center for Education Statistics, U.S. Department of Education.

of current policy as outdated and counterproductive. Some states have pursued policy initiatives to entice better-qualified college graduates into the teaching profession. Competitive teaching salaries produce larger numbers of college graduates aspiring to careers in education; once hired, they are more likely to stay in the profession longer than are teachers who experience instruction as a low-paid stepping stone to a "real" career.[99] During the 1970s, real wages of teachers nationally declined by about 20 percent. Comparatively sharp increases in teachers' pay during the 1980s essentially eliminated that deficit, although teachers effectively were no better off after those raises than they had been back in the early 1970s.[100]

(continued)

TABLE 7.3 Partial List of Programs Supported by the Goals 2000: Educate America Act 2000 of 1994 (PL 103-227)

Undergraduate International Studies and Foreign Language Program

International Research and Studies Program

Fulbright-Hays Faculty Research Abroad Program, Doctoral Dissertation Research Abroad Program, and Group Projects Abroad Program

Endowment Challenge Grant Program

Administration projects, demonstration projects, research projects, training and resource center projects, and administration projects under the Cooperative Education Program

Law School Clinical Experience Program

Projects under the Minority Science Improvement Program

Business and International Education Program

Centers for International Business Education Program

Dwight D. Eisenhower Leadership Development Program

Innovative projects for community service under the Fund for the Improvement of Postsecondary Education

Research in Education of Individuals with Disabilities Program

Early Education Program for Children with Disabilities

Services for Children With Deaf-Blindness Program

Grants for personnel training, and for parent training and information centers, under the Training Personnel for the Education of Individuals with Disabilities provision

Postsecondary Education Programs for Individuals with Disabilities

Programs for Children with Severe Disabilities

State Systems for Transition Services for Youth with Disabilities Program

Secondary Education and Transitional Services for Youth with Disabilities Program

Special Studies Program to assess the impact and effectiveness of programs and projects assisted under the Individuals with Disabilities Education Act

Technology, Educational Media, and Materials for Individuals with Disabilities Program

Program for Children and Youth with Serious Emotional Disturbance

Vocational Rehabilitation Service Projects for Migratory Agricultural and Seasonal Farmworkers with Disabilities

Community-based Special Projects and Demonstrations for Providing Supported Employment Services to Individuals with the Most Severe Disabilities and Technical Assistance Projects Rehabilitation Long-Term Training

Vocational Rehabilitation Services Projects for American Indians with Disabilities

Experimental and Innovative Training Program

Rehabilitation Continuing Education Programs

Licensing is being employed in some states to mandate teaching competence, to induce more creative teacher-training programs, and to improve classroom performance. Conventional licensing, based on completing specified teacher training programs and achieving acceptable scores on subject-matter multiple-choice examinations, would be supplanted by measures of how well the prospective teachers conduct their classes.

Attracting and retaining teachers—particularly in specialties such as mathematics and natural science, and teachers from minority backgrounds—is a major concern of education policymakers at the state and local level. State and federal programs have been developed to recruit teachers by forgiving at least part of their education loans. However, it is unclear whether such programs have been successful in drawing nontraditional or higher-quality educators into the profession, nor is it clear to what extent teaching career decisions may be affected by greater degrees of loan forgiveness.[101] Some states also have employed alternative programs for licensing teachers, usually involving shorter training periods.

It is important to note that contemporary education policy, emphasizing the devolution of authority to successively lower levels, has arisen from what is perceived to be overcentralized control. This seemingly overcentralized control originated in a reaction against what appeared in the early twentieth century to be a chaotic state of public education characterized by far too many school boards and related entities. With a primary goal of increasing the efficiency of the education system, the early twentieth-century reform movement was designed to adapt mass-production principles to the education of rapidly growing numbers of students, many of whom were the offspring of recently arrived immigrants and thus seen as needing rapid acculturation and Americanization. The scientific management movement produced "teacher-proof" schools characterized by "centralized decisionmaking, inflexible work rules and schedules, and standardized curriculum,"[102] as well as a drastic reduction in the number of school districts and elementary schools.

Contemporary restructuring concepts run the gamut, from creating school-site councils (Kentucky, Chicago, Los Angeles); overhauling state departments of education into support centers rather than regulatory mechanisms (Kentucky, Virginia); awarding waivers of state rules and regulations; creating new curricula tied to assessing student performance (Arizona, California, Vermont); enhanced funding for demonstration projects in nongraded schools; site-based management; year-round schooling (Washington, Texas); subcontracting public school district management out to private, for-profit corporations (Duluth, Minnesota) or to a university team (Chelsea, Massachusetts, which works with Boston University); and channeling corporate or foundation money into "break-the-mold" schools (the New American Schools Development Corporation).

The process of restructuring and reorganizing public education in the United States promises to be messy and highly politicized. This is inherent in the constraints imposed by the accessibility of teachers, administrators, and policymakers to public and media scrutiny. In contrast, corporate restructuring is not subject to the openness of democratic processes and can be undertaken in private without much concern to alternative viewpoints. As noted by The Business Roundtable: "Restructuring education . . . will be much more difficult than restructuring corporations. Education is a public institution with public visibility. An immense number of groups and organizations are powerful stakeholders."[103] Unresolved questions in implementing school reorganization include how best to involve parents, incompatibilities between restructuring and school-site decisionmaking, and public knowledge about the advantages and drawbacks to both the current and proposed future arrangements.

(continued)

One of the reputed virtues of more centralized policymaking is its greater concern for equity, by reducing disparities in available resources and by making it easier to transfer resources to areas where they are most needed. Modern labor markets and evolving high-technology communications require uniform competency levels, skills, and certification; thus, centralization, to some extent, is beneficial. In contrast, decentralization provides for greater diversity and recognizes the presence of different cultural environments. Bierlein finds that "there is a basic tension between decentralization on one hand and the tendency of the modern state to assert or reassert centralized control over the educational system on the other."[104]

Accountability of schools is complicated in a decentralized setting, because current accountability measures focus more on inputs than on outputs of the education process and because it is difficult to monitor complex comparisons among alternative strategies. Whether decentralization will enhance efficiency is also debatable. Economies of scale generally work in favor of larger, more centralized organizations, but supporters of radical decentralization allege that implementing their proposals will allow funds to be diverted to areas of greater need.

The debate over education restructuring addresses the distinction between "top-down" and "bottom-up" management. As Bierlein expresses the dilemma, "Should the mandate come down from above, or should the top simply allow, encourage, and guide those at the bottom to change? Or is some combination of these the best?"[105] The 1988 decentralization of Chicago's 594 schools was mandated by the Illinois legislature, which specified the precise composition and authority of each school council. In sharp contrast, the Dade County School Based Management/Shared Decision Making restructuring model resulted in local school boards with strong authority over personnel and budget decisions.

States and individual school districts also have resorted to issuing "warranties" on their graduating students, in an effort to restore public and business confidence in the quality of the educational process. In general, warranty programs permit employers to send graduates lacking in certain basic skills (such as reading, writing, mathematical calculations, or higher-level skills such as computer literacy and team problem-solving) back to high school for remedial training. Some districts have also adopted a "certificate of employability," which attests to work habits and general skill level. One consequence of such arrangements has been to redirect teachers and school administrators away from reliance on "social promotion" of students who lack basic educational skills.

The drive for accountability lies at the heart of much of the contemporary debate over education policy. Beginning in the 1980s, states rapidly expanded the use of educational achievement tests as one means to attain accountability. The National Commission on Testing and Public Policy reports that 127 million standardized tests are administered annually to precollege students, and that 20 million school days are devoted each year to those tests.[106] This amounts to about three tests per student each year. What is most needed is a way systematically to link the results of these tests with curriculum, goals, outcomes, rewards, and sanctions.[107]

Merit pay plans were implemented spottily in some school districts during the 1960s and 1970s, but recently have become a major component of education policy reform plans. The basic premise of merit pay proposals is to provide greater salary rewards to teachers who have demonstrated superior levels of performance, the reward usually taking the form of a bonus added to the base salary. This runs directly counter to the egalitarian emphasis of teachers' unions and the patterns of seniority-driven salary steps incorporated into contracts that originally provided for salary parity for women teachers and for teachers at all precollege levels. Similarly, career ladder programs are designed to reward high-performing teachers with promotions to higher levels within the teacher ranks and with salary stipends, in return for their assuming more demanding responsibilities. Relatively little research has been conducted to evaluate the efficacy of merit pay and career ladder policies, in part because of a widespread reluctance to connect teachers' rewards to students' performance. An alternative to merit pay and career ladders is the concept of group rewards, providing collegial, rather than competitive, opportunities for advancement. This alternative approach is supported more strongly by the American Federation of Teachers than by the National Education Association. Some states provide salary bonuses for exceptional collective performance, but in general these programs are badly underfunded.[108]

Some states have also implemented incentives for students. These include "guaranteed tuition assistance" programs providing college financial support for the families of students who perform well academically and who meet income eligibility criteria. Often part of broader state goals of economic development, such programs are tied to core curricula course work, overall high school grade point average, standardized test scores, abstinence from drug usage, enrollment in state colleges or universities, or low family income. They may tap students as early as the lower elementary grades, and provide one step along the route to a national policy of universal access to higher education.

Just as positive incentives have been proposed to enhance educational quality, negative group or individual sanctions have also gained currency. At least fourteen states have adopted "academic bankruptcy" provisions that permit state agencies to intervene in school districts that do not attain required outcomes or requirements. Districts may be required to implement corrective actions, may be taken over by state officials, or the local school board may be dissolved. Examples of districts that have suffered the "death penalty" include the Jersey City School District in New Jersey in 1989, the Hedrick Public Schools in Iowa, and the Central Falls School District in Rhode Island.

Student-directed sanctions have also been attempted. At least fourteen states during the mid-1980s enacted "no pass/no play" provisions requiring students to maintain minimum grade-point averages to remain eligible for extracurricular sports and other activities. Limited research on the subject, however, indicated minimal impact of these provisions.[109] Extensions of such student sanctions are the more contemporary "no attend/no drive" or "no pass/no drive" rules adopted by at least a dozen states. Depending on the particular state statutes, driver's licenses may be denied or suspended for students who fail to meet minimum requirements by dropping out, receiving failing grades, or not attending classes. Some states and school districts have also adopted sanctions against parents who do not assume responsibility for their children's education. "No attend/no welfare" provisions adopted by, for example, the Chicago Public Schools or the state of Wisconsin, can lead to court supervision, fines, and imprisonment of parents, or to reduced welfare benefits for families whose children accumulate too many unexcused absences.

Case Study

The Kentucky Reforms as a Model for the Future?

IN A 1989 ruling, the Kentucky Supreme Court ruled unconstitutional the state's entire system of public schools, on grounds that there was no justifiable basis for the extreme disparities in the amount of financial resources available to school districts. The court acted in response to a suit filed against the state's education system by sixty-six school superintendents from districts with low property tax bases.

Direct results of that ruling included a complete overhaul of the state's system for financing public schools, and corresponding changes in how Kentucky's public schools were organized and administered, through the 1990 Kentucky Education Reform Act (KERA). To pay for the required changes, an increase of almost $1 billion in taxes for the first fiscal biennium followed the court's ruling. The possibility that other states would follow suit gave rise to questions of funding equity in state education policy, in addition to the traditional concern over the quality of education. Funding issues are plagued by the obvious political complexities associated with redistribution of a fixed funding pie from wealthier to poorer residents of a state, combined with limitations on the right of wealthier neighborhoods to increase their tax levies for the purpose of funding higher than average expenditures, and loss of local control over funding decisions.

Several specific changes were undertaken by Kentucky,[110] in pursuit of the goals established by that state's Supreme Court. School councils were formed, for site-based decision making. Local school boards were stripped of the power to hire and fire school personnel, with the exception of the school district superintendent. All positions within the state department of education were eliminated, and all employees were terminated, at the end of the 1990–1991 state fiscal year. The revamped department rehired many of its previous workers and was restructured to establish regional service centers. A new, governor-appointed State Board for Elementary and Secondary Education was established, replacing the elected Superintendent of Public Instruction. The Board, in turn, hires a Commissioner of Education to oversee the state system. An independent legislative Office of Education Accountability was established, to monitor the outcomes of the restructured educational system. Both district-and school-level rewards and sanctions were developed. The first three primary grades were replaced by an ungraded "primary school program." In an effort to establish better coordination between material taught in the classroom and material over which students are tested, matching curriculum frameworks and performance-based assessments were developed. Additional funding was made available to the schools, to provide extended school days, weeks, or years for students who require additional support. Developmentally appropriate half-day preschools were established for all at-risk four-year-olds. The nonschool needs of students and families were supported by a network of family and youth resource centers. A statewide fiber-optic system, telephones in every classroom, and other technological innovations are under development.

Financial rewards are provided for schools experiencing an increase in the proportion of students that perform above an established threshold. The amount of that award is determined by applying the percentage set by the legislature to the salary levels of each certified staff member employed in the schools, and that award is to be distributed by majority decisions taken by the school staff. The other side to this provision is that schools failing to show improvement, or with declining performance, will lose revenue or autonomy. Schools that do not show advances in student achievement scores must develop an improvement plan, but become eligible for special state grants. After two years, if no improvement has occurred, a Distinguished Educator will be assigned to make extensive changes in how that school is run. Failure to improve after the third year results in declaration of a "school in crisis," which means that all certified staff are placed on probation, parents are given the right to transfer children to a successful school within the district or to one outside the district, personnel may be reduced or transferred if overstaffing results from declines in student enrollment, and the Distinguished Educator is empowered to make binding decisions about retention, dismissal, or transfer of school staff. Evaluations will be held every six months until the school is no longer in crisis. Schools evidencing declines of up to 5 percent must develop an improvement plan, become eligible for improvement grants, and will have at least one Distinguished Educator assigned with the power to implement changes.

Central office staff are eligible for rewards when the entire school district is successful. Likewise, the superintendent and school board may be dismissed if the entire district is declared to be in crisis. Additionally, an Office of Educational Accountability has been created as an independent arm of the legislature, to monitor the education system and the implementation of the Educational Reform Act.

Conservatives have generally been critical of KERA, arguing that the reforms were more faddish than successful. Opposition to the 1990 legislation was central to the 1995 gubernatorial campaign of Republican Larry Forgy, who nearly won the election with 49 percent of the vote. Between the 1989–1990 and 1993–1994 academic years, state and local expenditures per student increased by 40 percent, rising from $3,079 to $4,291. The expenditure gap between rich and poor districts declined substantially, and preschools for low-income children became widespread. An ungraded primary school program from kindergarten to third grade permitted students to progress at their own pace. Expenditures of $136 million vaulted Kentucky to rank seventh among the states in the ratio of computers to students. Counseling centers for Family Resources and Youth Services and tutoring programs operating after school were established in over 800 schools. From 1992 to 1994, increased student achievement was recorded in 78 percent of Kentucky's schools; average scores advanced 22 percent for fourth-grade students, 13 percent in the eighth grade, and 9 percent among high school seniors.

Support for the reform program, however, as measured by public opinion polls, fell to just 40 percent approval in March 1996 from 57 percent three years earlier. Opposition centered around uncertainties associated with the ungraded primary schools structure and expert criticisms of the state's assessment test as conceptually flawed and overstating gains from the reforms. Gains in student performance do not

(continued)

show up consistently when measured by national tests such as the National Assessment of Education Progress and the American College Test taken by high school seniors.[111]

Case Study Questions

1. Do you feel that your state's education system is in need of the kind of dramatic actions taken in Kentucky? Why or why not?
2. How can you tell that a school is in a state of "crisis?" What indicators would you use to make that determination?
3. If your high school had to be taken over by a school district or by state officials, what changes would you make? What should the school do to get out from under receivership?
4. Do you believe that a Kentucky-style program should be implemented nationwide? What problems can you foresee in any attempt to nationalize the Kentucky experience?
5. What do you think are some of the major advantages of the Kentucky program? What are its principal disadvantages?

Suggested Readings

Bierlein, Louann A. *Controversial Issues in Educational Policy.* Newbury Park, CA: Sage, 1993.

Murnane, Richard J., and Frank Levy. "Education and Training." In *Setting Domestic Priorities: What Can Government Do?,* ed. Henry J. Aaron and Charles L. Schultze. Washington, DC: Brookings Institution, 1992, pp. 185–222.

National Commission on Excellence in Education. *A Nation At Risk: The Imperative for Educational Reform.* Washington, DC: U.S. Government Printing Office, 1983.

Notes

1. National Commission on Excellence in Education, *A Nation at Risk: The Imperative for Educational Reform* (Washington, DC: U.S. Government Printing Office, 1983), p. 5.
2. Ibid, p. 5.
3. Ibid., pp. 5–6.
4. Ibid., pp. 7–8.
5. Ibid., p. 13.
6. Bell, H. Terrel, "Reflections One Decade After *A Nation at Risk,*" *Phi Delta Kappan* 74 (8) (1993), p. 597.
7. Conference Board, *Ten Years After "A Nation at Risk"* (New York: Conference Board, 1993), p. 20.

8. Ibid., p. 28.

9. Business Roundtable, *The Business Roundtable Participation Guide: A Primer for Business on Education* (New York: Business Roundtable, 1990), p. 85.

10. Conference Board, op. cit., p. 29.

11. Quoted in Katherine S. Manegold, "Clinton Tells Educators Youths Are Not Getting Practical Skills for Jobs," *New York Times*, 23 February 1994, p. B12.

12. Quoted ibid., p. B12.

13. Louann A. Bierlein, *Controversial Issues in Educational Policy* (Newbury Park, CA: Sage, 1993), p. 2.

14. D. C. Berliner, "Educational Reform in an Era of Disinformation," paper presented at the meeting of the American Association of Colleges for Teacher Education, San Antonio, TX, February 1992.

15. Bierlein, op. cit., p. 2.

16. Richard J. Murnane and Frank Levy, "Education and Training," in *Setting Domestic Priorities: What Can Government Do?*, ed. Henry J. Aaron and Charles L. Schultze (Washington, DC: Brookings Institution, 1992), p. 191; Ina V. S. Mullis et al., *Trends in Academic Progress* (Washington, DC: U.S. Department of Education, 1991).

17. Richard M. Jaeger, "'World Class' Standards, Choice, and Privatization: Weak Measurement Serving Presumptive Policy," paper prepared for the 1992 annual meeting of the American Educational Research Association.

18. David K. Cohen and James P. Spillane, "Policy and Practice: The Relations between Governance and Instruction," *Review of Research in Education* 18 (1992), pp. 3–49.

19. *The New Standards Project 1992–1995: A Proposal* (Rochester, NY: University of Pittsburgh, Learning Research and Development Center, and National Center on Education and the Economy, 1992).

20. U.S. Department of Education, *America 2000: An Education Strategy* (Washington, DC: U.S. Department of Education, 1991).

21. Lauren B. Resnick, "Learning in School and Out," *Educational Researcher* 16 (December 1987), pp. 13–20; Stephen F. Hamilton, *Apprenticeship for Adulthood: Preparing Youth for the Future* (New York: Free Press, 1990).

22. Thomas Bailey and Donna Merrit, "School to Work Transition and Youth Apprenticeship in the United States," paper prepared for the Manpower Demonstration Research Corporation, New York, May 1992; Charles Dayton et al., "The California Partnership Academies: Remembering the 'Forgotten Half,'" *Phi Delta Kappan* 72 (March 1992), pp. 539–545.

23. Murnane and Levy, op. cit.

24. David Stern et al., "Benefits and Costs of Dropout Prevention in a High School Program Combining Academic and Vocational Education: Third-Year Results from Replications of the California Peninsula Academies," *Educational Evaluation and Policy Analysis* 11 (Winter 1989), pp. 405–426.

25. Murnane and Levy, op. cit.; Robert H. Meyer, "Educational Performance Indicators and School Report Cards: Concept," paper presented at the meeting of the Association for Public Policy Analysis and Management, 1991.

26. Legislative Research Commission, *The Kentucky Reform Act of 1990: A Citizen's Handbook* (Frankfort, KY: Legislative Research Commission, September 1991).

27. Susan H. Fuhrman and Richard F. Elmore, *Takeover and Deregulation: Working Models of New State and Local Regulatory Relationships.* New Brunswick, NJ: Rutgers University, Consortium for Policy Research in Education. CPRE research report RR-024 (April 1992).

28. James Coleman, *Equality of Educational Opportunity Report* (Washington, DC: U.S. Government Printing Office, 1966); Educational Testing Service, *ETS Policy Notes: Testing* (Princeton, NJ: Educational Testing Service, 1991); E. A. Hanushek, "The Impact of Differential Expenditures on School Performance," *Educational Researcher* 18 (May 1989), p. 62.

29. Jeannie Oakes, *Multiplying Inequalities: The Effects of Race, Social Class, and Tracking on Opportunities to Learn Mathematics and Science* (Santa Monica, CA: RAND Corporation, 1990).

30. Edwin A. Sexton and Janet F. Nickel, "The Effects of School Location on the Earnings of Black and White Youths," *Economics of Education Review* 11 (March 1992).

31. Peter Passell, "An Economics Lesson: "The Candidates' Plans for Education," *New York Times*, 3 November 1996, pp. 20–21.

32. Bierlein, op. cit., p. 38.

33. National Center for Education Statistics, *Digest of Educational Statistics 1990* (Washington, DC: Office of Educational Research and Improvement, 1991).

34. Bierlein, op. cit., p. 16.

35. John Portz, "Problem Definitions and Policy Agendas: Shaping the Educational Agenda in Boston," *Policy Studies Journal* 24 (3) (1966), pp. 371–386.

36. M. E. Rasell and L. Mishel, *Shortchanging Education: How U.S. Spending on Grades K–12 Lags Behind Other Industrial Nations* (Washington, DC: Economic Policy Institute Briefing Paper, January 1990).

37. Public Agenda Foundation, *First Things First: What Americans Expect From the Public Schools* (New York: Public Agenda Foundation, 1994).

38. S. M. Elam, L. C. Rose, and A. M. Gallup, "The Twenty-third Annual Gallup Poll of the Public's Attitudes Toward the Public Schools," *Phi Delta Kappan* 73 (1) (September 1991), pp. 41–56.

39. Bierlein, op. cit., p. 52.

40. Linda Darling-Hammond and Carol Ascher, *Creating Accountability in Big City Schools* (New York: Columbia University, Teachers College, March 1991); Murnane and Levy, op. cit.

41. South Carolina Department of Education, Division of Public Accountability, *What Is the Penny Buying for South Carolina?* (Columbia, SC: South Carolina Department of Education, Division of Public Accountability, 1 December 1990).

42. Carnegie Forum on Education and the Economy, *A Nation Prepared: Teachers for the Twenty-first Century* (New York: Carnegie Corporation, 1986).

43. T. Toch, *In the Name of Excellence* (New York: Oxford University Press, 1991); Bierlein, op. cit.

44. Michael W. Kirst, *Who Controls Our Schools? American Values in Conflict* (New York: Freeman, 1984); Toch, op. cit.

45. Bierlein, op. cit., p. 26.

46. Dan Balz, "GOP Takes Long Look at Results of Election," *Washington Post*, 27 November 1996 (printed in *Des Moines Register*, p. 5A).

47. Bierlein, op. cit., p. 38.

48. Rita Mae Kelly and Dennis Palumbo, Series Editors' Introduction in Louann A. Bierlein, *Controversial Issues in Educational Policy* (Newbury Park, CA: Sage, 1993), p. x.

49. Bierlein, op. cit., p. 3.

50. "Union Members Dump Leader Who Backs Vouchers," *People's Weekly World*, 29 October 1994, p. 4.

51. Quoted in Tim Wheeler, "Fraud Suspected in Privatized Schools," *People's Weekly World*, 29 October 1994, p. 4.

52. George Judson, "Company to Manage Schools in Hartford," *New York Times*, 5 October 1994, p. A11.

53. Quoted in Emile Schepers, "Daley Cranks Up School Privatization Drive," *People's Weekly World*, 5 November 1994, p. 10.

54. Tom Post with Seema Nayyar, "Is School Out for Whittle?" *Newsweek*, 7 November 1994, p. 82.

55. J. E. Barry, "Politics, Bilingual Education, and the Curriculum," *Educational Leadership* 40 (1983), pp. 56–60.

56. U.S. Department of Education, *America 2000*, op. cit.

57. Sam Dillon, "Bilingual Education Effort Is Flawed, Study Indicates," *New York Times*, 20 October 1994, p. A19.

58. U.S. Department of Education, *America 2000*, op. cit.

59. John E. Chubb and Terry M. Moe, *Politics, Markets, and America's Schools* (Washington, DC: Brookings Institution, 1990).

60. Murnane and Levy, op. cit. See also Elizabeth A. Kelly, *Education, Democracy, and Public Knowledge* (Boulder, CO: Westview Press, 1995).

61. National Center for Education Statistics, *The State of Mathematics Achievement: NAEP's 1990 Assessment of the Nation and the Trial Assessment of the States* (Washington, DC: U.S. Department of Education, 1991).

62. Murnane and Levy, op. cit., p. 208.

63. John F. Witte, "Private School Versus Public School Achievement: Are There Findings That Should Affect the Educational Choice Debate?" *Economics of Education Review* (forthcoming); Richard J. Murnane, "A Review Essay: Comparisons of Public and Private Schools: Lessons from the Uproar," *Journal of Human Resources* 19 (Spring 1984), pp. 263–277.

64. Murnane and Levy, op. cit.

65. David K. Cohen and Eleanor Farrar, "Power to the Parents? The Story of Education Vouchers," *Public Interest* 48 (Summer 1977), pp. 72–97; Richard J. Murnane, "Family Choice in Public Education: The Role of Students, Teachers, and System Designers," *Teachers College Record* 88 (2) (Winter 1986), pp. 169–189.

66. Peter Passell, "After Years of Trying to Fix Education, Why Isn't it Fixed?," *New York Times*, 13 October 1994, p. C2. See also Simon Hakim, Paul Seidenstat, and Gary W. Bowman (eds.), *Privatizing Education and Educational Choice: Concepts, Plans and*

Experiences (Westport, CT: Praeger, 1995); Andrew Coulson, Markets Versus Monopolies in Education: The Historical Evidence. *Education Policy Analysis Archives* 4(9) (12 June 1996) [electronic file].

67. E. A. Hanushek et al., *Making Schools Work* (Washington, DC: Brookings Institution, 1994).

68. Jorgenson, quoted in Passell, op. cit., p. C2.

69. Peter Passell, "An Economics Lesson: The Candidates' Plans for Education," *New York Times*, 3 November 1996, pp. 20–21.

70. Ronald A. Wolk (ed.), "Quality Counts: A Report Card on the Condition of Public Education in the 50 States," *Education Week* 16, 22 January 1997, supplement.

71. National Education Goals Panel, *The National Education Goals Report* (Washington, DC: U.S. Government Printing Office, 1995).

72. U.S. Department of Education, Office of Educational Research and Improvement, *Study of Curriculum Reform* (Washington, DC: U.S. Government Printing Office, October 1996), p. 9.

73. Ibid., p. 4.

74. Gary Orfield, *Deepening Segregation in American Public Schools* (Cambridge, MA: Harvard University, Graduate School of Education, 1997).

75. Kirst, op. cit., p. 36.

76. D. G. Armstrong, K. T. Henson, and T. V. Savage, *Education: An Introduction* (New York: Macmillan, 1985); T. Toch, *In the Name of Excellence* (New York: Oxford University Press, 1991); Bierlein, op. cit.

77. J. W. Guthrie, W. I. Garms, and L. C. Pierce, *School Finance and Education Policy* (Englewood Cliffs, NJ: Prentice-Hall, 1988).

78. Bierlein, op. cit., p. 13.

79. K. Alexander, "The Common School Ideal and the Limits of Legislative Authority: The Kentucky Case," *Harvard Journal on Legislation* 28 (1991), p. 353.

80. Bierlein, op. cit., p. 31.

81. David K. Cohen and James P. Spillane, "Policy and Practice: The Relations between Governance and Instruction," *Review of Research in Education* 18 (1992), pp. 3–49.

82. Carnegie Commission on Science, Technology, and Government, *In the National Interest: The Federal Government in the Reform of K–12 Math and Science Education* (New York: Carnegie Commission on Science, Technology, and Government, February 1991); Murnane and Levy, op. cit.

83. Murnane and Levy, op. cit.

84. Peter Applebome, "Dilapidated Schools Are Bursting at Frayed Seams," *New York Times*, 25 August 1996, p. 8.

85. U.S. Congress, Office of Technology Assessment, *Testing in American Schools: Asking the Right Questions* (Washington, DC: U.S. Congress, Office of Technology Assessment, 1992).

86. Robert E. Slaven and Nancy A. Madden, "Modifying Chapter 1 Program Improvement Guidelines to Reward Appropriate Practices," *Educational Evaluation and Policy Analysis* 13 (Winter 1991), pp. 369–379.

87. Bill Zlatos, "Scores That Don't Add Up," *New York Times*, 6 November 1994, sec. 4A, pp. 28–29.

88. Lyn Nell Hancock, Pat Wingert, and Peter Annin, "Parents 'Crazy' for Federal Cash," *Newsweek*, 31 October 1994, pp. 54–55.

89. Jennifer Steinhauer, "Scholarships for the Genuinely Special," *New York Times*, 30 October 1994, sec. 4, p. 2.

90. Lyn Nell Hancock and Pat Wingert, "Silence in the Classroom," *Newsweek*, 3 October 1994, p. 48.

91. Ibid.

92. Peter Applebome, "Latest 'Best Hope' In U.S. Education: Chartered Schools," *New York Times*, 12 October 1994, pp. A1, B8.

93. Michael Mintrom and Sandra Vergari, "Advocacy Coalitions, Policy Entrepreneurs, and Policy Change," *Policy Studies Journal* 24 (3) (1996), pp. 420–434.

94. Murnane and Levy, op. cit., p. 218.

95. Peter Applebome, "Revamped Kentucky Schools Are a Study in Pros and Cons," *New York Times*, 25 March 1996, pp. A1, A6.

96. Murnane and Levy, op. cit., p. 220.

97. David C. Paris, "Schools, Scapegoats, and Skills: Educational Reform and the Economy," *Policy Studies Journal,* 22 (1) (1996), pp. 10–24. See also J. E. Stone, "Developmentalism: An Obscure but Pervasive Restriction on Educational Improvement, *Education Policy Analysis Archives* 4 (8) (23 April 1996) [electronic file].

98. National Education Goals, *Federal Register* 59 (111) (June 10, 1994), 30191–30215, p. 30191.

99. Richard J. Murnane et al., *Who Will Teach? Policies That Matter* (Cambridge, MA: Harvard University Press, 1991).

100. Murnane and Levy, op. cit.

101. David M. Arfin, "The Use of Financial Aid to Attract Talented Students to Teaching: Lessons from Other Fields," *Elementary School Journal* 86 (March 1986), pp. 404–423.

102. Bierlein, op. cit., p. 41.

103. The Business Roundtable, *The Business Roundtable Participation Guide: A Primer for Business on Education.* New York: Business Roundtable, 1990), p. v.

104. Bierlein, op. cit., p. 53.

105. Ibid., p. 55. See also Diane Ravitch, *National Standards in American Education: A Citizen's Guide* (Washington, DC: Brookings Institution, 1995); Michael W. Apple, "Being Popular About National Standards," *Education Policy Analysis Archives* 4 (10) (June 30, 1996) [electronic file].

106. Educational Testing Service, *ETS Policy Notes: Testing* (Princeton, NJ: ETS, 1991).

107. B. S. Romzek and M. J. Dubnick, "Accountability in the Public Sector: Lessons from the Challenger Tragedy," *Public Administration Review* 47 (1987), pp. 227–238.

108. L. M. Cornett and G. F. Gaines, *Focusing on Student Outcomes: Roles for Incentive Programs—The 1991 National Survey of Incentive Programs and Teacher Career Ladders* (Atlanta, GA: Southern Regional Education Board, Career Ladder Clearinghouse, January 1992); Bierlein, op. cit.

109. Bierlein, op. cit.

110. M. H. Miller, K. Noland, and J. Schaaf, *A Guide to the Kentucky Education Reform Act of 1990* (Frankfort, KY: Legislative Research Commission, April 1990).

111. Peter Applebome, "Revamped Kentucky Schools Are a Study in Pros and Cons," *New York Times*, 25 March 1996, pp. A1, A6.

8

Health Policy

SMOKING AND HEALTH

One of the central concerns confronting public health policy is how to deal with the consequences of smoking cigarettes, cigars, and other tobacco products, and the use of chewing tobacco. These have been associated with cancer, emphysema, and other severe health problems that add greatly to the costs of treatment, prevention, and the search for potential medical cures. Severely complicating policy decisions is the political power of tobacco growers and companies that manufacture tobacco products. The Democratic and Republican political parties both are funded heavily by tobacco interests, which benefited greatly by the November 1994 election of a Republican congressional majority committed to reducing government restraints on economic activity and stimulating corporate profits. Other pressure groups, such as Action on Smoking and Health (ASH), have fought against the political power of the tobacco lobby.

When the Democrats controlled Congress, in April 1994, executives of the nation's seven largest tobacco companies appeared before congressional committees investigating that industry's activities. All denied that their firms had manipulated levels of nicotine in their products, and they claimed that they did not know that nicotine was addictive. They also stated they did not believe in a causal link between cigarettes and cancer. By July 1995, however, the Justice Department began to investigate possible securities fraud against Philip Morris, one of the industry giants, and at least one of the executives who had testified before Congress the previous year was under suspicion of perjury. The Food and Drug Administration, supported by President Clinton, announced that it would try to regulate cigarettes, against the fierce opposition of the industry, by banning cigarette sales from vending machines and thus limiting access to minors. Over 400 lawsuits had been filed against U.S. tobacco companies, but no one ever had received compensation. In 1994, research documents from Brown & Williamson, the third-largest U.S. tobacco company, were leaked to the media, leading Congress to hold its initial hearings and stimulating both class-action lawsuits and federal criminal investigations.

In 1995, more documents were released regarding corporate knowledge of the hazards of smoking. The leadership of at least two major tobacco corporations had known as early as 1969 that cigarettes contained habit-forming ingredients leading to addiction. Studies had examined how best to attract children to the stimulants in nicotine, and an abortive electric-shock experiment was conducted on college students to associate smoking with stress.

ASH, a national, nonprofit scientific and educational antitobacco organization, notes that more people die from tobacco each year than from alcohol, guns, AIDS, car accidents, and airplane accidents combined, and called for government action to reverse this situation instead of subsidizing tobacco growers and cigarette manufacturers. ASH favors eliminating all cigarette advertising and subsidies to the tobacco industry, mitigating the harmful effects of secondhand smoke inhaled by nonsmokers, vigorous enforcement of laws prohibiting the sale of tobacco products to minors, and making smokers and tobacco companies pay for the medical and social problems they cause. ASH has been instrumental in establishing nonsmoking sections on airplanes, banning smoking on most domestic flights, establishing legal rights to nonsmoking areas in public places, forcing broadcasters to provide free air time for antismoking messages, eliminating broadcast cigarette advertisements, raising smokers' insurance rates, strengthening health warnings in cigarette advertising, banning smoking on public buses, and requiring smoke detectors in airplane lavatories.

The activities of groups such as ASH regarding secondhand smoke are particularly important, because the Occupational Safety and Health Administration has estimated that as a result of secondhand smoke about 47,000 people a year die from heart disease, 150,000 suffer nonfatal heart attacks, and 3,000 die from lung cancer. So-called passive smoking, from inhaling secondhand smoke, is estimated to increase the risk of heart disease by about 30 percent, since it reduces the blood's ability to carry oxygen and the heart's capacity to use oxygen, which promotes blood clots and stimulates the production of fatty deposits and cholesterol.[1] Another lobbying group, the Coalition on Smoking and Health, was formed by the American Heart Association, the American Lung Association, and the American Cancer Society to fight the use of tobacco and its consequences.

During the 1996 presidential campaign, Republican presidential candidate Bob Dole suffered from his comments on national television suggesting that smoking might not be addictive. The Democratic campaign seized on this departure from what most of the public has come to believe. Bill Clinton endorsed stricter federal laws to limit the sale of tobacco products to minors and proposed that tobacco be regulated like a drug. His Justice Department launched a criminal probe of tobacco-industry executives. However, the Democratic party also had benefited from tobacco industry money.

THE RPI INPUTS TO HEALTH POLICY

The Rationality Input

AIDS

Policy debates regarding the AIDS (acquired immune deficiency syndrome) epidemic illustrate the role and the limitations of scientific research in the health policymaking process. From the initial identification of AIDS cases in the United States in 1981, over 250,000 people had been officially identified as having AIDS by 1991[2] and over 150,000 of those people died of the disease; perhaps 1.25 million additional cases had remained undiagnosed. By 1991, AIDS had become the ninth leading cause of death.[3] Long-term projections[4] suggest an increasing number of AIDS deaths annually well into the next century.

The dominant paradigm of the AIDS disease has been developed by the U.S. Public Health Service and other scientific experts. This model attributes AIDS to infection with HIV (human immunodeficiency virus), transmitted through bodily fluids sexually and intravenously. Other views, however, counter the dominant hypothesis.[5] Some[6] suggest that HIV is merely a marker of AIDS and that the cause of the disease lies in the prolonged use of recreational drugs, which weakens the immune system and leads to other clinical problems. Evidence for this reasoning is found in the fact that the groups with the greatest risk of contracting AIDS—intravenous drug users and male homosexuals—are disproportionately substance abusers. Proponents of this view note that some patients with AIDS and related diseases fail to test positively for HIV infection.[7] It has been argued[8] that drug therapy actually may induce AIDS because it kills both infected and uninfected immune system cells and that other treatments discovered in the roughly $4 billion annual AIDS research program are equally flawed. If AIDS in fact is not transmitted through bodily fluids, then public policy promoting safe-sex or needle exchange would not be effective in preventing the spread of this disease.[9]

Cancer

Similar patterns are evident in research on cancer. Debates about the extent to which the federal government should be involved in regulating workers' exposure to cancer-causing workplace risks has mobilized scientific investigations on both sides. Federal reports[10] detailing the evidence of risk and extrapolating future levels of danger for workers exposed to known and suspected carcinogens were countered by an Oxford University study[11] suggesting that occupational exposures accounted for only 1 percent–5 percent of all cancers, against a projected 40 percent in the federal documents. Critiques[12] of extrapolation methods used by the federal researchers argued that risk ratios were used improperly and misleadingly. However, a reanalysis sponsored by the proindustry American Industrial Health Council[13] produced results that were close to the higher work-related incidence of cancer suggested by government figures. Expert evidence regarding the carcinogenic nature of asbestos was well established by the 1950s, based on a century of research conducted in many countries and published in the medical literature.[14] Asbestos was connected with diseases such as asbestosis, lung cancer, and mesothelioma, and with occupations including mining and construction, especially regarding workers who handled raw asbestos or worked with asbestos insulation.

It probably is accurate to conclude that contemporary research findings have not resolved the controversy over the source of cancer hazards. Increases in many forms of cancer—breast, colorectal, brain, non-Hodgkin's lymphoma, testicular, and kidney—cannot be attributed only to smoking, improved diagnoses, and increased access to medical care. Childhood cancers are related to exposure to pesticides, and farmers' higher rates of some kinds of cancers may be caused by contact with agricultural chemicals.[15] However, other researchers[16] hold that natural carcinogens in foods or in the ground (such as radon) are more dangerous than these products.

Risk Assessment

Debates over the proper role of rational analysis in policymaking occur when ideological and institutional imperatives raise questions about the limits of rationality. In 1990, the Bush administration's Office of Management and Budget (OMB) criticized traditional risk assessments as they were carried out by the Environmental Protection Agency (EPA) and the Occupational Safety and Health Administration (OSHA) for constructing worst-case scenarios that provided a large margin of public safety. The OMB report stated, in part, that "[c]onservatism in risk assessment distorts the regulatory priorities of the Federal Government, directing societal resources to reduce what are often trivial carcinogenic risks while failing to address more substantial threats to life and health,"[17] as with household radon measurements taken in basements. The report attacked the practice of mixing together the science and policy aspects of risk assessment, and complained that continuing to use conservative or worst-case assumptions would distort risk assessment, "yielding estimates that may overstate likely risks by several orders of magnitude," and diverting attention toward minute or trivial risks. Risk managers, rather than risk assessors, should be given responsibility for establishing margins of safety, according to OMB. Similar attacks on the federal regulatory function have come from conservatives wanting to reduce the government's role in health policy.[18]

Several different methods can establish the seriousness of a health hazard, and whether the public or policymakers perceive a threat to be "real" depends largely on what degree of proof is necessary before a policy decision is required. Epidemiological studies alone do not seem to be adequate for this purpose. Pennsylvania State University history professor Robert Proctor argues, for example, that "it is virtually impossible to detect, from epidemiology alone, the effect of a carcinogen that increases human cancer risk by less than about 30 percent."[19] However, saccharin was estimated by the Food and Drug Administration (FDA) to increase the risk of bladder cancer by about 3 percent, which would mean about 1,200 extra cases of bladder cancer each year. Robert Proctor concludes:

> If a hazard is sufficiently widely dispersed—asphalt road dust or pesticides in foods or microwave radiation, for instance—it may be difficult to find unexposed controls. Many such cancers are presumably preventable, though the magnitude of the hazard may be difficult or even impossible to ascertain.
>
> Epidemiology . . . is good at revealing certain kinds of hazards and bad at revealing others. Strong carcinogens affecting large numbers of people are fairly easy to identify—those often turn out to be "lifestyle" factors, like smoking, or clear-cut occupational hazards, like asbestos and uranium mining. Low-grade occupational or toxic hazards may be more elusive, since exposures tend to vary over time and space.[20]

In her detailed study of agenda setting, Denise Scheberle[21] found that scientific consensus about health risks was necessary, but not sufficient, for concerns about both radon and asbestos to achieve a prominent place in policy debates. Media involvement and the participation of activists serving as policy entrepreneurs were both critical for the unfolding of each policy issue, with interactions among experts more consequential for the outcome of the radon debate and political developments more meaningful to the asbestos policy story.

Preventive medicine is a method for reducing people's risk of suffering from health problems. An example of how preventive medicine fits in with the rational approach to health policy is provided by the federal government's program known as Healthy People 2000, which was initiated by the U.S. Department of Health and Human Services in September 1990. The degree to which the Healthy People 2000 goals are attained is monitored by annual reports prepared through cooperation among agencies such as the National Center for Health Statistics of the Centers for Disease Control and Prevention, the National Committee on Vital and Health Statistics, and the Office of Disease Prevention and Health Promotion. Three broad goals and 300 objectives, organized into twenty-two priority areas, were defined in the 1990 initiative: (1) to increase the span of healthy life, (2) reduce health disparities among different societal groups, and (3) achieve universal access to preventive services. Following receipt of over 550 public comments, proposed revisions to the program's goals were considered, leading to nineteen new objectives and 111 new sub-objectives directed toward addressing health risks or disparities based on age, sex, race, or ethnicity.[22]

The Power Input

Cancer Research

The role of political power—particularly the role of competing interest groups—in setting national health policy is evident in the policy struggles that have surrounded the question of health research. Much of the impetus for the current policy debate in cancer research, for example, comes from sharply divergent perspectives on the sources of modern cancers. One point of view—that industrial pollutants are responsible for a sizable proportion of all cancers—is represented by Samuel S. Epstein's 1978 book, *The Politics of Cancer.* This thesis was received enthusiastically by many medical, environmental, labor, and occupational health organizations. Support for this view was also provided by an interagency federal government report[23] that predicted that over the next few decades the proportion of cancer deaths due to several carcinogens commonly present in workplaces could increase by up to 40 percent. In response to documented health problems associated with asbestos, labor unions and asbestos victims' groups exerted pressure for government action. The White Lung Association lobbied for federal regulation of asbestos, and the Asbestos Workers' Union informed workers of health problems through its *Asbestos Worker* magazine.

As health problems associated with asbestos mounted, and as medical evidence accumulated that linked asbestos to a number of diseases, courts became active in adjudicating worker compensation for exposure to this carcinogen. In 1933, the first out-of-court settlement was reached in a worker's effort to achieve redress. In 1937, the first court case awarded damages to an asbestos worker for asbestosis.[24] In a landmark 1973 decision, *Borel v. Fiberboard Paper Products* (493 F.2d 1076 (5th Circuit, 1973), *cert. denied,* 419 U.S. 869 (1974)), the liability of asbestos companies increased greatly through application of the legal theory of strict liability, which permitted victories for workers who proved that asbestos companies had not warned them adequately about health risks. By 1982, 30,000 claims had been filed against 260 asbestos firms.[25] Legal problems forced the Manville Corporation, the nation's largest manufacturer of asbestos, which was facing $2 billion in court costs and settlements to individuals, into bankruptcy protection.

Studies published during the 1950s linking smoking to cancer led tobacco industry leaders in 1954 to form the Tobacco Industry Research Committee, renamed the Council for Tobacco Research in 1964. Allegedly set up to fund independent impartial research, its actual purpose was to foster the interests of tobacco manufacturers, growers, and warehousers. By 1994, the council's annual research budget was about $20 million; since its inception it had spent nearly $250 million and had published 5,000 scientific papers.[26] Similarly, the Tobacco Institute is the industry's public relations arm, supporting its legal position, tracking workplace smoking bans, and disputing studies about the consequences of smoking.

Health Insurance

One of the principal industry pressure groups in health insurance is the Health Industry Association of America, which has worked to preserve privately financed health care coverage through educational lobbying. Also active in the struggle against national health insurance is the American Medical Association

(AMA), which maintains an intensive advertising campaign designed to convince the public and policymakers of alleged drawbacks to national insurance.

Over time, however, opposition by the nation's medical establishment to reform of health care has waned. In 1992, the 74,000-member American Academy of Family Physicians supported limits on doctors' fees. During that year's presidential campaign, the 77,000-member American College of Physicians similarly endorsed negotiated ceilings on health care spending for doctor and hospital fees. In that election, of the 20 percent of voters who said that health care was the most important factor in their choice among presidential candidates, 67 percent voted for Bill Clinton, compared to just 19 percent for George Bush and 14 percent for H. Ross Perot. A Pennsylvania special Senate election held in 1991 to replace Republican Senator John Heinz, who was killed in an airplane crash, helped to bring health care reform to the national policy agenda through the dramatic come-from-behind victory by Democratic candidate Harris Wofford, based largely on his strong support of planned national health care.

In 1996, faced with mounting public concern about access to health insurance, particularly for workers who change jobs and their families, Congress passed legislation co-sponsored by Senators Edward Kennedy (D-Massachusetts) and Nancy Landon Kassebaum (R-Kansas). The Kennedy-Kassebaum bill, which passed the Senate on a unanimous 100 to 0 vote, provided for cross-job portability by requiring insurance companies to cover workers who changed jobs if they had been insured previously and sharply limited exclusions for pre-existing medical conditions. This legislation was much less far-reaching than the failed Clinton health initiative in 1994, and contained compromises that minimized opposition from health care insurance groups such as the Health Insurance Association of America, which had been instrumental in the defeat of the earlier Clinton plan.

Health Care Reform and Public Opinion

The role of public opinion in driving health policy decisions can be seen clearly in the 1994 debate over health care reform. Precisely because public sentiment regarding health care was fragmented and volatile, policymakers were able to propose a wide array of conflicting ideas that would not have been aired if there had been consensus about the proper direction to follow.

In general, public opinion about health care policy has been mixed and based on incomplete information. Just 28 percent of the respondents to a 1994 *Los Angeles Times* poll said that they knew "only some" or "not much at all" about "the details of the health care proposals that are currently being considered by Congress." In the same survey, just 9 percent reported that they felt "the nation's health care system is basically sound," while 22 percent replied that it "needs some improvement," 22 percent that it "needs many improvements," and 41 percent that it needs "a fundamental overhauling." A separate *NBC News/Wall Street Journal* survey taken at the same time found 61 percent agreeing that "Congress should pass a health care reform bill this year," but 34 percent felt that Congress should "continue to debate the issue and act next year." In the same survey, 70 percent believed that "Congress and the president should continue their efforts to reform the health care system," and just 26 percent wanted to "leave the system as it is now."

That the public was undecided and volatile on the direction in which the U.S. system of health care should evolve was clear from changes in support for and opposition to President Clinton's health plan. As tracked by surveys conducted by Yankelovich Partners, support for the Clinton solution collapsed from an initially strong 57 percent in September 1993 to only 37 percent in July 1993; in contrast, over the same time opposition to the Clinton proposal rose sharply, from 31 percent to 49 percent. Public opinion on health care options, as the Clinton proposal unraveled in 1994, showed clear support for postponing action. For example, a poll conducted for *Newsweek* magazine in early August 1994 showed that 65 percent believed Congress should "take more time to examine the various proposals and start over next year," while only 31 percent preferred that "health-care-reform legislation be passed this year."[27]

Nonetheless, there is somewhat surprising evidence, given the intensely negative antigovernment flavor of policy debates following the Republican capture of Congress in 1994, that public sentiments have not been uniformly, nor even in the majority, opposed to a major government role in health care. For example, a 1994 Yankelovich Partners survey found 61 percent agreeing that "the federal government should guarantee health care for all Americans"; 33 percent disagreed with that notion. Similarly, a February 1994 survey by *ABC News/Washington Post* showed 77 percent agreeing that the federal government could make the health care system better, versus 21 percent who believed that it could not do so.

The public, however, clearly did not see the Clinton plan as the way to resolve the health care crisis; in a March 1994 *ABC News/Washington Post* poll, 47 percent believed that "Clinton's [health care] plan creates too much governmental involvement in the nation's health care system"; just 14 percent felt that his plan created "not enough government involvement"; and 34 percent felt that it created "about the right amount." A central worry about the Clinton plan shared by a strong majority of the population was its threatened creation of "another large and inefficient government bureaucracy," a sentiment agreed to by 62 percent of respondents to the February *ABC News/Washington Post* poll. In a late October 1994 Gallup poll, there was no clear consensus as to how the nation's health care problems could be handled best: 40 percent opted for "regional organizations of consumers created by state governments," 29 percent preferred "the current system that relies on doctors, hospitals, and health insurance companies," and only 22 percent found the federal government to be optimal.

Further public confusion was evident regarding even the fundamental proposition that a crisis exists in health care. A March 1994 poll by *NBC News/Wall Street Journal* found that only 22 percent agreed that "the system is in crisis." In sharp contrast with the tenor of much public debate, a larger percentage (26 percent) felt that "the system has problems, but they are not major," although 50 percent did feel that "the system has major problems, but is not in crisis." That the Clinton proposal was not a preferred solution, however, was evident from the findings of a September 1994 poll by Yankelovich Partners: only 29 percent expected that as a consequence "the quality of medical care available to you will get better," while 28 percent felt it would "get worse," and 34 percent assumed there would be "no effect." The lack of a clear sense of public urgency for action on health care also was clear from an August 1994 Gallup poll showing that 68 percent agreed that Congress should "deal with health care reform on a gradual basis over several years," versus just 28 percent who favored that "Congress try to pass a comprehensive health care reform plan this year [1994]."

The societal conflicts underlying the battle over health policy are clear from examining the bases of support and opposition to Clinton's proposal. Support for the Clinton initiative was stronger among African-Americans, those with lower educational attainment, those with lower incomes, the elderly, and Democrats. Respondents who were more likely to favor a gradual resolution of the nation's health care problems included whites, women, the middle-aged, those with more education and higher incomes, Republicans, and Bush voters from 1992. Groups that were relieved that Congress failed to enact reform legislation in 1994 included whites, older respondents, those with more education and higher incomes, people living in Western states, Republicans, 1992 Bush voters, and conservatives.[28]

By the mid-1990s, skepticism about the future of the health care system was endemic. A July 30, 1996, Harvard University survey found only 12 percent agreeing that the American system of health care was improving, against 49 percent who saw it deteriorating. In addition, 61 percent were very concerned that they would not be able to afford needed health care when a family member got sick, and 43 percent were very concerned about the affordability of mental health care. Seventy percent felt that inadequate health insurance had become a bigger problem in the past five years. In fact, the number of uninsured Americans grew from 39.7 million at the time of President Clinton's 1993 health initiative to 41 million by mid-1996.[29]

The Ideological Input

Controlling Health Care Costs

Much of the contemporary debate over health care policy—although the emphasis of the arguments changed drastically after the Republican takeover of Congress after the 1994 elections—has concerned alternative proposals to implement national health insurance protection. The tenor of that debate has been accented heavily by ideological conflicts over changing health care financing from private insurance premiums to government funding. As this debate evolved, the Republicans argued, in opposition to the multitude of proposals about financing, that the Clinton plan and a number of alternatives would transfer the one-seventh of the country's gross national product devoted to health care from private care providers and insurers to government.

An alternative to national health insurance would be to require that all Americans carry private insurance. This approach is much more acceptable to conservative, probusiness interests, because it would preserve the basic structure of privately funded and self-financed (rather than government-paid) health care. President Bush proposed a variant of this approach that provided tax credits for low-income citizens but little assistance for others. Congressional Republicans' alternatives to Bush's approach required all families to carry insurance or pay an income tax surcharge equal to the health insurance premium.

A third possible arrangement for restructuring American health care is to provide mandatory health insurance coverage through employers. Currently, about 56 percent of the population are covered by employer-sponsored health insurance. This arrangement could be extended to cover all full-time employees and their dependents and could add coverage for people without strong employment ties. Such a strategy would require instating a high payroll tax in the absence of employer coverage to encourage firms to fund health insurance themselves. In addition, tax-financed subsidies would be required to provide coverage to non-worker families and to make it less attractive for firms to seek private insurance premiums. A variant of this scheme was preferred by the Clinton administration when it pursued its unsuccessful proposal of mandated coverage combined with purchasing alliances among firms. Under the employer mandate system, however, some firms would benefit while others would not. In general, health costs would rise for firms currently not extending coverage to workers' dependents.

Leading analysts of the cost containment debate, such as Theodore Marmor of Yale University, focus on the integral role played in this debate by questions of health insurance and access to health care.[30] Proponents of a Canadian-style, single-payer system of national health coverage argue that government should set benefits, pay for them with new taxes, and regulate spending through strict price, wage, and budget controls. This would provide virtually identical benefits for everyone. Those opposed to what they regard as an intrusive system maintain either that cost controls would not be guaranteed to remain effective, with the risk of explosive expansion of coverage costs, or that stringent controls might stifle innovative medical research and technology. A more purely market-driven alternative, favored by more conservative elements in the debate, would be designed to make people more responsible for their own health costs and would trust that competitive economic forces would hold down health care spending. Different market-driven versions of health care changes would, for example, provide vouchers to Medicare recipients to buy private insurance or would tax workers on their employer-paid insurance to give them a reason to pick a low-cost plan. Proponents also argue that cost-effective treatments are more likely to emerge from competitive market pressures, because unneeded clinics or hospitals would be weeded out.

In September 1994, congressional Democratic leaders gave in to a threatened Republican filibuster on health care legislation. The "true believers" in the administration's original universal health care proposal, including Hillary Clinton, favored an all-or-nothing pursuit of that goal, featuring attacks by President Clinton on special interests—particularly doctors, insurance companies, and small business—and Congress for inaction, with the administration claiming credit for standing up for the interests of middle-class Americans.[31] In contrast, the inclination of the president and most of his aides was to seek the best compromise possible, in a retreat from his January 29, 1994, State of the Union warning to Congress that "If you send me legislation that does not guarantee every American private health insurance that can never be taken away, you will force me to . . . veto the legislation."

Whether cost control in the way that doctors and hospitals are paid for their services can be achieved through market-based mechanisms or whether alternatives to market forces are needed is at the heart of the ideological component of the debate over health policy. One point of view is taken by Henry J. Aaron: "[M]arket-based competition alone cannot control growth of health care spending. Effective control will require the imposition of budget limits on hospitals and fee controls on other providers to overcome the incentive of insured patients and their physicians to disregard cost in choosing care, even when benefits are slight."[32]

In contrast to proponents of a market-based approach, other policy analysts[33] emphasize market failures that have caused rapid increases in health expenditures due to increasingly expensive medical technology, insurance claims paying as much as health care providers charge, and decentralization of health care policymaking. The private health insurance system profits by providing coverage to those who are less likely to need care, which forces higher-risk groups onto publicly supported systems.

Abortion

The issue of abortion rights has emerged as one of the most ideologically charged elements of contemporary health care policy. One of the most emotion-laden and controversial aspects of the abortion debate concerns the extent to which government power should be used to protect women's right of access to abortion services and the right of health care workers to provide such services. This controversy intensified after the murder of two doctors and a bodyguard providing abortion services in Florida. These events highlighted a larger problem of violence and intimidation. The National Organization for Women, Legal Defense and Education Fund[34] reported that since 1977 there have been over 600 clinic blockades, 300 bomb threats, nearly 200 instances of arson or attempted arson, bombings, or fire-bombings directed against abortion providers, and nearly 200 death threats. Generally, liberals favor protecting abortion workers, while conservatives fight to preserve the right to protest against abortion.

On May 26, 1994, President Clinton signed into law the Freedom of Access to Clinic Entrance Act (FACE), in response to the terrorist acts and murders committed against abortion providers and other clinic employees. The legislation permits the Justice Department to bring criminal charges that carry penalties of up to ten years in prison for violations that cause bodily injury, life in prison for deadly actions such as the murder of abortion clinic doctors, and fines between $10,000 and $250,000. In addition, governments, organizations, and persons who feel they are victims of clinic blockades, can file civil suits to recover compensation for damages. FACE also provides for court injunctions to punish clinic blockades. Following the adoption of FACE, groups opposed to access to abortion services filed lawsuits to prevent implementation of the legislation. In Virginia, a suit filed by the American Life League claiming that their constitutional rights were violated by the law was thrown out by a federal judge as groundless, following intervention by the Legal Defense and Education Fund of the National Organization for Women. Comparable lawsuits were filed by abortion opponents in other states and the District of Columbia.

AIDS

Ideological aspects of policymaking are also clearly present in the debate over AIDS. The contemporary state of policymaking regarding AIDS may be seen as an interplay between politics and science. Far from a case of richly promising scientific research opportunities being squandered by bureaucratic ineptitude, public policy researchers David A. Rochefort and Roger W. Cobb argue that:

> The special difficulties encountered in AIDS policymaking . . . reflect a volatile struggle over the proper role of government, means/ends relationships in AIDS policy formulation, and utilitarian and moral values. . . . Though many past science-related causes have benefited from an irresistible coalignment of instrumental and expressive standpoints, AIDS concerns repeatedly set the two at odds, resulting in fierce debates that make for good political theater but fitful decision-making.[35]

The claim that AIDS is communicated principally by intravenous drug users sharing dirty syringes and by unprotected homosexual intercourse "enhance the disease's moral dimension, injecting notions of culpability, deservingness, blame, and punishment."[36] Indeed, perhaps 50 percent or more of intravenous drug users are HIV-infected, and nearly 60 percent of all pediatric AIDS cases are related to intravenous drug use.[37] Great hostility against people with AIDS appears in many places: in the results of opinion polls, in violent acts against those who are HIV-positive, in portrayals of the infected population in the popular media, and in the success with which conservative groups have mobilized opposition to what they characterize as sinful lifestyles. The stigmatization of persons with AIDS has been likened to earlier tendencies to keep cancer or syphilis patients at arm's length on grounds that they induced their own illnesses through their inability to end abusive personal habits that may have brought on their disease. Even worse, the behaviors associated with AIDS often are seen as a consequence of self-indulgence and social delinquency, rather than of just weak will-power.[38]

This perspective is at the heart of the conservative policy position on AIDS. The characterization of AIDS as largely a consequence of "unnatural," even "perverted," sexual activity makes it far easier to treat persons with AIDS as anything but innocent victims worthy of sympathy and support. At best, large segments of the public may be willing only grudgingly to endorse policies designed to mitigate the ravages of AIDS, while believing that the only real solution lies in a complete change of lifestyle for groups at high risk of contracting the disease, who deplete national resources to combat problems they brought on themselves. Distinguishing "good AIDS" from "bad AIDS" makes it possible to thwart research or prevention programs by creating the perception that victims of the disease have only themselves to blame. This is consistent with the general tendency in U.S. social policy to direct limited, stigmatizing, and coercive policy efforts toward groups that are seen in negative terms.[39]

Liberal perspectives on AIDS and related health and policy problems also play a role in policymaking. Starting in the Netherlands in the early 1980s, programs to exchange drug addicts' dirty (infected) syringes for clean needles spread to the United States by the late 1980s. State governments and the National Academy of Sciences supported such programs. In 1991, the National Commission on AIDS advised the president and Congress that legal barriers to the purchase of needles and syringes should be dropped. However, Congress prohibited the state use of federal funds for needle-distribution programs. Intense and repeated community opposition severely limits opportunities to experiment with this initiative.[40]

Needle-exchange programs have met with intense community opposition and with arguments from conservatives who view such programs as immoral or dangerous. AIDS-prevention "programs in which people who inject drugs exchange used needles for sterile ones are the most controversial and least legislated of all the responses to ID [injection drug] use and HIV transmission."[41] Arguments that needle exchanges can reduce HIV transmission rates without increasing drug use are countered by assertions that supplying drug-using equipment abets further criminal behavior and undermines respect for the law by making government an accessory to illegal activity.

In a 1988 *New York Times/CBS News* poll, a majority of respondents who viewed drug addiction as an illness supported needle exchange, but only about one-fourth of those who saw addiction as a crime agreed with needle-exchange programs,[42] choosing instead to attack what they regarded as a personally destructive and morally reprehensible form of behavior. Only 25 percent of the respondents said that they had any sympathy for those who contract AIDS while sharing needles used to inject illegal drugs. In New York City, efforts by medical and AIDS activist communities to implement a needle-exchange program failed, largely due to opposition from city and community leaders responding to demands for the preservation of social order.

By late 1992, condom distribution programs had been implemented in some large cities, including New York City, Chicago, Los Angeles, Philadelphia, and Dallas. The Massachusetts Board of Education called on all its local school systems to permit condom distribution, although relatively few did so. Rational arguments for condoms as a logical way to provide for safer sexual activity were met by the view that parents and religious institutions, not government, should regulate sexual behavior, with an emphasis on chastity and sexual faithfulness that would be threatened by sex education and condom programs. In New York City, condoms were distributed to students in 1986 through school-based health clinics. The city's Board of Education ended that brief experiment, but in September 1990 Schools Chancellor Joseph A. Fernandez announced a new attempt to distribute condoms to all of New York's high schools without mandatory counseling or parental consent. Strong opposition from religious leaders, the Board of Education, and parents fearful that their control over their children's sexuality might be threatened by the program nearly defeated the proposal (it passed the Board by a 4 to 3 vote); in 1993, a state appellate court ruled that parental consent was necessary, thereby invalidating the policy. Other cities, such as Falmouth, Massachusetts, replayed the New York debate. National exposure of the condom distribution issue came in July 1993, when Dr. Joycelyn Elders, President Clinton's nominee for surgeon general, was attacked for having supported condom distribution to teenagers when she was director of health for the state of Arkansas.

Unclarity about the chances of infection makes it easy to manipulate public fears regarding the threat posed by AIDS. Various estimates based on interpretations of epidemiological evidence have created different levels of public concern. Fear of the rapid and supposedly easy spread of AIDS among heterosexuals, beyond the previously highly infected groups of Haitians, homosexual males, and intravenous drug users, was fanned in the 1980s. However, more recent research has mitigated heterosexual fears of rampant transmission, by regarding the most heavily infected groups as socially marginal and beyond the pale of the white middle class.[43]

Application of RPI to Health Policy: The United States Versus the World

The United States spends more per capita on health care than any other country—about 50 percent more than in Canada, the second-highest spending country, and nearly double the per capita expenditures of Germany or France.[44] The focus of the U.S. health policy debate at the end of the twentieth century is directed far more toward controlling the increasing cost of the nation's medical services than with deciding how best to expand coverage. Emphasis is placed particularly on the fact that U.S. expenditures on health have grown from under 6 percent of the nation's gross domestic product (GDP) in 1960 to about 14 percent today, and are anticipated by the year 2000 to constitute about 17 percent of GDP.[45] Measured another way, the consumer price index for medical care in the U.S. (where 1982–1984 = 100) has exploded from 34.0 in 1970 to 211.0 in 1994.

This growth rate of health costs is faster than for many other advanced industrial economies in the world, resulting in a much higher level of per capita health care expenditures compared to other countries with sophisticated health care delivery systems. Comparative data on health costs are shown in Table 8.1.

The high cost of U.S. health care is attributable at least partly to the fact that the financial incentives built into the health care system do not discriminate well between treatments that are more or less beneficial, and to the related difficulty that often there is no clear agreement among physicians on diagnostic and therapeutic procedures. Combined with the greater availability of advanced medical technology, costly medical procedures are performed even when many physicians believe they are not appropriate and possibly harmful.[46]

Health care in the United States has evolved in patterns very different from those in most other advanced industrial societies. U.S. health care has been segmented, to ensure that certain groups of citizens have access, in contrast to corporatized systems of government-regulated private insurance or nationalized systems in which government assumes responsibility directly for health care.[47] Canada, Japan, and Western Europe all have universal coverage, with standard payment schedules determined through direct negotiation among government authorities, doctors, and hospitals. Most other advanced countries have also set limits on overall national medical expenditures. Primarily for that reason, universal medical care in other countries has not threatened to bankrupt those societies, and none spends more than 10 percent of its gross national product (GNP) for health care. In contrast, that mark was surpassed in the U.S. in 1985, and now over one-seventh of the entire national economy is devoted to its health care system. What is more, it could be argued that

TABLE 8.1 Real Health Expenditures Per Capita, United States and Selected Countries, 1960–1990, Selected Years (in 1990 U.S. dollars)

Year	United States	Canada	West Germany	Japan	United Kingdom
1960	$ 592	$ 468	$ 345	$ 104	$303
1965	781	616	448	230	363
1970	1,059	840	608	383	445
1975	1,291	1,036	918	546	590
1980	1,601	1,215	1,120	772	665
1985	2,010	1,546	1,232	917	753
1990	2,566	1,794	1,287	1,113	909

Source: Adapted from Charles L. Cochran and Eloise F. Malone, *Public Policy: Perspectives and Choices* (New York: McGraw-Hill, 1995), p. 336; Congressional Budget Office calculations based on data from the Health Data File of the Organization for Economic Cooperation and Development, 1991.

Notes: Expenditures in different countries are expressed in a common currency (U.S. dollars) using OECD estimates of a purchasing power parity (PPP) rate of exchange among national currencies. PPP is an estimate of the exchange rate at which a dollar can buy the same basket of goods in each country.

The word *real* is used here to mean adjusted for general inflation, rather than for inflation in the prices of health services, which is almost certainly different. Nominal current values have been converted to 1990 currencies using the gross domestic product implicit deflator.

the U.S. population is not getting the expected results of such a mammoth investment of national resources. Of the twenty-four advanced countries in the Organization for Economic Cooperation and Development, the U.S. ranks twenty-first from the top in infant mortality, seventeenth in male life expectancy, and sixteenth in female life expectancy.[48]

Compared to other advanced countries, the U.S. also suffers from much more expensive private administrative expenses. U.S. hospitals devote 20 percent of their budgets to billing administration, versus only 9 percent for Canadian hospitals. The number of national health administrators in Canada, covering 30 million people, is comparable to the number of administrators required to run just the Blue Cross system in Massachusetts, for 2.7 million people. Additional costs in the U.S. are imposed by the more than 1,200 private health insurance companies, each of which requires massive separate costs for its underwriting, marketing, and administrative staff. The federal Health Care Financing Administration (HCFA) has estimated that such overhead costs account for about 14 percent of the premiums paid by those who are insured.

The extent of what is identified widely as a crisis in U.S. health care has been described by the editors of Consumer Reports, who support a "single-payer," Canadian-style form of universal health coverage:

> Health care now consumes about 16 percent of state and local tax revenues. In the years since 1986, private businesses have spent about as much on health care as they earned in after-tax profits. For many small businesses, insurance has become unaffordable; three out of four concerns employing ten or fewer people simply do not provide health benefits. At any given time, roughly 35 million Americans—most of them employees of small businesses or their dependents—have no health coverage at all.[49]

The scope of conflict over health care policy is clear from the fact that about one-seventh of the entire U.S. annual national income is devoted to health care. Extrapolating current trends leads to the conclusion that by the beginning of the next millennium the proportion would rise to about one-fifth,[50] and could go as high as 30 percent by 2030. The Medicare program for the elderly and the Medicaid program for those with lower incomes increased from 5 percent of all federal spending in 1970 to 17 percent in 1994.

Perceived need for health insurance reform varies with demography. About 83 percent of those under sixty-five have health insurance coverage, compared to virtually universal Medicare coverage for those over sixty-five. The incomes of 28 percent of those who are uninsured are below the poverty line ($14,763 for a family of four in 1993), but 40 percent of the uninsured have incomes at least double the poverty level. Many of the uninsured are young and healthy: one-third are aged eighteen to twenty-nine, and 20 percent are between the ages of twenty-nine and forty. Uninsured adults and children receive about sixty to seventy percent as much health care as the insured.

Rationing of health care is an essential component of any health care policy. The principal distinction among the many proposals to overhaul the nation's health care system is that some plans emphasize a greater role for government regulation or ownership of the medical industry, while other arguments are supportive of private, market-driven control and ownership. Highly advanced medical technology, such as CT scanners, are extremely expensive, and in vitro fertilization, to help childless couples produce offspring, costs perhaps $100,000 per successful birth.

How to determine what is socially useful and what is not must be done by some mechanism, governmental or otherwise. Governments tend to ration goods, like access to health care, by making politically based decisions about how scarcity can be imposed to some degree on all citizens; in contrast, private, market forces tend to ration by price, by making some procedures unavailable to most of the population who can't afford them. The basic dilemma of the health care controversy revolves around the facts that controlling government spending makes it difficult to expand coverage, and expanding benefits almost certainly is going to be accompanied by higher costs. Some room certainly exists for reducing waste and excessive administrative costs in both private and government components of health care coverage; these have been estimated at $200 billion annually, which would be enough savings to provide quality care to all Americans without additional government spending.[51]

Governments at all levels, but particularly the federal government, are involved in funding the national cost of health care. About 42 percent of all health care spending comes from government sources; 55 percent of hospital services and 34 percent of physician bills are government-funded. Nearly three-quarters of all government hospital spending comes from the federal government, which also accounts for over 80 percent of government expenditures for physicians' costs. Only about 35 percent of hospital costs and 47 percent of doctors' payments are funded by private insurance.

As noted by Henry J. Aaron, there are two major problems plaguing the U.S. health care system, both involving finances.[52] The first problem is that the costs of health care are high and in most recent years have risen much more rapidly than general prices. Health care costs amount to about 15 percent of the domestic economy, and that figure has been rising steadily. The second problem, which is the issue that caused the 1994 Clinton health care reform initiative to founder, is that an estimated 35 million Americans do not have health insurance. Worse yet, possibly 70 million people may lack health care coverage at some point during any given year, although one-half of them obtain insurance coverage within six months.[53] Furthermore, access to medical care, especially for lower-income residents of isolated neighborhoods, often is unavailable, difficult to reach, and available only through facilities that are beyond their ability to pay.

Aaron argues that three fundamental issues must be addressed by any plan that purports to provide universal access to health care. The first problem is that some people's medical care financing must be subsidized because they are too poor to pay for health insurance on their own, including those not in the workforce, the unemployed, and both full-time and part-time workers who earn so little that health insurance is unaffordable. The second problem involves people who deliberately refuse to acquire health insurance although their incomes are adequate; they would have to be required to obtain insurance. Finally, those who are most likely to use health care resources are also the most likely to acquire health insurance.

Health care policy decisions must engage at least two major realities. First, the public agrees that serious problems exist in the American health care system. An August 1991 *CBS News/New York Times* poll found 79 percent agreement that "because of rising health care costs we are headed toward a crisis in the health care system." However, there is uncertainty regarding the severity of the problems of American health care. A Louis Harris and Associates poll from April 4–7, 1994, showed that 54 percent of respondents felt that "[t]here are some good things in our health care system, but fundamental changes are needed to make it better," whereas 31 percent agreed with the statement that "[o]ur health care system has so much wrong with it that we need to completely rebuild it," and just 14 percent opted for "[o]n the whole, the health care system works pretty well and only minor changes are necessary to make it work." Second, health care costs, particularly Medicare assistance to the elderly and Medicaid assistance to low-income Americans, have become tempting targets of Congress and others for reducing expenditures to balance the federal budget. Thus, there is a political tradeoff between the desire to balance the budget and a desire to meet national health care needs. A May 1993 *CBS News* poll showed pronounced public ambivalence about national priorities: 50 percent found "reforming health care" to be "the more important problem facing the country," but 44 percent opted for "reducing the federal budget deficit."

HISTORY OF HEALTH POLICY

Before Medicare and Medicaid (1965)

There are two fundamental themes involving government's role in U.S. health care policy. First, the role of government in large part has been to support the efforts undertaken by private institutions to correct health problems such as insurance coverage, to address threats to public health like those posed by the various causes of cancer, and to deal with specific diseases such as AIDS. Second, government has been instrumental in developing and sustaining the system that delivers health care to the nation.

One complication in the national health debate is that policymakers have to shoot at a moving target, because changing social and economic circumstances have been associated with changes in the nation's leading health issues. For example, in 1924, cancer surpassed tuberculosis as a reported cause of deaths in the U.S., and by 1934 cancer had become the nation's second-leading killer. Heart disease remains the single most deadly health threat. By the 1920s, the

U.S. government was spending $10 million annually to study tuberculosis, which by that time had become widespread from rapid and largely unregulated industrial growth. It was not until 1928 that the first federal spending ($50,000) for cancer research was approved by the Senate, but that bill was killed by a House committee. In 1937, the National Cancer Institute was established. As late as 1938, the total budget for the national Public Health Service was $28 million (compared, for example, to over $26 million allocated that year to the Department of Agriculture).[54]

Cancer research has identified a long list of carcinogens (cancer-causing substances) as being of industrial or occupational origin. Chimney soot was identified as carcinogenic in 1775, fumes from smelting in 1820, paraffin in 1875, uranium mine dust in 1876, lubricating oil used by mule spinners in 1887, aniline dyes in 1895, X-rays in 1908 for sarcoma and in 1930 for leukemia, coal tar in 1915, radium-dial paint in the 1920s, nickel ores in 1932, asbestos in the 1930s, and betanaphthylamine in the 1930s. It was not until the 1970s, however, that legislation began to address these concerns over worker health, through the Occupational Safety and Health Act of 1970, which required employers to provide work environments that were "free from recognized hazards that are causing or are likely to cause death or serious physical harm" to workers, and the Clean Air Act, which imposed strict standards for urban air quality through threatened withholding of federal funds. In addition, DDT (in 1972) and a number of other carcinogens were banned.

Starting in 1913 with Iowa, states have been active in combating health problems associated with asbestos exposure, by writing worker's compensation laws to cover asbestos-related diseases; by 1945, such legislation had been passed by twenty states. Action at the state level was essential, in large part because, apart from a 1938 report by the Public Health Service, the federal government was almost completely inactive in moving to protect the public from exposure to asbestos. This lack of federal action is attributable[55] to the fact that the federal government was promoting the development of the industry, due to wartime use of asbestos for defense production and to help maintain an essential component of the economy. Asbestos was sold from the federal stockpile, and there were determined efforts taken in concert with industry and agencies such as the U.S. Navy, to prevent the dissemination of information about asbestos to workers, the general public, and government oversight agencies.

Asbestos problems confronted state governments most clearly with regard to public school buildings. In several states, school districts closed their schools temporarily because of concerns about unsafe levels of asbestos. In addition, the National Education Association and other groups requested action by the national government to regulate the presence of asbestos in schools.

As late as 1960, U.S. spending on health care constituted only 5.3 percent of GNP, not appreciably different from the rate of spending on health care in most other industrialized countries. The current situation of much higher spending on health care is traceable to two programs: Medicare and Medicaid. Medicare provided federal funding to cover medical treatment for people over sixty-five.

Medicaid assisted low-income Americans, and its costs were shared by national and state governments.

Prior to the advent of Medicare and Medicaid, there was a considerably less extensive network of health insurance coverage by private companies. Treatments had been left almost entirely to the discretion of doctors, and almost any physician's test or treatment was reimbursed. Doctors tended to charge reasonable fees for their services, since many patients had insurance coverage only for hospitalization but not for routine doctors' bills. However, to overcome their fierce opposition to these programs, private health care providers were promised that under Medicare they would be paid based on "usual and customary" fees for given services, similar to the arrangement that massive private health insurers like Blue Shield already provided. The system of health care administration that the U.S. has today is an outgrowth of the private and public health insurance arrangements that evolved throughout the 1960s and 1970s, in which workers expected that their employers and themselves would pay the costs to supply medical coverage during their working years and into their retirement.

Health Maintenance Organizations, or HMOs, are intended to control health costs by replacing traditional insurance coverage with membership in managed care plans. Enrollment in HMOs has doubled since 1985, but they have a long history. The first HMOs were Kaiser Permanente, in California, and the Health Insurance Plan of Greater New York, which emerged in the 1940s as alternatives to traditional, fragmented, fee-for-service medicine. Known originally as prepaid group-practice plans, doctors on salary provided medical services within a single location for a fixed monthly fee paid by the members or their employers. Doctors participating in the plan were paid the same amount whether participating members were well or required care. Thus, a leading goal of these prototype HMOs was to keep members well by providing preventive services that were not covered by conventional insurance policies. Through coordinating the delivery of all treatments, controlling access to hospitals, and limiting referrals to more expensive specialists, prepaid group practices endeavored to cut the costs of health care delivery.

From Medicare to the Clinton Plan of 1994

Managed Care

In the early 1970s, prepaid group practices (the HMO concept) were enhanced by the Nixon administration, but only as a means to fend off demands for national health insurance. The term "health maintenance organization" was coined to denote health delivery groups that would be granted formal recognition for having satisfied government expectations. One consequence of this politically motivated endorsement of the HMO concept was that a much larger number of medical practitioners—now numbering about 550 nationally—adopted the label even though many of them differed greatly from the prototypes. Some of these have been formed by hospitals, others by physician groups, and others by entrepreneurs. All provide some version of health care for their members for fixed monthly premiums, but some operate under restrictive arrangements similar to those offered under traditional prepaid group plans, while others are composed of loose affiliations of doctors that function essentially like the fee-for-service, decentralized care that had been delivered in the pre-HMO era. HMOs vary in size from a relative handful of doctors to others with large networks of physicians. Larger HMOs generally provide more choice, but their size makes them more difficult to evaluate as to the use of services and the quality of the care provided.

Variants of HMOs also have emerged, particularly for employees reluctant to participate in standard HMO arrangements. Preferred-provider organizations, or PPOs, consist of networks of doctors and hospitals that have agreed to provide discounted services to people covered by their sponsoring organizations. Unlike HMOs, PPOs often do not tightly manage access to or the quality of medical care provided through their networks. Cost control is difficult, because patients covered by a PPO may seek care from any doctor participating in the network at any time.

Yet another variant is the gatekeeper PPO, networks of hospitals and physicians who have agreed to provide discounts but with even less quality control and tighter control of the type of medical services provided. A more restrictive version is the exclusive-provider organization, or EPO, which pays no benefits at all if a member employee visits a medical care provider outside the network. Unlike HMOs, EPOs are regulated by state insurance laws, rather than by the statutes regulating HMOs. Thus, EPOs may not have all the consumer safeguards available with HMOs such as formal grievance procedures.

A more recently evolved alternative is the opt-out HMO, also known as a point-of-service HMO, that pays around 60 to 70 percent of the cost of visiting physicians outside of the network. The drawback to the patient is the likely loss of HMO grievance procedures and quality assurance. Yet another arrangement, known as specialized networks, is structured for specific medical problems such as mental illness or substance abuse. These are designed to reduce inpatient hospital treatment for such traditionally expensive and difficult-to-treat medical problems. After calling the network to receive permission, an employee is sent to health care providers offering discounts to the sponsor.

Medicare has come close to fulfilling its original mandate to protect the elderly from prohibitively expensive health care, at least for recipients who are relatively healthy and who have doctors who do not charge excessive fees. Some of the major gaps in coverage are plugged by "medigap" insurance. Nonetheless, costs for hospital deductibles, copayments, and prescription drugs add up to out-of-pocket expenses that make medical coverage nearly prohibitive for many of the elderly. Lengthy hospital stays, even with Medicare coverage, can destroy the fragile finances of patients. Part A of Medicare, which covers hospital services, picks up only costs above the deductible payments that must be borne by the patient. Part B of Medicare, which covers medical services, pays for 80 percent of allowed doctors' charges; the beneficiary pays the rest. Since 1992, allowed charges have been determined by the doctor's skill and by the time needed to perform particular procedures, after adjusting for geographic variation in office rent and prevailing salary levels. Doctors who do not accept the charges permitted by Medicare may bill up to 20 percent above the Medicare fee level, paid by the beneficiaries. With few exceptions, Medicare does not cover prescription drugs consumed outside of the hospital.

Environmental Health

Environmental sources of health problems received increasing attention during the 1970s. An example of this evolution in health policy is provided by radon gas, estimated by EPA to be responsible for 7,000–30,000 lung cancer deaths annually, or 5 to 20 percent of all deaths from lung cancer.[56] Radon gas occurs through the natural decay of uranium in rocks and soil, with the gas seeping into homes through foundation posts and cracks in basements, where in turn it decays into other products that can cause cancer when inhaled. Radon is probably the most important cause of lung cancer among non-smokers, and is commonly regarded as second only to cigarette smoking as a cause of death from cancer. The seriousness of radon was recognized by the late 1970s, growing out of fear that efforts to insulate homes in reaction to the energy crisis were trapping the gas and its byproducts inside homes and producing carcinogenic levels of indoor air pollution. Radon problems became dramatically better known through the mass media following the discovery in the mid-1980s in Boyertown, Pennsylvania, of home levels of radon nearly 1,000 times greater than EPA guidelines. Media interest elevated radon to the status of a national problem requiring action. In 1992, the EPA estimated that the residents of about six million homes were incurring risks from radon exposure equivalent to smoking half a pack of cigarettes a day.[57]

The health effects of environmental contamination were addressed by Congress in its 1980 "Superfund" legislation, known formally as the Comprehensive Environmental Response, Compensation, and Liability Act (CERCLA). This act gave the Environmental Protection Agency the power to respond to health threats arising from hazardous substances, including indoor air pollutants such as radon. In 1985, a coalition of senators from northeastern states raised the issue of radon in Congress. Following hearings the next year, Congress enacted the Superfund Amendments and Reauthorization Act of 1986 (SARA), which authorized EPA to conduct a national radon survey and to develop methods for reducing indoor radon levels.[58]

Another environmental health problem that attracted attention from health policymakers is asbestos. Following decades of not acting on the accumulating evidence of diseases related to asbestos, the federal government finally began to respond in 1973, when EPA declared its Asbestos National Emission Standard for Hazardous Air Pollutants. However, EPA did not ban the manufacture of most asbestos products until 1989.[59] An estimated 30 million tons of asbestos insulation, tiling, piping, and other products have not yet been removed from homes, schools, and other buildings, and much of that has decayed to the point of producing new hazards. In 1986, the Asbestos Hazard Emergency Response Act required that every school be inspected and that facilities with asbestos hazards begin to clean up the problem by July 1989. Estimates of the cost of school asbestos cleanup range between $3 billion and $6 billion, and the overall cost of removing asbestos altogether has been put at more than $2 trillion.[60]

Worker Health and Safety

In 1978, Joseph Califano, then secretary of the Department of Health, Education, and Welfare (HEW), weighed in on behalf of the arguments presented in an interagency document addressing industry threats to workers' health and safety. Addressing the AFL-CIO National Conference on Occupational Safety and Health, Califano argued in favor of preventive medicine over an emphasis on medical treatments, because far more people die from chronic diseases, especially heart disease, cancer, and accidents, than from infectious diseases. Califano noted that only about 4 percent of the $48 billion that the federal government then spent for health care was devoted to prevention.

Relying on this evidence, in 1978 Congress amended the National Cancer Act to require HEW to issue an annual report listing known or suspected carcinogens and the degree to which human populations had been exposed to them. Within a month, Secretary Califano established a National Toxicology Program, with an initial budget of $41 million, to improve research and detection of toxic substances. Subsequent reports in 1980 by President Carter's Council on Environmental Quality and by the Centers for Disease Control reinforced the expectation of an impending wave of occupational disease and called for a national surveillance capacity similar to that for infectious diseases. Opposition to this movement was most visible from the American Industrial Health Council, an industry body formed in 1977.

In general, the Carter administration had focused on public health concerns, particularly preventive medicine, rather than on high-cost advanced curative medical technology. Carter's director of the National Cancer Institute (Arthur Upton) shared the concern of prevention as a top priority. However, with the election of Ronald Reagan in 1980, the government's orientation shifted strongly in favor of "regulatory relief" for industry and away from the preventive health perspectives favored by environmentalists and workers' representatives. A particular target of the Reagan deregulators was OSHA, which the Reagan administration regarded as overstaffed. OSHA's monthly inspection rate fell by 17 percent between 1980 and 1981, and its staffing declined by almost 30 percent between 1980 and 1985.[61] Follow-up inspections declined by over half, and there was a drop of nearly 30 percent in major citations issued.

AIDS

Probably no modern health problem has riveted the public's attention as much as AIDS. Definitions of what constitutes AIDS have been a focus of the controversy between competing visions of health care policymaking.[62] Local health care providers and facilities are required to report new AIDS cases, as defined by the Centers for Disease Control and Prevention (CDC), to their state and territorial health departments, which then must relay the information to CDC. The initial definition of AIDS was devised in 1982 to monitor the demographic distribution and spread of the disease, and changed again in 1985 and 1987. The 1987 reworking defined a person with AIDS as having one of twenty-three specific conditions and meeting other criteria, such as a positive HIV test.

Both political and medical practice difficulties[63] with the 1987 revision arose when increasing numbers of HIV-infected people became seriously ill without developing any of the twenty-three conditions. The official definition, then, could seriously underestimate the scope of the disease and might reduce the hold that AIDS had acquired on the national policy agenda. As the 1987 list of AIDS-defining conditions was symptomatic of diseases among gay men, it was argued that the government's policy was discriminatory toward women and intravenous drug users, indirectly harming African-Americans and Hispanics. This restrictive definition of AIDS also limited eligibility for Social Security Disability Insurance, Supplemental Security Income, and Medicaid. Private health insurers generally adopted the CDC rules for approving reimbursements for AIDS-related services, and federal funds to states were allocated in proportion to the size of the AIDS target population within a geographic district.

In 1991, CDC tried again to revise the AIDS definition, proposing to include all persons with low counts of CD4+ lymphocyte immune system cells in the blood stream. However, women's and other groups favoring a broader definition blocked implementation of this redefinition through demonstrations, testimony before Congress, and other activist tactics.[64] Consequently, on January 1, 1993, the new federal definition of AIDS included three more illnesses typically present in HIV-infected women and drug users as well as the CD4+ cell test.

The U.S. Supreme Court has intervened in the question of whether insurance coverage may be denied to people with AIDS and those with HIV-positive diagnoses. In the 1992 case of *McGann v. H&H Music Co.* (742 F. Supp. 392 (S.D. Tex. 1990), *affirmed* CA-5 (1992), *cert. denied* November 9, 1992), the Court allowed the health plans of self-insured employers to limit coverage for care related to AIDS and HIV.

Pressures on Medicaid from the extremely high costs associated with treating AIDS patients may cause state legislatures to become involved more directly in allocating Medicaid resources among competing health needs.[65] State policies regarding Medicaid coverage for AIDS-related health care are determined primarily by how prevalent the AIDS problem is in each state, attitudes of the legislators, and constituency characteristics. Legislators' attitudes about AIDS funding are related to their political ideology, party affiliation, and gender. Liberal legislators are less likely than conservatives to regard hospital care, physician care, nursing home care, or maternal and child health programs as having higher priority for Medicaid funding than for AIDS-related care. Liberal and Democratic state legislators favor increasing taxes, if necessary, to finance Medicaid coverage of AIDS-related care and to provide AZT treatments to Medicaid recipients who are infected with HIV but do not yet manifest overt symptoms. Women legislators, liberals, and Democrats are more likely to support extending eligibility for Medicaid coverage to people with AIDS.

The Looming Debate Over National Health Insurance

During the Bush administration, a number of competing plans were introduced for national health insurance, which would entitle everyone in the nation, regardless of economic or employment status, to selected services from doctors, hospitals, and other health care providers. Among the Bush-era plans considered by Congress were the Comprehensive Health Care for All Americans Act (sponsored by Representative Mary Rose Oakar, D-Ohio), the National Health Insurance Act (sponsored by Representative John Dingell, D-Michigan), the Mediplan Health Care Act of 1991 (sponsored by Representative Pete Stark, D-California), and the Universal Health Care Act of 1991 (sponsored by Representative Marty Russo, D-Illinois). With variations, the legislation included limited cost sharing by patients, payment of most costs to health care providers by the government, and tax policies to finance the plan. Costs for various services and overall care provider budgets would have to be negotiated through federal or state public authorities, and private insurance premium payments would be replaced by public expenditures through taxes on businesses and households.

Congressional Republicans introduced other plans, using tax credits or vouchers to require everyone to have private insurance coverage. These included the Affordable Health Insurance Act of 1991 (sponsored by Representative William Dannemeyer, R-California), the Comprehensive Health Care Access Improvement and Cost Containment Act of 1991 (sponsored by Representative Michael Bilirakis, R-Florida), the Health Equity and Access Improvement Act of 1992 (sponsored by Representative Amo Houghton, R-New York), and the Comprehensive American Health Care Act (sponsored by Senator Mitch McConnell, R-Kentucky). The evolving cost dimension of the American health care system from 1960 to the dawn of the Clinton administration is summarized in Table 8.2, which identifies trends within several major categories of health expenditures.

The Clinton Plan of 1994

In 1994, a major effort was undertaken by national policy planners to overhaul the existing health care system, with all of its complexities and inadequacies. President Bill Clinton and his wife, Hillary, convened meetings involving large numbers of policy experts to help set the policy agenda. The membership of the planning groups was initially kept secret, on grounds that interest groups would exert too much pressure on the decision-making process at its preliminary stage and thus foreclose attractive options if the names were made public. Later, the lists of participants were released after the Clintons had crafted their basic proposal.

TABLE 8.2 U.S. Health Expenditures, 1960–1993, by Type of Expenditures (in billions of dollars)

Type of Expenditure	1960	1970	1980	1985	1987	1989	1990	1991	1992	1993
Hospital	$9.3	$28.0	$102.7	$168.2	$194.1	$231.8	$256.5	$282.3	$306.0	$326.6
Physician	5.3	13.6	45.2	83.6	104.1	127.3	140.5	150.3	161.8	171.2
Dental	2.0	4.7	13.3	21.7	25.3	28.6	30.4	31.7	34.7	37.4
Other professional	0.6	1.4	6.4	16.8	22.6	32.2	36.0	40.4	46.4	51.2
Home health care	0.0	0.2	1.9	4.9	5.9	6.1	11.1	13.2	16.8	20.8
Drugs and other medical nondurables	4.2	8.8	21.6	37.4	45.4	54.4	61.2	67.1	70.8	75.0
Vision products and other medical durables	0.8	2.0	4.5	7.1	8.1	9.6	10.5	11.3	12.0	12.6
Nursing home care	1.0	4.9	20.5	34.9	40.6	48.9	54.8	60.6	65.5	69.6
Other personal health care	0.7	1.3	4.0	6.1	7.7	9.5	11.4	13.8	15.8	18.2
Program administration and net cost of private health insurance	1.2	2.8	12.1	25.3	19.4	32.3	38.3	37.0	39.5	48.0
Government public health activities	0.4	1.4	7.2	12.3	14.6	19.0	21.6	22.9	23.7	24.7
Research	0.7	2.0	5.6	7.8	9.1	11.3	12.2	12.9	14.2	14.4
Construction	1.0	3.4	6.2	8.6	9.2	10.8	12.1	11.9	13.2	14.6

Source: Health Care Financing Administration, Office of the Actuary; data from Office of National Health Statistics.

Notes: Research and development expenditures of drug companies and other manufacturers and providers of medical equipment and supplies are excluded from research expenditures, but are included in the expenditure class in which the product falls.

The Clinton reform initiative was criticized strongly and consistently by opponents. Particularly disliked was the provision to force everyone to buy insurance through government-created purchasing cooperatives, which became an easy target since lobbyists could claim that the proposal would take away the right to choose one's own doctor who would prescribe necessary treatments and place that decision in the hands of much-maligned faceless bureaucrats in faraway offices who might deny access to needed medical services. In fact, most Americans could not make such a choice under the health system in effect when the Clinton proposal was released, because about 85 percent of the U.S. companies that provide health insurance offer only one plan.

Proponents of the Clinton reform argued that effective cost containment would be possible only if coverage were extended to everyone, so that private health insurers would not be able to deny coverage or to raise premiums arbitrarily for more risky individual cases, or for entire segments of the population. The goal of universal coverage was to prevent the possibility that those who currently have insurance coverage might lose it, and to provide coverage to those who now do not have it. A worker changing jobs might encounter a situation in which the new employer's health insurer would have more restrictive provisions that could deny coverage on grounds of a "preexisting condition" such as diabetes or cancer.

The essence of the Clinton proposal was to achieve managed competition, in which health insurance purchasing alliances would provide access to both the sale of health insurance and the purchase of health care, presumably at lower prices than are currently available.[66] This goal would be achieved by large-scale coordination among several such alliances acting together within an area to promote competition among insurers and to provide services competitively. Hospitals' and doctors' costs would be negotiated through these alliances. This arrangement was designed to consolidate insurance markets, reduce the administrative costs that occur when many groups compete with each other, minimize information problems and confusion among insurance buyers, and reduce the number of competing insurance plans.

The Progressive Policy Institute, the center-right "think tank" of the Democratic Leadership Council, from which Bill Clinton derived many of his policy ideas, touted the virtues of managed competition, as exemplified by health plans for federal workers and for public employees in California and Minnesota. Nine million Americans are covered under the Federal Employees Health Benefits Plan, which provides a market-based choice among a variety of competing private insurance plans subject to control by the Office of Personnel Management. About 120,000 people are covered by Minnesota public employee protection, which became more market-oriented during the 1980s and was credited with helping to reduce the rate of growth in medical care premiums. The California Public Employees Retirement System covers 800,000 people and is acclaimed for reducing administrative costs, spreading risk, and providing choice to the insured. Citing what it saw as success stories, the Progressive Policy Institute concluded, "These systems . . . demonstrate that managed competition can dramatically control health costs, and that in well-structured health markets consumers can make informed choices based on the relative value of competing options."[67]

Opponents of the Clinton proposal argued that rapidly growing federal government commitments to provide health protection would crowd out private and other government investment in economic growth, foster continued federal budget deficits, lower take-home incomes, reduce the rate of jobs formation, and further restrict already-limited discretionary spending within the federal budget. Those opposed to universal coverage point to the recent experience of European countries, which generally have more generous health care provisions than the U.S. The growth in European unemployment between 1974 and 1994, from 3 to 11 percent, with little growth in the number of private jobs available, was used by those who favored cost containment over universal coverage as a sign of what would happen in the U.S. as a result of high payroll taxes and required medical benefits. The likelihood of rapid increases in government health care spending is enhanced greatly by the aging of the baby boom generation born soon after the end of World War II, since older people require several times as much health care spending per capita as young adults. It is projected that by 2030, 20 percent of the U.S. population will be at least sixty-five years old, as contrasted to about 12 percent in the early 1990s.

The debate over health care reform involved two primary goals. The first was cost containment, by controlling spending on health care by government and private sources. The second was universal coverage, by expanding and protecting access to health insurance to nearly everyone in society. Arguments against the Clinton health care proposals were predicated largely on fears that the national government would be creating vast new spending programs, amounting to hundreds of billions of dollars, and would dictate to businesses the levels of benefits for those under sixty-five years of age (and therefore not covered by Medicare). The anti-Clinton argument held that it would be attractive politically to expand coverage to new categories of medical needs that now are either minor cost items or not yet known. The opponents feared that a strong political coalition would form in favor of steadily increasing health benefits and spending.

The 1994 congressional debate over health policy sharpened as support for the Clinton proposal waned and last-minute efforts prior to adjournment of the 103rd Congress were undertaken to work out at least a partial resolution to the problems confronting the nation's health care system. House Majority Leader Richard Gephardt (D-Missouri) proposed a standard insurance package, with employers paying 80 percent of the costs for their workers and creation of a new Medicare program for the unemployed and for workers in small companies. Gephardt's proposal included subsidies to help low-income workers and small firms, plus standby price controls taking effect after the year 2000. It required HMOs and other health plans to use any doctor willing to accept a plan's payment rates. The plan provided that the self-employed and workers in businesses with fewer than 100 employees could buy coverage either from a private insurance company or from a new component of Medicare. Under the Gephardt proposal, all participants would receive the same benefits the elderly have under Medicare and unlimited hospital care without having to make copayments, a $500 deductible per individual and $750 deductible per family, coverage for prescription drugs, comprehensive mental-health benefits, and a cap on annual family medical expenses. If competition from Medicare failed to hold down the costs of private insurance and medical treatment, Gephardt proposed that a national health cost commission would set doctors' and hospitals' fees.

Retiring Senate Majority Leader George Mitchell (D-Maine) suggested an essentially voluntary program, with subsidies providing coverage for 95 percent of the population by 2000, and proposed that if that level of coverage was unattained, Congress could require companies to pay 50 percent of the costs of a standard package. Pregnant women and children under age nineteen would receive either partial or total subsidies through government vouchers to pay the full costs of their health care, if they qualified because of low income.

The Mitchell plan required a standard package of benefits for all firms currently offering health insurance. It avoided establishing a federally run insurance plan, instead allowing broader participation in the same network of private insurers used by members of Congress and other federal employees, and tried to use existing market incentives to hold down the cost of health insurance coverage. Small groups needing coverage could band together to buy lower-cost insurance; "community rating" zones would be established to spread the risk of covering dramatic changes in individual health histories and avoid the possibility of canceling group coverage because of such individual changes; and the plan would require insurance companies to cover preexisting medical conditions. Home care would be provided for senior citizens or disabled persons. Rather than relying on government insurance or price controls, Mitchell proposed to replace Medicaid with a program that would allow low-income families to buy private insurance coverage.

The Contemporary Agenda

Disjointed Federal Government Action

Several agencies within the federal government play different roles in making and implementing health policy. Traditionally, the U.S. Department of Labor, in advocating the interests of its labor constituency, has been cautious in pursuing matters related to environmental and occupational health. In contrast, the U.S. Public Health Service, regarding itself as a neutral body providing scientific expertise, has emphasized minimizing the risk of public exposure to health hazards. As a result of this division of loyalties by major components of the national executive branch, it is important to notice that the National Institute for Occupational Safety and Health was established within the Public Health Service, rather than within the Labor Department, which, however, incorporates the Occupational Safety and Health Administration. One consequence of this division of authority has been to concentrate research within the Public Health Service and to make advocacy the specialized task of labor's institutionalized supporters.[68] Research coordination also is facilitated through professional associations, such as the Section on Health Policy of the American Statistical Association.

Medicaid

Medicaid, a joint federal-state program to finance medical care for the poor, currently covers about one-half of all nursing-home stays. In different states, between 25 percent and 50 percent of those admitted to nursing homes apply for Medicaid coverage immediately, and 4 percent to 18 percent more become eligible after entering a nursing home because their costs are so extreme that they are driven into poverty as their assets disappear. To qualify for Medicaid, patients cannot own assets exceeding a maximum determined by the state. Within federally set limits—which do not include the applicant's home, household goods, and personal effects—each state decides how much of a couple's assets the spouse remaining at home may keep. When a couple's assets fall below the minimum, the spouse at home may keep all of that amount and is allowed to continue to live in the family house. After both are dead, however, the state can recover from the couple's estate what its Medicaid program spent on them. How much income the spouse remaining at home may have is also determined by each state, again within federally established limits. Asset and income limits are adjusted for inflation annually.

Medicaid expenditures absorb a major portion of many state budgets. On average, 13.6 percent of all state government expenditures were devoted to Medicaid in Fiscal Year 1991, a marked increase from 10.2 percent of all expenditures in 1986.[69] That state governments find it difficult to incorporate these costs into their budget planning is evident from the fact that Medicaid programs frequently require supplementary appropriations beyond their initial allocations.[70] A study by the U.S. General Accounting Office[71] concluded that, especially during the economy's periodic downturns, the pressure on state governments to limit spending is making it increasingly difficult for state Medicaid programs to meet the needs of their recipients and to pay health service providers adequately.

Focus on the States

The impact of devolving policy authority to state governments is especially clear-cut in health care administration. A close examination of recent experiences at the state level provides a great deal of evidence about the range of future developments in this key policy area. Public health has always been primarily the province of state officials, with the federal government playing generally a supportive role. This situation promises to be accentuated in the future.

The state that has gone the furthest toward providing a form of universal health care is Hawaii. Although that state spends less on medical care—about 8 percent of its gross state product—than the rest of the U.S., Hawaii exceeds national averages in life expectancy, time spent in hospitals, and infant survival rate. Contributing to Hawaii's health advantages are nearly universal access to health insurance and a heavy emphasis on primary and preventive care. Only 9.2 percent of Hawaiians do not have health coverage from some source, compared to about one-seventh of the entire country. The noncoverage rate for each state is presented in Table 8.3.

In 1974, Hawaii enacted its Prepaid Health Care Act, which requires all employers to provide health insurance coverage for full-time workers. As a result of the need to compete for relatively scarce labor, most workers' dependents also

TABLE 8.3 Health Insurance Noncoverage, by State, 1994

State	Percentage Not Covered	State	Percentage Not Covered
Alabama	19.2%	Montana	13.6%
Alaska	13.3	Nebraska	10.7
Arizona	20.2	Nevada	15.7
Arkansas	17.4	New Hampshire	11.9
California	21.1	New Jersey	13.0
Colorado	12.4	New Mexico	23.1
Connecticut	10.4	New York	16.0
Delaware	13.5	North Carolina	13.3
District of Columbia	16.4	North Dakota	8.4
Florida	17.2	Ohio	11.0
Georgia	16.2	Oklahoma	17.8
Hawaii	9.2	Oregon	13.1
Idaho	14.0	Pennsylvania	10.6
Illinois	11.4	Rhode Island	11.5
Indiana	10.5	South Carolina	14.2
Iowa	9.7	South Dakota	10.0
Kansas	12.9	Tennessee	10.2
Kentucky	15.2	Texas	24.2
Louisiana	19.2	Utah	11.5
Maine	13.1	Vermont	8.6
Maryland	12.6	Virginia	12.0
Massachusetts	12.5	Washington	12.7
Michigan	10.8	West Virginia	16.2
Minnesota	9.5	Wisconsin	8.9
Mississippi	17.8	Wyoming	15.4
Missouri	12.2	U.S. total	15.2

Source: Bureau of the Census, U.S. Department of Commerce.

are covered, although such provisions are not required under the legislation. The law mandates minimum coverage of 120 hospital days, doctors' services, diagnostic and laboratory services, and maternity benefits. Insurance providers must accept all workers, regardless of their health history. One major consequence of this universal coverage is that health insurance firms share proportionately the risks of having to cover people having serious health problems that potentially may be expensive to treat, thus saving administrative overhead expenses associated with having to screen prospective policyholders' health histories.

At least one-half of Hawaiians' health insurance premiums are paid by their employers; workers' shares are limited to no more than 1.5 percent of wages. Businesses employing fewer than eight workers—which generally have more difficulty than larger firms affording their employees' health care costs—are protected by a "premium supplementation fund," but it seldom has to be used. The Hawaiian health care system contains controls on medical technology, to avoid waste and duplication of resources, through a health-planning agency and a law requiring hospitals and other care providers to justify an increased number of beds or improved medical equipment.

The Hawaii Department of Health established a State Health Insurance Plan (SHIP) in 1989, using $10 million in seed money provided by the state legislature, to extend health coverage to the unemployed and to those who work too few hours to be covered by their employers. Many Hawaiians who received this benefit have incomes too low for them to afford health insurance on their own, although their incomes were too high to qualify for Medicaid coverage. SHIP benefits are less comprehensive than what is provided to the broader population, with emphasis on primary and preventive care as opposed to more expensive inpatient hospital services. Benefits include twelve doctors' visits annually, but just five days of hospitalization. Most SHIP recipients must make a $5 copayment to help pay for medical services and pay monthly premiums calibrated to income levels. Other care is subsidized by the state.

The success of the Hawaii health care arrangement is traceable in large part to the fact that only two major insurers—the Hawaii Medical Service Association (HMSA)—a Blue Cross/Blue Shield entity—and Kaiser Permanente, a traditional HMO with doctors working for salary in health centers—dominate the state's insurance market. Small employers are offered uniform health policy rates for their workers independent of health history. Their concentrated market power permits Hawaii's two insurers to control health care costs. Doctors' fee increases are limited to cost-of-living raises, and their standard fee structure is set for a bundled package of medical procedures that doctors in other states have been able to bill separately. Doctors do not have to participate in the program. In that case, payments go directly to the patients, and the doctors must collect fees from them.

In addition, possibly as an outgrowth of its history of outpatient clinics designed to treat plantation workers, HMSA's insurance policies promote preventive and outpatient care. The fact that most policies have few deductibles encourages patients to get early medical attention before hospitalization may be required, and they pay only minimum rates for hospital stays rather than the higher semiprivate room rates that predominate in the rest of the nation. Perhaps for these reasons, the Hawaiian hospital system has little excess capacity and typically is 80 to 90 percent full.

There are problems with the Hawaiian medical care system, as in other states. The expense of new technology and rising wages for medical personnel absorb most of the money that is saved from high capacity rates, sharing services and equipment across hospitals, and low marketing costs. Medicaid and Medicare have failed to pay adequately for the cost of care provided to their recipients, resulting in hospitals charging the state's insurers exorbitant rates and the insurers passing those costs along in the form of higher premiums. Hawaii's Medicaid system is chronically in deficit and requires additional legislative appropriations. Because of this underfunding, some areas of the state do not have medical services, in large part because a number of doctors and dentists refuse to treat Medicaid recipients. Also, higher partial payments by workers have been mandated by some employers trying to defray their escalating health care costs. In general, the problems with Hawaii's health care payment system arise from the absence of universal access, even though the state does provide universal insurance coverage. As the editors of Consumer Reports conclude,

> Hawaii's clearest lesson may be an unintended one: the pernicious effects of cost shifting when public insurance and private insurance exist side by side. As long as the government can pay less and shift the cost to private insurers, and as long as private insurers can pass the costs on in the form of higher premiums, the crisis in health care will continue.[72]

Another leading state and local government experiment in health cost containment is under way in Minneapolis, Minnesota, where half the population belongs to HMOs, the largest of which enrolls almost a third of a million participants. This approach operates from the presumption that managed care provision through HMOs delivers health services more efficiently than do market-driven, fee-for-service health care programs. A major consequence of Minneapolis's HMO experience has been to reduce the number of hospitals in the area by half, as previous excess capacity was forced out of the local health care delivery system by the HMOs' insistence on heavy price discounts. This resulted in many hospital mergers, in part because HMOs popularized outpatient services and doctors became comfortable with the reduced need for hospitalization.

However, contemporary problems confronting health care delivery nationally have had an impact on the Minneapolis HMO system. Premiums have grown rapidly, more use is being made of medical services, drug prices have risen, and the escalating costs of new medical technology continually bring pressure to bear on established HMO cost structures. Some employers have attempted to reduce administrative costs by limiting their employees' choices of competing HMOs, and many small businesses are unable to participate in

Contemporary Controversy

Cost Containment

The U.S. health care system is caught between two realities: Its costs are increasing very rapidly, yet it fails to provide even basic coverage for large numbers of citizens who are uninsured or otherwise unable to afford adequate health service provision. The problem, of course, is that there is no easy way—at least not one that is feasible politically—to provide simultaneously for both lower costs and wider availability of service. Expanding health care service to more (let alone all) of the population requires greater funding levels, and cutting funds for health care delivery almost certainly will necessitate reduced coverage for those who will not be able to afford quality medical care with their own resources.

Owing to the strong commitment by federal and state governments to provide doctors' and hospitals' payments, control of health care costs is largely a function of the degree of governmental commitment to limiting expenditures. Until 1984, the Medicare program reimbursed hospitals under its Part A for "reasonable costs" associated with providing services to those receiving benefits. One of the executive-branch

---

their options. Thus, 300,000 people in Minnesota remain uninsured through either HMOs or traditional health insurance plans. Partial coverage of the uninsured has been provided through state legislative action, but this remains inadequate to cover the gaps in coverage.

The 1990s and Beyond

Among the developments toward the end of the 1990s that suggest future directions for American health policy is a movement by companies to work together to find the lowest possible health insurance rates. For example, in May 1995, ten large corporations, with 240,000 employees between them, joined in common bidding for the services of over 100 health maintenance organizations through a standardized contract,[73] and other firms were expected to join. Similar actions have been taken in other metropolitan areas, including Minneapolis, San Francisco, Houston, Orlando, Cleveland, Cincinnati, and St. Louis. Related efforts were contemplated by major companies to negotiate with Medicare-serving HMOs to cover medical care for their retired employees.

Future developments regarding Medicaid must take into consideration trends in patterns of expenditures for that program and recent developments regarding the Republican-led drive to force a balanced budget. Medicaid expenditures on inpatient hospital care have dropped from 31.3 percent of total

agencies involved in health policy is the Health Care Financing Administration (HCFA). Among its other duties, HCFA oversees the conversion of the process of paying for health service from one of retrospective cost reimbursement, in which the doctor or hospital was paid after submitting a bill to the government, to a prospective payment system under which payments are made at predetermined rates representing average national costs for treating patients with comparable diagnoses. Diagnosis-related groups, or DRGs, were used to classify hospital patients and the charges associated with their care.

The Omnibus Budget Reconciliation Act of 1989 established a three-part system of payment for doctors, replacing the previous "reasonable" charge payment system with a "fee schedule" based on a "relative value scale" that was to be phased in over four years, beginning January 1, 1992. This revised system was designed to give doctors incentives to take part in efforts to limit cost increases. The 1989 legislation also limited how much doctors could charge Medicare patients above approved payment levels.

In 1995, the Republican congressional majority committed itself to balancing the federal budget within seven years—by 2002. Central to the Republican plan was the need for deep cuts in projected spending on Medicare, without which the plan's objectives could not be attained. The primary budgetary problem is that the trust fund that pays for Medicare expenditures is in chronic danger of running out of money. In fact, in fiscal year 1995 the trust fund suffered its first loss ($35.7 million) since 1972, with much heavier losses in fiscal year 1996 ($4.2 billion in the first half). Democrats argued

(continued)

Medicaid costs in 1970 to less than 25 percent today, while the proportion of spending devoted to care at skilled nursing homes and at intermediate care facilities has declined from a peak of 35.3 percent in 1975 to about 27 percent in the early 1990s. Expenditures for intermediate facility care of the mentally retarded has grown rapidly, from only about 2 percent of total Medicaid costs in 1973 to about 12 percent now. Home health care costs expanded from under 1 percent in the early 1970s to over 5 percent in the 1990s. The most dramatic reductions in the use of Medicaid funds came in physician care—from about 13 percent in 1970 to only about 6 percent today. Some reduction also occurred in Medicaid spending for drugs, from 8.4 percent in 1970 to a low of 5.6 percent in 1980, but this was followed by more recent increases in this category.[74]

Nearly 250,000 Americans have been diagnosed with AIDS.[75] The average cost of treating an AIDS patient has been estimated at over $100,000.[76] An estimated 45 percent of persons with AIDS are likely to receive Medicaid benefits for their care,[77] and Medicaid is becoming the primary payer for AIDS-related hospitalizations, especially in large cities that have been hit hard by the disease—for example, New York City, Los Angeles, and San Francisco. The fact that the fastest spread of HIV is among intravenous drug abusers, their sexual partners, and their children is critically important for publicly funded health insurance, because these groups generally have lower incomes and do not have private health insurance.[78] This means additional upward pressure

that the Republican budget plan would result in lower-income Medicare recipients paying for tax cuts that also were included in the Republicans' fiscal strategy.

Medicare, together with Medicaid, the joint federal-state health program for the poor, constitutes the fastest-growing part of the federal budget. Its projected costs were $286 billion by 2000, 62 percent above its 1995 level. Because the congressional Republicans' budget plan omitted any changes in Social Security or military spending, and because interest on the national debt must be paid regardless of other budgetary developments, Medicare expenditures—roughly 25 percent of remaining "discretionary" spending—are a tempting target for budget cutters. Between one-fourth and one-third of the total saving needed to produce a balanced budget without raising taxes would come from reducing Medicare spending by an average of $35 to $45 billion for each of the seven years. At the end of 1995, President Clinton proposed to trim projected spending on Medicare by $124 billion over seven years. Republicans called that proposal insufficient, preferring their own plan that would reduce projected Medicare spending over seven years by $270 billion.[85] Democrats and most independent policy analysts concluded, in contrast, that limiting Medicare expenditures almost certainly would lead to higher costs or lower spending for the elderly. In the face of these counter-arguments, Republicans shifted their position, now maintaining that savings were needed to keep Medicare fiscally solvent, rather than purely for the sake of helping to balance the budget. The Republicans' target was to reduce projected Medicare spend-

on Medicaid expenses, all the more so because private health insurers deny or limit coverage for people diagnosed with HIV.[79]

Another dimension for future development regarding health policy concerns implementation of the 1990 Americans with Disabilities Act (ADA), which extended basic civil rights and access to government protections previously unavailable to the estimated 20–50 million Americans having a recognizable physical or mental disability. It has been estimated[80] that the combined costs of Medicare, income replacement programs through Social Security, education, rehabilitation, disabled veterans' services, health-related services, and other public and private social services may reach $500 billion annually during the 1990s.

The movement toward making personal assistance services more readily available through independent living and control by consumers receiving those services, and away from control of disabled persons' lives by health care professionals, is another aspect to the evolving debate over health policy. This change fits the contemporary emphases on cost containment and on local, community-based control over service delivery. There is debate about who should be entitled to publicly provided and/or paid services, how much assistance should be provided, and who should control its administration.[81] Future public policy issues surrounding the provision of personal assistance services should become increasingly important as more people live through catastrophic accidents and illnesses but suffer from residual functional impairments, and as the population of baby boomers approaches old age.

ing by $270 billion, or 14 percent, over the seven years of their balanced-budget program. This was intended to stem what they regarded as the unrestrained growth of Medicare costs, which were about $159.5 billion in 1994 and had expanded at the rate of about 10 percent per year.

The fundamental point of contention in this debate is Medicare hospital costs, which are funded by a 2.9 percent payroll tax, paid equally by employers and employees, that is channeled into the Health Insurance Trust Fund—the only money that may be used to pay hospital costs. Although the hospital fund had been in surplus for several years, and had helped to minimize the amount the federal government had to borrow to finance its activities, the trust fund was predicted to run out of money completely by 2002. Prior to the Republican-led efforts in the 104th Congress, the House and Senate had provided a number of short-term solutions to the impending Medicare funding crises. As part of President Clinton's 1993 legislation to reduce the deficit, Congress subjected all income to coverage by the Medicare payroll tax, raised the amount of Social Security benefits that could be taxed, and directed the higher tax revenue to the Medicare trust fund. Other solutions that have been discussed are to increase the Medicare recipients' premium for doctor and outpatient services, raise the deductible beyond $100 a year, charge new Medicare beneficiaries additional monthly charges if they opt out of an HMO, and require copayments for users of home health care services and certain other charges.[86]

Corporations, under pressure to improve their "bottom line" performance, have limited or eliminated health care benefits for their retired employees, and sometimes for their current workers. These retrenchments have become a flash point for union job actions, and are likely to become more salient for future public policymaking. For example, in 1995, the AT&T corporation and its 90,000 workers who were organized through the Communication Workers of America (CWA) and 20,000 other workers organized by the International Brotherhood of Electrical Workers came into conflict over a number of contract issues. Among the bargaining points were wages, pensions, job security, and whether employees would pay for part of their medical coverage. The unions firmly rejected the company's push to shift some of its health care costs onto retirees. The new three-year contract that was agreed to in June 1995 stipulated that no pensioners would have to pay toward their health care. Retirees were offered the same health benefits as active employees.[82] In a climate of frequently poisonous labor-management relations characterized by cuts in jobs, limited wage increases or reduced labor costs, eliminated or reduced worker benefits, and greater use of overtime to increase profits, health care increasingly has led to conflict as workers tried to maintain what they had won in previous efforts.

Mental health policy also is in flux. The decentralization of community mental health centers during the Reagan administration was accompanied by budget reductions that produced changes in the administration of mental health facilities. Local centers have been forced to seek wider bases of financial support and have targeted services more to the chronic mentally ill. Health

Case Study

Cancer and the Future of Health Care Policy

ALTHOUGH MUCH of the contemporary debate regarding U.S. health care policy has been consumed with problems such as AIDS and issues surrounding health care financing, heart disease and cancer have been and remain the two deadliest health problems in the country. Cancer has been a particular source of continuing public anxiety, partly because it has become linked closely with environmental contamination and with concern for workplace safety. In addition, cancer has been far less tractable to medical countermeasures. Whereas heart disease death rates fell by 55 percent between 1950 and 1987, cancer death rates, adjusted for age differences, actually increased about 6 percent. From 1958 to 1988, lung cancer incidence rates rose 425 percent for males and 121 percent for females; kidney cancer increased 35 percent for men and 22 percent among women; male colon cancer grew by 21 percent, esophagus cancer by 20 percent, prostate cancer by 12 percent, and skin cancer 126 percent. During the same time, age-adjusted death rates from all forms of cancer rose 3 percent, but cancer's general incidence grew much more quickly (44 percent).[87] Robert Proctor has noted:

> More than a thousand people die of cancer every day in the United States. For every American alive today, one in three will contract the disease and one in five will die from it. Cancer is the plague of the twentieth century, second only to heart disease as a cause of death in the United States and most other First World nations. While most other diseases are on the decline, cancer is on the rise.[88]

Issues related to care of the elderly are also central to the policy debate surrounding cancer, which is primarily a disease of the elderly. There are also racial and social class elements to the cancer story, as African-Americans die at significantly higher rates than do whites from all major forms of cancer except skin cancer, with poverty being the best explanation of these stark differences across racial groups.[89] Adjusting for age differences, the mortality rate for African-Americans was 27 percent greater than that for

policy initiatives must also address high rates of mental illness among the homeless and problems confronting those displaced from institutions.

Among future health policy developments will be discussions regarding capitation[83] as a means of limiting costs. Capitation involves payment for medical services for each enrolled client, over a limited time, and for specified services. This system forces health care providers to manage more carefully their provision of services within a fixed budget and thus to share the financial risk.[84] Supporters of capitation like its consistency with long-term planning because payments often are made in advance, as well as its consolidation of funding sources, increased resource base, greater flexibility, targeting resources to patients most in need of assistance, cost-effectiveness, and coordinating care

whites, and the odds of surviving five years or more from cancer were only 38 percent for African-Americans, contrasted to 53 percent for whites.[90]

The racial demographics of cancer are not improving. Among African-Americans, between 1956 and 1986, death rates from cancer increased 66 percent for men and 10 percent for women, after adjusting for the fact that people now live slightly longer; mouth cancer incidence rose 70 percent for men and 30 percent for women, while lung cancer exploded upward by 259 percent among men and 440 percent among women. Also, death rates have risen more quickly for African-Americans than for Americans of European ancestry. Since 1955, cancer death rates grew 17 percent for white men and 2 percent for white women, as compared to 66 percent among African-American men and 10 percent among African-American women.[91]

The gendered basis of the health policy debate is perhaps no more clearly evident than in the area of breast cancer research. The statistical and epidemiological evidence on increased incidence is startling. The age-adjusted incidence of breast cancer increased 45 percent from 1960 to 1985.[92] Furthermore, the more widespread use of mammography could explain at most only one-third of this overall increase. This gender difference is heightened by racial, and therefore also social, differences. From 1979 to 1986, the incidence of breast cancer increased 29 percent among whites and 41 percent among African-Americans, and the increased use of mammographic screening was estimated to account for only about 40 percent of the reported increase for whites and just 25 percent among African-Americans.[93]

The policy complexities and political complications that have evolved around the problem of cancer provide the focus of this case study. These difficulties are clear from the dismal facts of established treatments. Since President Richard Nixon declared war on cancer in 1971, over $25 billion has been spent on research by the National Cancer Institute, but five-year survival rates for leading cancers (of the lung, colon, breast, and stomach, among others) have changed little. The only perceptible progress may be in improved early diagnosis, which is credited with a modest growth in five-year survival rates from 49 percent in the mid-1970s to 53 percent in the 1990s.[94] However, 95 percent of all lung cancers are fatal, no matter how they are treated, and standard treatments for colon cancer and other leading cancers—chemotherapy, surgery, and radiation—show little benefit and actually may increase the risk of other problems such as leukemia.[95]

(continued)

among providers. Drawbacks include "skimming" healthy patients and avoiding those who require more intensive care, shifting providers' costs to other parts of the health care system not under capitation, substituting less qualified medical staff, underserving clients to reduce costs, and the crowding out of moderate users by higher-rate users.

Health care policy must contend with the political climate in Washington and in state governments favoring reduced expenditures in general, and particularly cuts in social services, including health. The defeat of major efforts to reform the nation's health care system, even with the support of the Clinton White House, combined with the impetus toward balancing the federal budget, demonstrates the strength of antireform forces in this continuing struggle.

With the rise of environmentally conscious groups and ideas in the 1970s, strong criticism emerged regarding the manner in which the battle against cancer had been conducted previously. A major component of the recent debate has revolved around the possible environmental origin of many common cancers. Cancer is more preventable to the extent that it is attributed to avoidable, naturally occurring phenomena, and the emphasis of national cancer policy accordingly should be changed away from treatment and toward prevention. This position has been taken by some researchers,[96] and by the United Nations's World Health Organization.[97] In contrast, the traditional argument has been that cancer was the result of luck, genetics, or the aging process. The outcome of this debate leads to profoundly different policy implications, depending on which side prevails. As interpreted by Robert Proctor,[98] the choice is between "the elusive search for cures" and prevention.

A large part of the contemporary policy debate surrounding cancer treatment and prevention is uncertainty about the origins of the disease, and particularly about the sources of its pronounced growth. One study[99] comparing fourteen types of cancer that showed increased mortality rates from 1973 to 1990 found that the second-fastest increase was for the category of "site unknown." Most research links smoking to much of the overall growth in cancer incidence, but incidence rates for multiple myeloma, non-Hodgkin's lymphoma, and cancer of the brain, breast, and testicles, which have not been shown to be related to smoking, also have grown in recent decades.[100]

Profoundly different world views are at the heart of the debate over cancer's origins. Environmental activists attribute much of the contemporary cancer problem to the concentration of industrial power. It has become generally accepted that chemical carcinogens were responsible for the bulk of cancer cases.[101] A group opposed to the use of pesticides, the Rachel Carson Trust, argued that as much as 60 to 90 percent of cancer cases in the world today are caused by environmental and occupational factors, and that 90 percent of those cases are due to primarily man-made chemical carcinogens.

The power perspective on policy formation is evident in the politics of cancer. This is perhaps most evident in the area of breast cancer, where groups such as the National Breast Cancer Coalition (NBCC) attempt to pressure governmental institutions to fund research on breast cancer. Founded in 1991, NBCC is a "peak" association comprising over 300 organizations nationally. It was instrumental in the effort to achieve congressional approval in 1992 for a substantial increase (to $410 million) in total federal funding of breast cancer research—$200 million for the National Cancer Institute and $210 million in the Department of Defense—and a further gain to $465 million in 1995. NBCC delivered 2.6 million messages to the Clinton White House, one message for each woman living at the time with breast cancer, and gained the endorsement of President Clinton, Hillary Rodham Clinton—who was leading the president's health care reform effort—and Secretary of Health and Human Services Donna Shalala for a National Breast Cancer Summit. In turn, the summit of scientists, industry representatives, media leaders, general citizens, government officials, and the NBCC established the National Action Plan on Breast Cancer, with the NBCC leading the charge to implement the plan's recommendations. Putting their cause into perspective, this group argued in a recent fundraising letter (emphasis in original):

> During the eight years of the Vietnam War, 54,000 Americans died. This year [1995] alone, 46,000 women will die of breast cancer. In the ten years of the AIDS epidemic,

nearly 133,000 Americans have died of AIDS. In that same time, we've lost more than 404,000 women to breast cancer. Every three minutes, a woman in the United States is diagnosed with breast cancer. Every eleven minutes, a woman dies of breast cancer.

NBCC monitors activities of the National Cancer Institute. Activists in the breast cancer policy arena are trained through NBCC's Project LEAD (for Leadership, Education, and Advocacy Development), which is designed to educate participants in both leadership skills and current scientific research. Annual Advocacy Training Conferences are held to train citizen activists in networking and organizing. In a classic effort to engage in direct lobbying, NBCC also conducts a series of Congressional Education Forums for members of Congress and their staff "to provide the facts on breast cancer to those who have the power to change the course of this epidemic." With the coming to power of Republican majorities in the 104th Congress, the organization's priorities became far more intensely focused on attempting to maintain what they had gained previously:

> We want the Republican leadership to know in no uncertain terms that any cost-cutting that jeopardizes breast cancer research or treatment that could save women's lives will not be tolerated. This is a war that must be fought with every ounce of courage and support from you and me, the research and medical communities, and every member— Republican and Democrat—in Congress.
>
> Please help us. In just a few short years, the National Breast Cancer Coalition has made a difference. And if you join with us, we can continue to make a difference. . . . until the day when women no longer have to live in fear of this dreaded disease . . . until the day when we can all rest assured that we, our daughters, and our granddaughters are safe from the disease that is terrorizing our lives.[102]

By the mid-1990s, it had been determined that a damaged p53 gene, which normally prevents the growth of tumors, was responsible for perhaps 60 percent of all cancers and up to 90 percent of cervix cancer. This knowledge brings with it hope for a possible "cure" for a wide range of cancers. After $28 billion expended in the "war on cancer" since passage in 1971 of the National Cancer Act, most of the decline in death rates was attributable to reduced incidence of smoking and earlier diagnosis, and the promise of p53 therapy might be more hope than success.

Case Study Questions

1. If, as evidence suggests, heart disease and cancer are among the leading causes of death, why has AIDS treatment and prevention received so much attention?
2. Which do you believe would be more productive in the struggle against cancer: a greater emphasis on prevention or a greater emphasis on the search for a cure for certain forms of cancer?
3. If the federal and state budgets are balanced through major spending cuts, do you believe that health care expenditures for cancer research and prevention should not be reduced at all, should be reduced only a little, or should be reduced greatly? Defend your answer.
4. Who do you believe is primarily to blame for the crisis of contemporary health care in the U.S., and why?

Suggested Readings

Aaron, Henry J. "Health Care Financing." In *Setting Domestic Priorities: What Can Government Do?*, ed. Henry J. Aaron and Charles L. Schultze. Washington, DC: Brookings Institution, 1992, pp. 23–61.

Editors of Consumer Reports. *How to Resolve the Health Care Crisis: Affordable Protection for all Americans.* Yonkers, NY: Consumer Reports Books, 1992.

Marmor, Theodore R. *Understanding Health Care Reform.* New Haven, CT: Yale University Press, 1994.

Mueller, Keith J. *Health Care Policy in the United States.* Lincoln: University of Nebraska Press, 1993.

Proctor, Robert N. *Cancer Wars: How Politics Shapes What We Know and Don't Know About Cancer.* New York: Basic Books, 1995.

Notes

1. "Smoke Takes Greater Toll on Nonsmokers, Researchers Say," *New York Times,* 5 April 1995, p. A11.

2. Centers for Disease Control and Prevention, *HIV/AIDS Surveillance Report* (Washington, DC: U.S. Department of Health and Human Services, 1993), p. 6.

3. Centers for Disease Control, *HIV/AIDS Surveillance Report* (Atlanta, GA: Author, October 1992), p. 2.

4. T. R. Sexton and J. Feinstein, "Long-Term Projections of the AIDS Epidemic," *Interfaces* 21 (1991), pp. 64–79.

5. R. S. Root-Bernstein, *Rethinking AIDS: The Tragic Cost of Premature Consensus* (New York: Free Press, 1993).

6. E.g., P. H. Duesberg, "The Role of Drugs in the Origin of AIDS," *Biomedicine and Pharmacotherapy* 46 (1992), pp. 3–15.

7. M. Navarro, "69 U.S. Patients in Limbo: Caught in Medical Enigma," *New York Times,* 21 October 1992, p. B7.

8. Duesberg, op. cit.

9. G. Kolata, "Debunking Doubts that H.I.V. Causes AIDS." *New York Times,* 11 March 1993, p. B13; L. K. Altman, "At AIDS Talks, Science Confronts Daunting Maze," *New York Times,* 6 June 1993, sec. 1, p. 20.

10. Kenneth Bridbord, Pierre Decoufle, Joseph F. Fraumeni, David G. Hoel, Robert N. Hoover, David P. Rall, Umberto Saffiotti, Marvin Schneiderman, and Arthur C. Upton, *Estimates of the Fraction of Cancer in the United States* (Washington, DC: U.S. Department of Health, Education and Welfare, Occupational Safety and Health Administration; Centers for Disease Control, *Recommendations for a National Strategy for Disease Prevention* (Atlanta, GA: Centers for Disease Control, 1978).

11. Richard Doll and Richard Peto, *Causes of Cancer* (New York: Oxford University Press, 1981).

12. Thomas H. Maugh II, "Industry Council Challenges HEW on Cancer in the Work-place," *Science* 202 (1978), pp. 602–604; Thomas H. Maugh II, "What Proportion of Cancers Are Related to Occupation?" *Lancet* 2 (1978), pp. 1238–1240.

13. Reuel A. Stallones and Thomas Downs, *A Critical Review of Estimates of the Fraction of Cancer in the United States Related to Occupational Factors* (New York: American Industrial Health Council, 1978).

14. House Committee on Education and Labor, *The Attorney General's Asbestos Liability Report to the Congress*, 97th Congress, 1st Session, 1981.

15. Devra Lee Davis, "Preventive Healthcare Strategies," *Medical World News* (January 1992), p. 58; Devra Lee Davis, Aaron Blair, and David G. Hoel, "Agricultural Exposures and Cancer Trends in Developed Countries," *Environmental Health Perspectives* 100 (1192), pp. 39–44.

16. E.g., Bruce N. Ames, R. Magaw, and L. S. Gold, "Ranking Possible Carcinogenic Hazards," *Science* 236 (1987), pp. 271–280.

17. Office of Management and Budget, "Regulatory Program of the United States Government," *SIRC Review* (October 1990), pp. 9–21.

18. E.g., Albert L. Nichols and Richard J. Zeckhauser, "The Perils of Prudence," *Regulation* (November–December 1986), pp. 13–24; Richard B. Belzer, "The Peril and Promise of Risk Assessment," *Regulation* (Fall 1991), p. 41.

19. Robert N. Proctor, *Cancer Wars: How Politics Shapes What We Know and Don't Know About Cancer* (New York: Basic Books, 1995), p. 263.

20. Ibid.

21. Denise Scheberle, "Radon and Asbestos: A Study of Agenda Setting and Causal Stories," *Policy Studies Journal* 22(1) (1994).

22. U.S. Department of Health and Human Services, *Healthy People 2000: National Health Promotion and Disease Prevention Objectives* (Washington, DC: U.S. Public Health Service, National Center for Health Statistics, 1991); U.S. Department of Health and Human Services, *Healthy People 2000 Review, 1995–96* (Hyattsville, MD: Public Health Service, 1996).

23. Bridbord, Decoufle, Fraumeni, Hoel, Hoover, Rall, Saffiotti, Schneiderman, and Upton, op. cit.

24. House Committee on Education and Labor, Subcommittee on Compensation, Health, and Safety, *Asbestos-Related Occupational Disease*, Hearing, 95th Congress, 2nd Session, 1978.

25. S. J. Marcus, "Asbestos: Regulating by Litigating," *Technology Review* 85 (1982), pp. 76–77.

26. Proctor, op. cit., p. 106.

27. Robert J. Samuelson, "Will Reform Bankrupt Us?" *Newsweek*, 15 August 1994, p. 51.

28. "The Demographics of Health Care Politics," *The Public Perspective* (September/October, 1994), p. 28.

29. Gene Guerrero, "Largely Meaningless Health Care Reform Enacted: Americans Demand Much More," *Public Citizen* (November/December 1996), p. 9.

30. Theodore R. Marmor, *Understanding Health Care Reform* (New Haven: Yale University Press, 1994).

31. Steven Waldman and Bob Cohn, "Death Rattle for Health Reform," *Newsweek,* 5 September 1994, pp. 30–32.

32. Henry J. Aaron, "Health Care Financing," in *Setting Domestic Priorities: What Can Government Do?* ed. Henry J. Aaron and Charles L. Schultze (Washington, DC: Brookings Institution, 1992), p. 24.

33. David F. Drake, *Reforming the Health Care Market: An Interpretive Economic History* (Washington, DC: Georgetown University Press, 1994); Betty Leyerle, *The Private Regulation of American Health Care* (Armonk, NY: Sharpe Press, 1994).

34. NOW Legal Defense and Education Fund, Untitled mailing, 1994.

35. Rochefort and Cobb, op. cit., pp. 163–164.

36. David A. Rochefort and Roger W. Cobb, "Instrumental Versus Expressive Definitions of AIDS Policymaking," in *The Politics of Problem Definition: Shaping the Policy Agenda,* ed. David A. Rochefort and Roger W. Cobb (Lawrence: University Press of Kansas, 1994), p. 160.

37. Editorial, "AIDS, Sex and Needles," *New York Times,* 29 March 1987, p. IV: 24; State ADM Reports, *Straight to the Point: State Legislatures Revisit the Needle Exchange and Prescription-for-Needles Controversy* (Washington, DC: Intergovernmental Health Policy Project, George Washington University, May 1992).

38. Susan Sontag, *AIDS and Its Metaphors* (New York: Farrar, Straus, and Giroux, 1989); Rochefort and Cobb, 1994, op. cit.

39. R. Shilts, "Good AIDS, Bad AIDS," *New York Times,* 10 December 1991, p. A31; David A. Rochefort, *American Social Welfare Policy: Dynamics of Formulation and Change* (Boulder, CO: Westview Press, 1986).

40. W. Anderson, "The New York Needle Trial: The Politics of Public Health in the Age of AIDS," *American Journal of Public Health* 81 (1991), p. 1508; U.S. General Accounting Office, *Needle Exchange Programs: Research Suggests Promise as an AIDS Prevention Strategy* (Washington, DC: U.S. General Accounting Office, March 1993).

41. State ADM Reports, op. cit., p. 2.

42. David A. Rochefort and P. E. Pezza, "Public Opinion and Health Policy," in T. J. Liman and L. S. Robins, eds., *Health Politics and Policy* (New York: Delmar), pp. 247–269.

43. V. H. Masters, V. E. Johnson, and R. C. Kolodny, *Crisis: Heterosexual Behavior in the Age of AIDS* (New York: Grove Press, 1988); National Research Council, Committee on AIDS Research and the Behavioral, Social, and Statistical Sciences, *The Social Impact of AIDS in the United States* (Washington, DC: National Academy Press, 1993); G. Kolata, "AIDS Groups Dismayed by Report They See as Discounting Concerns," *New York Times,* 7 February 1993, p. 30.

44. George J. Schieber, Jean-Pierre Poullier, and Leslie M. Greenwald, "Health Care Systems in Twenty-Four Countries," *Health Affairs* 10 (Fall 1991), pp. 22–38.

45. Charles L. Cochran and Eloise F. Malone, *Public Policy: Perspectives and Choices* (New York: McGraw-Hill, 1995), p. 331.

46. Robert H. Brook and Mary E. Vaiana, *Appropriateness of Care: A Chart Book* (Washington, DC: George Washington University, National Health Policy Forum,

1989); John Wennberg, "Outcomes Research, Cost Containment, and the Fear of Health Care Rationing," *New England Journal of Medicine*, 25 October 1990, pp. 1202–1204.

47. Cochran and Malone, op. cit., p. 335.

48. Editors of Consumer Reports, op. cit., p. 45.

49. Editors of Consumer Reports, *How to Resolve the Health Care Crisis: Affordable Protection for All Americans* (Yonkers, NY: Consumer Reports Books, 1992), p. 42.

50. Samuelson, op. cit., p. 50.

51. Editors of Consumer Reports, op. cit., p. viii.

52. Aaron, op. cit., p. 36; See also Henry J. Aaron, *Serious and Unstable Condition: Financing America's Health Care* (Washington, DC: Brookings Institution, 1991); Theodor J. Litman and Leonard S. Robins, eds., *Health Politics and Policy* (New York: Wiley, 1984); Paul Starr, *The Social Transformation of American Medicine* (New York: Basic Books, 1982).

53. Katherine Swartz and Timothy D. McBride, "Spells Without Health Insurance Distribution of Durations and Their Link to Point-in-Time Estimates of the Uninsured," *Inquiry* 27 (Fall 1990), pp. 281–288; Henry J. Kaiser Family Foundation, "Survey Shows Widespread Public Concern About Health Insurance Coverage and Costs," Press Release, Menlo Park, CA, 8 April 1992.

54. Proctor, op. cit., pp. 21, 22.

55. C. A. L. Twight, "Regulation of Asbestos: The Microanalysis of Government Failure," *Policy Studies Review* 10 (1990), pp. 9–39; B. Castleman, *Asbestos: Medical and Legal Aspects,* 3rd ed. (Clifton, NJ: Prentice Hall, 1990).

56. U.S. Environmental Protection Agency, *A Citizen's Guide to Radon,* 2nd ed. (Washington, DC: U.S. Environmental Protection Agency, 1992), p. 2.

57. U.S. Environmental Protection Agency, *National Residential Radon Survey: Summary Report* (Washington, DC: U.S. Environmental Protection Agency, 1992).

58. U.S. General Accounting Office, *Indoor Radon: Limited Federal Response to Reducing Contamination in Housing,* RCED-88-103 (Washington, DC: U.S. General Accounting Office, 1988).

59. Scheberle, op. cit., pp. 74–86.

60. Michael Fumento, "The Asbestos Rip-Off," *American Spectator*, October 1989, pp. 21–26.

61. W. Kip Viscusi, *Risk by Choice: Regulating Health and Safety in the Workplace* (Cambridge, MA: Harvard University Press, 1983); Rogene A. Buchholz, *Public Policy Issues for Management* (Englewood Cliffs, NJ: Prentice-Hall, 1992).

62. Office of Technology Assessment, *The CDC's Case Definition of AIDS: Implications of Proposed Revisions: HIV-Related Issues Background Paper 8* (Washington, DC: U.S. Government Printing Office, 1992).

63. Office of Technology Assessment, 1992, ibid., p. 2; J. Osborn, "The Changing Definition of AIDS: What's in a Name?," *Journal of American Health Policy* 1 (1991), pp. 19–22.

64. M. Navarro, "More Cases, Costs and Fears Under Wider AIDS Umbrella," *New York Times*, 29 October 1992, p. A1.

65. Robert J. Buchanan and Robert L. Ohsfeldt, "The Attitudes of State Legislators and State Medicaid Policies Related to AIDS," *Policy Studies Journal* 21 (4) (1993), pp. 651–671.

66. Alain Enthoven and Richard Kronick, "A Consumer-Choice Health Plan for the 1990s," *New England Journal of Medicine* 320, 5 & 12 January 1989, pp. 29–37, 94–101; John Garamendi, *California Health Care in the Twenty-first Century: A Vision for Reform* (Sacramento: California Department of Insurance, February 1992); Aaron, op. cit.

67. Will Marshall and Martin Schram (eds.), *Mandate for Change* (New York: Berkley Books, 1993), p. 118.

68. David Rosner and Gerald Markowitz, "Research or Advocacy: Federal Occupational Safety and Health Policies During the New Deal," *Journal of Social History* 18 (1985), pp. 365–381.

69. M. Tolchin, "Despite Billions in Tax Increases, States Cut Back, *New York Times*, 30 October 1991, p. A8.

70. M. C. Kimball, "Medicaid Shortfall Hits Twenty-nine States," *Health Week*, 4 June 1990, pp. 4, 66–67.

71. U.S. General Accounting Office, *Medicaid Expansion: Coverage Improves but State Fiscal Problems Jeopardize Continued Progress*, GAO/HRD-91-78 (Washington, DC: U.S. Government Printing Office, June 1991).

72. Editors of Consumer Reports, op. cit., p. 243.

73. Milt Freudenheim, "Ten Companies Join in Effort to Lower Bids by H.M.O.'s," *New York Times*, 23 May 1995, p. C2.

74. Buchanan and Ohsfeldt, op. cit.

75. Centers for Disease Control, 1992, op. cit.

76. F. J. Hellinger, "Forecasts of the Costs of Medical Care for Persons with HIV: 1992–1995," *Inquiry* 29 (1992), pp. 356–365.

77. A. Pascal, *The Costs of Treating AIDS under Medicaid: 1986–1991* (Santa Monica, CA: RAND/UCLA Center for Health Care Financing Policy Studies, May 1987).

78. M. A. Baily, L. Bilheimer, J. Woolridge, et al., "Economic Consequences for Medicaid of Human Immunodeficiency Virus Infection," Annual Supplement, *Health Care Financing Review* (1990), pp. 97–108.

79. Office of Technology Assessment, *AIDS and Health Insurance: An OTA Survey* (Washington, DC: U.S. Government Printing Office, 1988).

80. David Pfeiffer, "Overview of the Disability Movement: History, Legislative Record, and Political Implications," *Policy Studies Journal* 21(4) (1993), p. 731.

81. Margaret A. Nosek and Carol A. Howland, "Personal Assistance Services: The Hub of the Policy Wheel for Community Integration of People with Severe Physical Disabilities," *Policy Studies Journal* 21 (4) (1993), p. 789.

82. "AT&T and Unions in Accord on New Three-Year Contract," *New York Times*, 10 June 1995, p. 46.

83. D. Mechanic and L. H. Aiken, "Capitation in Mental Health: Potentials and Cautions," in *Paying for Services: Promises and Pitfalls of Capitation*, ed. D. Mechanic and L. H. Aiken (San Francisco: Jossey-Bass, 1989), pp. 5–18.

84. Joan R. Bloom, Garry Toerber, Jaclyn W. Hausman, Brian Cuffel, and Thomas J. Barrett, "An Analysis of Capitation for Mental Health Services," *Policy Studies Journal* 22 (4) (1994), pp. 681–690.

85. Michael Wines, "President Yielding to G.O.P., Will Offer Plan Erasing Deficit," *New York Times*, 6 December 1995, p. A1.

86. Robin Toner, "Medicare Target Could Be Elusive, Many Experts Say," *New York Times*, 16 May 1995, pp. A1, A11; David E. Rosenbaum, "In Political Wars, Medicare Is the Latest Battlefield," *New York Times*, 2 May 1995, p. A9; Robin Toner and Robert Pear, "Medicare, Turning Thirty, Won't Be What It Was," *New York Times*, 23 July 1995, pp. 1, 12.

87. L. A. G. Ries et al., *Cancer Statistics Review: 1973–1988* (Bethesda, MD: National Institutes of Health, 1991).

88. Proctor, op. cit., p. 1.

89. Ann Gibbons, "Does War on Cancer Equal War on Poverty?" *Science*, 253 (1991), 260.

90. Catherine C. Boring et al., "Cancer Statistics for African Americans," *CA* 42 (1992) 7–17.

91. American Cancer Society, *Cancer Facts and Figures for Minority Americans 1991* (New York: American Cancer Society, 1991); Boring et al., op. cit.

92. Andrew G. Glass and Robert N. Hoover, "Rising Incidence of Breast Cancer," *Journal of the National Cancer Institute* 82 (1990), pp. 693–696.

93. Jonathan M. Liff et al., "Does Increased Detection Account for the Rising Incidence of Breast Cancer?," *American Journal of Public Health* 81 (1991), pp. 462–465.

94. B. A. Miller et al., *SEER Cancer Statistics Review 1973–1990* (Bethesda, MD: National Cancer Institute, 1993).

95. Gastrointestinal Tumor Study Group, "Adjuvant Therapy of Colon Cancer—Results of a Prospectively Randomized Trial," *New England Journal of Medicine* 310 (1984), pp. 737–743.

96. E.g., John Higginson, "Present Trends in Cancer Epidemiology," *Proceedings of the Canadian Cancer Conference* 8 (1969), pp. 40–75; John Cairns, "The Cancer Problem," *Scientific American* (November 1975), pp. 64–78.

97. World Health Organization, *Prevention of Cancer* (Geneva: World Health Organization, 1964).

98. Proctor, op. cit., p. 55.

99. John Bailar, "Some Recent Trends in Cancer: Cancer Undefeated," manuscript, 1994.

100. Lawrence K. Altman, "Lymphomas Are on the Rise in U.S. and No One Knows Why," *New York Times*, 24 May 1994; Sheila H. Zahm and Aaron Blair, "Pesticides and Non-Hodgkin's Lymphoma," *Cancer Research (supp.)* 52 (1992), pp. 5485s–5488s.

101. Samuel S. Epstein, "Environmental Determinants of Human Cancer, *Cancer Research* 34 (1974), pp. 2425–2435.

102. National Breast Cancer Coalition, Untitled fundraising letter (Washington, DC: National Breast Cancer Coalition, 1995).

9

Family and Welfare Policy

GOSPEL OF LIFE

In a bold declaration entitled *Evangelium Vitae,* or *Gospel of Life*, Pope John Paul II addressed a number of controversial moral issues such as abortion, euthanasia (mercy killing of the aged or sick), and use of human embryos for medical research. A 194-page document was released in April 1995, which represented a solemn pronouncement of the church's "ordinary magisterium," or teaching authority, which was binding on the world's one billion Roman Catholics. The pope's pronouncement was heralded as the clearest, most impassioned, and most commanding encyclical of his sixteen-year reign, summoning people to "resist crimes which no human law can claim to legitimize."

In the encyclical, the pope decried a "culture of death" that he believed threatened human dignity and freedom. He advocated the creation of an alternative "culture of life" that respected human dignity from conception to death. The pope also focused on what he called "a new cultural climate" in the West, a culture that supported abortion on demand and tolerated mercy killing. The pope bluntly asserted that public opinion had been used in some countries to justify "crimes against life" in the name of individual freedom. He was highly critical of legislation in many countries that did not punish "practices against life." The legalization of such practices was viewed as "both a disturbing symptom and a significant cause of grave moral decline."

The pope perceived abortion to be a form of "murder" and a violation of the biblical commandment against killing. Anyone who promoted choice in abortion was perceived to be sharing in what he perceived to be the sin of destroying life. Medical experiments on human beings also came under attack in the encyclical. In condemning such "crimes against life," the pope called for every family, as well as every parish and church institution, to incorporate the *Gospel of Life* into its mission. In abundantly clear language, the pope denounced laws that permitted acts of abortion and euthanasia as "inherently unjust," promoting the freedom of the strong to act against the weak.

Reaction to the pope's declaration was immediate and somewhat predictable. Pamela J. Maraldo, president of the Planned Parenthood Federation of America, stated that the pope's encyclical was "a political and social document that is out of step with the developed world." The pro-choice Democratic Senator Edward Kennedy stated that it was wrong for any public official "to legislate the law of their church." American evangelist Billy Graham, on the other hand, praised the pope "for a forceful and thoughtful defense of the sacredness of human life in the face of the modern world's reckless march toward violence and needless death."[1]

The pope's encyclical was representative of the action of a moral leader in contemporary society. Whether or not such pronouncements actually influence governmental policy in the United States is a matter of speculation. At any rate, the pope is certainly an influential figure trying to exert influence on policies that address moral issues of our day. In the encyclical, the pope's sweeping plea to replace the contemporary "culture of death" with a new "culture of life" is emblematic of conflict underlying the debate over family and welfare policy.

THE RPI INPUTS INTO FAMILY AND WELFARE POLICY

The Rationality Input

Family policy can be viewed from the perspective of objectively measuring the costs and benefits of certain actions. From this perspective, various research designs are employed in an effort to evaluate the advantages and disadvantages of specific governmental action. For example, a 1983 study of the effects of guaranteed income in two cities (Seattle and Denver) provides an illustration of how evaluations are utilized. In these two locations, a guaranteed income was found to significantly lower earnings and work effort for participants in the program.[2]

The Seattle-Denver Income Maintenance Experiment (SIME/DIME) was perhaps the most comprehensive attempt to evaluate the impact of guaranteed income on behavior.[3] This experiment was undertaken in the late 1960s and early 1970s to measure the effect of cash transfers on work efforts of recipients. A sophisticated methodology guided the study, utilizing what was termed a factorial design.

The SIME/DIME experiment examined the impact of one or more treatments (social programs) on behavior. Families or individuals were enrolled in a pilot program (treatment) offering a specific benefit or service. Enrollment was based on random assignment, and information was collected for the group that was subject to the program as well as for a control group that received no special treatment. As with any classical experimental design, differences between the experimental and control groups were attributed to the effects of the treatment.

The primary focus of SIME/DIME was to test the effect of two programs on work effort. The two programs that were examined were (1) a program of cash transfers and (2) a program of job counseling, education, and training. The relationship between cash transfers (through a negative income tax) and marital stability was also tested. A number of inferences were drawn at the conclusion of this extensive and costly pilot program.

The SIME/DIME program was launched in Seattle, Washington, in 1970 and extended in 1972 to a second site in Denver, Colorado. The experiment involved almost 5,000 families and had a larger sample size than all other tests of income maintenance programs combined. Four different treatment combinations were measured: (1) a negative income tax only, (2) counseling/training only, (3) a negative income tax and counseling/training, and (4) no treatment.

The experiment tested eleven negative income tax plans (varying by level of guaranteed income and tax rate) to provide information about how guaranteed income could affect behavior. Families enrolled in the experiment were told about the negative income tax plan in general, how benefits would be calculated, and how long the experiment would last. Administrators spelled out in considerable detail the filing and record-keeping responsibilities for recipients, what counted as income, what counted as deductible expenses, and other items, along with the penalties for misrepresentation.

The experiment was fairly complex, with many different types of treatment. For example, within the counseling/training treatment, three variations were tested: (1) counseling only, (2) counseling combined with a 50 percent subsidy for approved education/training, and (3) counseling combined with a 100 percent subsidy for approved education/training. Families were informed of their eligibility for the counseling/training subsidy program at the time of enrollment. A counselor arranged either individual or group sessions for participants who desired counseling.

The primary data for analysis came from a series of face-to-face interviews administered three times a year during the treatment period and for at least one year beyond. Interviews took about forty minutes each, were administered in the family's homes, and were identical for both experimental and control group families. The sample was restricted to families with household heads between eighteen and fifty-eight years of age in order to focus on people most likely to be participants in the labor force.

The findings of the study revealed that husbands in the guaranteed income experimental group worked considerably less (annual weeks of work were 2.8 less during the second year of the treatment) than husbands in the control group (husbands who did not receive any money from the program). It was also revealed that work levels increased after the conclusion of the experiment.

This suggested that reductions in work effort were the result of the income guarantees. The response of wives to the experiment was larger in percentage terms, with an average decrease in annual hours worked of approximately 20 percent. Data were collected for two groups; in one group the experiment lasted three years, in the other group the experiment ran for five years. Wives displayed similar patterns as husbands in readjusting their work habits after the conclusion of the experiment.

The SIME/DIME study hypothesized that the counseling/training component of the experiment would increase the average annual earnings and hours of work. It was believed that as people were trained and counseled they would be better able to compete in the free market. In contrast to expectations, however, counseling/training reduced annual earnings. Researchers were somewhat at a loss to explain this finding but speculated that counseling/training may have raised client expectations unrealistically, discouraging them from taking jobs that were readily available. It was inferred that counseling/training may have raised expectations for earnings but did not provide an abundance of marketable skills that would enable clients to acquire higher-paying positions.

The SIME/DIME study also provided interesting insights into the impact of guaranteed income on marital stability. One hypothesis concerning the impact of America's guaranteed income welfare plan was that it contributed to marital dissolution. It was theorized that families were encouraged to break up so that single mothers could collect welfare payments. To remedy this perverse incentive to dissolve family bonds, it was believed that a negative income tax (a guaranteed income) should be adopted. This would promote marital stability, since both single-parent and two-parent families would be eligible for benefits. Contrary to expectations, however, the data collected in the SIME/DIME experiments indicated that more marriages actually dissolved in the group of families receiving government funds (experimental group) than in the control group (families not receiving money). This finding was true for both black and white families. The rate of marital dissolution among Chicano families was unaffected by government payments.

The SIME/DIME study ultimately came up with a number of clear policy statements. First, in regard to marital stability, the study concluded that it was unlikely that any guaranteed payment program would be neutral with respect to marital stability. Second, in regard to work effort, the study found that higher levels of guaranteed income reduced the amount of work individuals performed. Third, in regard to counseling/training, the study concluded that hours worked and earnings (both during and after the program) were actually lower for those receiving counseling/training. Ironically, counseling/training had the effect of reducing the income of program participants.

The SIME/DIME experiment demonstrated that rational analysis could be applied to the study of complex human behavior. The rational analysis of SIME/DIME produced many findings that were contrary to anticipated results. The research served to influence the direction of welfare policy and slowed the expansion of benefit payments.

The Power Input

Liberal Interest Groups

The power input appears in interest group and elite behavior. Women's groups such as the National Organization for Women (NOW), the National Women's Political Caucus (NWPC), and the Women's Equity Action League (WEAL) are examples of groups that have mobilized to influence family policy concerning issues such as employment, health, reproductive rights, and violence against women.

Prominent among women's interest groups is the National Organization for Women (NOW). NOW was organized in 1966 to address issues of sex discrimination. Betty Friedan, a founder, stated that the goal of NOW was to bring women into full participation in the mainstream of American society, *now*.[4] Picketing government organizations such as the Equal Employment Opportunity Commission (EEOC) and filing sex-discrimination complaints against companies that received federal funds were examples of the group's activities. A specific agenda was enumerated at the national NOW conference in November 1967 (Table 9.1).

The agenda of NOW helped to focus attention on women's and family issues. Support for many of these issues grew, and in 1972 Congress passed the Equal Rights Amendment (ERA). By the end of 1972, twenty-two states had approved the ERA, yet while the ERA gained a sympathetic hearing with many supporters, powerful forces also were mobilized in opposition to the Amendment. By the deadline of June 30, 1982, the ERA was still three states short of the thirty-eight states needed for ratification. The inability of ERA supporters to generate sufficient support for the Amendment represented a stinging defeat for groups categorized as "family liberals."

The struggle over defining the "proper" role of women in American society, however, did not abate with defeat of the ERA. Women's advocacy groups

---

TABLE 9.1 National Organization of Women Policy Agenda, National Conference, November 1967

---

1. Enforcement of laws prohibiting gender discrimination in employment.
2. Provision of adequate, quality child care for families of employed women and of students in educational and training programs.
3. Maternal leave rights for employed women.
4. Fair tax treatment for employed women, including tax credits for child care expenses and nondiscriminatory tax treatment of two-income families.
5. Equal access to all fields of education.

Source: M. Margaret Conway, David W. Ahern, and Gertrude A. Steuernagel, *Women and Public Policy* (Washington, DC: CQ Press, 1995), p. 7.

achieved some success by pursuing an agenda that focused on issues such as the plight of battered women. In Santa Clara County, California, women's advocacy groups were able to fashion improvements in the enforcement of abuse laws. In the early 1980s an organization called the Mid-Peninsula Support Network for Battered Women persuaded local California communities to adopt policies that responded more effectively to domestic disturbance calls. Women's groups took pride in their claims of sensitizing police officers to the problem of domestic violence.

Conservative Interest Groups

Conservative interest groups also have been active in promoting family values and family policy. In 1995, Pat Robertson headed a powerful network whose goals included the shaping of family values in the country. Robertson was able to exert influence as founder and president of the Christian Coalition and as founder of the American Center for Law and Justice, a Christian civil rights group that opposed liberal legal centers. In addition to Robertson's influence in these organizations, he remained chairman of the Christian Broadcasting Network (CBN), an organization that included twice-daily religious broadcasts on 300 TV stations in seventy countries.

Other media figures (such as radio commentator James Dobson) also actively promoted a "family" perspective that had distinctively conservative overtones. In 1995, Dobson's daily half-hour program, *Focus on the Family*, was heard weekly by about 5 million Americans. Dobson's book *Dare to Discipline* sold more than 2 million copies and helped to launch his radio career. In his radio broadcasts, Dobson argued that when parents tried to teach their children traditional values, they felt hostility from the wider culture. Values of the wider culture were believed by Dobson to be reinforced in the national media, television, and the movie industry. As an alternative to this mainstream culture, Dobson stressed the everlasting nature of biblical values.

The conservative group Christian Coalition represents another interest group that is active in the development of family policy, activity that is felt increasingly in the halls of Congress. On May 17, 1995, the 1.4 million-member Christian Coalition presented Congress with a set of ten policy priorities that focused on school prayer, education vouchers, abortion, pornography, the rights of parents, and family-based tax breaks.[5] House Speaker Newt Gingrich promised a vote on each item of the Family Contract.

Some analysts attributed the Republican capture of the House of Representatives and Senate in 1994 to the activism of groups such as the Christian Coalition, whose fervor and enthusiasm contributed to the election of "family conservatives" across the nation. The power input therefore interacts with ideology, since interest groups are strongly influenced by ideological predispositions. Conservative interest groups influence policies ranging from abortion, the ERA, school curriculum, rights of homosexuals, and pornography.[6]

The Ideology Input

In contemporary American society the concept of "family policy" addresses an array of issues that deal with various matters. Issues commonly associated with what has come to be known as "family policy" include abortion, "alternative lifestyles," welfare, pornography, child abuse, and the role of women in American society. Debate over these issues has generated a great deal of heat and emotion, as little common ground has been found among starkly differing perceptions of "correct" behavior.

Conservatives argue that since the foundation of American society is based on personal liberty, government has no place or role in family matters. If government is to play a role, conservatives usually favor policies that uphold mainstream thought and behavior. Liberals, on the other hand, are more accepting of government intervention aimed at protecting real or perceived "rights," such as the rights to higher pay, abortion, "artistic expression," and alternative lifestyles. Conservatives view many of these "rights" as subversions of revered values that have served to benefit the country over time.

The rhetorical conflict over "family policy" consists of attempts to shape interpretations or to put a favorable "spin" on data. In general, family conservatives express alarm at the following trends. In 1960, 5 percent of births were out of wedlock; in 1991 out-of-wedlock births comprised 30 percent of total births. In 1960, 9.1 percent of families were headed by a single parent, in 1991 28.6 percent of all families were headed by a single parent. In 1972, 600,000 abortions were performed in the United States, by 1991 there were 1.7 million abortions. The rate of births to unmarried teenagers increased almost 200 percent between 1960 and 1991, and between 1980 and 1987 the abortion rate among girls under the age of fifteen increased by 18 percent.[7]

Depending upon the "spin," one could interpret such data as representing a dangerous breakdown in values, or from an another perspective, the data could be viewed as a release from oppressive relationships. To former drug czar William Bennett, divorce data represented an indicator of "social decomposition."[8] To feminist author Shere Hite, however, divorce represented a sign of rebellion against a repressive, patriarchal system that no longer suits modern needs. According to Hite (whose works on sexuality have sold more than 20 million copies worldwide), an increase in the divorce rate can be positive, since many people will free themselves from "oppressive" relationships.[9] What today is considered to represent a conservative "spin" generally characterized early American views on the issues of welfare and charity.

Early American Values: Welfare and Charity

In regard to the issues of welfare and poverty, early American orientations nurtured a strident belief in the value of individualism in conjunction with the view that discipline and hard work could convert rags to riches. The doctrine of self-help and "bootstrapping," or picking oneself up by one's bootstraps, became synonymous with early American philosophies. In other countries, poverty was more accepted as a "blessing" that should inspire charity in the rich and meekness in the poor. In the United States, however, poverty was more likely to be associated with sloth and sinfulness. Relief efforts also tended to be less popular in America, with individualism, independence, hard work, and honest labor revered as cures for the disease of impoverishment.[10] America adopted an attitude toward compassion that was both hard-headed and warm-hearted. American justice mandated punishment for indolence and lack of ambition. Mercy, however, was granted to people who turned away from past misdeeds. Compassion was permitted for the poor who were mistreated but the "undeserving" were chastised.[11]

Colonial values guarded against providing relief for the "unfit." In the late 1600s and early 1700s, the minister Cotton Mather warned his church members not to misapply charity and advised congregants to find work for the idle. He believed that charity should be dispensed with "due care" to suitable objects. The teachings of the apostle Paul were cited for guidance, specifically the maxim found in 2 Thessalonians 3:10, which declared it to be a breach of God's law to "bestow upon those the Bread of Charity, who might earn and eat their own Bread, if they did not shamefully idle away their Time."

In the colonial period, therefore, social policy reflected a theology prodding the poor onto the "right path." Positive incentives induced individuals to follow "correct" paths in accordance with the belief that hard work would lead to respect, prosperity, and independence. The Protestant Ethic guided early American attitudes, particularly in New England where the Pilgrims inculcated and fostered their strong religious beliefs. The Protestant Ethic not only provided a "carrot" for proper behavior but also wielded the "stick" of hunger, dishonor, dependence, and poverty, which were promised to the indolent.[12]

Social Darwinists, "Family Conservatives," and Welfare

The writings of the Social Darwinist Herbert Spencer advanced a radical strain of the conservative argument against welfare. Spencer proclaimed that the unfit must be eliminated as nature intended. This Social Darwinist view achieved a relatively high level of popularity in the late nineteenth century. In 1876, a report to the New York State Board of Charities complained that "idleness" was frequently, if not universally, hereditary in character. The report recommended that vigorous efforts be instituted in order to break the line of pauper descent.[13]

Social Darwinist philosophy was also expounded in the late nineteenth century by the Yale University and Johns Hopkins University professor, William Graham Sumner, who provided intellectual justification for what became known as the "politics of anticompassion." This view advanced the notion that nature had her own remedies against vice and simply removed gene pools that had lost their usefulness. Others agreed with the core beliefs of Social Darwinism advanced by Sumner and Spencer. Simon Newcomb, a fellow professor of Sumner at Johns Hopkins University, argued that increasing the amount of charity would simply increase the number of beggars in the country. He emphasized the survival of the fittest and removal of those who were unfit. Newcomb held the view that man was by nature poor, miserable, and worthless, concluding that we should discourage or prevent the bringing forth of children by the "pauper and criminal" classes. No amount of repression would be too severe to attain these objectives.[14]

"Family conservatives" today do not criticize welfare on the grounds of distorting some Darwinian pattern of survival but claim instead that welfare undermines family composition. Pat Robertson, founder of the Christian Coalition and chairman of the Christian Broadcasting Network (CBN), articulated the views that the American family was under siege, undermined by popular culture and government policies such as welfare, no-fault divorce, and tax laws. For Robertson, the family was the foundation of society, and therefore an erosion of family values undermined the very fabric of the nation. Robertson contended that the loss of "moral infrastructure" was particularly troublesome for African-Americans, who were believed to be victims of a welfare system that robbed them of the "spiritual foundation for achievement."[15]

In general, "family conservatives" viewed contemporary changes in family structure as a symbol of deteriorating moral values. Evidence for such a deterioration included the high rates of divorce in American society, the large numbers of children born out of wedlock, the growing acceptance of cohabitation without marriage, and increased participation in the labor force by mothers with young children. In order to reverse this erosion of moral behavior, "family conservatives" advocated policies such as parental control of school curricula, voluntary prayer in the schools, eliminating no-fault divorce, restricting second and third marriages, opposition to the Equal Rights Amendment (ERA), ending the legalization of abortion, and limiting support for day care.

In 1980, Phyllis Schlafly, leader of the Eagle Forum and organizer of a STOP ERA movement, charged that demands by working mothers for publicly funded day care promoted government control of family life. Fifteen years later, Ralph Reed, executive director of the Christian Coalition, echoed many of the positions enunciated by Schlafly. Reed promoted a ten-point legislative program termed the Contract with the American Family (Table 9.2).

The contract of the Christian Coalition stressed school prayer, parental rights, limits on abortion, restrictions on pornography, promotion of private charity, and tax relief for married couples. This agenda was no surprise to anyone who even remotely followed the debate over family policy. These policy positions advanced by "family conservatives" such as Reed found little common ground with the positions advocated by those who were characterized as "family liberals."

"Family Liberal" Perspectives

"Family conservatives," for the most part, saw government activity as contributing to family problems. In contrast, "family liberals" viewed government as a vehicle for positive change, which could include the establishment of a

TABLE 9.2 Christian Coalition Contract

1. *Religious Equality Amendment*   Called for changing the U.S. Constitution to allow citizen-initiated prayers in public places and for events where attendance was voluntary, such as graduation ceremonies and sporting events.
2. *Education*   Called for repeal of the Clinton administration's program to set national educational standards and the Clinton administration's establishment of what the coalition called a national school board.
3. *School choice*   Contract would give tax credits or subsidized vouchers to parents with children in private schools and encourage privatization of public schools.
4. *Parental rights*   Contract-endorsed legislation to strengthen the rights of parents to control the upbringing of their own children.
5. *Tax relief*   Called for a $500 tax credit for children, a flat tax, elimination of the marriage penalty, and allowing a homemaker to put up to $2,000 a year in an individual retirement account.
6. *Abortion*   Called for a ban on late-term abortions in which forceps are used to remove the fetus from the uterus; called for a change in the policy that required (rather than permitted) states to use Medicaid dollars for abortions in rape and incest cases, called for an end to taxpayer subsidies to Planned Parenthood and other groups that permitted abortion.
7. *Charity*   Contract promoted private charity as an alternative to government welfare by allowing taxpayers to designate tax payments for charities.
8. *Pornography*   Contract called for enactment of laws to keep pornography off the Internet computer system; would make it easier for parents to block pornographic programs on cable television and would make possession of child pornography illegal.
9. *Arts*   Contract would halt federal funding of National Foundation on the Arts and the Humanities, the Corporation for Public Broadcasting, and the Legal Services Corporation.
10. *Crime*   Contract called for restitution to victims before a criminal is released from prison, and encouraged work and study requirements for prisoners.

Source: Kenneth Pins, "Coalition Presents Legislative Agenda," *Des Moines Register*, 18 May 1995, p. 4A.

"safety net" for poor children and the redress of injustices against women.[16] "Family liberals" also distinguished themselves in regard to their interpretation of concepts such as authority, obligation, and sexuality.

"Family liberals" advanced the view that authority and family responsibility should be shared in an equitable manner. This was enunciated in the Equal Rights Amendment (ERA), which for family liberals symbolized the formal recognition that women were autonomous from and therefore equal to men. Issues of pay equity became important not only for the sake of material rewards but also as a means of increasing the self-esteem of women.

The question of authority in family relationships was directly linked to controversies over the ordination of women. Certain religious denominations (such as the Catholic Church as well as the orthodox branch of the Jewish religion) refused to ordain women, a practice accepted for many years in other religions.

To "family liberals" the presence of female authority figures in religious institutions sent clear and positive signals regarding the role of women in American society. Family liberals encouraged the placement of women in positions of greater authority in religious organizations.

The issue of obligation also established clear cleavages between family conservatives and family liberals. While family conservatives viewed abortion as an assault on a mother's principal obligation to bear children, family liberals contended that the legal right to an abortion was necessary to ensure women's autonomy from men. The issue of obligation also raised the question of who was responsible for caring for young children. Family liberals advocated government support for child care as a way of allowing women to enter the labor force, contending that children would not be impaired by child care and that the number of hours spent with children was less important than the presence of "quality time" spent between parents and children. Family liberals contended that children of dual-career households would not be affected adversely by the career choices of their parents. In contrast, family conservatives advocated the position that children suffered when others besides family members participated in child care.

Sexuality presented another point of contention. Family liberals advanced a new vision of family life, attacking old conceptions of homosexuality such as the view that homosexuality represented a fundamental perversion of nature. Some family liberals contended that lesbians and gay men were not a threat to families, but represented an essential thread in the fabric of American family life. Gays and lesbians claimed that they did not threaten the American family and, turning the tables on the conservatives, argued that threats emanated from family conservatives who were involved in the manipulation of ignorance, bigotry, and economic injustice. Anti-gay feelings were characterized as part of a cultural offensive against egalitarian social principles and marginalized people in America.[17]

Confusion surrounding a precise definition of family was expressed in popular movies such as the 1993 film *Mrs. Doubtfire*. The closing statement of the Twentieth Century Fox film starring Robin Williams provides an example of contemporary attempts to broaden the definition of family. In responding to a letter from Katie McCormick, a child concerned about the separation of her parents, her brother Andrew's contention that they were not a "real family" any more, the question of whether she had lost her family, and whether there was anything she could do to get her parents back together, Mrs. Doubtfire responded:

> Oh My Dear Katie:
>
> You know some parents when they're angry they get along much better when they don't live together. They don't fight all the time and they can become better people and much better mommies and daddies for you and sometimes they get back together, and sometimes they don't dear. And if they don't, don't blame yourself. Just because they don't love each other anymore doesn't mean that they don't love you. . . .

There are all sorts of different families, Katie. Some families have one mommy, some families have one daddy or two families, and some children live with their uncle or aunt and some with their grandparents, and some children live with foster parents, and some live in separate homes in separate neighborhoods in different areas of the country, and they may not see each other for days, weeks, months, or even years at a time. But if there's love dear, those are the ties that bind and you have a family in your heart forever.

All my love to you puppet

You're going to be all right

Bye-Bye

Application of RPI

Family policy appears to be predominantly ideological due to the intensity of the debate and the unwillingness of those in the struggle to compromise. It appears that in such a context, rational analysis can only be used as a tool by one side or another to attack nonbelievers. Power is subordinate to ideology in the sense that interest groups are captive to their visions and predispositions. Groups such as the conservative coalition or lobbyists representing lesbians and gays are less concerned about the material benefits that they can extract for their supporters than they are concerned with shaping society in accordance with the views of their clients. They advance policy that is consonant with their lifestyles or moral convictions. In this sense, the ideological dynamic truly motivates policy.

Family policy in a sense can be seen as a struggle for the soul of the nation's norms, values, and expectations. Compromise is anathema in such a context, as zealotry drives out concession. Compromise, where "half a loaf" is viewed as better than "no loaf at all," is possible for distributive policies, but agreement is elusive between ideologically based groups when issues such as abortion, pornography, and homosexuality are debated. Debates can take the tenor of a holy war, or jihad, between believers and infidels. Policy is likely to reflect the outcome of a struggle between forces who believe that they are protecting virtue and those who wish to redefine virtue in a manner that is more suitable to their desires. "Bible thumping" moralists are portrayed by their adversaries as narrow-minded, bigoted, old-fashioned, or out of touch with modernity. Advocates of a looser interpretation of morality are portrayed by their opponents as miscreants, sinners, destroyers of virtue, perpetrators of abominations, or worse.

Turnout rates in school board elections where "moralistic" candidates have run suggests that the majority of the voting population are apathetic in the battle over family policy. The intensity of advocates for both sides, however, appears to be quite high. The "moralists" who wish to "save the soul" of the nation coalesce as a highly committed group pitted against others who are equally committed to preserving "rights" such as the ability to maintain an alternative lifestyle or have an abortion. In the 1996 reelection of President

Clinton, "family" issues were subordinated to issues of paying bills, quality schools, and crime. Clinton coopted the issue of welfare well before the election, and received credit from most voters for passage of welfare reform.[18]

There is little doubt that conflict over family policy will continue as ideological interest groups polarize the policy debate. Issues such as abortion, gay/lesbian rights, welfare, and pornography continue to arouse intense emotions. Unresolved issues include questions of (1) family composition (policies that affect childbirth, marriage, divorce, parenting, adoption, and foster care); (2) economic support (policies that affect families' ability to provide for their dependents' basic needs); (3) child-rearing (policies that concern parents' ability to nurture their children); and (4) family care (policies that concern families' ability to care for the chronically ill).[19]

Family policy is ideologically based yet in a certain sense can be viewed as a classic example of an oxymoron, or a figure of speech in which opposite or contradictory terms are used together to form a phrase. The term *policy* suggests specific government action, while the term *family* connotes a degree of independence from government activity. Fundamental liberties and freedoms enunciated in the U.S. Constitution help to ensure that government does not intrude too much into personal matters dealing with family or religion. Family policy would seem to militate against this dictum.

HISTORY OF FAMILY AND WELFARE POLICY IN THE UNITED STATES

Early American Family and Welfare Policy

When coming to the new world, early colonists believed that the family stood at the center of their social order. Colonists defined families as "little cells of righteousness" that enforced the laws of God, taught religion, instilled morality, taught the work ethic, and inculcated deference to authority. As teachers of such values, colonial families operated as the key units for survival and social stability.[20]

During the colonial era, public sector involvement in family affairs dealt with the issue of poverty. Early colonial leaders did not look kindly upon indolence, and in 1692 a Massachusetts poor law empowered officials to put the able-bodied idle into workhouses. American Poor Laws were modeled after the English Poor Laws, which divided the poor into three groups: (1) poor children, (2) the old and afflicted, and (3) the able-bodied poor. Local governments appointed overseers to raise money, aid the old and afflicted, apprentice the children, and set up workhouses for the able-bodied.[21]

To prevent strangers from becoming a burden on towns, colonial leaders passed ordinances known as settlement laws. These laws permitted towns to restrict the entry of strangers who were deemed objectionable for political, religious, or economic reasons. Persons with skills or resources were usually welcomed by town residents; others would be *warned-out,* or told to leave. *Warned-out* individuals who did not leave voluntarily might be fined or removed forcibly, with those who returned after removal subject to severe penalties such as whippings.[22]

Towns tried to restrict entry by strangers yet assumed responsibility for their own poor, a group termed the *indigenous poor.* Families were obligated to provide support for immediate relatives. Parents and grandparents were obliged to provide for their children; adults provided support for their parents. Local governments intervened only when the immediate family could not deliver support. The *deserving poor* (such as the aged, sick, disabled, and mothers of young children) received *outdoor relief,* which was defined as discreetly provided assistance. *Indoor relief* referred to relief provided through the system of poorhouses. This form of relief was reserved for the *undeserving poor* such as alcoholics, persons with disorderly temperaments, and the idle who refused to work.[23] The notion of poverty as a local responsibility and the assignment of the poor to poorhouses gained general acceptance in the nineteenth century. By 1884, there were about 600 poorhouses in New England and eventually most states passed laws designating poorhouses as the primary method of caring for the needy. The philosophy underpinning this strategy prevailed until the Great Depression.[24]

Modern Period of Family and Welfare Policy in the United States

The attitude that had supported a minimal level of government intervention in family matters changed dramatically with the onset of the Great Depression. Prior to the Great Depression, the prevailing view in America had been that pauperism was an outcome of individual deficiencies and that government intervention to help the destitute should be discouraged. Rewards (wealth) and punishments (poverty) were thought to encourage hard work, prioritize thrift, improve productivity, and ensure the survival of the fittest in American society.

The experience of the Great Depression, however, undermined the Social Darwinist view that success or failure was the result of personal actions. The years between the stock market crash of 1929 and entry into World War II were among the bleakest in America's economic history.[25] Millions of hard-working, sober, and earnest people (who before the Depression considered themselves to be quite successful) were thrown out of work, lost their businesses, or forfeited their farms. For the most part, individualistic explanations of failure gave way to systemic explanations for poverty, and blame shifted away from the individual to society, business, or the capitalist system. Voluntary agencies attempted to mitigate the hardships of the Depression yet found that they could not cope with the magnitude of the crisis. President Hoover called for local businesses to "spread the work" and encouraged private charities to step up their efforts. These efforts, however, could not reverse the economic devastation, and Hoover was thrown out of office three years after the great stock market crash of October 1929. Hoover's inability to alter the course of the Great Depression produced one of the greatest electoral landslides in American history when Franklin D. Roosevelt was elected president in 1932.

At the time Franklin D. Roosevelt took office in March 1933, over one-third of the labor force was jobless, and nearly one family in six was dependent on some sort of assistance. In an effort to break this pattern, job programs were instituted for the massive numbers of the unemployed. Relief became a matter of national concern, and millions of federal dollars were expended for public works projects and welfare.

In 1935, the Roosevelt administration was able to pass the Social Security Act, which authorized payments to the elderly, the blind, the unemployed, and dependent children (Aid to Dependent Children, or ADC). The Aid to Dependent Children provisions of the Social Security Act assisted children under sixteen years of age who were in homes without breadwinners because of death, absence, or incapacity. Administrative control, eligibility standards, and payment levels for this program were left to the discretion of states. Over time, significant changes were made in the aid to dependent children program, later named Aid to Families with Dependent Children, or AFDC. In 1950, the Social Security Act was amended to permit coverage of the mother or any other needy adult with whom a child was living. Other amendments expanded the role of government in the lives of the poor. In 1956, amendments required states to provide "casework," or social services, to needy families. In 1962, amendments to the Social Security Act permitted applicants to qualify for aid solely on the basis of need. Prior to 1962, "suitable home rules" allowed government workers to make surprise visits to investigate the "moral behavior" of recipients. Changes in the Social Security Act would eventually make AFDC synonymous with a welfare state that was clearly broken.

In the 1970s, government began to play a major role in the family issue of abortion. Prior to 1973, the courts held that it was up to the states to decide the circumstances under which women could obtain an abortion. There was little uniformity between states with some (such as New York) allowing abortion on demand during the first twenty-four weeks of pregnancy and others (such as Texas) banning abortion except when the mother's life was threatened. In 1973, the Supreme Court struck down the Texas law, as well as all similar laws, with its landmark *Roe v. Wade* decision. In this decision, the majority argued that the Due Process Clause of the Fourteenth Amendment implied a "right to privacy" that protected a woman's freedom to choose, during the first three months of pregnancy, whether or not to have an abortion. For sixteen years, the Supreme Court reaffirmed and broadened the scope of its decision in *Roe v. Wade*.

Welfare remained an important issue for the Nixon, Reagan, and Clinton administrations. The Nixon administration attempted to reform the welfare system with the Family Assistance Plan (FAP), a strategy to benefit "poor working fathers" as well as families with absent or unemployed fathers. Nixon's plan proposed levels of federal relief that when combined with food stamps would amount to approximately two-thirds of the 1969 poverty level. The FAP was lauded as a major attack on poverty, since it increased welfare payment levels in a number of states and increased funding for about 20 percent of existing AFDC recipients.[26]

The Nixon plan embraced a strategy of what was commonly termed the *negative income tax* (NIT). For Milton Friedman, the originator of the idea of the negative income tax, payments directly to the poor would eliminate existing programs such as Social Security, Medicare, public housing, public health, farm price supports, and the minimum wage.[27] All families earning less than a predetermined income level would receive a government check. Supporters claimed that the guaranteed income plan would save money in the long run by greatly lowering administrative costs, taking power away from the "welfare bureaucracy," and giving more of the money to recipients.

In a message to Congress, Nixon proposed that the welfare system should be replaced by an entirely new system that would be more effective. He proposed a minimum federally guaranteed income of $1,600 for a family of four. Nixon's plan to assist low-income families passed in the House of Representatives in 1970, but the Senate failed to approve the bill.[28] With the end of the Nixon presidency, talk of welfare administered through a guaranteed income died.

The Reagan administration ostensibly was committed to reestablishing family values in America, promoting self-reliance, and advancing the notion that welfare would serve only as a family's last resort and temporary safety net. Fears that welfare would become a "way of life" for generations of the dispossessed instead of a short-term helping hand motivated the general thrust of policy during the Reagan administration. Reagan encouraged states to formulate their own plans to promote self-reliance. States were given the authority to develop "workfare" programs through which the poor were required to work in order to pay back benefits. The Reagan administration further stimulated development of plans to find nonsubsidized jobs for welfare recipients. Reagan proposed repeal of the Aid to Families with Dependent Children program, permitting states to acquire the discretion to retain, replace, or abolish welfare. Ironically, Reagan's goal was finally realized in 1996 under the administration of the "New Democrat" Bill Clinton.

Fueling support for reform in welfare were the rising costs of the AFDC and other programs. By the late 1980s, government's role in assisting children had taken on major proportions. Table 9.3 describes the estimated public expenditures in child-related categories for fiscal year 1989.

One can see from Table 9.3 that the public sector has taken over responsibility in a multitude of family activities including income support, training, nutrition, housing, health, and education. The AFDC program that came under fierce attack totaled more than $8 billion in 1989. This sum represented only a small amount of the total public sector aid to children.

TABLE 9.3 Estimated Public Expenditures on Children, Fiscal Year 1989 (in billions of dollars)

	Amount
Federal Programs	
Social Security (to children through dependent and survivor benefits)	$ 13.73
Aid to Families with Dependent Children	8.31
Food stamps	7.81
Child nutrition	5.16
Women, Infants, and Children	2.19
Compensatory education	4.17
Education for the handicapped	2.13
Medicaid	4.69
Social services block grant	1.52
Foster care and adoption	1.52
Head Start	1.39
Housing assistance	3.63
Job Training Partnership Act	.90
State and local programs	
State elementary and secondary education	101.75
Local elementary and secondary education	90.49
State Medicaid	3.62
State and Local AFDC	6.86

Source: Adapted from Isabel Sawhill, "Young Children and Families," in *Setting Domestic Priorities*, ed. H. Aaron and C. Schultze (Washington, DC: Brookings Institution, 1992), pp. 166–167.

By the late 1980s, welfare reform was a high-profile issue that led to legislation such as the Family Support Act of 1988. This Act required all states to adopt a program that would mandate education, work, or training for most AFDC mothers with children over the age of three. States also were directed to spend 55 percent of funds from the federal program (Job Opportunities and Basic Skills program) on individuals who were identified as likely to become long-term welfare recipients. Two-parent families receiving AFDC were required to have at least one parent enrolled in the JOBS program or complete sixteen hours a week of community service work. The 1988 Family Support Act also directed states to establish automatic payroll deductions (for child support) from parents of AFDC children who were not living with the children.[29]

The Clinton administration presided over fundamental changes in welfare. As a candidate for President in 1992, Clinton claimed that he was a "New Democrat" and pledged to "end welfare as we know it." As President, Clinton presented his welfare reform plan in 1994. This plan included a five-year time limit on benefits, coupled with $9.3 billion in investments (additional spending) over five years in an effort to ensure jobs for people leaving welfare. The 1994 Clinton plan was not adopted, and after the Republicans won control of Congress in 1994, they began drafting their own proposals, two of which were vetoed. The third time, however, was the charm, and in 1996 Clinton finally agreed to a welfare reform plan.[30]

On August 22, 1996, Clinton signed into law a welfare bill that ended six decades of guaranteed help (AFDC) to the nation's poorest children, set a five-year limit on payments to any family, and gave states vast new powers to run their own welfare and work programs. The heart of the 1996 welfare law abolished the Aid to Families with Dependent Children program, which provided monthly cash benefits to 12.8 million people, including 8 million children. The AFDC program was replaced by a system of block grants and vast new authority for the states.[31] Work requirements for most people seeking welfare were established; states that did not comply with federal requirements could lose some of their grant funding. How the law impacted certain recipients is described in Table 9.4.

TABLE 9.4 Impact of 1996 Welfare Plan on Recipients

---

1. *Single mother, youngest child over five years old:* The mother is required to work within two years of receiving benefits.
2. *Single mother, youngest child less than five years old:* The mother is exempted from work requirements if she proves that she cannot find suitable, affordable child care.
3. *Unmarried mother under eighteen:* The unmarried mother will generally have to live with an adult and attend school in order to receive welfare benefits.
4. *Missing father:* A woman will be required to provide information about the father of her child as a condition for receiving welfare. If she does not cooperate, she will lose at least 25 percent of her family's welfare benefit.
5. *Legal immigrant family:* Noncitizens (even if legally immigrated) generally will be ineligible for food stamps and Supplemental Security Income. Immigrants arriving on or after August 22, 1996, generally will be ineligible for welfare or any other "means-tested benefit" financed by the federal government. States will be allowed, but not required, to cut off cash assistance, Medicaid, and social services for noncitizens now receiving such aid.
6. *The chronic welfare family:* About half of all Aid to Family with Dependent Children recipients are people who have received benefits for five years or longer. The new law sets a five-year lifetime limit for aid from federal block grant funds.
7. *Convicted drug abuser or drug dealer:* If convicted of a drug felony under federal or state laws, a person may not receive cash welfare benefits or food stamps. A state may override this ban.
8. *Childless nonworker:* A person eighteen to fifty years old who is not raising children and not working may receive food stamps for only three months in a three-year period.

Source: Francis X. Clines, "Clinton Signs Bill Cutting Welfare: States in New Role," *New York Times*, August 23, 1996, p. 10A.

Contemporary Controversy

The Battle over School Curriculum in America's Heartland

THE CONTROVERSY surrounding school curriculum reached its full intensity in 1995, as a furor arose over a proposal to include instruction about homosexuality in the Des Moines public schools. The Des Moines school district's education plan proposed to increase substantially gay/lesbian/bisexual materials in school libraries and multimedia centers. A Sexual Orientation Advisory Committee that had been previously created recommended a number of highly controversial long-range and short-range goals for the district (Table 9.5).

Both the long-term and short-term goals proved to be unacceptable to the leading newspaper in the state, as well as to a vocal group of citizens who stridently expressed their displeasure with the committee at a public forum. To many in the state of Iowa, mandatory cross-cultural training, discussions about contributions of gay, lesbian, and bisexual people, information about roots of homophobia, and other recommendations of the Advisory Committee smacked of heavy-handed government indoctrination. The *Des Moines Register*, the leading newspaper in the state of Iowa, stated that the new proposal to teach about gays, lesbians, and bisexuals in the Des Moines schools went "too far." The *Register* asserted that the new proposal would contradict the moral instruction that some students received from their families:

> Public schools exist to serve all students, many of whom learn from their parents and religious leaders that practicing homosexuality is a sin. It's not the place of public schools to tell students that their faith is misguided. It is the place of the public schools, when students are old enough, to discuss the range of viewpoints that exist. . . . Some of the proposal, however, is not about informing or helping children. Its overall tone promotes creation of a society that embraces gays and lesbians and bisexuals as practicing a way of life that is simply different, not objectionable. That's a worthy goal, one that must be pursued in the larger arena of public opinion, not gained by indoctrination of a captive audience in public-school classrooms.[33]

Shortly after the new proposal was released by the Advisory Committee, an eight-hour public forum was held before the school board. A number of the community's

The new welfare bill was hailed as the biggest shift in social policy since the Great Depression. President Clinton praised the bill for restoring America's basic bargain of providing opportunity and demanding in return responsibility. Others, however, were highly critical. Marion Wright Edelman, president of the Children's Defense Fund and friend of Hillary Rodham Clinton, claimed that enactment of the bill represented a "moment of shame." Christopher Dodd, chairman of the

TABLE 9.5 Recommendations of the Des Moines Sexual Orientation
Advisory Committee

Long-range goals	1. Infuse specific information into courses about the history and contributions of gay/lesbian/bisexual persons. 2. Promote equality and justice. 3. Avoid heterosexual bias in language. 4. Include the following in the curriculum: • Diverse and honest biographical information about the contributions of famous gay, lesbian, and bisexual people; • Discussions of individual autonomy versus institutionally imposed conformity; • Discussions of the nature of families, including same-gender families; • Presentations of information on gender/sexual orientation and diversity; • Discussions of how homophobia impacted the governmental response to the HIV/AIDS disease; • Presentations of information about the history of gay, lesbian, and bisexual issues and their impact on movements throughout history. 5. Provide mandatory cross-cultural awareness training.
Short-range goals	1. Provide students with information regarding the psychological roots of homophobia. 2. Create student awareness of homophobic thinking and behavior and to compare homophobic thinking and behavior with other forms of prejudice and oppression. 3. Include information about gay/lesbian/bisexual issues into the ninth-grade curriculum. 4. Provide support for gay/lesbian/bisexual staff members. 5. Continue current strategies to support gay/lesbian/bisexual youth. 6. Provide information about why gay, lesbian, and bisexual teenagers are considered to be at risk.

Source: *Des Moines Register,* January 2, 1995, p. 9A.

(continued)

Democratic National Committee, denounced the measure as an "unconscionable retreat." Paul Simon, Senator from Illinois, stated that "This isn't welfare reform, it's welfare denial."[32] Clinton, however, expressed hope that the partisan edge could be eliminated from frustration over welfare. A primary motivation of Clinton was to neutralize the welfare issue in an election year. He was successful in defusing the issue and was reelected by a significant electoral college margin.

religious leaders expressed support for the plan, while other religious leaders strongly protested the recommendations of the Sexual Orientation Advisory Committee. Supporters expressed their belief that homosexuality should be presented realistically and honestly as part of the way the world is. Opponents insisted that both the Old and New Testaments clearly characterized homosexuality as a sin, citing passages in *Leviticus* 20:13: "If a man lies with a male as with a woman, both of them have committed an abomination: they shall be put to death," as well as *Romans* 1:26-27: "For this reason God gave them up to degrading passions. Their women exchanged natural intercourse for unnatural, and in the same way also the men, giving up natural intercourse with women, were consumed with passion for one another. Men committed shameless acts with men and received in their own persons the penalty for their errors."[34]

After about a month of debate on the issue a poll was taken of all Iowans age eighteen or older. According to the poll, 59 percent of respondents opposed curriculum that addressed the issue of homosexuality in Iowa schools; 33 percent favored such curriculum; 5 percent said it would depend on the circumstances; and 3 percent were unsure. Attitudes were linked to age groups; the eighteen to twenty-four age group

Case Study

The Entertainment Industry and Family Values

PRESSURE ON Hollywood to reverse its course as a purveyor of symbols is not new in American history.[37] In the 1930s, the film industry adopted a formal production code limiting the depiction of sex and violence on the screen. In the 1980s, Tipper Gore (wife of Vice President Al Gore) and the interest group Parents Music Resource Center waged a high-profile campaign that pressured record companies to label certain albums with Parental Advisory stickers. In the 1992 presidential campaign, Vice President Dan Quayle attacked the popular television comedy *Murphy Brown* for promoting single-motherhood. In the 1996 presidential race, Senator Robert Dole revisited earlier attacks on Hollywood's values.

On May 31, 1995, in a speech delivered at a Los Angeles fundraiser, Bob Dole stated that Hollywood was mainstreaming deviancy and accused the entertainment industry of promoting rape, violence, and casual sex. In addition, Dole asserted that music groups such as *Cannibal Corpse*, *Geto Boys*, and *2 Live Crew*, represented examples of "mindless violence and loveless sex," singling out executives at Time Warner's music division for egregious behavior stating that: "You have sold your souls . . . for the sake of corporate profits." Furthermore, Dole noted:

expressed majority (52 percent) support; 72 percent of respondents 65 or older opposed the curricular change. In addition to the strong opposition by the elderly population, the proposal was opposed by "born again" Christians (76 percent), Republicans (71 percent), and residents of the county (Polk) where the plan would be implemented (69 percent).[35]

On January 23, 1995, the Des Moines Schools Superintendent, Gary Wegenke, "pulled the plug" on the controversial proposal and dissolved the committee that drafted it. Wegenke stated that the proposal was no longer being considered and was a "dead issue" as far as he was concerned. Wegenke, maintaining that he had no plans eventually to add information about homosexuality to the curriculum, at the same time didn't rule out the option. The school superintendent also contended that gay and lesbian students have a right to a safe learning environment and that people in Des Moines valued diversity and tolerance. Bill Horn, an opposition organizer to the Des Moines proposal, called Wegenke's recommendations to drop the plan, "very, very wise." Wegenke also received good reviews in the community for juggling what was seen as a hot-potato issue.[36]

An extreme of depravity has mobilized a mainstream of worried parents and concerned citizens. Across America, people are alarmed that our sense of decency is being dulled and our ability for outrage smothered by an entertainment industry that ridicules our values. . . . One need not be a conservative Republican, as I am, to object to corporations making millions from gangsta rap that revels in the pleasures of ripping women apart. Or to a movie industry raking up profits by dulling respect for human life. Or to television story lines with heavy-handed, cruelly wrong messages that casual, meaningless sex is the norm in adult America. . . . The heat from this issue won't let up in a week or a month or a year. I, and others who care about the family, will continue to speak out about the threat you posed to our children and our culture until you show some sign that you recognize the responsibilities of freedom and are ready to shoulder your share.[38]

In September 1996, during the presidential campaign, Dole revisited his attacks on the entertainment industry, speaking before an audience at the Roman Catholic-run Chaminade College Preparatory School in the San Fernando Valley of California:

Our popular culture owes a duty to the fragile world of children. The market is not the only standard by which we live. It is possible to entertain us without debasing us. Free expression does not require the destruction of children's character.[39]

Other politicians were even more outspoken in decrying values promoted in the media. Former Secretary of Education William Bennett sent letters to Time Warner's directors demanding that the company stop distributing rap music that contained violent or sexually degrading lyrics. Bennett stated that he hoped to shame the company into action. The chairman of the Warner Music Group, Michael Fuchs, responded to political criticism of his organization with statements supporting the right of free expression.

(continued)

This argument was not persuasive to cultural conservatives who questioned the principle of pushing anything that sold in the marketplace. Filmmakers such as Mark Canton, chairman of the Columbia-Tri Star Motion Picture Group, echoed the sentiments of the Warner Music Group, noting that it was essential that Hollywood retain the right to make creative choices with diversity and freedom."[40] Dole's views on Hollywood were well received by Christian conservatives such as Ralph Reed, who told the *Washington Post* that it may have been a defining moment for Dole's presidential candidacy.

Ironically, controls on the content of material in the entertainment industry may not come from politicians but from retailers. Retailers such as Blockbuster Video and Wal-Mart have refused to carry NC-17 videos. Director's cut versions of the film *Natural Born Killers* was banned by these outlets as well as by Kmart. As a result of retailer pressure, record labels and musicians have designed different covers and booklets, omitted songs from albums, electronically masked objectionable words, and even changed lyrics. An album cover for John Mellencamp's CD *Mr. Happy-Go-Lucky* was altered; songs were dropped from albums by Jackyl and Catherine Wheel; a Nirvana song title was changed; and songs by dozens of groups were altered to remove obscenities. Albums by Tupac Shakur and Snoop Doggy Dogg were barred from Wal-Mart because of its policy not to carry any album affixed with the "parental advisory" label denoting explicit lyrics.

The economic clout of Wal-Mart was considerable. In 1995, Wal-Mart was the single largest seller of pop music in the country, accounting for sales of an estimated 52 million of the 615 million compact disks sold in the United States. Wal-Mart, as well as other outlets such as Blockbuster, have had an impact on the music and film industries and reportedly have induced changes in the way the entertainment industry operates. This has been interpreted both positively (to those who wish to protect family values) and negatively (to those who see such actions as censorship). Representatives of the music industry claim that "the fact that stores like Wal-Mart are deciding how music should sound is creating a chilling effect." This effect also applies for the film industry. The director of *Natural Born Killers,* Oliver Stone, stated that he would think twice before directing a movie with explicit sexual content because of the economic power of retailers. Other directors shoot different versions of the same scene for the video and television versions of their movies. They then market the different versions to the appropriate outlet.

Suggested Readings

Abramovitz, Mimi. *Regulating the Lives of Women.* Boston: South End Press, 1988.

Hunter, James. *Culture Wars: The Struggle to Define America.* New York: Basic Books, 1991.

Klein, Ethel. *Gender Politics.* Cambridge, MA: Harvard University Press, 1984.

Piven, Frances Fox, and Richard Cloward. *Regulating the Poor.* New York: Vintage Books, 1971.

Olasky, Marvin. *The Tragedy of American Compassion.* Washington, DC: Regnery Gateway, 1992).

Zimmerman, Shirley. *Understanding Family Policy: Theoretical Approaches.* Newbury Park, CA: Sage, 1988.

In 1996, Blockbuster (run by a former Wal-Mart executive) followed policies that replicated those of Wal-Mart, with similar impact. Blockbuster had enormous marketing power in the video market as its 4,500 outlets accounted for 25 percent of all video rentals nationwide (a number expected to double in the next four years). This retailing muscle, combined with a willingness to use it as Blockbuster saw fit, persuaded motion picture studios to edit their films in such a manner as to be acceptable to the huge retailer. The most often cited example of re-editing for Blockbuster is the film *Showgirls*. *Showgirls* originally was rated NC-17, was then edited to receive an "unrated" classification, and when this version still did not meet Blockbuster's standards, was edited again to receive an "R" rating. Lesser known cases range from unrated B movies like *Sgt. Kabukimamn,* which was trimmed to a PG-13 film for eventual distribution by Blockbuster, to better-known films like *Wide Sargasso Sea,* edited from an NC-17 rating to an R rating.[41]

Case Study Questions

1. What kind of ideological, power, and rational pressures influence the entertainment industry?
2. Do you consider American culture to be "polluted"? What forces, if any, should have the right to define and limit cultural influences?
3. Do you think that retailers should be allowed to regulate the content of the material found in their stores?
4. Do companies such as Wal-Mart have too much power in setting acceptable standards? Should the government be involved more actively? Should anything be sold as long as there is a buyer?
5. If greater controls were placed on films or songs, how do you feel the nation as a whole would be affected? Would such controls hurt society through limitations on expressions of ideas?
6. What type of material do you feel is most objectionable in songs or movies?
7. Who should decide what is objectionable? Is society harmed by actions of retailers such as Blockbuster Video and Wal-Mart? Should legislation force them to accept certain types of material?

Notes

1. Kenneth L. Woodward, "Life, Death, and the Pope," *Newsweek,* 10 April 1995, pp. 56–59.

2. Thomas Dye, *Understanding Public Policy,* 7th ed. (Englewood Cliffs, NJ: Prentice-Hall, 1992), pp. 366–367.

3. Felicity Skidmore, "Overview of the Seattle-Denver Income Maintenance Experiment Final Report," in *Evaluation in Practice,* ed. R. Bingham and C. Felbinger (White Plains, NY: Longman, 1989), pp. 58–96.

4. Ethel Klein, *Gender Politics* (Cambridge, MA: Harvard University Press, 1984), p. 23.

5. Kenneth Pins, "Coalition Presents Legislative Agenda," *Des Moines Register,* 18 May 1995, p. A3.

6. Shirley Zimmerman, *Understanding Family Policy: Theoretical Approaches* (Newbury Park, CA: Sage, 1988), p. 69.

7. William J. Bennett, *The Index of Leading Cultural Indicators* (New York: Simon & Schuster, 1994), pp. 18–70.

8. Bennett, op. cit., p. 8.

9. "Hite Book Targets Family 'Myths'," *Des Moines Register*, 22 May 1995, p. 4A.

10. Frances Fox Piven and Richard Cloward, *Regulating the Poor* (New York: Vintage Books, 1971), p. 46.

11. Marvin Olasky, *The Tragedy of American Compassion* (Washington, DC: Regnery Gateway, 1992), p. 8.

12. Ibid., p. 10.

13. Olasky, op. cit., p. 68.

14. Ibid., p. 71.

15. Allen D. Hertzke, *Echoes of Discontent* (Washington, DC: Congressional Quarterly Press, 1993), p. 96.

16. James D. Hunter, *Culture Wars: The Struggle to Define America* (New York: Basic Books, 1991), p. 195.

17. Hunter, op. cit., p. 189.

18. Gloria Borger, "Fresh Start," *U.S. News & World Report*, 18 November 1996, p. 37.

19. Steven V. Roberts, "The Heavy Hitter," *U.S. News & World Report*, 24 April 1995, pp. 34, 39.

20. Mimi Abramovitz, *Regulating the Lives of Women* (Boston: South End Press, 1988), pp. 52–53.

21. Anthony Champagne and Edward Harpham, *The Attack on the Welfare State* (Prospect Heights, IL.: Waveland Press, 1984), p. 91.

22. Abramovitz, op. cit., p. 80.

23. Olasky, op. cit., p. 11.

24. Piven and Cloward, op. cit., p. 47.

25. Champagne and Harpham, op. cit. p. 94.

26. Ibid., p. 100.

27. Milton Friedman, *Capitalism and Freedom* (Chicago: University of Chicago Press, 1962).

28. Champagne and Harpham, op. cit. p. 100.

29. Theresa Funiciello and Sanford Schram, "Post-Mortem on the Deterioration of the Welfare Grant," in *The Reconstruction of Family Policy*, ed. E. Anderson and R. Hula (Westport, CT: Greenwood Press, 1991), p. 152.

30. Alison Mitchell, "Two Clinton Aides Resign to Protest New Welfare Law," *New York Times*, 12 September 1996, p. A14.

31. Francis Clines, "Clinton Signs Bill Cutting Welfare; States in New Role," *New York Times*, 23 August 1996, p. A10.

32. Ibid., p. A1.

33. "Teaching About Homosexuality," *Des Moines Register*, 2 January 1995, p. A8.

34. William Simbro, "Both Sides Use Bible to Boost Arguments on Homosexuality," *Des Moines Register,* 8 January 1995, p. A1, A4.

35. Thomas A. Fogarty, "Poll: 59% Oppose Teaching About Gays," *Des Moines Register*, 23 January 1995, p. A1.

36. Kellye Carter, "Wilson Reveals Secret: 'I Am Gay'," *Des Moines Register*, 25 January 1995, p. A8.

37. Joe Klein, "Off to the Culture War," *Newsweek*, 12 June 1995, pp. 28–29; Thom Geier and Jim Impoco, "Shame Isn't Fleeting," *U.S. News & World Report*, 19 June 1995, p. 57; Jim Impoco, "The Race to Bash Hollywood," *U.S. News & World Report*, 12 June 1995, p. 8.

38. Bob Dole, "Responsibility, Not Censorship," *Des Moines Register*, 20 June 1995, p. A9.

39. Adam Nagourney, "Attacking Drugs, Dole Takes on Entertainment Industry," *New York Times*, 19 September 1996, p. A14.

40. Bernard Weinraub, "Films and Recordings Threaten Nation's Character, Dole Says," *New York Times,* 1 June 1995, p. A1; Bernard Weinraub, "Filmmakers Discount Criticism by Dole," *New York Times,* 2 June 1995, p. A10; Mark Landler, "Time Warner Seeks a Delicate Balance in Rap Music Furor," *New York Times*, 5 June 1995, pp. A1, D8.

41. Neil Strauss, "Wal-Mart's CD Standards Are Changing Pop Music," *New York Times*, 12 November 1996, pp. A1, B11.

10

Crime Policy

OKLAHOMA CITY BOMBING

On April 19, 1995, a bomb weighing thousands of pounds ripped through the Alfred P. Murrah Federal Building in Oklahoma City, Oklahoma, collapsing all nine floors on the building's north end. Shortly after the blast, an FBI agent discovered a twisted piece of truck axle that had been blown two blocks from the blast. The piece of axle bore a vehicle identification number (VIN) that was ultimately used to track down the rented van, 270 miles away, to Elliot's Body Shop in Junction City, Kansas. A composite drawing of two men (John Doe 1 and John Doe 2) was developed after questioning the clerk at the body shop. The images of these two men as well as a promise of a $2 million reward for information leading to their conviction was flashed around the world. The FBI, however, using the most modern technology did not have very far to look.

On April 20, one day after the blast, FBI agents fanned out through Junction City showing the drawings of the John Does to bartenders and motel proprietors. The owner of the Dream Land Motel, about a half-mile outside town, recognized the face of John Doe 1 and stated that he had checked into the motel on April 14 and checked out on April 18, the day before the bombing. The man had identified himself by his real name, Tim McVeigh. Using its national computer network, the FBI soon discovered that McVeigh was already in custody, in Perry, Oklahoma. McVeigh had been arrested by an Oklahoma state trooper about sixty miles north of Oklahoma City on charges of driving an unregistered car and carrying an unregistered handgun. Even with their modern technology, the FBI was lucky in apprehending their suspect in the bombing. Two days after the arrest, McVeigh was almost set free from county jail in Oklahoma on a $500 bond. Right before he was to be free, word arrived from the FBI that McVeigh was one of the two most wanted men in America. As McVeigh was led out of his cell in front of a jeering crowd, some shouted "baby killer" to the man who allegedly had blown up a building with a large day care center directly in the path of destruction.

A motive for the Oklahoma City bombing was not immediately clear. One of the more than 2,600 calls to the FBI (immediately following a $2 million reward offer) told authorities that McVeigh was a disenchanted army veteran who hated the government and had vague ties to the Michigan Militia, a militaristic organization formed in 1994. This group claimed to have about 10,000 to 12,000 members, and had stockpiled weapons, conducted regular exercises, espoused theories about government plans to confiscate guns, and feared an impending takeover of the United States by the United Nations.

One member of the Michigan Militia, named Mark Koernke, preached a scenario (familiar to those on the extreme right of the American ideological spectrum) that predicted that a conspiracy of wealthy bankers, politicians, and media elites would use UN troops flying in black helicopters to launch a coup against the United States. Americans would be enslaved with computer chips planted in their hands in order to track their movements. All "true patriots" were instructed to organize, preferably in small groups of no more than six to eight to avoid infiltration.

It was reported that McVeigh was influenced by a book he had read in 1989, entitled *The Turner Diaries*. This book described a right-wing revolt and race war that would begin with the bombing of FBI headquarters in Washington, DC. McVeigh also was said to have been particularly agitated about the FBI raid in Waco, Texas, where eighty-six men, women, and children died after the U.S. Bureau of Alcohol, Tobacco, and Firearms (ATF) attempted to seize weapons. Shortly after his arrest, FBI agents showed McVeigh pictures of children murdered in the Oklahoma City blast. McVeigh showed no remorse and no emotion, simply repeating his name, rank, and old serial number. McVeigh told agents, "I am a prisoner of war."

Others who held similar beliefs toward the federal government continued to criticize and mock government officials such as President Clinton (called "the Slick One"), Attorney General Janet Reno (called "Butch Reno"), and the Bureau of Alcohol, Tobacco, and Firearms (referred to as "Burn All Toddlers First"). Events such as the Waco, Texas, incident in 1993 (in which David Koresh and his followers were killed) and the 1992 shoot-out at Ruby Ridge, Idaho (where Randy Weaver's wife and son were killed) were cited as evidence of a government that was out of control and allegedly out to destroy the lives of "patriotic" citizens. Such citizens claimed to be committed to traditional American values and expressed a desire to save America from surrender to a loosely defined "New World Order."[1]

It appears that rationality, power, and ideology were all connected in the strange cycle of events associated with the Oklahoma City bombings. The law enforcement community used rationality in the speedy identification and arrest of the suspect McVeigh. Modern technology, a clear problem-solving orientation, and administrative efficiency all contributed to the speedy arrest. Ideology also appears to be directly linked to the Oklahoma City incident. The bombing of the Murrah Federal Building in 1995 and the subsequent arrest of McVeigh graphically illustrate the power of specific world views/ideologies. It appears evident that deeply held convictions can lead to action (often very destructive action), which in turn may produce public policies to counter the action. In the sense that political perspectives (loosely defined here as ideologies) were associated with the Oklahoma City bombing (and crime policy in general), they are relevant to this discussion.

To some extent, it appears that perception of power may have been linked to the bombing of the Murrah Federal Building. Power and ideology were interrelated in the sense that belief in an impending coup against the American government was perceived to originate from a conspiracy of wealthy bankers, politicians, and media elites. Powerful interests in American society were viewed as the enemy of ordinary citizens. From this perspective, the powerful controlled the weak, suppressed those who dared to dissent, and engaged in action detrimental to average citizens. From such a perspective, criminal activities such as the blowing up of federal buildings (representing evil governmental forces) might be justified in the name of striking a blow against the oppressor.

This chapter will review crime policy historically with an emphasis on drug abuse in the United States. Data show that many violent crimes are committed under the influence of illegal drugs and that significant proportions of the prison population are serving sentences that are linked to drug use or drug trafficking. This chapter looks at crime policy from an ideological perspective (that examines different philosophies of how to deal with crime), a rational perspective (viewing methodological tools of social scientists), and a power perspective (examining whether some groups set the agenda in crime/drug policy to the detriment of others). Discussions of the controversial issues of drug legalization and spousal abuse are provided in an effort to spark interest and debate. The issue of spouse abuse is illustrated through the O.J. Simpson murder trial, which gripped the nation's conscience and focused attention on a number of fundamental problems: racial polarization, equal justice for all, and spousal abuse.

THE RPI INPUTS TO CRIME POLICY

The Rationality Input

Research methods and objective analysis are necessary to develop effective crime policy. As with other policy areas, researchers have applied scientific principles systematically to discover the effectiveness of specific policy initiatives. For example, since the early 1960s crime-related research has led to a number of general observations about rehabilitation programs (in general they have not been successful), frequency of police patrolling neighborhoods in squad cars (they have few or no demonstrable effects on crime rates), and the benefits of job training, schooling, and racial integration (minimal).[2]

A typical method of studying criminal behavior is cross-sectional research or a comparison of similarities and differences at one point in time. Cross-sectional studies are akin to taking a "snapshot." In contrast to this static view, longitudinal research traces developments over time and is akin to a motion picture. A third method for conducting crime policy research is to conduct experimental research measuring the effects of an intervention. Innovative interventions have been tried from time to time in efforts to rehabilitate prisoners or reduce the rate of recidivism.

Boot Camp Experiments

One of the most compelling new ideas in criminology involved *boot camps*, an appealing concept in terms of cost and "get tough" image. Advocates of boot camps, or shock incarceration programs, claimed that they would instill discipline, boost self-esteem, teach decency, and ultimately establish respect for the law. The concept was endorsed by President Clinton, Vice President Gore, and many others.[3]

The popularity of boot camps grew in the early 1980s as alternatives to traditional correctional programs. Between 1983 and 1993, forty-one boot camps opened in twenty-six states. One example of the boot camp philosophy was witnessed in Louisiana in 1987. In the first phase of Louisiana's adaption of the boot camp, offenders were to spend ninety to 180 days in a medium-security prison and participate in activities such as daily work, physical exercise, drills, group counseling, drug education, and rehabilitation. Successful completion of the first phase of the program would result in parole. In a second phase of the program, offenders were to be placed back into the community under intensive supervision. This phase required contact with supervisors, adherence to a strict curfew, performance of community service, work, and screening for alcohol and illegal drugs. Restrictions were relaxed gradually if offenders successfully complied with requirements.

The effects of this intervention were monitored carefully. Research conducted by the National Institute of Justice (NIJ) found that individuals who completed the program, in general, had more positive attitudes, were more optimistic about their futures, and were more likely to report their prison experiences as beneficial. However, the research also noted that only 57 percent of participants completed the program and that the program did not seem to have much of an impact on recidivism when controlling for age and past criminal history. When these variables were considered, researchers found that graduates of boot camps experienced rates of jailing for new offenses and parole violations similar to rates for those who did not participate in the program. Participants in the boot camp program expressed satisfaction that the length of their prison time was reduced, that they had received discipline, that the program had helped "pass the time," and that it had taught them self-confidence.

However, since these participants were just as likely as nonparticipants to commit crimes after release from the program, at least one aspect of the program was considered a failure.[4]

In 1996, twenty-one states operated boot camps for juvenile offenders and thirty-seven states ran similar programs for adult inmates. Criminal justice experts, however, concluded on the basis of their study that the only offenders who seemed to benefit substantially from boot camps were those who received intensive counseling and drug treatment in camp and in transitional programs after they left. Studies showed little difference between the recidivism rates of those who completed boot camp programs and those who did not. Offenders had lower recidivism rates in programs where there were at least three hours or more of therapeutic treatment such as education, counseling, and drug treatment, and where some kind of intensive supervision that existed.[5]

Kansas City Patrol Experiment

Another example of research that utilized a rational approach to policy was the Kansas City Patrol Experiment, conducted in the early 1970s by the Police Foundation, a nonprofit organization established by the Ford Foundation. The ultimate purpose of the Kansas City experiment was to determine whether or not police patrols made a difference in the reduction of crime rates, police response times, and citizen perceptions of the police.

The basic research design of the Kansas City Patrol Experiment looked at the impact of three different levels of police protection. One area of the city was assigned two to three times the normal number of police patrol cars (proactive patrol), another area had no patrol cars (reactive patrol), and a third area representing a control group was assigned the regular number of patrol cars. A team of investigators conducted the research over a one-year period. They hypothesized that crime would increase in the area with fewer patrols, decrease in the area with more patrols, and remain the same in the area where the number of patrols remained unchanged. In short, they anticipated that the level of patrolling would have a direct impact of reducing crime. The researchers also hypothesized that an area with greater police presence would also have quicker response times to reported crimes and would be associated with more positive attitudes toward the police.

The results of the experiment did not support the hypotheses. The researchers found that the number of patrol cars assigned to designated areas by the Kansas City police force made little statistical difference in the amount of crime committed in the various areas, that no change at all occurred in the amount of time it took the police to respond to reported crimes, and that the number of patrols had only a marginal impact on the citizens' perceptions of the police.[6] Counter to expectations, citizens living in areas with greater patrolling (the proactive patrol) felt more apprehensive about being robbed or raped than those living in other areas. Citizen respect for police declined slightly in the area of the proactive beats and increased slightly in the control area.

The potential policy impact of the Kansas City Experiment is of considerable interest. Some caution, however, must be exercised. It is important not to misinterpret rational studies, not to overgeneralize findings, and to state precisely what was found. The Kansas City experiment did not show that police made no difference and were useless in controlling crime. The experiment, however, did show that changes in the amount of patrolling did not alone affect (over one year's time in one city) the incidence of crime or perceptions of the police. The Kansas City Patrol Experiment offered an interesting piece of evidence for the view that one police procedure (patrolling by squad cars) had little impact on crime rates and perceptions of the police, in one city.

From the perspective of applying research to policy, a case can be made for reevaluating policies on squad car patrolling if other experiments supported the Kansas City findings. If rational experimentation concluded that squad car police patrolling had little effect, there would be no compelling reason to tie up large numbers of uniformed police in the task of driving through the streets waiting for something to happen. By cutting back on such patrols, a substantial amount of manpower could be made available for other tasks such as investigation, surveillance, or community service.[7] The Kansas City experiment is illustrative of how analysts can use the rational perspective to formulate more effective and cost-efficient public policy.

The Power Input

An example of how interest groups influence crime policy is found in activities of the National Rifle Association and other groups. A report from the National Criminal Justice Commission, an organization founded in 1977 to conduct research in the field of criminal justice, provides some insights into the relationship between crime policy and various vested interests such as the National Rifle Association. The Commission comprised a group of thirty-four citizens charged with examining criminal justice policy in the United States and making recommendations regarding how crime policy could make the nation safer. In discussing the role of special interest groups, the Commission stated:

> Many special-interest groups focus on crime. One group, the National Rifle Association (NRA), is a leading example of an organization that tries to convince the public to support prison expansion. Although known primarily for its vigorous opposition to gun control legislation, the NRA in recent years has entered the battle over crime policy with a flourish. Its agenda appears to be to divert public fear of violent crime away from support of gun control legislation and toward tougher law enforcement and prison expansion. The clout of the NRA is enormous: it counts 3.4 million members and a budget of approximately $140 million, and has the largest single political action committee in the nation. It may have more influence over crime policy than any other private organization.[8]

The influence of the NRA can also be seen in electoral campaigns. The National Criminal Justice Commission reported that on the eve of the vote on the

1994 federal crime bill the NRA bought full-page advertisements in major newspapers urging Congress to increase its allocation for new prison construction from $13 billion to $21 billion and to eliminate crime-prevention programs. The NRA also backed the first federal "three strikes and you're out" initiative, funded a similar successful ballot initiative in California, and financed a successful campaign to persuade the Texas legislature to spend $1 billion on new prisons.[9] The "three strikes" provision was the most widely publicized component of the 1994 federal anti-crime bill. This provision mandated life in prison for anyone convicted of a third violent felony, if the felony was prosecuted in federal court. Federal judges were instructed to count earlier violent felony convictions in either state or federal courts when applying the three strike rule.

The National Criminal Justice Commission reported that numerous entities, business and government, profited financially or politically from fear:

> The more fear can be inflamed, the more intense public passion about crime becomes and the easier it is to gain votes by proposing harsher sentences and more prisons. It is also easier for private companies to get new business, for retailers to expand the market for home security devices, and for unions of correctional officers to increase their salaries. And through it all, this fear can be used to get additional "raw material" to feed the growth of jails and prisons.[10]

Specific interests that would benefit from increased public spending on crime control include the private correctional industry and depressed rural areas. The private correctional industry incarcerated only a small proportion of the overall correctional population in the mid-1990s, but the rate of growth of private facilities was more than four times the rate of growth of state facilities. The Corrections Corporation of America (CCA), the largest private prison company, had profits in 1993 of $4 million on $100 million of revenue. This represented a 57 percent increase from the previous year. Founders and officers of CCA included people with major political influence among both Democrats and Republicans. Communities also look to prisons as a source of economic growth.

While most offenders came from cities, since 1980, the bulk of new prison construction has taken place in economically depressed rural communities. Demographers consider the punishment of crime to be a leading rural growth industry. Rural areas housed such a large portion of the prison population that 5 percent of the national increase in rural population from 1980 to 1990 was accounted for by prisoners.[11]

The Ideological Input

The ways in which people conceptualize the problem of crime depend to a large extent upon ideological perspectives. The response to drug use was shaped by the ideological predispositions of different administrations, as well as by unexpected events and budget constraints.[12] Ideological differences are evident in debates over drug strategies, as well as in the issue of drug legalization. For example, the "supply strategy" in drug policy was based upon the assumption that punishment was an effective deterrent to criminal drug trafficking and drug use. A "demand strategy" rejected these assumptions and accepted the view that prevention, education, or treatment programs were more viable alternatives. Ideological perspectives relating to crime policy in general have been characterized as falling into liberal or conservative camps.

The Conservative View

Under the conservative view, criminals should be dealt with firmly to teach them a lesson, and the roots of crime are believed to be in the individual criminal, not in the environment in which the criminal lives. Conservatives tend to emphasize individual responsibility in explaining criminal behavior. In the 1996 Presidential race, Republican candidate Bob Dole echoed this refrain, stating, "Americans are tired of being guinea pigs in a discredited liberal-leaning laboratory of leniency. What works in combating crime is no mystery. It begins with the understanding that the cause of crime can be explained with one simple word: Criminals. Criminals. Criminals."[13] Borrowing a line that was used originally by Georgia Governor Zell Miller in reference to President Bush at the 1992 Democratic National Convention, Dole claimed that Clinton "talks like Dirty Harry, but acts like Barney Fife." This line contrasts Clint Eastwood's tough San Francisco police officer with the bumbling deputy sheriff on the old *Andy Griffith Show*.[14]

Some conservatives maintained that the roots of criminal behavior were biological. Biological theories of crime were pioneered by Cesare Lombroso. In the late 1800s, Lombroso argued that some people were born with a greater or lesser tendency to become criminals. Borrowing heavily from Charles Darwin's theory of evolution, Lambroso contended that such people could be identified by examining the size and shape of their heads. According to Lambroso, man had evolved over thousands of years, from primitive to sophisticated human beings and that some people simply had not evolved as far as others. These people could be identified by physical characteristics that were vestiges of an earlier evolutionary stage. In more recent times, there has been a resurgence of interest in biological explanations for crime. A new group of researchers termed *neo-Lombrosians* by their critics sought to demonstrate that biological characteristics played a role in the predisposition of some individuals toward criminal behavior. During the 1960s, neo-Lombrosian studies tried to link certain chromosomes to criminal behavior. Political criticisms of biological studies, however, have been effective in discrediting such studies.

Another explanation for crime embraced by conservative thinkers related to the concept of culture. According to Edward Banfield, a lower-class culture was linked to crime. This culture was characterized by traits such as a short time horizon (live for today, don't worry about the future), a taste for risk, an acceptance of violence, and little concern for others. These traits were believed to keep the lower classes mired in poverty even as opportunities rose for others:

[T]he lower-class individual lives from moment to moment. If he has any awareness of a future, it is of something fixed, fated, beyond his control: things happen to him, he does not make them happen. Impulse governs his behavior, either because he cannot discipline himself to sacrifice a present for a future satisfaction or because he has no sense of the future.[15]

Banfield believed that the benefits of criminal behavior tended to be immediate and that its costs accrued at some time in the future. A "present orientation" was believed to be a product of the environment in which an individual was raised, and was not necessarily determined biologically. Both the biological and cultural approaches to crime, however, referred to specific attributes of individuals. Under the conservative perspective, certain characteristics (either by birth or cultural predisposition) differentiated criminals from law-abiding citizens. A variant on the conservative perspective (the neoconservative view) focuses upon rational choice and the decline of community.

The rational-choice theory views criminal behavior as an outcome of choices made by offenders. This theory suggests that potential offenders rationally evaluate the properties of offenses such as the type of payoff and perceived risk. If payoffs appear to be large and risks small, people will choose to engage in criminal behavior. In contrast to the rational-choice view, the decline of community perspective focused upon acceptable standards of behavior. According to the community decline perspective, a decline in the observance of appropriate conduct is associated with further inappropriate behavior. Small towns and villages where people know their neighbors are said to possess a sense of community that reinforces acceptable norms of behavior. The sense of community, however, is fragile and difficult to sustain in larger cities. Small violations in social norms (such as a window left unrepaired) send a message to the entire community. Consonant with this theory is the view that if a window is broken and unrepaired, all the rest of the windows will soon be broken.[16] Such perceptions of decline can send a neighborhood spiraling down a pathway to more and more disorder as citizens who previously were law-abiding no longer feel constrained by social norms. Criminal behavior becomes more acceptable. As it seeps into community life, the inclination for others to engage in similar behavior increases.

Crime policy recommendations are similar for neoconservatives and conservatives. Both emphasize punishment and incapacitation. From the rational-choice perspective, policymakers must increase the costs and decrease the benefits of crime. One method of increasing the costs is to increase the probability of being caught and punished severely. Policy remedies emanating from the community decline perspective include reestablishing and maintaining informal social ties that bind the community together.

The Liberal View

The liberal view of crime differs fundamentally from the conservative perspectives. While conservatives and neoconservatives focus upon individual impulses or calculation, liberals insist that policymakers must attack the *root causes* of crime. They maintain that attention should be directed toward environmental concerns such as the character of society in which criminals live. For liberals, crime reflects the character of society more than the character of those who committed the crimes; they blame the environment more than individuals. Liberals contend that root causes of crime such as slums, racism, ignorance, poverty, unemployment, prenatal neglect, pollution, overcrowded housing, drug addiction, hopelessness, and injustice need to be addressed.[17]

More recently, liberal attempts to ameliorate crime have focused upon the education/treatment/prevention dimensions of drug abuse. A number of innovative prevention/education programs have been implemented. One such effort was the Drug Abuse Resistance Education program, better known as Project DARE. Project DARE was developed in 1984 as a joint effort between the Los Angeles Police Department and the Los Angeles Unified School District in an effort to teach students how to resist taking drugs. A seventeen-week curriculum was delivered primarily to fifth- or sixth-graders with police officers conducting group discussions, identifying alternatives to drug use, engaging in role-playing, and encouraging parental involvement.

In the early 1990s, the DARE program was offered in over 450 cities throughout the United States and in several other countries. Research indicated mixed results from the DARE curriculum. A study of Los Angeles suggested that DARE students accepted significantly fewer offers to use drugs and reported significantly lower levels of substance use than control group students. Evaluations in North Carolina, however, found that the DARE program had no significant effect on self-reported drug use, intentions to use drugs, or self-esteem.[18]

Critics of the drug education strategy claimed that education may lead to experimentation with drugs. They contended that drug education would increase curiosity and encourage experimentation. Furthermore, critics complained that drug education could be successful in providing information about drugs, but education would be much less successful in modifying behavior or changing attitudes.[19]

In general, liberals have pressed to improve the life chances of "at risk" children in programs such as Head Start, which emerged from President Lyndon Johnson's War on Poverty in the 1960s and provided special preschool preparation to disadvantaged children before they entered kindergarten or the first grade. More recently, a number of drug prevention programs have been targeted to children in the sixth as well as seventh grades. One such program (Life Skills Training, or LST), was designed at the Cornell University Medical College. The LST program taught skills such as how to deal with anxiety, how to cope with problems, how to overcome shyness, and how to resist peer pressures. Studies reported that rates of marijuana use were one-half to three-quarters lower among students who participated in LST than among those who did not.[20]

Another program, Students Taught Awareness and Resistance (STAR), was developed at the University of Southern California's Institute for Health Promotion and Disease Prevention Research to teach resistance to drugs. The program was aimed at students in their first year of junior high school. Curriculum focused on media, family, and peer influences as students engaged in role playing. Five-year follow-up studies reported that rates of tobacco, marijuana, and alcohol use for participants in STAR were 20 to 40 percent lower than for students who did not participate in the program. By the ninth and tenth grades, STAR graduates used cocaine at half the rate of other students.[21]

Another prevention program, termed "Smart Moves," was tailored for inner-city neighborhoods and was adopted in Boys and Girls Clubs. This program provided after-school prevention classes, as well as recreational, educational, and vocational activities. The Smart Moves program approached prevention in a comprehensive manner, working at the individual, family, and community levels to change attitudes toward drug use. A 1987 evaluation found that boys who participated in Smart Moves were more likely to refuse marijuana and cocaine, and were less willing to try drugs.[22]

In general, liberals are more willing to accept government responsibility for altering environments in an effort to reduce crime rates. Two activists in the Democratic Leadership Council summarized the following differences between liberal and conservative attitudes toward crime:

> The terms of the debate have become chiseled in stone: liberals blame crime on poverty, while conservatives blame it on the moral decline in the country. Liberals insist that the only way to attack crime is to attack the conditions that give rise to it. Conservatives insist that the only way to attack crime is to incarcerate criminals. Liberals believe that everyone is a product of his or her society and that someone who commits a crime is, in essence, as much a victim as the person against whom the crime is committed. Conservatives believe that each person is responsible for his or her own actions and that any suggestion to the contrary is an open invitation to murder and mayhem. A conservative who opposes more spending on prisons has become as much an anomaly as a liberal who favors the death penalty.[23]

Application of RPI

Rationality, power, and ideology all intermingle in the dance of policymaking. The issue of crime is addressed largely at the state and local levels where city, county, and state police all assume crime-fighting responsibilities. On one level, crime policy is rational. Evidence is collected; standard operating procedures are followed; leads are pursued; cases are developed for presentation to a jury; and judges make decisions based upon existing law. In a large sense, standardized, objective, routinized processes direct behavior and provide for uniformity in action.

From the managerial perspective of service delivery and personnel direction, a rational approach holds intuitive appeal. Law enforcement becomes a profession much like other professions such as accountancy or engineering. Skills are taught in police academies or training programs, and expectations of performance are learned on the job. The FBI or other national crime-fighting organizations can be called upon to provide technical assistance on an array of problems. Standard responses to problems from crowd control, to hostage taking, to dealing with persons wishing to jump off of tall buildings are formulated. These "micro-level" policies can evolve by trial and error as administrators learn what seems to work and what does not.

The salience of the rational input in crime policy is most applicable to the relatively narrow range of managerial options. From the broader perspective of "macro" crime policy, reflected in major policy shifts, other forces appear to be operative. While at the "micro" level rationality plays a role in crime policy, at the "macro" level major changes in policy (such as the change from strategies addressing "root causes" of crime to strategies that would make criminals more accountable for their actions) seem to be influenced by the ideological or power inputs.

Fundamental changes in approach appear to occur only after "paradigmatic" shifts in ideological sentiments. One such shift appears to have occurred as liberal crime solutions aimed at "root causes" were discredited and perceived as being "soft" on criminals. The alternative view of being "tough" on criminals by "locking them up and throwing away the key" has worked to the advantage of numerous politicians. The Contract with America, formulated in 1994 at a conference of Republicans from the House of Representatives, reflected this shift in popular sentiment, calling for "tough punishment for those who prey on society."[24]

The influence of ideology appears to be especially relevant to capital punishment. Death penalty opponents often argue that if life is sacred, then the murderer's life, too, is sacred, and for the government to punish the offender by execution is barbaric, causing the government to descend to the murderer's level. As an example of this view, Amnesty International stated that while governments have a duty to protect citizens from criminals, "physical elimination" was barbaric in today's world. Furthermore, the death penalty is viewed as "unleashing a brutalizing force on society." "Just retribution" arguments are identified as pro-death penalty rhetoric that holds great emotional appeal but these arguments are rejected by many who believe that vengeance is rooted in a "culture of violence" and represents an act of "desperation."[25] In contrast to the view of Amnesty International is the position that a person who commits capital murder simply cannot and should not expect to be given a pat on the back and told to "go and sin no more."[26]

Because of the highly emotional nature of the capital punishment debate, it is best seen through the ideological visor of emotion, gut feelings, faith, and rigid beliefs. Some people embrace the ideological view that swift and sure retribution is necessary to punish transgression. This is perceived to be just from a moral point of view and effective in ensuring social order for society. Furthermore, some believed that capital punishment could assuage the fears of those threatened by crime, dispensing justice through the biblical imperative of "an eye for an eye." The legitimacy of taking a life for a life has been supported in societies throughout history. To some, life is not a right but a privilege that can be removed at any time by the proper authorities.

In opposition to the policy prescription of capital punishment is the fundamental moral principle that a higher order controls the lives of individuals and therefore that the government or others should be very careful about using its power of execution. The question that remains to be answered is whether any crime warrants the taking of another life. Is such a penalty cruel and unusual punishment? Is it moral? Is it necessary and proper? Is it just? Can a jury of peers decide to take another life or should those matters be left to another authority? Such questions are unlikely to be answered by a computer printout, a reason for crime policy being more ideological than rational.

HISTORICAL PERSPECTIVES ON CRIME POLICY

Early History of Crime in the United States

Since the founding of the American colonies, each generation has felt threatened by the specter of rising crime and violence. On the eve of the Revolutionary War, many colonists feared that if rebellion came, the harmony of the world would be confounded and the order of nature subverted. In 1767, Benjamin Franklin petitioned the British Parliament to stop solving its crime problem by shipping convicted felons to the American colonies. Franklin complained that transported felons were corrupting the morals of the poor and terrorizing the rest of the population with many burglaries, robberies, and murders. Although Franklin complained, when the framers of the Constitution met in 1787, crime was not an important issue. Analysis of records in Massachusetts found that approximately the same number of prosecutions for theft occurred before 1776 as after 1776. It appeared that the small towns and villages of which the infant republic was composed were able to enforce a communal consensus to maintain an orderly society.[27]

There is some historical evidence, however, of high levels of crime in the United States when compared with the rates in other nations. For example, the city of Cleveland, Ohio, whose population in 1920 was one-tenth the size of London's, had six times as many murders and seventeen times as many robberies. Chicago was one-third the size of London in 1920, but had twelve times as many murders and twenty-two times as many robberies.[28] Criminal behavior expanded significantly after 1920 when the Eighteenth Amendment to the United States Constitution (prohibiting the manufacture and sale of alcohol) went into effect. The "roaring twenties" were associated with high levels of violence, bootleg alcohol, and the growth of crime syndicates. Mobsters such as Al Capone and Meyer Lansky became media celebrities, and the focus of attention. New and more violent crime syndicates arose and displaced older groups that had dominated in earlier periods of the nation's history.[29] The era of prohibition spawned a growth in illegal behavior, and by 1933 prohibition was repealed. With the end of prohibition and the subsequent period of economic decline marked by the Great Depression, crime rates dwindled. Homicide deaths dropped by 50 percent between 1933 and the early 1940s. The rate of other serious offenses dropped by one-third. Crime increased somewhat after World War II, yet remained well below the levels reached in the 1920s and early 1930s. These levels were not approached again until the early 1960s.

Some researchers claim that in different periods of time certain activities are considered to be acceptable, but that as time passed these actions fall into disfavor and are declared illegal. In essence, therefore, any social problem can be viewed as time-, place-, and context-bound.[30] The history of drug use provides an example of how this phenomenon has evolved over time; in some periods of time drug use was permitted, while in others it was defined as a crime.

Drug use is not a modern phenomenon. Archaeologists have found evidence in ancient ships of the transportation of alcohol dating back to ancient times.[31] Poppy seeds (the source of opium) dating back several thousand years were found in what is now Turkey, and ancient Greeks such as Aristotle wrote about the poppy and its product, opium. In the Americas, European explorers found that the Indians used a variety of drugs such as coca, peyote, and certain types of mushrooms. These drugs were used to relieve fatigue, to achieve a psychological uplift, and for religious purposes. In the 1700s and 1800s, "cash cropping" in commodities such as opium, tea, coffee, grains, and grapes for alcohol consumption was a common practice.[32]

Alcohol consumption in America can be traced back to the time of the founding of the republic. In 1790, yearly per capita consumption of alcohol approximated six gallons of pure 200-proof alcohol. By the year 1810, consumption had risen to an all-time high of 7.10 gallons but declined following public agitation by religious leaders in the 1820s. A number of secular organizations such as the Washingtonians (recovering alcoholics), the Independent Order of Rechabites of North America, the Sons of Temperance, and the Independent Order of Good Templars also campaigned against alcohol consumption.[33] By the late 1840s, antialcohol and prohibition sentiment achieved a considerable degree of popularity.

A growing perception of the dangers of some legally sold drugs marked a period of antidrug activism in the late 1800s. In 1890, most pharmacies and a variety of other stores in America or Britain sold opium pills, pure morphine, opium for smoking, coca leaf products, pure cocaine, and a variety of drinks containing alcohol mixed with opiates or cocaine. Many common patent medicines contained opium, and consumers drank cocaine-containing beverages such as Coca-Cola, Coca Cordial, and New Ola.[34] Sentiment turned against the use of such drugs, as many middle-class consumers became addicted to such medicines and drinks. Estimates of the number of opiate addicts in the United States prior to World War I range from 100,000 to 300,000.[35]

In the late 1800s, cities and states in America began passing antinarcotics legislation. In 1875, the city of San Francisco passed an ordinance prohibiting the smoking of opium in smoking houses, or what became known as *smoking dens*. Following the lead of San Francisco, western states began adopting similar legislation, and by 1914, a total of twenty-seven anti-narcotics laws were in effect at the city and state level.[36] At the national level, in 1883, Congress raised the tariff on opium prepared for smoking; in 1887, it prohibited the importation of opium by individuals living in the United States who were not American citizens, and in 1909, Congress banned its importation altogether.

Finally in 1914 the Harrison Act made the importation, sale, or possession of opiates (except for medical purposes) illegal. Between the period of antidrug activism around the turn of the twentieth century and the early 1960s, drugs were perceived to represent deviant behavior, largely confined to minority groups as well as to specific professions such as musicians. This perception, however, changed beginning in the 1960s and early 1970s, a period characterized as the "modern" period of crime in America.

Modern Crime Period in the United States

Crime Rates and Incarceration

Crime levels increased dramatically in the United States during the 1960s. In 1962, there were 4.5 murders per one hundred thousand population, a rate that more than doubled to 9.4 by 1972. Similar increases were noted for robbery and auto theft. In 1959, the robbery rate per one hundred thousand was 51.2; in 1968 these rates rose to 131.0. Increases in the rates of auto theft were particularly prominent.[37] A number of explanations have been presented for the large increase in crime rates since the early 1960s. Simple demographics, or the large growth in the age group most prone to crime, explained much of the increase. In 1950, there were about 24 million people aged fourteen to twenty-four. By 1960, there were just under 27 million, and by 1970 there were approximately 40 million. The increase in the number of teenagers in the early 1960s was attributed to the baby boom phenomenon (a child born in 1946 would have been sixteen in 1962). Age alone, however, accounted for only a portion of the increase in crime in the 1960s. One study conducted by researchers at the Massachusetts Institute of Technology found that the murder rate during the 1960s was more than ten times greater than what one would have expected from the changing age structure of the population alone. Explanations for the increase not attributed to demographics included: a critical mass of young persons setting off a "chain reaction" effect, the media's celebration of a culture of personal liberation, increased access to drugs, and the decline in the deterrent force of the American legal system.[38]

Perhaps the most accurate information dealing with crime comes from the crime victimization survey, first conducted in 1966. This survey initially involved questioning 10,000 households. By 1991, approximately 50,000 housing units and other living quarters were included in the sample, which was praised for its ability to detect crimes that were unreported to the police in addition to reported crimes. Victimization studies suggest that less than 50 percent of all crimes actually were reported.[39] A more accurate reading of crime rates therefore should include nonreported as well as reported crimes, data that are compiled in the victimization studies. In the absence of victimization data, "crime waves" might simply reflect a greater willingness on the part of the police to make arrests or an increase in the proportion of people who report crimes. Similarly, "crime drops" might reflect a diminished willingness to make arrests or a decrease in the proportion of crimes that are reported.

Victimization surveys revealed a decline in crime since the explosion of the 1960s. Since 1973, crime rates have declined for personal crimes (including violent crimes such as rape, robbery, and assault) as well as for household crimes (burglary, larceny, and motor vehicle theft). Table 10.1 provides a summary of victimization rates per 1,000 persons aged twelve or older.

Crime victimization rates have declined in practically every area since 1973. Both overall personal and household crimes registered declines in excess of 25 percent. Declines in crimes of violence have been more muted than for personal or household crimes. Crimes of violence declined by almost 4 percent. Reduction in violent crime continued in the 1990s. The Department of Justice reported that on the basis of their National Crime Victimization Survey violent crime fell by more than 9 percent in 1995. During the 1996 electoral campaign, President Clinton proclaimed that the 9 percent yearly drop was the largest decrease in a decade and asserted that his policies, including putting more police officers on the streets and regulating the sale of handguns and assault rifles, had helped contribute to the decline.[40]

Republicans offered alternative explanations for the drop in crime. They claimed that reductions in crime could be traced to the massive national imprisonment binge that began in the 1970s and escalated rapidly when Republicans

TABLE 10.1 Victimization Rates for Personal and Household Crimes

	Victimization Rate							Percent Change 1973–1991
	1973	1981	1983	1985	1987	1989	1991	
Personal crimes	123.6	120.5	107.9	99.4	98.0	97.8	92.3	−25.3%
Crimes of violence	32.6	35.3	31.0	30.0	29.3	29.1	31.3	−3.9
Rape	1.0	1.0	.8	.7	.8	.7	.8	−11.6
Robbery	6.7	7.4	6.0	5.1	5.3	5.4	5.6	−17.2
Assault	24.9	27.0	24.1	24.2	23.3	23.0	24.9	No change
Crimes of theft	91.1	85.1	76.9	69.4	68.7	68.7	61.0	−33.0
Household crimes	217.8	226.0	189.8	174.4	173.9	169.9	162.9	−25.2
Burglary	91.7	87.9	70.0	62.7	62.1	56.4	53.1	−42.1
Larceny	107.0	121.1	105.2	97.5	95.7	94.2	88.0	−17.7
Mot. Veh. Theft	19.1	17.1	14.6	14.2	16.0	19.2	21.8	14.3

Source: National Crime Victimization Survey Report, 1992, p. 6.

controlled the White House and Senate during the 1980s. Other factors that contributed to declining crime rates included a sizable drop in the number of violence-prone teenagers, a healthy economy, burgeoning grass-roots anticrime campaigns, and declining strife in urban narcotics markets. Drug turf wars between rival gangs, a staple of the late 1980s and early 1990s, became increasingly rare as battles succumbed to what criminologist James Lynch termed the "routinization of the drug trade."[41] The linkage between crime and drugs has been well documented. When George Pataki was elected Governor of New York in 1994 he discovered that half of all inmates incarcerated in New York prisons were serving sentences for drug offenses.[42] In 1992, a very high proportion of those arrested in major American cities tested positive at the time of their arrest for some type of drug.

In 1992, a majority of males arrested in the twenty-three cities listed in Table 10.2 tested positive for some type of drug at the time of their arrest. The

TABLE 10.2 Drug Use by Arrestees in Twenty-three U.S. Cities, by Type of Drug and Sex, 1992 (percent testing positive)

City	Male		Female	
	Any Drug	Cocaine	Any Drug	Cocaine
Atlanta, GA	69	58	65	58
Birmingham, AL	64	49	59	46
Chicago, IL	69	56	(NA)	(NA)
Cleveland, OH	64	53	74	66
Dallas, TX	59	41	66	48
Denver, CO	60	38	61	50
Detroit, MI	58	37	72	62
Ft. Lauderdale, FL	64	46	62	47
Houston, TX	59	41	54	44
Indianapolis, IN	52	23	50	25
Kansas City, MO	60	41	73	62
Los Angeles, CA	67	52	72	58
Miami, FL	68	56	(NA)	(NA)
New Orleans, LA	60	49	52	44
New York, NY	77	62	85	72
Omaha, NE	48	16	(NA)	(NA)
Philadelphia, PA	78	63	78	67
Phoenix, AZ	47	26	63	49
Portland, OR	60	35	73	54
St. Louis, MO	64	50	70	62
San Antonio, TX	54	32	44	25
San Diego, CA	77	45	72	37
Washington, D.C.	60	44	72	64

Source: Statistical Abstract of the United States, 1995, p. 207.

proportion of women arrestees testing positive for any drug ranged from 44 percent (San Antonio) to 85 percent (Manhattan, New York). The proportion of men arrestees who tested positive ranged from 52 percent (Indianapolis) to 77 percent (San Diego and Manhattan, New York). Both men and women were more likely to test positive for cocaine at the time of their arrest. Cocaine use by men appeared to be a particularly significant problem in Philadelphia, Manhattan, Atlanta, Chicago, and Miami. High levels of cocaine use by women arrestees were noted for Philadelphia, Cleveland, and Washington, DC.

Drug use and the reaction of policymakers to drug use has had a profound effect on the prison population. In 1986, 52 percent of prisoners reported that they had at some time used major drugs, and 35 percent reported that they had been under the influence of a major drug at the time they committed the crime that led to their current imprisonment.[43] Incarceration rates increased dramatically in the 1980s. The 1993 incarceration rate of 351 per 100,000 was over three times the rate that had prevailed for the previous fifty years.[44] A 1996 report observed:

> The United States now has 1.5 million people behind bars—one million in state and federal prisons and another half million in local jails. Compared to other countries, this is by far the highest rate of incarceration relative to population in the Western world.
>
> The population of Americans incarcerated on any given day would qualify as the sixth-largest city in the country and is equal to the total combined populations of Seattle, Cleveland, and Denver. The Rikers Island Correctional Facilities in New York City and the Los Angeles county jail system are the two largest penal colonies in the world and by themselves have budgets larger than many cities.[45]

Crime Strategies

Two basic strategies were employed in the 1970s and 1980s to combat crime. These differing strategies are observable in what has been termed the two "wars" waged against crime. The first war (1967–1980) was said to have addressed issues of poverty; the second (1980–present) was said to be waged against criminals. Both strategies had their own assumptions, philosophies, and underlying beliefs.[46] Chief strategists in the first war against crime were liberals who emphasized the goals of rehabilitation of offenders, reintegration of offenders into society, humane treatment, and constitutional rights. Chief strategists of the second war emphasized punishment, deterrence, and cost containment.

Conservatives desired a limited role for the federal government in crime control, while liberals called for an expansion of governmental responsibility. The liberal approach is summed up in the Katzenbach commission report, a 340-page document issued in 1967 by a nineteen-member Commission led by former Attorney General Nicholas Katzenbach. The commission report, in essence, supported the view that social programs financed and administered by the federal government were America's best hope for preventing crime. The commission advocated a focus on civil rights, education, and family counseling as the means to reduce crime. Although conservative in its crime rhetoric, the Nixon administration acted on most of the Katzenbach recommendations and funneled a great deal of federal money to the state and local level through the Law Enforcement Assistance Administration (LEAA). This agency in turn embarked upon ambitious initiatives for activities such as community crime prevention, offender rehabilitation, and law enforcement training.

By 1980, conservative critics of the first war on drugs were declaring that the "war" was lost and could not be won as long as basic strategies remained unchanged. These analysts claimed that the first war was fought according to intellectually and morally bankrupt philosophies. They advocated abandoning the "root causes" strategy of crime fighting and adopting strategies that called for swift, certain, and more severe penalties. In 1982, President Reagan phased out the LEAA, and in 1984 Congress passed a tough anticrime bill, the Comprehensive Crime Control Act. Some of the key provisions of the 1984 bill permitted pretrial detention of dangerous defendants, restricted the use of the insanity defense, and increased penalties for drug trafficking. The "get tough" approach to crime has continued in the 1980s and 1990s as prison populations have expanded greatly.

Policies toward Drug Use

In 1965, approximately 5 percent of high school seniors had used marijuana at least once in the preceding twelve months. This figure rose to 30 percent by 1970, 40 percent by 1975, and 49 percent by 1980, before declining to 38 percent in 1985. Overlapping the so-called drug revolution of 1960 to 1975 was a rise in heroin use in inner-city neighborhoods. The rise of cocaine use in urban areas constituted the next stage in the modern chronology of illicit drug use. As the heroin epidemic eased in the mid-1970s, the use of cocaine became increasingly popular. From 1975 to 1983, cocaine became a "status drug," with its use spreading rapidly among marijuana-using segments of the baby boom generation.

Beginning in 1984, authorities began to come across a form of purified cocaine termed "rock," and in 1985 vials were discovered that contained a product known as "crack." Both of these products (rock and crack) contained purified cocaine, and both products were marketed to low-end (i.e., poor) buyers. With the new marketing strategy, crack use expanded in large cities throughout the nation, and by the early 1990s crack began to dominate illicit drug markets in most inner-city neighborhoods.

General drug use declined in the 1980s, as monitored through the government-sponsored National Household Survey on Drug Abuse. In terms of the share of teenagers who admit using any illicit drug in the previous month, the National Household Survey on Drug Abuse found that rates of drug use have increased since 1992 (Table 10.3).

TABLE 10.3 Teenagers and Drug Use: Share of
People Who Admit Using Any Illicit Drug in
Previous Month, by Age Group (in percent)

Year	Age 12–17	Age 18–25
1979	16.3%	38.0%
1982	(NA)	(NA)
1985	13.2	25.3
1988	8.1	17.9
1990	7.1	15.0
1991	5.8	15.4
1992	5.3	13.1
1993	5.7	13.6
1994	8.2	13.3
1995	10.9	14.4

Source: 1995 National Household Survey on Drug Use; U.S. News &
World Report, 30 September 1996, p. 33.

Increases in teenage drug use were recorded for all illicit drugs since the low point of 5.3 percent for twelve- to seventeen-year-olds and 13.1 percent for eighteen- to twenty-five-year-olds in 1992. The rise in drug use on a percentage basis was greater for the younger (twelve- to seventeen-year-olds) teenage group. For this group, the proportion of people who admitted using any illicit drug more than doubled from 5.3 percent in 1992 to 10.9 percent in 1995. This rate, however, was still considerably lower than the 16.3 percent rate of 1979.

Policy responses to drug abuse have varied over time and have changed from administration to administration, with three general waves of governmental interest in drug policy.[47] The first wave of interest began early in the Nixon administration, peaked in 1971–1972, and ebbed quickly. This wave was characterized by "war on drugs" rhetoric, substantial increases in funding, and innovative treatment procedures. Not only did the Nixon administration emphasize treatment; the administration also promoted the new treatment of methadone maintenance. Mobilization of the Nixon administration's war on drugs was followed by a demobilization in 1973. "Victory" was claimed as well as disengagement from the war. Beginning in 1973, the federal budget for drug treatment and rehabilitation began to decline in absolute, as well as inflation-adjusted, dollars.

The Carter administration represented a second wave of government attention. The most notable policy initiative of the Carter years was a proposal to decriminalize marijuana. At marijuana decriminalization hearings conducted by Congress in 1977, representatives of the Carter administration recommended a relaxation of criminal penalties on marijuana. Administration spokespersons

Contemporary Controversy

Drug Legalization

Legalize

The controversy over drug and alcohol legalization has been simmering ever since the founding of the republic. As previously recounted, prohibition of alcohol as well as repeal of prohibitions on alcohol were issues of high saliency during the first half of the twentieth century. More recently, legalization of other drugs has been advocated by policy experts as well as by public officials. In 1988, the mayor of Baltimore, Kurt Schmoke, surprised a meeting of the United States Conference of Mayors by calling for congressional

put forth three reasons at the hearings: (1) current penalties for marijuana were counterproductive and inappropriate; (2) actual enforcement was ineffective; and (3) compared to other substances being abused, the health effects of marijuana were not that serious.

In 1977, Dr. Peter Bourne, director-designate of the Office of Drug Abuse Policy, proposed arguments in favor of decriminalization. The thrust of the decriminalization movement, however, was blunted when Bourne resigned under pressure. Bourne's short-lived directorship was shrouded by controversy as he was accused of writing prescriptions for one of his assistants. Some time later, journalist Jack Anderson reported that Bourne was seen sniffing cocaine at a Washington, DC, party. After Bourne's resignation, the movement toward decriminalization of marijuana lost credibility and momentum.[48]

The Carter administration also moved away from a "demand side" treatment/prevention/education emphasis back to more of a traditional law enforcement emphasis. In the 1971–1972 period, roughly 70 percent of drug spending went to treatment and prevention programs. In 1977–1978, this proportion of the drug budget declined to 55–56 percent. The trend initiated in the Carter administration continued over time. By the late 1980s, drug spending priorities had been reversed with only 30 percent of the drug budget going to "demand-side" expenditures of treatment/prevention and 70 percent allocated to law enforcement programs.[49]

The high priority assigned to drugs in fighting crime continued in the Bush administration. The overall strategy of the Bush administration could be summarized as one of continuing emphasis on law enforcement and interdiction. In 1989, President George Bush devoted his first prime-time speech to announcing a new war on drugs. The press noted that it was the most visible domestic initiative of his presidency.[50] It appeared that problems of drug abuse received

hearings to consider the legalization of some illicit drugs. Support for this position also was expressed by numerous liberal as well as conservative leaders. Mayor Schmoke cited three basic arguments in favor of decriminalization: (1) libertarianism (people should have a right to pursue their own decisions concerning drugs), (2) economics (decriminalization would take the profit out of drugs and reduce drug-related violence, and (3) health (money saved from law enforcement could be used for public education and treatment).[55]

In testimony before the Select Committee on Narcotics Abuse and Control, on September 29, 1988, Schmoke proposed a new approach to the problems of drug abuse:

> Our response to drug-related crime has been to try to prosecute our way out of it. But it is an effort that is destined to fail. The criminal justice system can handle, at best, only a small percentage of drug offenses . . . I propose that we begin a phased-in process of fighting drug addiction as a public health problem, not as a crime problem. I propose we . . . eliminate criminal penalties for marijuana possession and reallocate resources from interdiction efforts to drug-abuse prevention programs.[56]

(continued)

somewhat lower priority in the early years of the Clinton administration, with attention focused on welfare, tax, and health reform. In general, President Clinton's prescriptions for fighting drug abuse focused upon drug treatment on demand (helping communities dramatically increase their ability to offer drug treatment to everyone who needs assistance) and drug education in schools (to provide children with access to drug counseling, education, and outreach programs before drug addiction begins).[51]

A large number of Americans view drug use as a major problem of American society. It is interesting how politicians suddenly discover the issues of crime and drugs when they campaign in elections. The 1996 presidential election was no exception, as Bob Dole tried to portray Bill Clinton as soft on crime, too accepting of drugs, and weak in character. This effort was not successful, as Clinton deflected criticism with statistics indicating declining crime rates during his administration.

Residents of the United States continue to consume enormous quantities of illicit drugs. In the early 1990s, the Bureau of Public Affairs of the U.S. Department of State estimated that 65 percent of the world's supply of illegal narcotics was consumed in the United States. Analysts estimated that in the late 1980s the dollar value of illegal drug consumption ranged anywhere from $60 billion to $150 billion a year.[52] In a more conservative estimate, the Office of National Drug Control Policy estimated that in 1990 illegal drug consumers in the United States spent $18 billion for cocaine, $12 billion for heroin, $9 billion for marijuana, and $2 billion for other drugs.[53] In 1996, it was estimated that trafficking in illegal drugs was a $400 billion to $500 billion industry and rivaled the global oil trade for financial might.[54] Various ideas have been proposed in attempts to ameliorate the corrosive influences of illegal drugs. One such idea is drug legalization.

Other analysts advocated changes in existing policy, basing their conclusion on the perspectives that (1) attempts to enforce prohibitions were very costly, (2) prohibitions were ineffective, and (3) the outlawing of drugs produced major criminal activity.[57] Some policy experts believed that drug legalization was risky, yet recognized that it offered the benefit of lowering crime fighting costs, gaining new tax revenues from legal drug sales, increasing the quality of urban life, decreasing crime rates, and encouraging more ghetto residents to seek out legitimate career opportunities.[58]

Libertarian authors focused upon the perceived threats to liberty deriving from America's drug war. The libertarian philosophy (a philosophy that is considered by many to be an extreme form of contemporary conservatism) advocates maximizing individual choices and minimizing actions of the state. According to this view, the legitimacy of the United States rests in maximizing the security of citizens' lives, liberties, and property, not in saving people from falling into moral sin, political error, or illness. From this perspective, drug legalization should be encouraged since it prioritizes individual choice and reduces the role of the state.[59] The libertarian perspective expressed apprehension over the rise of a paternalistic public sector vigorously treating social problems. Libertarians contended that endorsing the expenditure of government funds for various treatment programs was a prescription for "statism and therapeutism" and that if people were not free to make their own choices, a "therapeutic state" could become a totalitarian state, masking its tyranny as therapy.

Various factors are commonly cited in making the case for drug legalization. Among the most commonly accepted arguments in favor of drug legalization are the views that drug laws have created evils (such as corruption, violence, street crime, and disrespect of the law) far worse than the drugs themselves; that laws have not succeeded in reducing demand; that too many people were taking drugs to be punished effectively; that the government must not interfere with personal behavior; and that if drugs were legalized prisons would be made more accessible to "real criminals."[60]

Don't Legalize

Opponents of legalization contend that some drugs are harmful to individuals and society as a whole and that government therefore has a responsibility to reduce the level of harm by promoting "correct" action and discouraging "incorrect" action. There is some evidence that legalizing drugs would increase the number of addicts and cause harm to society. For example, cocaine and heroin were found to be more addictive than alcohol, suggesting that there would be many millions more addicts if these substances were legalized.[61] The percentage of adults addicted to opiates and cocaine in 1913 (prior to their being declared illegal in the Harrison Act of 1914) is believed to correspond to the percentage of adults addicted to alcohol in North America today. A study of Jacksonville, Florida, in 1913 revealed that almost 1 percent of the entire population of Jacksonville was habitually using drugs. Because some users were not counted in the study, the author concluded that levels of drug use in large urban centers were much higher. Estimates based on very large surveys concluded that 47 million people, or about 2 percent of the U.S. population, used alcohol once or more weekly.[62] The experience of the Chinese with opium in the 1800s also supports the view that availability of drugs correlates positively with use (i.e., the greater the availability the greater the use). Reasons for discouraging use through governmental action include societal costs of lost productivity, subsidized medical care, and welfare assistance to users.

Drug abuse has been a particular concern of many congressional representatives from inner-city districts. Charles Rangel, Representative from New York and chairman of the Select Committee on Narcotics Abuse and Control, consistently voiced strong opposition to legalization initiatives, stating in the late 1980s:

> We have watched many of our young kids turn to dope to cope because they are without hope. Young Black children who have the capacity to become doctors and lawyers and engineers and scientists have given up . . . in exchange for the street corner hustling of cocaine and crack and marijuana. . . . Black America has watched and weeped as many lives have become twisted and have been snuffed out by the powerful lure of drug addiction. Under conditions that would make drugs cheaper and more readily available— as legalization would do—do we want to further these genocidal problems that we already have as a result of drug abuse?[63]

Mayors of New York, Philadelphia, and Newark also strongly condemned the idea of legalizing drugs. The former mayor of New York City, Ed Koch, compared drug legalization with "extinguishing a raging fire with napalm."[64] The mayor of Philadelphia, Wilson Goode, stated that "we have a moral and social responsibility to all citizens to protect them, to provide the best quality of life possible, and ensure a secure future. The legalization of drugs contradicts these precepts and the very foundation of our government and sense of community." Sharpe James, mayor of Newark, New Jersey, declared that "if the cost of reducing some crime in our cities is to enlarge the number of young addicts, then that is a price we cannot pay. We cannot sacrifice more of our boys and girls to low-cost drugs in the elusive hope of safer streets."[65]

Other arguments that favor keeping drug activity a criminal endeavor refer to the damage that drug use inflicts on others and on society at large. The view that drug abuse is a victimless crime is refuted by reference to medical costs and lower productivity. To counter libertarian arguments, opponents of legalization claim that the ideal of freedom must be balanced by the recognition of citizen rights to society as a whole.

Case Study

The Juice and Domestic Violence in America

ON THE night of October 25, 1993, Nicole Brown Simpson made two 911 calls stating that her ex-husband, the former football star O.J. Simpson, had broken into her house. She told the 911 operator that "He's f——— going nuts. . . . He broke the door. He broke the whole back door in. Then he came and he practically knocked my upstairs door down. No one could talk." Responding to a question asked by a 911 operator of whether this had happened before, Nicole Simpson responded, "Many times."[66] This message was played before the jury in the O.J. Simpson "trial of the century," underscoring the problem of domestic violence in the nation.

Prior to his arrest on charges of murder, Simpson seemed to exemplify a true realization of the American dream. He had risen from Potrero Hill, a poor neighborhood in San Francisco, to become, according to some, the most popular sports figure of his generation. After football, he moved to advertising various products. Sports columnist Ron Rapoport of the *Los Angeles Daily News* claimed that he became a professional "good guy," selling athletic shoes, orange juice, and above all Hertz rental cars. Mark Morris, who helped create Hertz ads for him, said that he had a certain "magnetic quality" that enriched advertising beyond the typical celebrity endorsement. *Los Angeles Times* columnist Peter King said that TV viewers came to think of him as "Uncle Juice— likable, honest and, more than anything, familiar."[67]

Following the arrest, however, a darker side of the former football star was revealed. The media reported that Simpson's first wife had told Simpson's biographer that he was a "terrible person" in his youth and had "lived on the brink of disaster." Simpson agreed with her account in a book titled *O.J.* and admitted that he "had a lot of hatred and defiance" in him. Simpson eventually divorced his first wife and married Nicole Brown, a former companion from suburban Los Angeles.

It was reported that Nicole and O.J. Simpson lived a glamorous life in West Los Angeles. At least eight times, however, police were called to their home to settle domestic fights. In 1989, the Los Angeles city attorney filed charges against Simpson for wife beating. He pleaded no contest to the charge. In 1992, the year Nicole and O.J. were divorced, Nicole consulted a therapist who later revealed that Simpson had beaten Nicole all through their marriage and stalked her after they were separated.[68] Only a month prior to the murders, Simpson reportedly told friends that he still hoped to reconcile with Nicole and might even get married again. Denise Brown, the sister of Nicole Simpson, told the *New York Times* that Nicole had broken up with O.J. a week and a half before she died. Nicole put her home in Brentwood up for lease just five months after she purchased it, and a news organization quoted a friend of Nicole's as stating that Nicole was concerned about her safety and that she had caught O.J. looking into her window.[69]

The arrest and trial of O.J. Simpson riveted media attention on spousal abuse and its relationship to crime in general. Though Simpson eventually was acquitted of all charges after the jury deliberated for less than four hours, the issue of spousal abuse gained a great deal of attention. Anita Hill, professor of law at the University of Oklahoma, stated after Simpson's acquittal that whatever you think of his guilt or innocence, there was uncontroverted evidence of his abusive behavior.

Women and victim advocacy groups were outraged at the verdict, claiming that the "quieter" message of the trial was that men could beat their wives, perhaps even kill them, and still go unpunished. Abuse experts worried that Simpson's release would force victims of battering to retreat and avoid seeking legal help. Following the trial, Denise Brown (sister of the slain Nicole Brown Simpson) told a gathering of candle-carrying protesters that the verdict in the O.J. Simpson trial was saying, "You can rape, you can stalk, you can kill, and it's quite all right." Women's groups continued to criticize the Simpson verdict. Demonstrators from the National Organization for Women (NOW) and other groups massed outside NBC's studios in Burbank, California, in protest over a planned interview with Simpson following the trial. The interview, however, never materialized as Simpson canceled his scheduled appearance after consulting with his lawyers.[70]

Spousal abuse had received some attention over the years, but previous incidents did not generate the media hysteria that surrounded the Simpson affair. Notable prior spousal abuse stories included that of John Fedders, the chief regulator of the Securities and Exchange Commission. Fedders resigned from his position in 1985 after he acknowledged that he'd broken his wife's eardrum, wrenched her neck, and left her with black eyes and bruises. In 1988, Hedda Nussbaum described how her companion, a New York lawyer named Joel Steinberg, systematically beat her and killed their adopted daughter. Neither of these events, however, generated the type of attention that surrounded the O.J. Simpson trial.

The Law and Domestic Violence—Changing Views over Time

Historically, the courts and the law in general have provided justification for some types of punishments to be carried out within families. British common law of the Middle Ages gave husbands the right to "chastise" women, children, and apprentices. In 1395, an Englishwomen tried to divorce her husband because he had attacked her with a dagger, slashed her, and broken her arm. The husband contended that his actions were reasonable and necessary for "reducing her errors." The English court ruled in favor of the husband. Common law in Wales allowed a husband to beat his wife a maximum of three strokes with a rod the length of his forearm and the thickness of his middle finger, if there was evidence that the wife was disrespectful. The English "Rule of Thumb" referred to a husband's right to "chastise his wife with a whip or rattan no bigger than his thumb." While the husband retained these accepted rights, "severe beating" or "extreme brutality" toward spouses were considered to be acts of "bad form."

Common law British traditions of "chastisement" were carried over into America. In 1824, the Mississippi Supreme Court ruled that a husband should be permitted to "modestly chastise his wife" without subjecting himself to "discredit and shame of all parties concerned." A North Carolina Court ruled in 1864 that beating a wife was a matter best left out of the courts unless "some permanent injury be inflicted or there be an excess of violence."[71]

The courts' views on spousal abuse, however, began to change over time. In 1871, in the landmark decision an Alabama court ruled that men no longer had a right to beat their wives. The court stated, "The privilege, ancient though it be, to beat her with a stick, to pull her hair, choke her, spit in her face or kick her about the floor or to inflict

(continued)

upon her other like indignities, is not now acknowledged by our law." Similar court rulings followed.[72]

Ideology and Spousal Abuse

Legal changes on issues such as wife beating appear to have occurred as a result of fundamental changes in thinking. What was perfectly accepted practice in 1395 England is considered to be unconscionable behavior in America today. The emerging ideology of feminism appears to have had some influence in these changing perceptions of acceptable conduct toward women.

The absence of wife-battering as a topic in criminal justice literature before 1970 and the rapid proliferation of interest in the topic thereafter indicate that a relationship exists between social definitions and the ideology of feminism that emerged after 1970. In 1970, a survey found that 25 percent of male respondents and 17 percent of female respondents approved of a husband's slapping his wife under certain circumstances. Feminists sought to change these views and to have the public accept the notion that beating a wife was a serious crime. To a significant degree this campaign succeeded.

In recent years, philosophical attitudes toward spousal abuse have begun to move away from being perceived as a private matter toward the view of abuse as a criminal act. This redefinition generated a wave of legislation designated to make the courts, police, and social agencies more responsive to this type of behavior. The ideology of the feminist movement is credited at least partially with bringing about change in spousal abuse laws:

> The prime reason for recent interest in spouse abuse and arrest as a deterrent strategy, as suggested, has been the rise of the new feminist movement, gathering force from about 1970 and affecting virtually every aspect of American life and thought, including the law. Although changed material circumstances may be the source of the new feminism, the ideological basis of the new feminism, in general, has been gender equality in most spheres of life.[73]

Power, Rationality, and Spousal Abuse

Interest group behavior also seems to have had an impact on defining the relationship between spousal abuse and the law. One of the goals of the feminist movement was to "empower" women and to change attitudes. Women began to use their power as an organized interest group in order to achieve their aims:

Suggested Readings

Gerstein, Dean, and Lawrence Green, eds. *Preventing Drug Abuse: What We Know.* Washington, DC: National Academy Press, 1993.

Gordon, Diana. *The Return of the Dangerous Classes: Drug Prohibition and Policy Politics.* New York: Norton, 1994.

Wilson, James Q. *Thinking About Crime*, 2nd ed. New York: Basic Books, 1984.

Wilson, James Q., and Joan Petersilia, eds. *Crime.* San Francisco: Institute for Contemporary Studies, 1995.

In a sense, women constituted themselves into an interest group after 1970, and as an interest group they developed sufficient organizational cohesion to bring pressure to bear on public policy decision makers to pass legislation and develop policies that benefited their needs and demands.

The feminist movement, concerned as it is with the direct experience of half the population and the relations of this half of the population with the other half, has the potential to thoroughly rearrange social concepts of acceptable behavior and appropriate thought.[74]

One empirical study of spousal abuse, conducted in 1984 (commonly known as the Minneapolis Experiment), is said to have had enormous impact in mobilizing support for more arrests in spousal abuse cases. The study was funded by the National Institute of Justice (NIJ) for the purpose of gaining information about deterrence. The Minneapolis Experiment concluded that a policy of arrests in misdemeanor assault cases (in contrast to policies of separation or mediation) resulted in lower recidivism rates on the part of abusers. This study started to be commonly cited in the areas of spousal abuse and served as a rationale for increasing arrests in cases of family violence.[75]

A number of underlying currents in American society were exposed in the trial of O.J. Simpson: differing perceptions of blacks and whites, the role of money or ability to hire the best attorneys, racism of police officers, the viability of the justice system itself, and not to be ignored, spousal abuse. Time will tell whether real changes occur in how society views spousal abuse and whether the Simpson trial produced real changes in people's attitudes or only a temporary jolt of interest.

Case Study Questions

1. Which of the three inputs of power, ideology, and rationality best explains the jury's verdict in the O.J. Simpson trial?
2. When should the police become involved in domestic abuse? Are the police too easy on domestic abuse offenders? What is an appropriate police action for domestic offenses?
3. Do you think tougher punishment for domestic abuse offenders could prevent more serious abuses later on? Why do you think this strategy might or might not work?
4. How do you explain the recent changes in domestic violence law?
5. What should the penalty be for spousal abuse?

Notes

1. *U.S. News & World Report*, 1 May 1995, pp. 10–11, 28–36, 38–40, 42, 47–54; *Newsweek*, 1 May 1995, pp. 24–32, 34–41, 44–51, 53–58, 60–61; *Newsweek*, 8 May 1995, pp. 26–39, 44–46.

2. David Farrington, Lloyd Ohlin, and James Q. Wilson, *Understanding and Controlling Crime: Toward a New Research Strategy* (New York: Springer-Verlag, 1986), pp. 1–2.

3. Bill Clinton and Al Gore, *Putting People First: How We Can All Change America* (New York: Times Books, 1992).

4. Doris MacKenzie, James Shaw, and Voncile Gowdy, "An Evaluation of Shock Incarceration in Louisiana," *National Institute of Justice Research in Brief*, NCJ 140567 (June 1993), pp. 1–7.

5. Jennifer Preston, "After Youth Boot Camp Comes a Harder Discipline: Staying out of Trouble," *New York Times*, 3 September 1996, p. A12.

6. Frank Fischer, *Evaluating Public Policy* (Chicago: Nelson-Hall, 1995), pp. 33–34.

7. James Wilson, *Thinking About Crime* (New York: Vintage Books, 1985), p. 68.

8. Steven Donziger, ed., *The Real War on Crime: The Report of the National Criminal Justice Commission* (New York: HarperPerennial, 1996), p. 82.

9. Ibid.

10. Ibid., p. 98.

11. Ibid., p. 94.

12. Elaine Sharp, *The Dilemma of Drug Policy in the United States* (New York: HarperCollins, 1994), p. 547.

13. Adam Nagourney, "Dole Attacks on Crime, but Clinton Is Ready," *New York Times*, 17 September 1996, p. A18.

14. Ibid.

15. Edward Banfield, *The Unheavenly City Revisited* (Boston: Little, Brown, 1974), p. 61.

16. Wilson, op. cit., p. 78.

17. Ramsey Clark, *Crime in America* (New York: Simon and Schuster, 1970), p. 17.

18. Dean Gerstein and Lawrence Green, *Preventing Drug Abuse: What Do We Know?* (Washington, DC, 1993), p. 95.

19. Stanley Einstein, "Drug Education: A Primer," *International Journal of the Addictions* 18 (1983), pp. 1157–1169.

20. Mathea Falco, *The Making of a Drug-Free America* (New York: Times Books, 1992), p. 37.

21. Ibid., p. 41.

22. Ibid., p. 60.

23. Morley Winograd and Dudley Buffa, *Taking Control: Politics in the Information Age* (New York: Holt, Company, 1996), p. 142.

24. Ed Gillespie and Bob Schellhas, *Contract with America* (New York: Random House, 1994), p. 37.

25. Amnesty International, "The Case Against the Death Penalty," in *Point Counterpoint*, 5th ed., ed. H. Levine (New York: St. Martin's Press, 1995), pp. 154–162.

26. James Anders, "The Case for the Death Penalty," in *Point Counterpoint: Readings in American Government*, 5th ed., ed. H. Levine (New York: St. Martin's Press, 1995), p. 165.

27. Wilson, op. cit., p. 224.

28. Charles Silberman, *Criminal Violence, Criminal Justice* (New York: Random House, 1978).

29. Ibid., p. 30.

30. David Rochefort and Roger Cobb, "Problem: An Emerging Perspective," in *The Politics of Problem Definition*, ed. D. Rochefort and R. Cobb (Lawrence: University Press of Kansas, 1994), p. 6.

31. Joseph Westermeyer, "The Pursuit of Intoxication: Our One Hundred Century-Old Romance with Psychoactive Substances," *American Journal of Drug and Alcohol Abuse* 14 (2) (1988), pp. 175–187.

32. Ibid., p. 181.

33. Franklin Zimring and Gordon Hawkins, *The Search for Rational Drug Control* (New York: Cambridge University Press, 1992), p. 54.

34. John Rouse and Bruce Johnson, "Hidden Paradigms of Morality in Debates About Drugs: Historical and Policy Shifts in British and American Drug Policy," in *The Drug Legalization Debate*, ed. J. Inciardi (Newbury Park, CA: Sage, 1991), p. 192.

35. David Courtwright, *Dark Paradise* (Cambridge, MA: Harvard University Press, 1982).

36. Edward Brecher, *Licit and Illicit Drugs* (Boston: Little Brown, 1972).

37. Wilson, op. cit., pp. 15–16.

38. Ibid., pp. 23–25.

39. Parviz Saney, *Crime and Culture in America* (New York: Greenwood Press, 1986), p. 18.

40. Fox Butterfield, "Violent Crime Shows a Drop of 9 Percent in Past Year," *New York Times*, 18 September 1996, p. A10.

41. "Popgun Politics," *U.S. News & World Report*, 30 September 1996, p. 33.

42. Morley Winograd and Dudley Buffa, *Taking Control: Politics in the Information Age* (New York: Holt, 1996), p. 152.

43. Alfred Blumstein, "Prisons," in *Crime*, ed. J. Wilson and J. Petersilia (San Francisco: Institute for Contemporary Studies, 1995), p. 399.

44. Ibid., p. 388.

45. Steve Donziger, ed., *The Real War on Crime: The Report of the National Criminal Justice Commission* (New York: HarperCollins, 1996), pp. 33–34.

46. John DiIulio, "Crime," in *Setting Domestic Priorities: What Can Government Do?*, ed. Henry Aaron and Charles Schultze (Washington, DC: Brookings Institution, 1992), p. 106.

47. Elaine Sharp, "Agenda-Setting and Policy Results: Lessons from Three Drug Policy Episodes," *Policy Studies Journal* 20 (4) (1992), pp. 538–551.

48. Ibid., p. 44.

49. Mathea Falco, *Winning the Drug War* (New York: Priority Press, 1989), p. 26.

50. Diana Gordon, *The Return of the Dangerous Classes: Drug Prohibition and Policy Politics* (New York: Norton, 1994), p. 167.

51. Clinton and Gore, op. cit. pp. 72–73.

52. David Teasley, "Extent of the Problem," *CRS Review: The Drug Problem* (Washington, DC: U.S. Government Printing Office, 1989), p. 5.

53. Bureau of Justice Statistics, *A National Report: Drugs, Crime and the Justice System*, NCJ-133652 (December 1992), p. 36.

54. John Omicinski, "Wealth of Booming Drug Trade Rivals That of Oil Industry," *Louisville Courier Journal*, 4 November 1996, p. 1A.

55. Kurt Schmoke, "Drugs: A Problem of Health and Economics," in *The Crisis in Drug Prohibition*, ed. D. Boaz (Washington, DC: Cato Institute, 1990), p. 10.

56. Select Committee on Narcotics Abuse and Control, *Legalization of Illicit Drugs: Impact and Feasibility, Part I* (Washington, DC: U.S. Government Printing Office, 1989), pp. 28–29.

57. Ernest Van den Haag and John LeMoult, "Legalize Illegal Drugs," in *Drug Abuse Opposing Viewpoints*, ed. J. Bach (San Diego: Greenhaven Press, 1988), p. 30.

58. Ethan Nadelmann, "The Case for Legalization," *Public Interest* (Summer 1988), pp. 32–50.

59. Thomas Szasz, *Our Right to Drugs: The Case for a Free Market* (New York: Praeger, 1992), p. 163.

60. James Inciari and Duane McBride, "The Case Against Legalization," in *The Drug Legalization Debate*, ed. J. Inciardi (Newbury Park, CA: Sage, 1991), pp. 45–79.

61. D. Courtwright, *Dark Paradise* (Cambridge: Harvard University Press, 1982), p. 45.

62. Avram Goldstein and Harold Kalant, "Drug Policy: Striking the Right Balance," *Science* 249, 28 September 1990, pp. 1513–1521.

63. Select Committee on Narcotics Abuse and Control, *Drug Legalization: Catastrophe for Black Americans* (Washington, DC: U.S. Government Printing Office, 1989), p. 83.

64. Select Committee on Narcotics Abuse and Control, *Legalization of Illicit Drugs: Impact and Feasibility*, Part I, op. cit., p. 231a.

65. Select Committee on Narcotics Abuse and Control, *Drug Legalization: Catastrophe for Black Americans,* op. cit., pp. 10, 83.

66. Bill Turque, "'He's Going Nuts'," *Newsweek*, 4 July 1994, pp. 22–25.

67. Steven V. Roberts, "Simpson and Sudden Death," *U.S. News & World Report*, 27 June 1994, pp. 26–29, 32.

68. Ibid., p. 26.

69. Turque, op. cit., 4 July 1994, p. 25.

70. "Now, O.J. the Pariah," *Time*, 23 October 1995, p. 87.

71. Roger Langley and Richard Levy, *Wife Beating: The Silent Crisis* (New York: Dutton, 1977), p. 39.

72. Ibid.

73. E. Marvin Zalman, "The Courts' Response to Police Intervention in Domestic Violence," in *Domestic Violence: The Changing Criminal Justice Response*, ed. E. Buzawa and C. Buzawa (Westport, CT: Auburn House, 1992), p. 80.

74. Ibid., p. 82.

75. Eve Buzawa and Carl Buzawa, eds., *Domestic Violence: The Criminal Justice Response* (Newbury Park, CA: Sage, 1990), p. 72.

11

Intermestic Policies

NAFTA, MEXICO, AND INTERMESTIC POLICYMAKING

The theme of this chapter is that, as international relations specialist Bruce Russet has stated, "Foreign policy is, in substantial degree, domestic policy."[1] The same point is emphasized by other authors who have analyzed American foreign policy as a process determined largely by how prominent an issue is at home and by its potential domestic impact.[2] This chapter will concentrate on several instances of how foreign policy developments are connected to national domestic policy. We pay particular attention to the large—and we believe growing—role in domestic policy and politics of immigration and trade.

Foreign policy basically has to do with the goals that the United States government wants to pursue in the world and the ways in which those goals will be achieved. Instruments to attain foreign policy objectives include diplomatic contacts, economic aid, technical assistance, and military action. Diplomatic efforts are undertaken to try by peaceful methods to settle disputes and conflicts that arise among nations or within nations. These diplomatic activities consist of a combination of positive offers of support and negative messages, including threats made either directly or implicitly, as the techniques for negotiation that the United States uses to execute its foreign policy.

National security policy, a crucial subset of a nation's overall foreign policy, has the primary goal of protecting the United States against dependency on other countries for economic, political, or military strength. Military actions or threats, intelligence-gathering, protecting national borders (both to keep some people in and to keep others out), and counterespionage activities are key elements in fostering national security. Among the major institutions involved in the national security decision-making process are the Department of Defense, the Department of State, and the National Security Council of presidential advisors, which has grown to rival the State Department in its influence over the foreign policy process. In its relations with Mexico in particular, the security policy of the United States has emphasized problems such as attempting to seal off the border to prevent an influx of undocumented workers and others that the United States has declared to be unwanted. Such policy also involves shutting down the inflow of illegal drugs into the United States through Mexico and sharing intelligence data concerning what the two nations might regard as "subversive" activities by anti-American pro-Cuban interests or by the revolutionary groups that have been operating against the Mexican government for decades.

Under Article II, Section 2, of the United States Constitution, the president is the "Commander in Chief of the Army and Navy of the United States." Since the Civil War administration of Abraham Lincoln, presidents have interpreted this authority broadly and have expanded it commensurately with the status of leader of a global superpower. In the case of the North American Free Trade Agreement, or NAFTA, treaty with Mexico, both the president and Congress were involved, although the primary impetus for negotiating the treaty clearly came from the White House. Since the administration of George Washington, the United States has been involved in over one hundred undeclared wars conducted under the authority of the president. American involvement in the Korean War of 1950–1953 and the wars in Southeast Asia that continued from about 1961 to 1975 took place without formal declarations of hostilities by Congress. (It may be worth noting, in the context of NAFTA, that the United States has fought one formal war against Mexico, from 1846–1848—in which the United States suffered nearly 20,000 military casualties—and has intervened frequently with military force or the threat of force in internal Mexican politics, most notably when President Woodrow Wilson ordered General John J. "Blackjack" Pershing to invade and temporarily occupy parts of Mexican territory from 1916 to 1917 to prevent the success of prorevolutionary peasant armies operating under Francisco [Pancho] Villa, who had raided United States border areas.)

That same portion of the Constitution gives to the president the power to make treaties, although agreement must be obtained from two-thirds of the senators present and voting when a treaty is brought before Congress for formal ratification. That consent usually comes in the end. However, an estimated 95 percent of all international pacts made with other countries since World War II (1939–1945) have taken the form of executive agreements, which do not require Senate consent. This mechanism has been used in setting up peace agreements at Yalta and Potsdam in World War II, and set the stage for American involvement in South Vietnam. Since the end of World War II, more than 8,000 such agreements have been put into force. Other constitutionally specified components of presidential power over foreign policy include the power to appoint ambassadors, consuls, and other public ministers, and the power to recognize foreign governments through receiving their ambassadors.

The still-unfolding example of the North American Free Trade Agreement, commonly referred to as NAFTA, demonstrates many of the consequences of the rational, power, and ideological (RPI) inputs into U.S. intermestic policy decisions and their implementation. Here is how the story has developed thus far, together with an assessment of how the RPI perspective clarifies our understanding of this evolving situation.

In 1994, the Mexican government confronted a major financial crisis. The problems with that country's economy had been building for some time, but had been hidden for the most part from international financial institutions and from national governments in the United States and in other leading industrial economies that feared for the stability of the world economy. In the international financial markets, confidence in the Mexican peso was collapsing, which threatened to produce a severe shortage of investment capital for Mexico. To combat this potential crisis, the Mexican government implemented an austerity program designed to reduce inflation and cut the scope of government spending by restricting the money supply and government spending and by raising interest rates to very high levels. The result was a sharp economic downturn, which diminished inflationary pressures but which also generated high unemployment and greater misery for the rural and urban underclass who had never benefited from the government's earlier efforts to assist Mexican and external (largely United States) businesses. Mexico's economic problems were aggravated by the armed peasant Zapatista uprising in the southern state of Chiapas and demonstrations in support of the uprising in the capital, Mexico City, and elsewhere throughout the country.

Complicating the situation further, and particularly for Mexico's northern neighbor, the United States, was the fact that the peasant revolt, as well as the government's economic problems, were associated with the passage of the North American Free Trade Agreement (NAFTA) in 1993. NAFTA had been adopted by the Democratic-controlled 103rd Congress at the insistence of President Clinton, even though the bill was originally introduced by George Bush during his term as Republican president, and despite the fact that it was opposed by a large majority of congressional Democrats. NAFTA's opponents argued that it would harm workers in the United States by holding down their wages through competition from cheaper labor in Mexico (and elsewhere), and that it would split Democrats into free trade and protectionist wings.

On November 17, 1993, the House voted 234 to 200 to pass HR 3450, to approve and implement NAFTA. On November 20, the Senate voted 61 to 38 to pass HR 3450. On December 8, President Clinton signed the bill, now known as PL 103-182. NAFTA took effect on January 1, 1994.

What was NAFTA intended to do? It ended all tariffs between the United States and Mexico over fifteen years, and dropped most other trade barriers between the two countries. It also changed United States laws to conform with the agreement, which had originally been signed by George Bush in December 1992. NAFTA also changed the United States–Canada Free Trade Agreement of 1988 (PL 100-449), and extended free trade ideas to all of North America. The goal was to create a huge market to compete against trade blocs emerging in Europe and Asia, and to expand in South America after consolidation of the Canada-United States-Mexico link.

NAFTA was considered by Congress under "fast-track" provisions, which protected the president's ability to negotiate trade agreements without worrying about congressional second-guessing. Fast-track allowed no amendments, and an up-or-down vote was required within ninety days after the bill was introduced; precise deadlines were set for the president to negotiate and sign agreements. Fast-track provisions are generally renewed for short periods, to guarantee that the president will keep Congress informed. This led to an unusual decision-making process, characterized by mock conferences to put together implementing language before the bill was introduced, and sufficient time for the Clinton White House to bargain and make changes to line up votes based on arguments that NAFTA would help to create more high-skill, high-wage jobs.

Where did NAFTA come from? In the spring of 1990, Mexican President Salinas de Gortari asked the United States government about negotiating a free trade agreement. Mexico wanted foreign capital and increased access to the United States for its economy to expand. President Bush was initially cool to the idea, but warmed up as a result of pressure from Texas business interests. In September 1990, Bush announced that negotiations with Mexico had begun, under the authority provided by PL 100-418 in 1988. At the time, Bush needed a success, because GATT (the General Agreement on Tariffs and Trade) was stalled and regional trading blocs were emerging in Europe and Asia that threatened to shut out the United States from exporting to those parts of the world. Bush lobbied hard for fast-track authorization, which was granted by congressional votes in May 1991. Following a Bush-Salinas summit meeting in July 1992, an agreement was initialed on August 12, as required formally by the fast-track rules.

On March 17, 1993, the new Clinton administration began to talk with Salinas's administration to work out side agreements that would enforce labor and environmental laws. By August 15, the major work had been accomplished by Mickey Kantor, the United States' Official Trade Representative. Trinational (United States-Canada-Mexico) commissions were set up to deal with labor issues, environmental concerns, and protection against the "dumping" of foreign-produced goods in the United States at below-production costs. The Democratic party was split on the issue, with the House leadership generally opposed. David Bonior (D-Michigan), the majority whip, and Richard Gephardt (D-Missouri), the majority leader, were strongly against NAFTA, while support from the House Speaker Tom Foley (D-Washington) was lukewarm. On September 14, Clinton signed the side agreements. He hired Bill Frenzel, a former Minnesota Republican member of the House, to lobby congressional Republicans.

On September 30, 1993, the House Ways and Means committee's subcommittee on trade approved draft implementation legislation. From October 18 to 22, the Ways and Means full committee finished deliberations, apart from funding. The Senate Finance Committee informally approved NAFTA, but with the addition of an amendment by Max Baucus (D-Montana) to restore the "Super 301" trade sanctions program that had lapsed in 1990. This required a yearly inventory of foreign trade barriers, with sanctions that could be applied if necessary.

On October 26, 1993, the House Agriculture Committee approved draft agriculture provisions, including amendments to protect domestic producers of peanuts, high-fructose corn syrup, fruits, vegetables, and fresh-cut flowers. On September 24, 1993, the District of Columbia circuit court ruled out the requirement of an environmental impact statement. On October 18, the administration proposed a retraining program for workers who lost jobs because of NAFTA. This provision was included in the legislation reported out by the House Ways and Means and Senate Finance committees. The final bill continued retraining through September 30, 1998.

On October 26, the administration submitted a $2.7 billion package to cover worker retraining and lost tariff revenue. Congressional budget rules require spending cuts or increased revenues to offset any revenue lost for the five years after enactment of NAFTA. On October 27, 1993, the House Ways and Means Committee approved the North American Development Bank for treating environmental impacts. The Senate Finance Committee agreed on October 28, and on November 3 NAFTA was sent to Congress, where it was introduced in the House on November 4 as HR 3450 by Dan Rostenkowski (D-Illinois), chair of the House Ways and Means Committee. The fast-track provision allowed two weeks in which to act.

A number of concessions were negotiated, to make the legislation more palatable. Mexico could not export sugar to the United States. Florida orange juice was protected by tariffs if the Mexican orange juice became too cheap. Tomato growers were protected with possible tariffs, as were the producers of other vegetables. Mexico would phase out its tariffs faster on flat glass, wines, appliances, bedding, and other commodities. On November 9, Ways and Means approved NAFTA, 26 to 12, by endorsing H. Rept. 103-361, Parts 1–3. On November 9, the House Energy and Commerce Committee agreed by voice vote to send the bill to the floor without a recommendation. The following day, the House Banking Committee, by voice vote, sent the bill to the floor with an unfavorable recommendation. Five other House committees with jurisdiction over various parts of NAFTA failed to act within the time limit.

On November 17, the House approved NAFTA by 234 to 200. The political dynamics of that decision are clear from the odd party breakdown in support of a Democratic president, following eleven hours of floor debate. A majority of Democrats split with their president, voting 102 in favor and 156 opposed; Republicans split heavily in favor, by a margin of 132 to 43; and the lone independent representative was opposed.

On November 18, six Senate committees met informally to consider that chamber's NAFTA bill, S 1627. This measure, identical to HR 3450, was introduced by majority leader George Mitchell (D-Maine). It was approved by the Senate Finance Committee, 16 to 3, and by voice votes in both the Agriculture and Foreign Relations committees. Sent by voice vote to the floor by the Commerce, Governmental Affairs, and Judiciary committees, the bill was reported jointly as S. Rept. 103-189. On November 30, the Senate voted 61 to 38 for NAFTA. The breakdown was twenty-seven Democrats and thirty-four Republicans in favor, and twenty-eight Democrats and ten Republicans opposed.

Immigration issues also were involved in the NAFTA experience. One of the selling points used by President Clinton in trying to persuade his party's members, and congressional Republicans, to vote for the resurrected NAFTA bill, which George Bush had not been able to push through the Democratic-majority 102nd Congress, was that passage of NAFTA would create job opportunities for Mexican workers "at home," so that they would not feel compelled to enter the United States in search of better jobs. The Clinton administration thus sold NAFTA in part as an anti-immigration initiative that, the president argued, would reduce incentives to migrate from Mexico.

NAFTA and its related issues of jobs, immigration, and free-market trade policies with other nations provides a useful starting point to discuss the interface between domestic and foreign policy. There are other aspects to this intermestic issue perspective as well. For example, military spending, along with the national security policy to which it is ultimately related, plays a powerful domestic role as well. It stimulates (and distorts) the nation's economy, creates jobs, and generates local sources of political power for the members of Congress who can claim that they have been bringing home the "bacon" of military spending to benefit their constituents. It also helps to accentuate the complexities that are involved in trying to satisfy the competing demands that come from different parts of the world. The implementation of NAFTA has, for example, stimulated new demands in western Europe for some version of a Trans-Atlantic Free Trade Zone that would link the economies of North America and Europe more closely.[3] By the end of 1996, however, a comprehensive study conducted at the North American Integration Development Center at the University of California, Los Angeles (UCLA) concluded that the first three years of NAFTA had at best only a very modestly positive impact on employment related to international trade, to the tune of a net gain of slightly less than 3,000 jobs (an estimated 28,168 jobs were lost, and 31,158 created). However, these figures do not take into account an estimated loss of 33,000 jobs in the United States caused by plants that relocated to Mexico to exploit the lower wages, weaker environmental regulations, and tax advantages available south of the border. These results differed sharply from projections of a net gain from NAFTA of about 200,000 jobs in the United States that were made by supporters during the 1993 congressional debate.[4]

THE RPI INPUTS TO INTERMESTIC POLICY

The Rationality Input

The Global Economy

Among the most significant developments related to the role of the United States in contemporary world affairs is the emergence and spread of what has come to be called the global economy. About one-fifth of the total national income of the United States derives from trade with the rest of the world. It has been estimated that nearly 80 percent of all the growth of United States domestic economic output in recent years has been attributable to exports.[5] Since the 1980s, the international financial position of the United States has changed drastically, from being the world's biggest creditor nation to being its largest debtor country. This rapid shift occurred because the United States has run a consistently large deficit in its balance of trade (exports minus imports) with other countries and because the nation's budget deficits have been financed increasingly by the governments of other countries and by foreign financial institutions. This dramatic change in the status of the United States from being a net exporter to its current position of running chronically huge balance of trade deficits from 1950 to 1995 is summarized in Table 11.1.

The greatest trade problems have arisen with Japan, which has been pressured heavily by the Clinton administration to reduce its barriers to importing foreign, and particularly American, goods. In 1994, for example, the United States' trade deficit was about $151 billion, and Japan accounted for nearly $66 billion, or just under 44 percent, of that total.

To resolve this problem, the Clinton administration followed the advice of experts in international economics to pressure Japan to open up its domestic markets to competition from foreign corporations, including, of course, American exporters. C. Fred Bergsten and Marcus Nolad, two analysts of the United States–Japan economic conflict, argue: "Japanese market limitations have a large and disproportionate impact on the United States because of the sectoral composition of the two economies and the interaction of their governments' policies."[6] However, although Japan is the primary source of that deficit (and China is a rapidly growing source, as well), the largest component of this country's trade is carried on within North America. Canada is the single largest market for products from the United States, and Canada and Mexico together account for about 30 percent of both all United States exports and imports. Table 11.2 shows the status of United States trade with leading countries and areas of the world in the early 1990s.

The European Union (EU), known as the European Community until 1994, has created a greatly changed reality in international commerce and finance. The EU is designed to provide a massive internal common market among at least a dozen European countries, and the United States and other countries worry that the resulting market will be closed to their exports. Comparably powerful trading blocs have been forming among the rapidly growing economies of East

Table 11.1 United States Exports, Imports, and Merchandise Trade Balance, 1950–1995 (millions of dollars)

Year	United States Exports and Re-exports, Excluding Military Grant Aid	United States General Imports f.a.s. Transaction Values[1]	United States Merchandise Balance f.a.s.[1]
1950	$ 9,997	$ 8,954	$ 1,043
1955	14,298	11,566	2,732
1960	19,659	15,073	4,586
1965	26,742	21,520	5,222
1970	42,681	40,356	2,325
1975	107,652	98,503	9,149
1980	220,626	244,871	–24,245
1985	213,133[2]	345,276	–132,143
1990	394,030[2]	495,042	–101,012
1991	421,730[2]	485,453	–66,723
1992	448,164[2]	532,665	–84,501
1993	465,091[2]	580,659	–115,568
1994	512,626[2]	663,256	–150,630
1995	583,865[2]	743,430	–159,565

Source: Office of Trade and Economic Analysis, U.S. Department of Commerce.

Note: Export values include both commercially financed shipments and shipments under government-financed programs such as AID and PL-480.

[1]Prior to 1974, imports are customs values—that is, generally at prices in principal foreign markets.

[2]In 1981, import value changed back to customs value.

Asia. In this climate, the argument has been made by U.S. national policy-makers that it would be a rational response for the United States to participate in its own trade bloc.

One answer to this perceived threat to national economic security was NAFTA, passed by Congress in 1993 and effective as of January 1, 1994. NAFTA created a North American regional trading bloc, linking together more closely the economies of Canada, Mexico, and the United States, spanning a combined population of about 400 million. Over fifteen to twenty years, NAFTA is intended to eliminate nearly all tariffs on trade among those three countries. At the same time, tariffs will be maintained on goods and services from other, non-NAFTA countries. This arrangement provides for an artificial version of what economists refer to as comparative advantage, which is the ability to produce goods more efficiently than anyone else. Tariffs are a government-supported way to help domestic firms beat the competition from abroad. Otherwise, comparative advantage will be gained by the country that has lower levels of production costs, because of the combination of more plentiful and hence cheaper raw materials, more efficient or lower-paid workers, or lower taxes.

Table 11.2 Trade Between the United States and Selected Leading Countries and Areas of the World, 1993 (in millions of dollars, not seasonally adjusted)

Country/Area	Trade Balance	Exports	Imports
Total	−$115,568.4	$465,091.0	$580,659.4
Japan	−59,354.9	47,891.5	102,246.4
China	−22,777.1	8,762.8	31,539.9
Canada	−10,772.1	100,443.3,	111,216.4
Germany	−9,629.9	18,932.2	28,562.1
Taiwan	−8,933.7	16,167.8	25,101.5
Italy	−6,751.9	6,463.8	13,215.6
Thailand	−4,775.4	3,766.2	8,541.5
Malaysia	−4,498.6	6,064.4	10,563.0
Nigeria	−4,406.7	894.7	5,301.4
Venezuela	−3,549.7	4,590.2	8,139.8
Indonesia	−2,665.1	2,770.3	5,435.4
Korea	−2,336.0	14,782.0	17,118.0
Sweden	−2,180.0	2,353.7	4,533.7
France	−2,012.5	13,266.8	15,279.3
Angola	−1,918.4	173.8	2,092.2
India	−1,775.6	2,778.1	4,553.7
Brazil	−1,420.8	6,058.0	7,478.8
Philippines	−1,364.4	3,529.2	4,893.6
Singapore	−1,120.2	11,678.0	12,798.2
Saudi Arabia	−1,046.6	6,661.2	7,707.8
Gabon	−912.8	48.2	961.0
Kuwait	−819.0	999.4	1,818.5
Sri Lanka	−798.5	203.2	1,001.7
Finland	−760.7	847.6	1,608.3
Norway	−745.1	1,212.4	1,957.5
North America	−9,108.4	142,025.4	151,133.8
Western Europe	−1,876.0	113,680.6	115,556.7
European Community	−967.2	96,973.4	97,940.6
European Free Trade Association	−3,112.1	12,703.8	15,815.9
Eastern Europe	2,578.4	6,104.2	3,525.7
Former Soviet Republics	1,889.7	3,983.8	2,094.2
Organization for Economic Cooperation and Development in Europe	−1,856.3	113,114.1	114,970.3
Pacific Rim countries	−97,956.6	131,595.4	229,551.9
Asia, Near East	1,433.8	16,820.9	15,387.1
Asia, NICS	−12,070.5	52,501.6	64,572.2
Asia, South	−3,370.1	4,062.8	7,432.9
Association of Southeast Asian Nations	−13,981.4	28,280.6	42,262.0
South and Central America	2,385.6	36,841.9	34,456.3
20 Latin American republics	2,281.7	73,547.8	71,266.1
Central American Common Market	511.0	4,770.0	4,265.9
Latin American Free Trade Association	1,108.1	65,002.7	63,894.5
Organization of Petroleum Exporting Countries	−12,239.6	19,499.5	31,739.2
Unidentified	343.8	343.8	NA

Source: Office of Trade and Economic Analysis, U.S. Department of Commerce.

This is the view of classical political economists such as Adam Smith[7] and David Ricardo,[8] who argued for free trade among nations as the means by which "automatic" market forces would make the world's economy more efficient since industries and services would survive only in those countries where they could be produced or delivered most efficiently, thereby making everybody wealthier through specializing in what each country does best. In practice, however, when businesses and workers that are hard pressed by cheaper imports from other countries call on their national governments for help, the political pressures tend to be almost irresistible to impose protective tariffs to eliminate or reduce the foreign competitor's price advantage. Foreign trade issues thus readily become intermestic, as domestic political realities lead to government intervention to protect what might be regarded in that country as vital industries from being destroyed by foreign competition.

The global scope of decisions involving international trade is also evident in the worldwide trade agreement that was at the heart of trading relations among most of the world's nations since the implementation of the General Agreement on Tariffs and Trade (GATT) on January 1, 1948. GATT had been designed initially to put back together the patterns of international trade that had been disrupted or destroyed by World War II. GATT provided a forum for the discussion of economic problems related to world trade among its 177 member countries accounting for 85 percent to 90 percent of all world trade. A total of eight rounds of frequently difficult and prolonged multilateral trade negotiations took place under the auspices of GATT. The last major action undertaken by GATT, called the Uruguay Round, began in 1986 in Punta del Este, Uruguay, and culminated on December 15, 1993, in an agreement among 117 signatory countries to reduce their tariffs on manufactured goods by an average of 37 percent and to eliminate completely the tariffs on certain industries, including drugs, medical equipment, and construction equipment. Members also were required to reduce subsidies for agriculture by an average of 21 percent, and were forbidden to restrict competition by foreigners in most service industries, such as computer software and advertising. Protection also was provided for patents, trademarks, and copyrights for movies, computer programs, books, and music.

In 1995, by international agreement, GATT ceased to exist. It was replaced by the World Trade Organization (WTO), which maintains a permanent committee to consider the environmental implications of international trade as well as arbitration boards to decide whether any country's domestic laws violate the provisions of GATT decisions. Decisions of the WTO cannot be vetoed by member nations, but whether WTO's decisions can be enforced will present a challenge to American and other decision-makers in the next century. Some of the difficulties facing the future of the WTO, and particularly the future role to be played in that structure by the United States, are suggested by the fact that it took a year—until November 29, 1994, for the House to approve the terms for U.S. WTO participation, by a vote of 288 to 146, and the Senate to approve on December 1. By the official ratification deadline of July 1, 1995, 100 countries had approved the WTO agreement. The extent to which the rational self-interest of the United States will be fulfilled by its future participation in the WTO largely will be determined by whether the WTO's decisions favor U.S. interests over those of other nations competing for shares of world markets.

Military and Diplomatic Globalism

Latin America

The extent to which rational self-interest drives the foreign activities of the United States also is evident from recent U.S. military and diplomatic initiatives. This is perhaps most clear-cut in the effort to keep foreign powers from exercising major influence in Latin America, which many residents of the United States consider to be their country's backyard. The special relationship the United States has felt for the nations south of its border perhaps is reflected best in the fact that the name originally given to the entirety of the New World—America, named in honor of Italian explorer Amerigo Vespucci—and its inhabitants—Americans—has been appropriated as a synonym for the United States and its residents. The large number of people in the U.S. who are of Hispanic ancestry, and particularly their concentration in politically important states such as Florida and California (formerly ruled by Spain and Mexico, respectively) provides a virtually permanent intermestic link between domestic U.S. politics and the role played by the United States in Mexico, Central America, and South America.

In 1823, President James Monroe declared that the United States had a special interest in the region. In the twentieth century, the Caribbean Sea came to be called an "American lake." The United States has intervened frequently with military force in the region, to restore order in favor of governments and domestic groups within the Latin American countries that supported United States interests and to protect American property and lives. These activities have included military occupation of Haiti, the Dominican Republic, and Nicaragua; the annexation of Cuba, Puerto Rico, and the Virgin Islands following the successful war with Spain in 1898; the military conquest of Mexico in the 1840s and later military interventions in that country to attempt to prevent the spread of the Mexican revolution early in the twentieth century; the military and economic quarantine of Cuba that has been maintained by the United States since the early 1960s in the face of almost universal condemnation by the other countries of the world; and the fact that much of the western and southwestern land mass of the United States formerly was dominated by Latino cultures and was annexed by a combination of conquest and purchase of the land.

By the 1980s, United States interests were challenged directly in three Central American countries. In El Salvador, a civil war threatened the hegemony of that nation's right-wing government; in Nicaragua, the United States clearly supported conservative *contra* military and political forces fighting against what Washington interpreted as a Cuban-style pro-Moscow leftist Sandinista government in Managua; and in Panama, where the Panama Canal was to be turned over largely to Panamanian control under the terms of treaties ratified in 1978, the country's military leader, General Manuel Noriega, refused to leave office despite being indicted by an American court for drug trafficking. In 1989, American troops invaded Panama to capture and imprison Noriega. The invasion resulted in perhaps several thousand dead Panamanian civilians and destroyed substantial sections of Panama City. In El Salvador, the United States maintained its support for a right-wing military regime that waged a bloody civil war against leftist opponents. The Nicaraguan situation resolved itself at least temporarily through an election in 1990 that brought a pro-Washington government to power. Elections in 1996 returned to power an even more conservative and pro-U.S. government. The opposition that arose within the United States to Washington's intervention in Central America in support of conservative governments and of both armed and legal political movements against left-leaning governments generally was weak and ultimately unable to reverse the direction of policy in the region.

Haiti became a focus of American regional policy largely for domestic reasons. Large numbers of Haitian refugees fled, many in unseaworthy boats, to avoid severely depressed economic conditions and brutal repression by a military dictatorship. Haitian refugees came into conflict with already established anticommunist Cuban refugees in Florida and were suspected by many in the United States of spreading the AIDS virus. Both the Bush and Clinton administrations returned the "boat people" home, often through military force. When the military regime deposed the democratically elected president, Jean-Bertrand Aristide, in 1992, the Clinton administration imposed military and economic sanctions designed to return Aristide to power temporarily, although powerful intelligence and military groups within the United States government were convinced that Aristide would pursue left-wing policies inimical to the economic and security interests of the United States. In 1995, tens of thousands of American troops were dispatched to the island nation to disarm supporters of the military regime and returned Aristide to his presidency. Continued economic difficulties in Haiti, however, meant that the intermestic link through the refugee crisis was not resolved. American troops returned from Haiti having suffered very few casualties and having prepared the way for a successor to Aristide who was more amenable to American interests.

Eastern Europe

Since the waning of Soviet influence in Eastern Europe in the late 1980s, that part of the world has become another major focus of United States foreign policymaking. The United States has pursued its self-interest in that part of the world by trying to put an end to the ethnic struggles that have destabilized Yugoslavia and created the potential for a wider European war that inevitably would involve American military power and have a major impact on United States economic affairs. The official dissolution of the Soviet Union by Russian

President Boris Yeltsin on Christmas day 1991 accentuated the economic dislocation that had been gripping the region since its socialist economies and its ruling communist parties began to unravel in the 1980s. Although Yeltsin's policies favoring American-style economic reforms produced massive hardships for many Russians, he was reelected president in 1996 with secret backing and advice from President Clinton's White House. It became clear that Yeltsin and Clinton had become mutually interdependent on each other's successes, both in winning elections and in pursuing economic strategies that fostered the privatization of public-sector institutions and activities.

A prime goal of American foreign policy became the spread of Western-style governments and capitalist economic structures to Eastern Europe and to the successor states of the former Soviet Union. In theory this would prevent further economic and political disintegration and intertwine those countries' economies more closely with those of the United States and of other capitalist economic powers. The difficulties of pursuing this self-interested goal became evident with the resurgence of political support for communist or former communist political forces in much of the region and by an upsurge of ethnic violence, particularly in the former Yugoslavia.

The disintegration of Yugoslavia in 1991 came about as the former provinces of Slovenia, Croatia, and Bosnia-Herzegovina declared independence. The sharpest divisions led to three-way conflict among ethnic Croats, Serbs, and Muslims for control of Bosnian territory. Following three years of protracted warfare, a combination of NATO air attacks, sweeping battlefield successes by Croat and Bosnian Muslim armed forces, and sustained diplomatic pressure from Western powers and Russia, the Bosnian conflict ended in late 1995, and 60,000 troops were brought in from dozens of countries—20,000 of them from the United States—to try to maintain the cease-fire. Even after the expiration of the original mandate by NATO, the United States succeeded in pressuring its allies to reauthorize the continued presence of its own and other Western troops in order to maintain the situation in the former Yugoslavia to its liking. This action was accompanied by serious discussions about expanding NATO farther to the East by incorporating some of the countries in Eastern Europe that NATO leaders believed had gone the farthest toward a pro-Western position and that would welcome NATO protection against a future in which a resurgent Russia might attempt to reassert its influence in the region.

The Power Input

Coordination of National Security

Formally, the State Department is the part of the executive branch that is concerned most directly with the nation's foreign relations. It supervises relations with the nearly 200 independent nations of the globe as well as with the United Nations and other multinational groups. However, because it is known for being rather slow and plodding in its decision making, the State Department is often shunted aside in favor of other agencies. Unlike other national-security-related agencies, such as the Department of Defense, which benefits from its connections with defense contractors and millions of active-duty and former military personnel, the State Department does not have a natural domestic constituency to provide support for its role. Rather, the State Department often is referred to as the "department of bad news" because its actions tend to attract opposition from "negative constituents" who oppose unpopular and costly foreign entanglements. The intermestic nature of foreign policy decisions is especially obvious in the ways that the nation's foreign policy often must be modulated to respond to the domestic demands from segments of the U.S. population that have common ancestral ties as well as business dealings and cultural linkages with other parts of the world.

The National Security Council (NSC) was established by the National Security Act of 1947 to advise the president on how to integrate domestic, foreign, and military policy related to national security. It serves as a form of "institutional memory" that provides continuity from one presidential administration to the next. Although its membership can change with each new presidential administration, the NSC usually consists of the president, the vice president, the secretary of state, the secretary of defense, the director of emergency planning, the chair of the Joint Chiefs of Staff, and the director of the Central Intelligence Agency (CIA). The president has the benefit of advice from the National Security Advisor, who on occasion overshadows the secretary of state as the person with the single greatest degree of influence over American foreign policy.

About forty government agencies are involved in the vital job of gathering the information from within the United States and abroad on which national foreign policy is based. These agencies constitute collectively what has come to be known as the national intelligence community. Defined formally by Executive Order 12036, issued by President Jimmy Carter in 1978, the major elements of the intelligence community include the Central Intelligence Agency, the National Security Agency, the Defense Intelligence Agency, various offices within the Department of Defense, the Bureau of Intelligence and Research within the Department of State, the Federal Bureau of Investigation, Army intelligence, Air Force intelligence, the Department of the Treasury, the Drug Enforcement Administration, and the Department of Energy.

These and other intelligence agencies undertake both overt, or open, and covert, or secret, operations to gather information about military and economic developments. Among the more spectacular covert policy actions of this community have been the subsidies that were paid to foster anti-Communist labor movements and conservative political parties in Europe following World War II, as well as the overthrow in 1953 of the Mossadegh government in Iran and the restoration to power of the shah (who was overthrown in turn by the Islamic revolution of 1979), the overthrow in 1954 of the Arbenz government in Guatemala that threatened corporate investments in that country, and the destabilization of Chile leading up to the military coup led by General Pinochet that overthrew the socialist Allende government in 1973. Efforts were undertaken over several decades to infiltrate and destabilize the Soviet Union and its Eastern European allies. Propaganda and dissemination of favorable information abroad about the United States is conducted by the United States Information Agency.

In 1947, the Department of Defense was formed to provide better coordination for the military activities of the nation's land, air, and sea armed forces, under the direction of a civilian secretary of defense. In the same year, a conference of the commanders of each of the military branches was constituted as the Joint Chiefs of Staff, to provide unified military strategy and policies. With about one million civilian and two million military personnel, and an annual budget of about a quarter of a trillion dollars, the Department of Defense has a very broad impact on American society and is linked closely to jobs and to the nation's economic performance. For that reason, the Department of Defense is central to the linkage between domestic and foreign aspects of the national security policy process. That link is particularly evident from the highly sensitive politics that are involved in any effort to close military installations, when local members of Congress typically do all they can to prevent economic losses from such changes.

The intermestic nature of the current and previous military commitments of the United States appears when examining how the power input operates through linkages with the civilian population and the domestic economy. These linkages are especially clear in the role played in U.S. national security policy by the National Guard and by military veterans.

The National Guard

A major component of the intermestic component of national security policy is the National Guard.[9] This is a component of the reserve military forces of the United States that fills both federal and state missions, unlike the other reserve components of the Army, Navy, Marine Corps, Air Force, and Coast Guard, which are purely national in orientation and are tied directly to the regular active-duty armed forces. During peacetime, the National Guard is commanded by the governors of the states and territories, and can be called into active-duty service by a governor to respond to natural disasters, civil disturbances, or other emergency situations. The Guard also may be called to active duty by the President or by Congress during wartime or to help with a national emergency, when it acts as the primary backup for active-duty Army and Air Force units. As "civilians" with clearly military roles that are traceable back to colonial militias, the members of the National Guard have fought in every American war from the Pequot War in 1637 to the Persian Gulf War of 1991, in which 75,000 National Guard personnel volunteered or were called up to active duty.

The Army National Guard comprises over 3,300 units spread throughout more than 2,000 communities in every state, as well as Puerto Rico, Guam, the Virgin Islands, and the District of Columbia. Army Guard units provide about 55 percent of the Army's overall combat capability, and 35 percent of its combat support. Similarly, the Air National Guard represents about one-third of the fighter and air transport capability of the United States Air Force, through its 88 flying units and 1,500 support units at 200 locations.

Known as "weekend warriors," National Guard members typically train one weekend per month in addition to fifteen days of annual continuous unit training. They receive education benefits, enlistment incentives for those in selected specialized careers, access to reduced-price military shopping facilities, and many of the other benefits provided to active-duty military personnel. As of 1996, the Army National Guard had an authorized force level of 373,000, with another 112,400 in the Air National Guard. The Army and Air National Guard combined accounted for about $10 billion of the federal budget for fiscal year 1996. The widespread location of National Guard units and their bases, and their consequent integration with local economies provides a great deal of power for the Guard as a source of both political and economic support for local business and political interests. The closing of active-duty military bases and the disposition of National Guard resources have become major items on the intermestic agenda of domestic problems associated with the nation's military establishment and with its foreign policy.

Military Veterans and Their Families

The importance of veterans in the intermestic link between domestic and international aspects of national policy is especially clear in the formation of a separate Cabinet-level agency, the Department of Veterans Affairs, which was created on March 15, 1989, to replace the older Veterans Administration. The Department of Veterans Affairs manages a wide array of programs for an estimated 26.5 million veterans now in civilian life and for many of their dependents and other family members. The policy decisions of the national government, and of virtually every state and local government in the United States, are influenced heavily by the lobbying power of organized veterans' interest groups (such as the Veterans of Foreign Wars and the American Legion) and by the obvious political and economic implications of such a vast segment of the population associated with military service. The economic survival of a very large number of local communities, and thus the political survival of many elected officials, is determined by the distribution of benefits to resident veterans and the availability of jobs and spillover economic benefits from the presence of military bases, military-related industry, and medical and other services provided to veterans and their family members.

The War Powers Act

To assert greater control over presidents who might commit the United States to unwise foreign military entanglements, in 1973 Congress passed the War Powers Act over the veto of President Richard Nixon. The law requires presidents to consult with Congress before sending American armed forces into combat situations. After troops have been dispatched, the president must report to Congress within 48 hours. The troops must be withdrawn within 60 days, unless in the meantime Congress passes a declaration of war or extends that time limit. In 1983, negotiations between Congress and the Reagan administration resulted in the passage of an eighteen-month limit on troop deployments in Lebanon. In 1991, Congress passed a resolution that authorized the use of force against Iraq if it did not withdraw from Kuwait pursuant to a United Nations resolution. Within days, the Desert Storm military offensive broke over the Middle East at the order of President George Bush. In general, the practice has been for presidents to commit troops first and inform Congress afterward.

The Role of Public Opinion

Recent evidence shows a strong and persisting connection between the foreign policy of the United States, the activities of domestic interest groups, and the climate of public opinion. For example, in an attempt to forestall stricter congressional pressures against South Africa when it was still ruled by a white-minority apartheid government, President Ronald Reagan in 1985 issued an executive order imposing his own milder form of sanctions. The following year, Congress imposed its own harsher version of antiapartheid sanctions on that country, although it had to override Reagan's veto of those measures. Public opinion was believed to influence this congressional action. Such influence in foreign policy has been referred to as "a compelling example of the growing impact of societal groups" on how the nation conducts its business abroad.[10] There is abundant evidence that the direction of national foreign and security policy changes when public opinion shifts.[11]

An example of the relationship of domestic public opinion to foreign policy adjustments is provided by a close examination of changes in United States policy toward South Africa's former apartheid regime. Two distinct trends in the results of United States public opinion polls on South Africa are notable. First, there was a sharp difference in attitudes between average citizens ("the mass public") and elites. Second, there was a much sharper change in mass public attitudes over time than in elite opinion; it was the shift of the mass public that translated into politically self-interested action by Congress to stiffen sanctions against the apartheid regime. In 1974, 75 percent of elite respondents to a national survey agreed that the United States "should take a more active role in opposing the policy of apartheid—that is, racial separation—in South Africa," but only 35 percent of the general public held the same view.[12] By 1982, a follow-up survey showed that 79 percent of elites and 45 percent of the mass public supported greater activity by the United States on this issue.[13] Although clearly very far from unanimous, average citizens were at least shifting their sentiments so that by the early 1980s a plurality of the public favored a more strongly antiapartheid foreign policy in southern Africa. In 1986, relatively mild sanctions were imposed by an executive order from President Reagan, whose Republican party had been far less vociferous in its opposition to South African apartheid than Democrats and liberals in Congress.

Interest Groups and Foreign Policy

South Africa and NAFTA

Domestic interest groups also endeavor to apply pressure to affect foreign policymaking. For the case of antiapartheid legislation, pressure came from civil rights groups, churches, labor unions, universities and colleges, and public interest groups—such as TransAfrica, the American Committee on Africa, the Washington Office on Africa, and the Free South Africa Movement.[14]

The governments of other countries also attempt to exert influence over the course of American foreign policy by lobbying Congress and the executive branch. When Congress was considering antiapartheid sanctions, the white-minority South African government campaigned against that action by open diplomatic action and by using agents to put pressure on legislators, as did American corporations defending their economic interests. Lobbying by agents of the South Korean government became a major issue in domestic American politics during the 1980s, and a number of Reagan administration officials lost their jobs (and some were imprisoned) for accepting funds illegally from lobbyists working for foreign governments. The Clinton administration faced considerable risk of political and legal problems as a result of its open solicitation of funds from Asian backers of Clinton's 1996 reelection campaign who may have passed funds illegally into the Democratic candidate's campaign treasury.

The interplay of power interests and the varying degrees of success achieved through the pressures that are exerted by interest group lobbying are illustrated nicely by a letter written by Senator Tom Harkin (D-Iowa) to one of the authors, in response to correspondence related to the senator's vote in support of the NAFTA legislation. Harkin's letter reads, in part:

> I carefully considered the concern expressed to me by Iowans such as yourself, closely followed the national debate, and gathered as much information about it as I could in order to make a sound decision. This was not an easy decision for me. Many good arguments were made by those favoring the agreement and those opposing it. Iowans were evenly split on the question according to a poll taken last year, with 36 percent in favor, 38 percent opposed, and 28 percent undecided.
>
> In deciding how to vote on NAFTA I tried to determine whether the people of Iowa and our nation would be better off with or without the agreement. I concluded that the balance tipped slightly in favor of supporting the agreement. Because it is impossible to predict the future with certainty, NAFTA involved a bit of a gamble, just like any action looking to the future. But I was satisfied that the odds were more favorable than unfavorable.
>
> For Iowa, NAFTA has two main potential benefits: reducing tariffs on our exports and promoting economic growth that will make Mexico a better customer for our products. NAFTA will reduce tariffs and trade barriers that restrict exports of a number of our most important products: agricultural commodities, such as corn, pork and soybeans; processed foods; and manufactured goods such as machinery, equipment and consumer products. Over time, the agreement is expected to promote the development of a middle class in Mexico that will be able to afford more of what

we have to sell in Iowa and in the U.S. as a whole. We know from experience that open markets and exports are decidedly in the best interest of Iowa and our nation.

I have long stood for free and fair trade and improved exports because it means economic growth and more jobs at home. Our State of Iowa stands to benefit from open markets and exports and this is the main reason I voted for NAFTA. Be assured that I am continuing to monitor the implementation of this agreement and will carefully consider any modification which may come before the Senate.[15]

Clearly, Senator Harkin's predicament on this vote reflected his desire to try to satisfy conflicting and somewhat amorphous demands from constituents and from his party's president, as well as from other sources. These cross-pressures are often an important component in the process of foreign and national security policy decision making, particularly when the intermestic dimensions of the policy options are evident. In Harkin's case regarding NAFTA, the absence of a clear majority of the public either supporting or opposing NAFTA made it relatively easy for his decision to be driven by the desire to support his party's president, by the strength of the generally pro-NAFTA arguments from business interests, and by divisions among labor unions, some of which back NAFTA and some of which are among its most vocal and emphatic opponents.

Latin America and the Middle East

Cuban exiles long have played a major role in domestic American politics. Most of those who fled Cuba since the communist revolution came to power on that island in 1959 brought with them a fiercely anticommunist, anti-Castro political agenda that came to dominate the politics of Miami and much of southern Florida. Conflicts also arose between these relative newcomers and the established Anglo communities, which felt threatened by cultural differences, and with disadvantaged populations—particularly African-Americans—who found the Cuban émigrés to be a source of economic competition and resented the favored status accorded many Cubans because of their professional training and entrepreneurial skills.

One massive wave of migration was launched deliberately by Cuban leader Fidel Castro in 1980, in retaliation for continued hostile actions by the United States. The resulting influx of tens of thousands of refugees, including many criminals and other undesirable elements from Cuban society, strained the state and local Florida governments and helped to make the Carter administration seem helpless in the face of foreign actions. Carter's inability to address this problem successfully may have contributed to his loss of popularity and his subsequent loss in the 1980 presidential election against Republican candidate Ronald Reagan and independent nominee John Anderson. A similar situation emerged in the summer of 1994, when Castro allowed large numbers of Cubans to leave the island unimpeded in the face of mounting economic difficulties that followed the collapse of socialist governments in Eastern Europe and the dissolution of the Soviet Union, Cuba's leading trading partner and chief financial benefactor. The Cuban refugees and Haitian emigrants were sent to holding camps at the United States naval base at Guantanamo, Cuba, and in Panama. In return for agreeing to prevent further such refugee problems for the United States, Castro concluded an agreement by which the United States would accept 20,000 legal Cuban immigrants each year.

The Middle East has provided another regular focus of the self-interested dimension of United States foreign policy and of the intermestic link between U.S. policy toward that region and the American political as well as economic structure. United States policy toward the Middle East is influenced heavily by its politically and economically active Jewish population and by the need to come to terms with the economic power that is exerted by the primarily Arab governments of the Middle East that control much of the world's supply of oil, in addition to the influence of huge segments of the American economy—such as automotive manufacturers and their supporting industries—that depend on low prices for gasoline and other petroleum-based products.

Perhaps the most central aspect of United States policy in the region is its steadfast support of Israel, as a generally pro-Western nation in a region that is vital for its oil production and that has been a focal point of several superpower confrontations through surrogate Israeli and Arab armies. Several wars have been fought in the Middle East since the end of World War II—most notably, between Arab states and Israel after the founding of the Jewish nation in 1948—but also the long Iran-Iraq war from which the Iraqi leader, Saddam Hussein, emerged as the battered victor. The Iranian Islamic revolution of 1979 that ousted the pro-American government of Shah Mohammed Reza Pahlevi accentuated American interest in the Middle East, particularly because the revolutionary forces held American embassy personnel hostage until Ronald Reagan was sworn in as president in January 1981.

On August 2, 1990, Saddam Hussein invaded and occupied Kuwait, which Iraq claimed as a missing province, notable for its extraordinarily large oil deposits and great wealth. Acting at the request of the Saudi Arabian king and other leaders opposed to Saddam Hussein, about half a million American troops were sent to the region. A massive air attack against Iraq and its forces in Kuwait was launched on January 16, 1991, by the United States and its allies. Following several weeks of pounding from the air, the Iraqi army was attacked by very strong ground forces that rolled back the invaders within about 100 hours and threatened to capture Baghdad and thus unseat Saddam Hussein. Although his popularity soared during and immediately after the Gulf War, to about 90 percent in major national polls, President Bush was confronted by 1992 with a sour economy and other problems.

The Ideological Input

Moral Idealism

Among the major elements of American foreign and national security policy is a long-standing tension between moralistic and realist perspectives on how to conduct the nation's business abroad. Perhaps in line with the arguments of some contemporary critics that the United States was a nation founded by "religious nuts carrying guns," a dominant tendency in the country's foreign policy has been the belief that the American experiment in democratic government and a capitalistic economic system provided an unsurpassed model that the entire world should emulate. Major foreign actions undertaken by the United States have been justified on the basis of moral principles.

This perspective defines the position of moral idealism, which views the world as fundamentally benign and other nations as willing to cooperate for the common good.[16] This perspective, as manifested in President Woodrow Wilson's proposal to set up the League of Nations after World War I, holds that the countries of the world should meet together and agree mutually to keep the peace among themselves. This view of international relations, commonly associated with more liberal and progressive political groups in the United States, leads to a heavy emphasis on fostering human rights. This view also favors nurturing peaceful relationships among potentially hostile groups within and between countries—especially groups that have sharp differences of religion or ethnicity, or that possess territorial ambitions that need to be contained to prevent continual warfare and massive human suffering.

One example of America's zeal to spread goodwill and technology around the world is the Peace Corps, which began in 1961 under President John Kennedy to stimulate American-style economic and political development, particularly in Latin America, where the United States believed that Cuban-style pro-Soviet governments might come to power through popular revolutions taking advantage of the economic misery and lack of political power that characterized (and still does characterize) much of that region's population. Similarly, moral imperatives were predominant over other considerations when the administration of President Bill Clinton returned Haitian President Jean-Bertrand Aristide to power despite bitter opposition from the previous military regime in Haiti and from conservative groups in the United States (apparently including the CIA) who feared that Aristide would impose a leftist regime and renege on his promise to turn over power when his term of office ended. In fact, following a new presidential election, Aristide was replaced by his hand-picked successor who was more supportive of capitalist-style economic changes that would benefit foreign investors and the Haitian middle class.

Political Realism

The opposing perspective, adopted more commonly by conservative elements within American society, is that of political realism. Proponents of the realist perspective tend to see the world as a dangerous place, with nations fighting for their own survival and for selfish interests. This point of view leads to seeing foreign policy decision making as dominated by a need for precise calculation of what actions best serve the interests of the United States and its allies. A common feeling among foreign policy "realists" is that a strong military, as well as a strong and competitive economy, are essential above all else, to meet the challenges that will be posed by all other countries. This view leads to actions such as selling weapons to virtually any government that supports the foreign policy goals of the United States. It also results in support for American business interests abroad and fosters free-market capitalism throughout the world. Another form taken by foreign policy realism is the determination never to negotiate with terrorists who have taken hostages to thwart United States policy goals, out of fear that the nation will appear weak and that more hostages might be taken in the future, once it is demonstrated that the government will submit to such pressure.

At different times in the history of the United States, one or the other of these two tendencies of moral idealism and political realism has been predominant. The foreign and national security policy of the Carter administration, for example, with its strong emphasis on human rights, was regarded by many analysts as being driven by primarily "idealist" motives. Until late in his presidency, Carter tended to tone down disputes with the Soviet Union, attempted to accommodate the Sandinista revolution in Nicaragua, and made it more difficult for U.S. security agencies to provide open support to right-wing dictators around the world. However, Carter's stand hardened and tended to drift much more toward a "realist" approach, following Soviet intervention in Afghanistan and in the wake of Cuban support for the successful Nicaraguan revolution against the U.S.-supported Somoza oligarchy. After Ronald Reagan came to power in January 1981, open hostility toward communism generally, and especially toward the "evil empire," as he called the Soviet Union, became the driving force behind the American international agenda of rolling back leftist revolutions and supporting capitalist economic development. Many of these same tendencies of the "realist" approach to world affairs were evident in both the Bush and Clinton administrations, which had to deal with a planet in which the chief ideological and military adversary of the United States had formally ceased to exist.

Application of RPI

Rationality, power, and ideology all influence policies that possess both domestic and international implications. Rationality mandates that one of the roles of government is to ensure national economic security. As the world becomes smaller and more interdependent, international trade agreements become especially critical. Many economists see severe domestic implications arising from the persistent negative trade balances that exist between the United States and many other nations. Domestic producers pressure the government to promote policies designed to benefit their products. Appeals to "level the playing field" and to stop the "dumping" of relatively inexpensive foreign products in the United States market reflect governmental initiatives to force other nations to accept more American goods in their own markets or to prevent other nations from selling their goods in the United States. Claims that the United States is pursuing only the goals of "national security" and "fairness" often are invoked in an effort rationally to promote American economic interests.

A second rational consideration is that of domestic tranquillity. As displayed very clearly in the contemporary controversy over immigration into the United States, the stability of the country's neighbors to the South may have a profound impact on the domestic tranquillity of the United States. A Latin America that is in constant turmoil or parts of which might be allied with forces that the American government believes are antagonistic to the interests of the United States is undesirable from the rational perspective of self-interest. Even instability in areas as far away as Eastern Europe, the Middle East, or Asia can be viewed as unacceptable to American interests.

Power influences on intermestic policy are seen clearly in the interest group pressures that are exerted by major ethnic groups in the United States such as African Americans, Irish Americans, and Jewish Americans. The direct and indirect lobbying efforts undertaken by these groups mandate more than a passing interest by the United States in the politics of South Africa, Northern Ireland, and Israel. The large network of military veterans and members of the National Guard also acts as a force influencing international diplomatic, military, and economic policies. For example, activating National Guard forces for long periods of time can negatively influence public opinion, which can affect the direction and scope of the nation's foreign policy.

Finally, ideological predispositions are an important component of intermestic policymaking. A dichotomy between moralistic and realistic approaches to U.S. foreign policy provides a useful guide to the contours of American intermestic policy. These two sources of influences over intermestic policy are not mutually exclusive; both factors contribute importantly to the international postures that have been advanced by the United States government in its efforts to deal with the interface between world affairs and domestic matters. Certain policies such as those related to international trade possess more of the realist approach to intermestic policy, while others such as the intervention in Somalia, which was advertised as a means to reduce the incidence of starvation and civil war in that region of Africa, were linked more closely to the moralistic dimension.

HISTORY OF INTERMESTIC POLICY IN THE UNITED STATES

Introduction

Intermestic and All That

This chapter takes its title from the idea, developed most fully by political scientists Stephen Hess and Michael Nelson,[17] that much of the national policy agenda addresses issues that connect United States domestic policy with foreign policy developments. Intermestic policies include decisions regarding issues such as foreign trade, immigration, or defense policy that clearly have an impact on those who live within the United States, even though the policy issue may have originated outside of this country. Invention of the term intermestic generally is attributed to a former president of the Council on Foreign Relations, Bayless Manning.[18]

Hess and Nelson argued that the intermestic mix of foreign and domestic policy is clear from the history of presidential elections. They found that foreign policy usually plays a dominant role in presidential campaigns, although generally foreign policy is not decisive in determining who wins the White House.[19] They suggest:

> In truth, the foreign-domestic distinction always has oversimplified reality, but historically, as long as the United States was able to seal off its economy from extensive international influences, the oversimplification was not serious. That situation is changing, as any trip to an appliance store, gas station, or abandoned steel mill will make clear. Already, traditional occupational interest groups are increasing their involvement in foreign policy issues. Their organizational purpose has stayed the same—to enhance their members' economic well-being—but in the new international economy new political strategies for achieving this goal are necessary.[20]

Intermestic Policy Actors

The primary actors in the intermestic policy arena are the president and Congress. Owing to inherent and constitutionally mandated powers, the presidency in particular, and the executive branch more generally, is the segment of government most intimately involved in daily intermestic policymaking and implementation. The power of the purse to control the national budget and governmental expenditure decisions, and its other roles in the treaty and executive appointment process, ensure that Congress also is a major institutional actor. It has been said by some analysts of U.S. foreign and national security policy that the constitutional and institutional imperatives in that area of national decision making are such that "the nation's foreign policy process continues to reflect an invitation to struggle between the president and Congress."[21]

Another sense in which there is a direct linkage between domestic and foreign policy relates to the presence of what are often regarded by the Department of State—usually the official source of pronouncements and interpretations of United States foreign policy—as "negative constituents," that is, large numbers of people within the country's borders who have family, ancestral, cultural, or commercial ties to another country and who try to influence United States foreign policy.

Ethnicity and Foreign Policy

A large number of residents of the United States—an estimated 40 million—regard themselves as being at least partially of Irish ancestry. Many Irish immigrants did indeed come to the United States, first during the great potato famine of the 1840s and later in the early twentieth century in search of better job opportunities and to escape British rule back home. The fact that so many

United States residents today think of themselves as "Irish," and often see themselves as being interested in developments that involve Ireland, has had important implications for the nation's foreign policy. Efforts have been made within the United States to raise money for the Irish Republican Army (IRA), which fought earlier in the twentieth century to free Ireland from British rule and which continues to struggle on behalf of Catholic rights in Protestant-dominated Northern Ireland. Northern Ireland remained a part of the United Kingdom after the southern counties of Ireland achieved independence from Britain in 1920.

This domestic United States support for at least informal intervention in Northern Ireland's affairs has led to tensions with the government of the United Kingdom and to divisions among United States residents of Irish extraction over how much and what kind of assistance to provide to Catholic citizens of Ireland who oppose British domination. Within the U.S., ideological cross-pressures exist between those who favor economic justice for Catholics in Northern Ireland and those who fear that IRA success might result in pressure from the overwhelmingly Catholic population of southern Ireland and at least some IRA supporters to limit access to abortion. The result is that at least some active or potential supporters of the IRA position within the United States have been "cross-pressured" on issues of economic and social liberalism.

Many other large "ethnic" groups coexist within the diverse population of the United States, and those groups frequently complicate the process of making the country's foreign policy. Polish, African-American, Hispanic, Jewish, or Arab groups attempt to influence the course of diplomacy, and economic and military assistance, toward Eastern Europe, sub-Saharan Africa, Latin America, and the Middle East. Some idea of the scope and diversity of these major internal constituencies related to foreign affairs is provided in Table 11.3.

Before the United States government, under President Woodrow Wilson, decided in April 1917 to enter World War I, it was unclear whether the country would be able to join forces with the Allied nations—principally Great Britain, France, and Russia—against Germany and its allies, given that the United States had fought two earlier wars against Great Britain, Russia was widely regarded as an undemocratic czarist autocracy, and France was commonly seen as a source of scandalous ideas and culture. Besides, a very large portion of the population in this country was (and is) of German ancestry, which led to military and police efforts to prevent violent reactions against American entry into the war.

Today, the Hispanic population of the United States is nearly as large as its African-American population. Fiercely anticommunist Cubans concentrated in states such as Florida exert pressure that drives United States foreign policy against ending the nation's embargo of Fidel Castro's Cuba, a policy that has been condemned by virtually every other country in repeated votes taken in the United Nations. These and other consequences of the increasingly diverse demographic mix within the United States are addressed in this chapter's case study on immigration.

Table 11.3 Ancestry of the Population of the United States, 1990 (groups with estimated size of 1 million or more)

Ancestry Group	Number	Percentage of Total Population
Total population	248,709,873	100.0%
German	67,947,873	23.3
Irish	38,735,539	15.6
English	32,651,788	13.1
African-American	23,777,098	9.6
Italian	14,664,550	5.9
American	12,395,999	5.0
Mexican	11,586,983	4.7
French	10,320,935	4.1
Polish	9,366,106	3.8
American Indian	8,708,220	3.5
Dutch	6,227,089	2.5
Scotch-Irish	5,617,773	2.3
Scottish	5,393,581	2.2
Swedish	4,680,863	1.9
Norwegian	3,869,395	1.6
Russian	2,952,987	1.2
French Canadian	2,167,127	0.9
Welsh	2,033,893	0.8
Spanish	2,024,004	0.8
Puerto Rican	1,955,323	0.8
Slovak	1,882,897	0.8
White	1,799,711	0.7
Danish	1,634,669	0.7
Hungarian	1,582,302	0.6
Chinese	1,505,245	0.6
Filipino	1,450,512	0.6
Czech	1,296,411	0.5
Portuguese	1,153,351	0.5
British	1,119,154	0.4
Hispanic	1,113,259	0.4
Greek	1,110,373	0.4
Swiss	1,045,495	0.4
Japanese	1,004,645	0.4

Source: U.S. Bureau of the Census, 1993.

Note: Data are based on a sample and are subject to sampling variability. Since persons who reported multiple ancestries were included in more than one group, the sum of the persons reporting ancestry is greater than the total; for example, a person reporting "English-French" was tabulated in both the "English" and "French" categories.

The United Nations

It should not be forgotten, that the United Nations (UN) is headquartered in the United States—in New York City. This fact alone means that there is always going to be an interaction between American foreign policy and the decisions that are made by the UN. Conservative groups in the United States are particularly fond of the slogan "U.S. out of the UN," which is sometimes accompanied by the added comment, "and the UN out of the U.S." The United States is perennially the country that owes the largest amount of unpaid "dues" to fund the activities of the United Nations; that fact becomes tied up in domestic budget disputes, because many groups from different parts of the American political spectrum oppose UN operations. In particular, congressional conservatives have been inclined to restrict national monetary commitments to the UN; they also commonly push for legislation designed to limit the amount and type of foreign assistance provided by the U.S. to other countries, and conservatives do not at all like the idea that American funds would be given to the UN and spent on multinational programs that are not subject to review by U.S. legislators. Congressional conservatives have focused their wrath on the question of whether U.S. funds should be used to provide for UN social welfare services that include abortion counseling.

Foreign Policy Before 1898

In general, the early history of U.S. foreign policy was characterized by a consensus against "foreign entanglements," in favor of isolationist concentration on developing the domestic economy and on expanding the borders of the young nation. In the twentieth century, however, the role of the United States in foreign policy grew to one of global involvement, to the extent of dominating the world's economy, serving often as the "world's policeman" to enforce peace agreements, fighting in major wars principally in Europe and Asia, and, particularly following World War II, containing what was seen as the pervasive threat of communism.

The initial thrust of foreign policy for the United States was to achieve independence from Great Britain, which was attained at the end of the Revolutionary War, with the official signing of the Treaty of Paris on September 3, 1783. The infant republic, still militarily weak, otherwise tended to hold back from major foreign involvements. That posture was necessitated in part because the country operated initially under the Articles of Confederation, which forbade the national government from levying and collecting taxes, controlling commerce, making commercial treaties, and raising an army (which was disbanded in 1783). Profoundly mistrustful of European governments, which commonly were regarded as rife with corruption, the nation's earliest generation of leaders emphasized avoiding entangling foreign alliances.

Although limited in its posture in Europe and in much of the rest of the world, the United States did attempt to establish its claim of influence in the Western Hemisphere through actions such as the Monroe Doctrine of 1823, which stated the nation's opposition to foreign intervention in its "backyard," in return for which the United States would stay out of European affairs. This isolationist posture vis-à-vis Europe continued throughout the nineteenth century, but contrasted sharply with U.S. expansion in North and South America and in the Pacific. In 1803, the Louisiana territory was purchased from France. In 1845, Texas was annexed. During the 1840s, the U.S. seized in warfare or purchased about half of the territory of Mexico. In 1867, Alaska was bought from the czarist Russian government. In 1898, Hawaii was annexed.

Wars with European Powers

The Spanish-American War of 1898 broke the United States out of its isolationist foreign policy mold. After defeating Spain, the United States gained control of Guam, Puerto Rico, and the Philippines. The United States did not enter World War I (1914–1918) until the declaration of war on Germany on April 6, 1917, when President Woodrow Wilson reversed his 1916 campaign pledge to keep the United States out of the war. That involvement, which resulted in the deaths of over 116,000 members of the American armed forces, helped to prevent the defeat of Great Britain, France, and its allies (Russia surrendered to Germany in 1917 following the Bolshevik revolution). The United States did not join the League of Nations, following prolonged debate and conflict between Congress and President Wilson.

During the 1920s, the nation went "back to normalcy," under conservative Republican presidential leadership. Military forces from the Great War were largely dismantled, government spending on defense shrank to only about 1 percent of total national income, and a period of isolationist introspection ensued.

World War II and Its Effects

Although the United States had supplied some assistance to the nations arrayed in opposition to the Axis powers (Nazi Germany, Fascist Italy, imperialist Japan, and other nations), the country did not become involved directly in World War II until the Japanese attack on Pearl Harbor, Hawaii, on December 7, 1941. War was declared on the Axis powers following the first attack by a foreign power on American soil since Washington, DC, was burned by the British in 1814.

At the price of over 400,000 wartime deaths, the United States emerged from World War II both very changed and in a world that could never be the same. By 1945, defense spending had risen to nearly 40 percent of total national income, and the number of foreign military bases had exploded from only three in 1940 to nearly 450. The national government had assumed a major goal of maintaining national security. Unlike most other major participants in World War II, the United States emerged with its economy intact and vastly larger than before the outbreak of hostilities. Also, the United States at the time was the sole possessor of nuclear weapons, which it had not hesitated to use against Japan to hasten the end of the war.

The Cold War and Beyond

Following the defeat of Germany and fascism in World War II, the major competitor with the United States for global supremacy was the Soviet Union. To recover from the loss of about half of its prewar industry and over 20 million lives in what it called its Great Patriotic War, the USSR established a security buffer by exercising control over much of Eastern Europe in the postwar years. At the same time, the United States forged an alliance among Western countries with itself as the dominant force. The Cold War had begun, during which time the United States positioned itself as the defender of democracy and capitalism against what it saw as totalitarianism and communism.

Throughout the Cold War, successive American administrations pursued the official doctrine of "containment," a policy first enunciated in 1947 by George F. Kennan, chief of the policy-planning staff at the Department of State. The first application of this global strategy came with announcement of the Truman Doctrine in 1947. In a historic address to Congress, President Harry Truman declared that the United States must help countries—specifically Greece and Turkey—in which communist movements were seen as likely to gain control unless the U.S. granted such help. Similarly, the Marshall Plan in Western Europe aimed at preventing communist groups from gaining power and socialist economies from taking root.

During the Cold War, which lasted from about 1947 until the collapse of the Soviet Union in 1991, the superpowers waged conflicts against each other more through wars by proxy than by direct confrontation. It is interesting to note, however, that the United States was more inclined than the Soviet Union to commit large segments of its military strength to combat. The war between Soviet-supported North Korea and United States-backed South Korea, a country that was divided between the two occupying powers when the Japanese surrendered control of Korea at the end of World War II, lasted from 1950 to 1953. During that conflict, which ended in an armistice and military stalemate after China intervened, the United States suffered more than 54,000 deaths and over 100,000 wounded. Large contingents of American troops have remained in South Korea ever since.

The United States also engaged in massive military involvement in Vietnam, beginning shortly after the Korean conflict came to its tentative end. After the Japanese surrendered control of Indochina to the French in 1945, Vietnamese and other communist forces under Ho Chi Minh defeated the French occupiers

Contemporary Controversy

Should the United States Police the World?

Wɪᴛʜ ᴛʜᴇ demise of the Soviet Union and the emergence of a post–Cold War world, in theory the United States should have achieved hegemonic control over global politics and economics to match its military supremacy. As the first president to face this brave new world from the beginning of his tenure in the White House, Bill Clinton has found instead that the United States is beset with severe problems in the international economy and with porous borders. Even in the military sphere, although unmatched by any competitor nation, a principal problem of the new era revolves around the recurring question of when, where, and how to project power in support of U.S. interests.

in a war that culminated in the decisive 1954 siege of Dien Bien Phu. Vietnam was divided into two countries—North Vietnam and South Vietnam—and elections that could have unified the country were canceled. Starting with only a handful of military advisers in the early 1960s, the American commitment grew to about 16,000 before the assassination of President Kennedy in 1963, and peaked at over 500,000 troops under Lyndon Johnson. In a war that escalated incrementally, over 58,000 Americans died in an effort to prevent what supporters of the war argued were the "dominoes" of the region falling under the control of Soviet and Chinese influence. As the casualties mounted and American frustration grew with the absence of a quick military victory, domestic discontent became explosive, and President Johnson declined to run for reelection in 1968. The Nixon administration both escalated the air war against North Vietnam and worked to extract American ground forces from the region. In April 1975, the South Vietnamese capital of Saigon (now called Ho Chi Minh City) fell to communist armed forces.

The closest that the two superpowers came to direct nuclear confrontation during the Cold War came in 1962. By that time, both countries had already acquired "overkill" capability to destroy their opponents' population centers, and their military and industrial power, several times over. In 1961, the Kennedy administration had half-heartedly supported an invasion of Cuba, which was controlled by a pro-Moscow communist government under Fidel Castro, the leader of a successful popular revolution against the Batista dictatorship (Castro took power on January 1, 1959). Following the failed American-sponsored invasion by anti-Castro exiles, the Soviet Union offered Cuba nuclear weapons to ward off future invasion threats, an offer that would also provide Soviet strategic advantages by placing atomic weapons within a few minutes' flight time of the United States mainland. The United States imposed a naval blockade

In many respects, this is not a new problem at all. Since achieving its independence in a war of liberation against the occupying power of Great Britain, with significant assistance from France, the United States has been involved in major foreign wars of varying intensity and scope since at least the Mexican War of 1846–1848. The problem of foreign wars carries with it very powerful intermestic implications, considering the many domestic linkages that exist with national security issues and military involvement. The United States has paid a very high price for its previous involvements in the military aspect of world affairs, and that price has had enduring effects in transforming the nation. This price can be evaluated in at least two obvious ways: in terms of money and in terms of human casualties.

The estimated financial costs of past wars in which the United States has been involved are summarized in Table 11.4. The primary message from these data is that wars can be terribly costly in purely monetary terms, with the possible exception of the Persian Gulf War of 1991 in which United States military forces played a role somewhat akin to that of mercenaries whose services were paid for almost entirely by other participating countries. World War II far and away provided the greatest financial impact on

(continued)

on Cuba, to prevent the entry of additional Soviet nuclear weapons. Following high tension over whether the confrontation would turn into a nuclear war, Soviet ships carrying new weapons to Cuba turned around. On October 28, 1962, the Soviet Union announced that it would withdraw its missiles, in exchange for a United States pledge not to invade the island and the removal of American missiles near the Soviet border. The United States has maintained an economic blockade against Cuba, in an attempt to overthrow or change the direction of the Castro government. This action, which has little official support from other countries in the United Nations, has endured despite Soviet and Cuban efforts to lift the embargo.

By the late 1960s, according to many analysts, the Soviet Union had essentially caught up with the previous American lead in strategic nuclear weapons that had led to American successes in earlier confrontations involving Cuba, Berlin, and other international hot spots. In May 1972, after long and difficult diplomatic exchanges, the United States and the Soviet Union signed the first of two Strategic Arms Limitation Treaties, known as SALT I. SALT greatly reduced the possibility of developing and deploying potentially destabilizing antiballistic missiles (ABMs). This interval of détente, or relaxed tensions, between the superpowers was short lived.

By the late 1970s, tensions again increased between the United States and the Soviet Union. Antagonism was clearest in Afghanistan, where Soviet troops had intervened to support a pro-Moscow government against Islamic fundamentalist forces that were backed by the United States. By the early 1980s, pro-Soviet governments that had been in power in Eastern Europe since the end of World War II were weakening, which led the Soviet government to crack down in Poland and elsewhere against what was perceived as possible contamination by antisocialist ideas.

Table 11.4 Estimates of Total Dollar Costs of American Wars (in millions of dollars, except percent)

	World War II	Vietnam Conflict	Korean Conflict	World War I	Spanish American War	Mexican War
Direct costs[1]						
Current dollars	360,000	140,600	50,000	32,700	270	82
Constant (1967) dollars	816,300	148,800	69,300	100,000	1,100	300
Percent of one year's GNP	188	14	15	43	2	4
Service-connected veterans' benefits[2]	96,666	32,288	19,512	19,580	2,111	26
Interest, payments on war loans[3]	5	5	5	11,000	60	10
Current cost to 1990[4]	466,000	179,000	72,000	63,500	2,441	120

Source: The Military Budget and National Economic Priorities, revised and updated by James L. Clayton.

Note: The U.S Department of Defense reported that, as of 1991, the total cost of the Persian Gulf War was $61.1 billion; this figure includes $7.4 billion from the United States and $53.7 billion in contributions from other countries.

[1] Figures are rounded and are taken from Claudia D. Goldin, *Encyclopedia of American Economic History.*
[2] Total cost to October 1, 1990. For World War I and later wars, benefits are actual service-connected figures from the *Annual Report* of the Veterans Administration. For earlier wars, service-connected veterans' benefits are estimated at 40 percent of total, the approximate ratio of service-connected to total benefits since World War I.
[3] Total cost to 1990. Interest payments are a very rough approximation based on the percentage of the original costs of each war financed by money creation and debt, the difference between the level of public debt at the beginning of the war and at its end, and the approximate time required to pay off the war debts.
[4] Figures are rounded estimates.
[5] Unknown.

The Reagan administration generally adopted a hard line toward the Soviet Union, as shown by its policy decisions to drastically increase defense spending, to support "freedom fighters" who opposed communist regimes throughout the world, to pursue advanced technology such as the Strategic Defense Initiative, or "Star Wars," and to inflate the anti-Soviet rhetoric through phrases such as "evil empire." When the Soviet Union collapsed in 1991, worries arose about who exercised command and control over that nation's nuclear arsenal. In 1992, the Bush administration concluded the Strategic Arms Reduction Treaty with four of the successor states to the Soviet Union—Russia, Ukraine, Belarus, and Kazakhstan.

In October 1993, Warren Christopher, President Clinton's secretary of state, enunciated six major foreign policy goals for the post–Cold War era

the United States, at a level of over $800 billion in direct costs measured in constant dollar terms. To this must be added another nearly $100 billion in service-related veterans'- benefits and an unknown additional amount of interest payments on war loans. The prolonged war in Vietnam has had the second-greatest impact, followed by the Korean War, World War I, the Spanish-American War, and the Mexican War. Omitted from this table are comparative figures for the Civil War, the American Revolution, and the War of 1812 (much of which was fought on the territory or future territory of the United States), as well as "minor" conflicts such as Somalia.

A more pronounced impact of U.S. involvement in foreign wars is measured by the "body count," or the human casualties that produce widows, orphans, lost relatives, and national soul-searching about whether the foreign involvement was worthwhile. Table 11.5 provides a summary of the human cost to the United States of its major foreign wars. Of the nearly two million total casualties suffered by the armed forces of the United States during these wars in the past century and a half, including two-thirds of a million fatalities in battle and from other war-related causes, the great majority were incurred in the Second World War, in which the United States was an active combatant from 1941 to 1945. Many other military casualties, however, were suffered in two of the major wars—in Korea and in Vietnam—that were part of the Soviet-U.S. confrontation during the Cold War.

President Clinton wrestled with the turmoil in Bosnia to find a way for the United States to practice a hybrid moralistic policy of protecting human rights and pragmatic desires to prevent the Bosnian war from spreading to other parts of Eastern Europe. After initially opposing the introduction of American ground troops into Bosnia, President Clinton pressured NATO (the North Atlantic Treaty Organization, consisting of most nations in Western Europe plus the United States and Canada) into launching air attacks against Bosnian Serb targets and re-supplied the Croatian military secretly until it was strong enough to overrun Serbian-held portions of Croatia in conjunction with a Muslim offensive in Bosnia. A tenuous peace agreement was negotiated in Dayton, Ohio, late in 1995, after Serb forces had been weakened and forced to retreat from much of the territory they had held previously. The treaty was signed in Paris, on December 14, 1995.

The division among United States policymakers about the best path to follow in Bosnia was apparent in Congressional efforts to express opposition to Clinton's decision

(continued)

following the dissolution of the Soviet Union late in 1991—economic security, promoting reform in Russia, creating a new framework in which NATO could be adapted to new world realities and needs, improved trading relationships with Asian economies, resolving deadlocks in the Middle East, and preventing the spread of nuclear weapons and the technology required to make them. The major themes of the Clinton administration related to foreign and national security policy have been summarized as: "enlargement of market democracy," to be achieved by "strengthening the rich democracies; by helping countries making the transition to pluralistic politics and market economies; by countering the troublesome 'backlash states' that opposed such changes, and by providing humanitarian relief where it could do the most good."[22]

Table 11.5 Casualties in Principal Foreign Wars of the United States

War	Number Serving	Battle Deaths	Other Deaths	Wounds Not Mortal	Total[1]
Mexican War	78,718	1,733	11,550	4,152	17,435
Spanish-American War	306,760	385	2,061	1,662	4,108
World War I	4,734,991	53,402	63,114	204,002	320,518
World War II	16,112,566	291,557	113,842	670,846	1,076,245
Korean War	5,720,000	33,629	20,617	103,284	157,530
Vietnam War	8,744,000	47,366	10,801	153,303	211,470
Persian Gulf War	467,539	148	145	467	760
Total	36,164,574	428,220	222,130	1,137,716	1,788,066

Source: U.S. Department of Defense.

Note: All data are subject to revision. For wars before World War I, information represents the best data from available records. However, due to incomplete records and possible difference in usage of terminology, reporting systems, etc., figures should be considered estimates.

[1]Excludes captured or interned and missing in action who were subsequently returned to military control.
[2]Vietnam figures provided by the U.S. Center of Military History, Reference Division, Washington, DC, February 1994.

to dispatch 20,000 American troops to Bosnia (with another 17,000 support personnel), as part of a 60,000-member NATO force, to help enforce the terms of the Dayton peace accord. Nearly half of the membership of the House of Representatives—a total of 201 members, of whom fifteen were Democrats—took the highly unusual act of signing a letter opposing the troop deployment.[23] A House vote on a motion introduced by Representative Bob Dornan, a California Republican and second-tier candidate for his party's presidential nomination, to cut off funds for the troop deployment failed only narrowly, by 210 to 218. A parallel Senate vote was not as close, with twenty-two (twenty-one Republicans and one Democrat) voting in favor of cutting funding and seventy-seven against. The Senate subsequently passed a resolution offered by Republican senators Bob Dole of Kansas (the Republican presidential front runner) and John McCain of Arizona that supported the mission under the conditions that the United States would lead an effort to arm and train Bosnian Muslim government forces, the government would support the American troops, reservations about President Clinton's decision to send troops would be expressed as well as agreement with Clinton that preserving the credibility of the United States was of paramount strategic interest.[24]

The congressional debate largely reflected the concerns of policymakers and of the general public over moral idealism. Senator Phil Gramm, a Texas Republican challenging Bob Dole for the party's presidential nomination, concluded, "When you get down to the bottom line as to whether we have a vital national security interest in Bosnia, the clear answer is no. . . . [Y]ou can't run foreign policy like social work. You can't look for some good to do around the world. We . . . can't fix everything that's broken. We can't right every wrong."[25] Pennsylvania Republican Senator Arlen Specter, also a contender for the 1996 presidential nomination, was unconvinced by President

Clinton's arguments for the troop deployment: "U.S. national security is not imminently threatened and we are not the world's policemen. It may be that at some point there will be consideration to the deployment of U.S. troops for international moral commitments or from some other standard. But the vital-national-interest context has been that which has traditionally governed the deployment of U.S. military personnel. In the absence of a vital national interest, it is my view that the Congress should support the troops without endorsing the President's policy. Our congressional action should show as much national unity as possible under the circumstances and project American leadership to the maximum extent possible consistent with congressional policy not to give the President a blank check."[26]

In contrast, support for the president's position, based on the need to maintain the integrity of American leadership in NATO, was expressed by Democratic Senator Bob Kerrey, of Nebraska, who had opposed Clinton for the 1992 presidential nomination: "Stability in Europe and the continued viability of NATO are our vital interests. And they are at issue today in the Balkans. . . . No one else in the world can do this, except the United States of America. We are doing it . . . to protect vital interests. And we are doing it in a good cause. . . . If we lead with the same vision of our post-war predecessors, we can achieve success in Bosnia."[27] A leading Democratic Senate liberal, Edward M. Kennedy of Massachusetts, argued that supporting Clinton's actions would prevent more serious conflicts: "This mission is the only chance to achieve peace in Bosnia. That peace is essential to prevent a wider war in Europe, a wider war would inevitably involve the United States, with vastly greater risk of casualties. Twice in this century, tens of thousands of Americans have lost their lives in World Wars that destroyed much of Europe. Containing such wars, before they spiral out of control will save future American lives."[28]

The American public was at best ambivalent about the president's actions. A *New York Times/CBS News* opinion poll showed that about two-thirds expected fighting to break out again, in spite of the heavy NATO troop concentration. The same survey revealed that only 36 percent agreed that it was "the right thing" to do, and 58 percent felt that the troops should be kept out of the Balkans. In other major international crises, public opinion also has been very divided or negative toward presidential initiatives. This was true early in the buildup of troops to fight Saddam Hussein in the Gulf War of 1991, although opinion turned around sharply in support of Bush after a highly successful military campaign. The specter loomed of a possible repeat of Clinton's earlier failure in Somalia, when American troops were forced to withdraw after suffering heavy casualties in warfare against warlord Mohammed Farah Adid's supporters. Potentially even more ominous was the concern of the administration's policymakers to avoid repeating the Vietnam War errors that drove Lyndon Johnson from the White House.[29]

Much of the uncertainty regarding the role of the United States in Bosnia has to do with the "exit strategy," that is, when and under what circumstances the troops would leave and what—or who—would replace them. The administration's stated goal was to withdraw the troops after about one year, which would allow time to equip and train the Bosnian army, as well as for civilian and other agencies to resettle refugees, provide aid, train new police forces, and construct a political infrastructure to conduct elections. That such policy decisions are not built purely on rationality is evident from testimony given by Secretary of Defense William J. Perry on November 30, 1995, before the House International Relations Committee, who admitted that limiting the mission

(continued)

to one year was based on judgment, rather than hard facts: "How long that breathing space is necessary, no one can estimate. A year of breathing space is a pretty good breathing space."[30] One major unresolved complication was who would pay for the civilian effort, estimated to cost $6 billion; although the United States committed itself officially to paying $600 million (or 10 percent), European leaders like French President Jacques Chirac stated publicly that the United States and Western Europe each should pick up one-third of the total cost. Tension also existed between European governments, which did not want to arm Muslim troops supporting the Bosnian government, and the Clinton administration, which made rearming and training the Bosnians a centerpiece of its Dayton peace strategy.

Similarly, opinions in the United States among policymakers and those who influence their decisions were sharply split as to whether the United States should pretend to be neutral in Bosnia. For example, Richard Perle, former Assistant Secretary of Defense during the Reagan Administration, stated:

> The idea that our forces in Bosnia could or should try to wrap themselves in a cloak of neutrality is simply wrong. . . .

Case Study

Immigration

THROUGHOUT THE history of the United States, immigration has shaped the character of the nation and its policy decisions. This is true today, just as it was when the first Europeans began to push indigenous Native American populations off their land in the sixteenth and seventeenth centuries. (It is worth keeping in mind, too, that the ancestors of the Indian peoples who met Columbus and other early European colonizers had probably migrated across a Bering Sea land bridge from Asia tens of thousands of years earlier). Table 11.6 summarizes the record in this century of immigrants and non-immigrant aliens admitted to the United States.

A massive outmigration of Europeans to North America in the early twentieth century provided a sharp impetus to population growth in the United States; changed the ethnic mix of the United States away from its once-predominant English, German, and African roots, toward a more heavily Irish and southern European mix. It may be surprising to realize that the actual number of immigrants coming to the United States is higher today than during the period of heaviest European immigration in the years before World War I. In 1994, more than 1.7 million people immigrated into the United States legally, together with a substantial but hard-to-estimate number of illegal immigrants.[33] Unlike the early-twentieth-century wave of immigration, the pattern at the

We will be far safer in Bosnia if we assume that we are likely to become targets and behave accordingly, rather than hiding behind a political fiction and merely encouraging others to train and arm the Bosnians while we distance ourselves in public. Those who would attack our troops will not be deterred or impressed by our resorting to surrogates for training the Bosnians. They are not subtle and they are not fools.[31]

A contradictory point of view is afforded by George Kenney, who resigned from the State Department in August 1992 to protest the policy taken by the Bush administration in the former Yugoslavia:

Arming and training Bosnian Muslims . . . cannot possibly help the peace agreement or advance United States interests. Abandoning neutrality would put our troops at greater risk, and our allies would hold us responsible for the consequences if war broke out again, unleashed in part by the emboldened Bosnians. . . .

The deployment of United States forces in Bosnia is already a difficult enough job without exposing our soldiers to reprisals by taking sides. Our enemies will likely include not only disgruntled Bosnian Serbs but also Islamic fighters who stay behind, with or without the Bosnian government's blessing.[32]

end of the century was for the greatest number of new arrivals to come from Mexico and the countries of Central and South America, with large numbers of immigrants also coming from Asian nations. Table 11.7 demonstrates the dominant countries of origin for the foreign-born. Currently, about 20 million residents of the United States were born outside of America. Of that total, nearly one-fourth entered the country between 1985 and 1990. The number of foreign-born persons entering the United States has increased steadily since the early 1960s, from 1.5 million between 1960 and 1964, to 5.6 million between 1985 and 1990. About 7.9 percent of the nation's population was foreign-born in 1990, and this was the highest proportion in forty years. One-third of the foreign-born were concentrated in California, with large numbers also residing in New York state (14 percent), Florida (8 percent), Texas (8 percent), New Jersey (5 percent), and Illinois (5 percent).

Policies affecting immigration clearly can have a significant impact on the structure and dynamics of society in the United States. It is not much of an overstatement to say that the future shape of the country's culture and its political balance of power depend critically on policy decisions that affect who can enter the country and who can live, work, vote, pay taxes, and establish citizenship here. A measure of the impact of immigration on the changing structure of American society is provided by the expanding number of people who speak a language other than English—31.8 million, or about 14 percent of the population age five and over, compared with 23.1 million, or 11 percent of the age-five-and-over population, in 1980. This amounted to an increase of nearly 40 percent during the decade of the 1980s, when concerns grew about the cultural impacts of immigration from Spanish-speaking countries particularly. Nearly 20 million people spoke Spanish in their homes.

(continued)

Table 11.6 Immigrant and Nonimmigrant Aliens Admitted to the United States in the Twentieth Century

Fiscal Years[1]	Immigrants	Nonimmigrants[2]	Total
1901–1910	8,795,386	1,007,909	9,803,295
1911–1920	5,735,811	1,376,271	7,112,802
1921–1930	4,107,209	1,774,896	5,882,090
1931–1940	528,431	1,574,071	2,102,502
1941–1950	1,035,039	2,461,359	3,496,398
1951–1960	2,515,479	7,113,023	9,628,502
1961–1970	3,321,677	24,107,224	27,428,901
1971–1977	2,797,209	45,236,597	48,033,806
1983	559,763	9,849,458	10,409,221
1984	543,903	9,426,759	9,970,662
1985	570,009	9,675,650	10,245,659
1986	601,708	10,471,024	11,072,732
1987	601,516	12,272,866	12,874,382
1988	643,025	14,591,735	15,234,760
1989	1,090,924[3]	16,144,576	17,235,500
1990	1,536,483[3]	17,145,680	18,682,163
1991	1,827,167[3]	18,962,520	20,789,687
1992	937,977[4]	20,793,846	21,767,823

Source: U.S. Department of Justice, Immigration and Naturalization Service.

[1]Fiscal year ending June 30 prior to 1977. After 1977 for fiscal year ending September 30.
[2]Nonimmigrant aliens include visitors for business or pleasure, students, foreign government officials, and others temporarily in the United States.
[3]Includes immigrants and legalized immigrants.
[4]Includes immigrants and 163,342 legalized immigrants.

The United States was unwilling to accept immigration from large numbers of refugees desperately trying to flee from Nazi and fascist terror in Europe or from Japanese aggressive expansion in Asia in the years before and during World War II (1939–1945). However, a selective influx of refugees, particularly intellectuals like Albert Einstein from Germany or Enrico Fermi from Italy, provided a major boost to U.S. scientific research and contributed to enhancing the economic and cultural life of the nation. During the Cold War confrontation with the Soviet Union and its allied governments in Europe, with Cuba in Latin America, and with China and other Asian communist countries, from the end of World War II until the early 1990s, large numbers of anticommunists leaving those countries were admitted into the United States. The domestic impact of that Cold War inflow almost certainly contributed toward pushing the political spectrum in the country faster toward the conservative right. This impact perhaps was felt most strongly in southern Florida, where the inflow of primarily anti-Castro Cuban émigrés started to arrive in the late 1950s. Miami and other cities in southern Florida became very heavily influenced by the generally conservative and frequently pro-Republican leanings of those

Table 11.7 The Foreign-Born Population in the United States, 1990

Place of Birth	Number	Percentage of Total
Mexico	4,298,014	21.7%
Philippines	912,674	4.6
Canada	744,830	3.8
Cuba	736,971	3.7
Germany	711,929	3.6
United Kingdom	640,145	3.2
Italy	580,592	2.9
Korea	568,397	2.9
Vietnam	543,262	2.7
China	529,837	2.7
El Salvador	465,433	2.4
India	450,406	2.3
Poland	388,328	2.0
Dominican Republic	347,858	1.8
Jamaica	334,140	1.7
Soviet Union	333,725	1.7
Japan	290,128	1.5
Colombia	286,124	1.4
Taiwan	244,102	1.2
Guatemala	225,739	1.1
Haiti	225,303	1.1
Iran	210,941	1.1
Portugal	210,122	1.1
Greece	177,398	0.9
Laos	171,577	0.9
Total	19,767,316	100.0

Source: U.S. Bureau of the Census, 1993.

immigrants, and contributed toward making Florida a state that conservative Republican candidates generally could count on in presidential elections. Prior to that inflow of Cuban émigrés, Florida had been a dependably Democratic state in presidential and congressional elections for several decades.

More recently, other evidence is available of the increasing diversity of the electorate attributable to rising immigration rates, combined with the relatively high birth rates among those new Americans.[34] According to the U.S. Immigration and Naturalization Service, over 2.3 million immigrants became naturalized citizens between the 1992 and 1996 presidential elections. This was the largest number of new citizens created between presidential elections since 1924, a previous peak of immigration, which at that time had come primarily from Europe. The latest wave of newfound citizens was far more likely

(continued)

to have come from the Middle East, Latin America, or Asia. An almost immediate implication of this massive wave of new naturalizations was the introduction into the electorate of large numbers of new adults who came into the U.S. political process with potentially very different ideas about the country's economic, social, and political life.

It is crucial to note that candidates for national, state, and local office must adapt to these new realities, to attract votes and campaign contributions, particularly in key states where these immigrant populations have been concentrated. These concentrations include crucial blocs of swing votes held by Asian-Americans in California, Mexican-Americans in states in the southwest, Russians and Caribbean-area immigrants in New York, and Arab-Americans in Michigan. The partisan leanings of the new ethnic voters were a bit difficult to decipher. For example, a national survey of Arab-American registered voters indicated that 42 percent identified themselves as Republicans, compared to 36.5 percent who called themselves Democrats and 21.4 percent as independents or as members of a third party. However, in elections, these new voters have been likely to swing between liberal and conservative candidates, and from Democrats to Republicans. The survey of Arab-American voters showed that 43.4 percent voted for Bill Clinton, as against 29.6 percent for Bob Dole, although a plurality had identified themselves as Republicans.[35]

The Clinton presidential campaign in 1996 made a major effort to attract funds and votes from the new sets of ethnic voters. An extensive ethnic outreach program was supported by the Democratic National Committee and through the Clinton White House. This effort led to some events that caused severe image problems for the Democrats, including allegations of unethical and illegal solicitation of funds from Indonesian and other Asian sources, domestically and abroad.

A major portion of national policymaking regarding immigration has to do with rules regarding naturalization, which is the process by which people originating from other countries can become citizens. Under Article I, Section 8 of the United States Constitution, Congress is empowered to "establish a uniform Rule of Naturalization." Precisely because this can be a difficult, time-consuming, and demanding process, many immigrants remain in the United States without taking out proper documentation. The major executive-branch agency involved with implementing national policy regarding foreign visitors is the Immigration and Naturalization Service, in the Department of Justice.

In 1892, Ellis Island opened as the immigration depot for New York City, and over many years came to symbolize the experience of the waves of immigrants, primarily from Europe, who entered the country in the early part of the twentieth century. Congress sharply limited immigration in 1921, setting up a national quota system that had the primary effect of limiting the influx of people from Asia—particularly China—and southern and eastern Europe. The Immigration and Naturalization Act of 1952 removed the last racial and ethnic barriers to naturalization. In 1965, the restrictive national origins quota system was abolished, with the chief consequence of opening up immigration from Asia, and family reunification became the primary means of entry into the United States.

Following almost fifteen years of heated legislative debate, in 1986 Congress passed the Immigration Reform and Control Act, to attempt to regain control of illegal and undocumented immigration and its consequences. There were four main provisions of that legislation.[36] First, in a major effort to overhaul the cumbersome procedures for naturalization, Congress established a May 4, 1988, deadline for applying for amnesty under a new policy. Nearly 1,400,000 illegal aliens met that deadline, of whom over half were in California. An estimated 71 percent had entered the United States from

Mexico. Second, employers were required to hire only employees who could establish their right to work in the United States. Violations were to be met with substantial civil and criminal penalties, known as "employer sanctions." Third, a supply of legal foreign workers for growers of perishable agricultural crops was guaranteed for fiscal years 1990 through 1993, to meet fears from the industry over prospective shortages of workers. Finally, border controls were enhanced substantially.

Whether the 1986 act, often referred to as the Simpson-Mazzoli bill (named after Senator Alan Simpson, a Wyoming Republican, and Romano Mazzoli, a Kentucky Democratic representative), was effective is a matter of dispute. A study by two United States Department of Labor analysts[37] concluded that the law failed to resolve "the problem of illegal migration into the United States" because "it did not mandate the establishment of a secure means of determining an individual's eligibility to work in the United States" that may be critical to the effective enforcement of any employer sanctions provisions. These authors concluded that initial declines in illegal immigration after passage of the 1986 law were artifacts of legalizing many resident aliens who had been part of the previous flow of illegals.[38] Future immigration policy debates will likely include discussions of how to reduce discrimination against resident aliens, verify employability, reduce incentives for employers to exploit cheap and relatively defenseless workers, induce Mexican workers to keep jobs in Mexico rather than becoming potential migrants into the United States, and provide for legitimate needs of industries currently relying on imported workers.[39]

The Immigration Act of 1990 was signed into law by President George Bush on November 29, 1990, amending the basic provisions laid down in the Immigration and Nationality Act. The law increased the quota on immigration to 700,000 annually for fiscal years 1992 through 1994, excluding refugees and some other categories of entrants not limited by law, and dropping to 675,000 beginning in fiscal year 1995. Within very detailed divisions, the law provided for 480,000 immigrants as family relatives of those already in the United States, 140,000 immigrants who meet priority job qualifications, and 55,000 "diversity immigrants" from countries that previously had not provided large numbers of entrants.

Issues related to immigration remain unresolved, and this policy area is highly volatile politically, as is clear from the passage of California's Proposition 187 in the November 1994 elections. The primary goal of the legislation—to ban state spending on illegal immigrants—was endorsed by a large (59 percent) majority. Opponents of the proposition argued that it was racially discriminatory.[40] The politically charged atmosphere surrounding the issue is clear from the fact that it was one of the principal tactics used successfully by California's Republican Governor Pete Wilson to win reelection in 1994 after at one point having been far behind his Democratic opponent, Kathleen Brown. Another indication of the political potency of illegal immigration is its adoption as a major campaign theme by congressional candidates, such as Dana Rohrabacher, a California Republican, who campaigned successfully for reelection to the House in 1994 partly on the basis of supporting Proposition 187 because "we can no longer afford to provide a treasure chest of benefits to every person who manages to cross our border illegally."[41] Congressional Republicans made a cutoff of government aid to *legal* immigrants a part of their national agenda, the Contract with America. Immigration is certain to remain a volatile issue, because the low birth rates among residents of the United States mean that in the future, in the absence of immigration, the country will confront

(continued)

a shrinking working-age share of the population. The policy question, then, becomes whether the United States will continue its previous policy of encouraging immigration as a way to expand the size of the future labor force.[42]

Case Study Questions:

1. Do you believe that immigration is better thought of as a problem that needs to be solved, or is immigration an opportunity for the United States to enhance its workforce and to create a more diverse society? Support your answer.

Suggested Readings

Allison, Graham, and Gregory F. Treverton (eds.). (1992). *Rethinking America's Security: Beyond Cold War to New World Order.* New York: Norton, 1992.

Crabb, Cecil V., Jr., and Pat M. Holt. *Invitation to Struggle: Congress, the President, and Foreign Policy,* 4th ed. Washington, DC: CQ Press, 1992.

Moran, Theodore H. *American Economic Policy and National Security.* New York: Council on Foreign Relations Press, 1993.

Nincic, M. *Democracy and Foreign Policy: The Fallacy of Political Realism.* New York: Columbia University Press, 1992.

Romm, Joseph J. *Defining National Security: The Non-Military Aspects.* New York: Council on Foreign Relations Press, 1994.

Small, Melvin. *Democracy and Diplomacy: The Impact of Domestic Politics on U.S. Foreign Policy, 1789–1994.* Baltimore: Johns Hopkins University Press, 1996.

Notes

1. Bruce Russett, *Controlling the Sword: The Democratic Governance of National Security* (Cambridge, MA: Harvard University Press, 1990), p. 50.

2. Melvin Small, *Democracy and Diplomacy: The Impact of Domestic Politics on U.S. Foreign Policy, 1789–1994* (Baltimore: Johns Hopkins University Press, 1996).

3. Nathaniel C. Nash, "Showing Europe That U.S. Still Cares," *New York Times,* 3 December 1995, p. 12.

4. Richard W. Stevenson, "Nafta's Impact on Jobs Has Been Slight, Study Says," *New York Times,* 19 December 1996, pp. C1, C3.

5. *Economic Report of the President* (Washington, DC: U.S. Government Printing Office, 1994), p. 208.

6. C. Fred Bergsten and Marcus Nolad, *Reconcilable Differences? U.S.-Japan Economic Conflict* (Washington, DC: Institute for International Economics, 1993), p. 200.

7. Adam Smith, *An Inquiry into the Nature and Causes of the Wealth of Nations* (London: Strahan and Cadell, 1776).

2. Are the problems of foreign trade and immigration related? Why or why not? Can both problems be "solved" using the same methods?

3. What are some of the advantages, both for the United States and for other countries, of an immigration policy that favors the admission of skilled workers and family members? What are some disadvantages, both for the United States and for other countries, of this policy?

4. How has American politics been affected by the policy of admitting large numbers of refugees from communist countries during the Cold War? Should such policies be continued today; why, or why not?

8. David Ricardo, *On the Principles of Political Economy, and Taxation* (London: Murray, 1817).

9. For a detailed discussion of the role of the National Guard in domestic U.S. politics, see Martha Derthick, *The National Guard in Politics* (Cambridge, MA: Harvard University Press, 1965).

10. N. Bodurtha, *America and South Africa. Shaping American Global Policy: The Growing Impact of Societal Relations* (Muscatine, Iowa: Stanley Foundation, 1993), p. 37.

11. L. A. Kusnitz, *Public Opinion and Foreign Policy: America's China Policy, 1949–1979* (Westport, CT: Greenwood Press, 1984); Bruce Russett, *Controlling the Sword: The Democratic Governance of National Security* (Cambridge, MA: Harvard University Press, 1990); R. H. Hinckley, *People, Polls, and Policymakers: American Public Opinion and National Security* (New York: Lexington Books, 1992); M. Nincic, *Democracy and Foreign Policy: The Fallacy of Political Realism* (New York: Columbia University Press, 1992); C. F. Hermann, "Changing Course: When Governments Choose to Redirect Foreign Policy," *International Studies Quarterly* 334 (1990), pp. 3–21.

12. J. E. Rielly, *American Public Opinion and U.S. Foreign Policy, 1975* (Chicago: Chicago Council on Foreign Relations, 1975).

13. J. E. Rielly, *American Public Opinion and U.S. Foreign Policy, 1983* (Chicago: Chicago Council on Foreign Relations, 1983).

14. A. O. Hero and J. Barratt, eds., *The American People and South Africa: Publics, Elites, and Policymaking Processes* (Lexington, MA: Heath, 1981); S. Metz, "The Anti-Apartheid Movement and the Populist Instinct in American Politics," *Political Science Quarterly* 101 (1986), pp. 379–395; R. Michael Smith, "Democratic Pressure on U.S. Foreign Policy Toward South Africa," unpublished manuscript.

15. Tom Harkin, Letter to Mack Shelley, 9 November 1995.

16. Charles W. Kegley, Jr., and Eugene Wittkopf, *American Foreign Policy, Patterns and Process,* 3rd ed. (New York: St. Martin's Press, 1987).

17. Stephen Hess and Michael Nelson, "Foreign Policy: Dominance and Decisiveness in Presidential Elections," in *The Elections of 1984,* ed. Michael Nelson (Washington, DC: CQ Press, 1985), pp. 129–154.

18. Ibid., p. 153.

19. Ibid., p. 129.

20. Ibid., p. 138.

21. Cecil V. Crabb, Jr., and Pat M. Holt, *Invitation to Struggle: Congress, the President, and Foreign Policy,* 4th ed. (Washington, DC: CQ Press 1992), p. x.

22. "Otherwise Engaged," *The Economist,* 30 October 1995, pp. 21–24.

23. Katharine Q. Seelye, "Nearly Half of House Members Sign Letter Opposing Bosnia Deployment," *New York Times,* 8 December 1995, p. A6.

24. Katharine Q. Seelye, "Senate and House Won't Stop Funds for Bosnia Force," *New York Times,* 14 December 1995, pp. A1, A10.

25. "Impassioned Words in the Senate: National Interest or Deadly Quagmire?," *New York Times,* 14 December 1995, p. A10.

26. Ibid., p. A10.

27. Ibid., p. A10.

28. Ibid., p. A10.

29. R. W. Apple, Jr., "Flimsy Bosnia Mandate," *New York Times,* 14 December 1995, pp. A1, A10.

30. Eric Schmitt, "Key Bosnia Question: Where Are Exits?," *New York Times,* 2 December 1995, p. 5.

31. Richard N. Perle, "'Neutrality' Won't Protect Our Troops," *New York Times,* 7 December 1995, p. A19.

32. George Kenney, "If the U.S. Takes Sides," *New York Times,* 12 December 1995, p. A19.

33. *Universal Almanac 1994* (Kansas City, MO: Andrews and McMeel, 1994).

34. Steven A. Holmes, "Influx of Immigrants Is Changing Electorate," *New York Times,* 30 November 1996, p. A10.

35. Ibid., p. A10.

36. D. M. Meissner and D. G. Papademetriou, *The Legalization Countdown: A Third Quarter Assessment* (Washington, DC: Carnegie Endowment for International Peace, 1988); B. Lindsay Lowell and Demetrios G. Papademetriou, "Introduction: Immigration and U.S. Integration, Policy Reforms, and Economic Change," *Policy Studies Review* 11 (2) (1992), pp. 76–86.

37. Lowell and Papademetriou, op. cit., p. 83.

38. See also D. G. Papademetriou, R. L. Bach, D. A. Cobb-Clark, R. G. Kramer, B. L. Lowell, S. J. Smith, and M. Shea, *Employer Sanctions and U.S. Labor Markets: First Report* (Washington, DC: U.S. Department of Labor, 1991).

39. Lowell and Papademetriou, op. cit., 1992.

40. Michael Barone and Grant Ujifusa, *The Almanac of American Politics 1996* (Washington, DC: National Journal, 1995), p. 81.

41. Quoted in ibid., p. 208.

42. Charles F. Bosner, Eugene B. McGregor, Jr., and Clinton V. Oster, Jr., *Policy Choices and Public Action* (Upper Saddle River, NJ: Prentice-Hall, 1996), pp. 106–107.

Conclusions

RATIONALITY, POWER, AND IDEOLOGY (RPI)

Public policies represent collective actions or inactions by governmental bodies of a society. Public policies also raise perplexing questions in regard to the economic, social, and political dynamics of societies, questions such as who profits or loses in policy decisions, how are social structures affected by policy pronouncements, and who has the power to govern? This book has investigated contemporary policy issues, generated a framework for understanding public policy, and hopefully has brought the sometimes esoteric study of public policy down to an understandable level. We particularly hope that we have increased the level of interest of readers who might not think the study of anything that has the label *public* could ever be of much value. We have sought to provide a model that is simple to understand and also uncovers the less visible, noninstitutional actors in the game of policymaking.

As stated in the introduction, the United States has faced many challenges in the past and will continue to face challenges in the future. For the most part, previous public policies achieved their goals and objectives. Numerous challenges remain. Affordable health care, a clean environment, a world-class educational system, safe streets, functional families, and economic security are but some of the challenges discussed in this book. Adequate responses to these and other challenges are essential if the future well-being of the American state is to be ensured.

Public policies are shaped by a multitude of forces and actors that interact with governmental institutions. Rationality, power, and ideology have been identified in this book as inputs that influence policymaking. We do not wish to suggest that these influences are exhaustive (the only forces that influence public policy) or mutually exclusive (no overlap between inputs); nevertheless we wish to suggest that a comprehensive discussion of these inputs is vital for understanding how public policy is made. For example, to understand how a complex public policy such as the delivery of health care to citizens is developed, it is helpful to know something about previous studies that have at least claimed to analyze American health care rationally, to know the major policy players as well as their relative influences, and to have some idea of the philosophical perspectives that shape the parameters of the policy debate.

Rationality

All of the inputs influence policy in their own manner. In contrast to the ideological or power perspectives, the rationality input contends that careful study and objective analysis can produce an optimal mix of public policies that will maximize benefits to all members of society. This perspective maintains that the usefulness of government spending can be estimated quantitatively and that public servants will be able to choose policies that maximize the utility of scarce public resources. Such analysis places dollar values on outcomes and compares the benefits to the costs of specific actions. For example, the benefits of providing early child care or inoculation against disease may be calculated and then compared to the program's costs. Costs might include the expense for the vaccine. Benefits might be calculated in terms of the reduction of future illnesses. Whether the cost of preventive medicine is more than the benefit can be determined rationally. Similarly, costs of programs that provide help to children at risk can be calculated and compared to increased prison expenses that may be linked to a failure to provide such programs. Rational studies often provide a baseline of estimates for impacts of certain types of policies, such as the implications of changes in tax structure. Both the executive (Office of Management and Budget) and legislative branches of government (Congressional Budget Office) have their own separate units that engage in rational analysis of policy implications.

The embrace of rational techniques has captured many social science disciplines as well as governmental bureaucracies. From the rational perspective, well-trained policy experts should be able to collect data, develop options, and choose alternatives that maximize results. Schools of public affairs, departments of public administration, and other academic units teach rational techniques that are intended to improve governance. Specific areas of teaching that enhance rationality in the policy process include studies of implementation, bureaucracy, the political environment, program evaluation, data analysis, research designs, administrative law, environmental impact analysis, cost-effectiveness analysis, cost-benefit analysis, and environmental assessment. Such rationalistic strategies have been utilized in controversial policy decisions such as the closing of military bases.[1] Economists usually are involved in the process of assigning costs and benefits of various outcomes.

The rational approach, however, is not without its problems, many of which relate to the ability to place hard dollar figures on subjective outcomes such as aesthetic beauty. Is the aesthetic attractiveness of a given outcome worth $10, $100, $1,000 or $10,000? Certainly many variables influence the ascribing of dollar figures to specific outcomes.

Disagreement over how to measure outcomes as well as benefits greatly impairs the general credibility of the rational perspective on public policy. Because of these problems, the rational input may be a poorer predictor of policy than other inputs such as power and ideology. Why is this the case? It appears that for all of the methodological sophistication that has been developed in the social sciences, rational studies are commonly dismissed out of hand. Academic journals become more esoteric and unreadable to ordinary citizens; studies become more and more contradictory on key issues; "experts" learn how to distort statistics and earn large sums of money contradicting each other. None of these factors adds luster to the perception that rationality is a key determinant or even a useful predictor of public policy. As a result of these shortcomings, scholars of public policy must look at other factors in order to explain policy outputs.

Power

The power to impose policy preferences for personal gain is a key component of public policy. Policy is often presented in a manner that suggests that all citizens will gain from government action, yet it is often the case that only some will gain and others lose. Actors involved in the struggle for advantage may be lobbyists representing certain industries, clientele groups representing beneficiaries of programs, or citizen groups seeking an ideal that is advocated by its members. The exercise of power can be observed in many areas such as environmental policy.

In conflicts over defining environmental policy, representatives of paper/logging companies (in an attempt to protect their economic interests) try to influence institutional actors to behave in a certain manner. By the same token, environmental organizations such as the Sierra Club use their assets (such as votes of members or money from their organization) to pressure institutional actors to intervene on their behalf.

Power may also be viewed as pluralistic (not dominated by a single group) because there is a separation among policy arenas. For example, economic elites of a community may not dominate in the arena of public school education. This particular policy area may not be especially relevant to many local elites who choose to send their children to private institutions.

Policy studies from a power perspective can also view policy as the result of group conflict. In this view, policy does not simply respond to those with the largest carrot or stick. Policy is not perceived to be unilaterally imposed by a small group of elites but as responding to coalitions of groups that are present in American politics. This perspective asks questions such as: What is the power of one group compared to another? What institutional actors are influenced? Which interest usually prevails? Do different interests prevail in different policy arenas?

It is likely that more powerful groups will be able to direct policy, and less powerful groups will be forced to abide by the results. The relative power of environmental versus industrial groups could be assessed in order to predict policy. An interactive effect with factors such as ideology also may be at work. Are logging companies more powerful or less powerful because of an increase or decrease in general probusiness or antibusiness sentiment? Are environmentalists able to sustain their agenda, even with relatively low numbers of activists because of philosophical (ideological) congruence of their agenda with the views of key institutional leaders? The pluralist perspective does not preclude interactive linkages between inputs. The pluralist view asserts that groups will marshal their forces in policy disputes.[2]

From the perspective of an *idealized democracy,* power comes directly from the people. From this perspective, issues such as environmental protection should be resolved by plebiscite, or polling of the population. The public could be polled, and if a plurality or majority of citizens voted to cut down forest X, or to preserve forest Y so that animal Z could maintain its habitat, policymakers would follow the views of the public. In a sense, this *idealized democracy* conception of governance is similar to the *representative model* of government, which asserts that elected representatives from specific districts are obligated to follow the wishes of their constituents. In contrast to the representative model, the *trustee model* of government contends that representatives are free to exercise independent judgment, even if their judgment is contrary to the desires of constituents. This model is based on the assumption that constituents trust their representative to make policy and do not have the time or interest to voice their opinions on all issues of the day. The ultimate check on representatives in the trustee model is at the ballot box, and in theory those representatives who displease constituents will be replaced by others.

The idealized democracy view of governance appears to be problematic on a number of grounds. One might, in theory, agree with the principle of power (including power to make policy) to the people, yet one could ask whether the people are really informed or simply manipulated and, if so, who is doing the manipulation. A majority of citizens may decide that they do not care a hoot about the environment and are willing to let logging companies do whatever they desire. They may have been convinced by a slick advertising campaign by the logging companies that their economic well-being would improve by loosening government regulations. Governance by plebiscite therefore may fail for two reasons: (1) citizens vote for things that might not be in their long-term best interest, and (2) citizens become pawns in the hands of others, who either manipulate their thinking through slick advertising campaigns or as in the "old days" simply buy their vote by plying them with alcohol or hard currency.

At the other end of the continuum from the idealized democracy perspective is the view that policy is formulated as a result of elite behavior, or the actions of the "real" holders of power. According to this perspective, public opinion is manipulated, the institutional structure is controlled, and the halls of Congress are populated by lobbyists who write legislation for their clients. In this scenario, the "golden rule" (those who have the gold make the rules) prevails, and policy is controlled directly by the desires of elites. In the example of environmental policy, logging companies would be allowed to cut down certain forests if elites who ran the county believed that it was directly or indirectly in their best interests to have this outcome occur.

Some interaction between power and rationality might occur, if elites were convinced (based on rationalistic studies) that environmental degradation may have adverse consequences on their economic health (trees won't grow as fast) or their physical well-being (they might not live as long). If that was the case, one would expect that policy would be somewhat more responsive to environmental priorities. Under the elite perspective, changes in environmental policy or other policy arenas would occur only if the real power holders in society desired to institute such changes.

To evaluate power influences, behind-the-scenes actors must be identified. Few would disagree with the notion that some groups or individuals have more power to shape policy than others. If one accepts this notion, a number of fundamental questions remain. Does greater concentration of power in policy matters render the ideals of democracy untenable? Is power exerted to enhance further the aims of the powerful? Are fundamental principles of American society (justice, equal opportunity, due process, liberty, and freedom) undermined or protected through the concentration of power in policymaking? Is the concentration of power a constant in American society, or does the dispersion of influence expand or contract over time? Do wielders of power prefer some values at the expense of others? Do wielders of power operate in the best interests of the entire society?

The power dynamic must be recognized as an important component of public policy. Who makes policy? To what ends? These are important questions, not only for understanding discrete policy decisions but also for the broad purposes of understanding more about governance in the United States. Power also can be seen as interrelated to ideology since power wielders may hold deeply felt beliefs, which may be constant or may change over time.

Ideology

Ideology affects public policy through the influence of basic philosophies on the behavior of members of the three branches of government and on others who possess political power. Members of Congress, the courts, and the executive branch of government often have been identified by their differing ideological predispositions. For example, when considering the executive branch, the presidency of Franklin D. Roosevelt was noted for its sharp policy departure from that of his predecessors, Herbert Hoover and Calvin Coolidge. It is believed that at least part of this policy departure can be traced to differing assumptions and differing philosophies concerning the role of government. The Great Depression (crisis) might account for some of the policy change; yet for the most part Herbert Hoover faced the same bleak economic conditions as Roosevelt did but acted to implement a different policy agenda.

Policy analysts need to explain why different leaders pursue different policies. A definitive answer to this question is not readily available, but the RPI model contends that ideology should be viewed as at least one component of the response. To use a more contemporary example, the policy thrusts of the Reagan administration differed from the agenda of the Carter administration. Reagan's policies of cutting taxes, increasing defense spending, reducing social spending, and devolving authority down to state and local levels did not occur spontaneously, but were by-products of a broader over-arching philosophy of governance. Similarly, the policy initiatives of the 1994 Republican Congress (led by Newt Gingrich and Bob Dole) differed qualitatively from initiatives that were pursued by the Democratic Congress. Again, deep policy disagreements over taxes, spending priorities, and devolution of government are traced to ideology. The Republican Party's Contract with America (which guided legislation after the 1994 election) and the Christian Coalition's Contract with the American Family both demonstrate how specific philosophical precepts can be converted into identifiable plans of action.[3]

Ideological differences in the court system also exist. Between 1899 and 1937, the Supreme Court was characterized as supportive of the rights of private property but unsure about definitions of reasonable and unreasonable regulation.[4] During this period, the Supreme Court vigorously protected private property by (1) upholding injunctions to prevent labor strikes, (2) striking down the federal income tax, (3) limiting the reach of antitrust laws, (4) restricting the powers of the Interstate Commerce Commission to set railroad rates, (5) prohibiting the federal government from eliminating child labor, and (6) preventing states from setting maximum hours of work. In later years, the Supreme Court began rendering decisions that upheld the ability of the federal government to regulate commerce, protect civil liberties, and ensure equal protection under the law.[5]

In recent times, ideological battles have surrounded Supreme Court nominations. After Ronald Reagan was elected president in 1980, the administration no longer sought out liberal judges for the Supreme Court. Reagan nominated the conservative justice William Rehnquist to be chief justice and Robert Bork to be associate justice. Liberals opposed the nomination of Bork to the Court and in 1987 rejected his nomination. In 1991, after another bruising battle in the Senate, the candidacy of Clarence Thomas was approved. The great drama surrounding the Thomas confirmation proceedings demonstrates that ideology plays a vital role in the shaping of decisions. In general, it was believed that liberal senators were highly critical of the conservative philosophies espoused by Justice Thomas and tried to derail the confirmation. The opposition of liberal senators to the nomination of Bork was enough to prevent his appointment to the Supreme Court, but Thomas triumphed in the face of adversity.

From the broad historical perspective, America always has been shaped by dominant streams of thought: taxation without representation, manifest destiny, states' rights, prohibition, rights of workers, women's rights, isolationism, civil rights, justice, social equality, democracy, freedom, and liberty. Good definitions of these concepts and agreed-upon methods of promoting these concepts through the "nitty gritty" of specific policies, however, have been problematic.

Ideological positions are transitory and fluid. American sentiment at times has swung between various positions. Sentiments surrounding the administration of Franklin D. Roosevelt were sympathetic to the view that the private sector had failed, that government could be a positive force in society, that the Republican party of Lincoln still could not be trusted by white Southerners, that the Republican party was hostile to ethnic Americans, and that the Republican party was associated with wealth, greed, and depression. In contrast to this general picture advanced by Franklin Roosevelt's supporters, champions of the "new" Republican party advanced the views that the private sector was a ladder to success, government inhibited both businesses and individuals, the Democratic party (dominated by minorities, feminists, cultural liberals, secular humanists, and advocates of alternative lifestyles) was undermining traditional American values, and the Democratic party could not be trusted to fulfill its promises. Democrats were linked to ideologies of high taxation, high spending, moral decline, lack of character/values, and a failed view of the world.

Enduring Policy Challenges

The study of public policy presents students with an opportunity to gain insight into American institutions and the forces that influence them. Policy is never made in a vacuum, and one must understand the actors who attempt to influence institutions. This book has enumerated an array of contemporary policy challenges that confront American policymakers and has attempted to peek behind the traditional institutional modes of analysis. This book also contends that less visible forces as well as clear institutional forces influence policy. Policy analysis therefore is incomplete without identification of these inputs. We have discussed rationality, power, and ideology to provide a deeper understanding of the contextual intricacies of the policy environment.

As in any period of America's past, public policy choices must be made and challenges confronted. A number of enduring problems can be identified on the basis of the general interest that they have generated. Identification of these problems should not imply that others do not pose as great or even greater dangers. Tax and deficit issues are prominent among the public policy challenges facing the nation. Some disagreement exists among economists concerning the exact point at which deficits pose a danger to the economy, but there is a general consensus about the benefits of savings and the negative effects of debt. Debt is said to have a negative impact on private sector investment; it transfers wealth from the middle class and working class to upper-income lenders and places a burden on future generations. According to economists, a steady accumulation of debt will erode the very foundation of the economy slowly just as termites eat away the foundation of a home.

The issue of who will bear the burden of taxation is a subject of continuous controversy and involves different interpretations of what is "fair." The Reagan Revolution of 1980 popularized what became known as "supply-side economics," which argued that tax reductions for businesses and higher-income individuals would stimulate economic growth. In previous eras, politicians contended that progressive taxes (higher taxes for higher earners) were necessary to enhance equity. Advocates of progressive taxes argued that those who earned more should pay more both in actual dollars and in percentage terms. Some have advocated a flat tax as a means of simplifying the complexity of filing income taxes, but others view it as a retreat from the ideal of progressivity.

Other challenges within the policy domain include health care and education. Perhaps the biggest problems of health care relate to the ability of the federal government to fund the Medicare and Medicaid programs. Health expenditures continue to eat up large proportions of federal revenue and grow at rates far exceeding those of other functional categories. In addition to the growth of expenditures, the extent of health coverage in the United States lags behind coverage in other nations. Education in America traditionally has been a strength—pulling millions of immigrants up to middle-class status. More recently, ominous rumblings have been heard from the education establishment. High school dropout rates are perceived to be relatively high; American children score below children of other nations on standardized tests; discipline problems gain headlines; teachers are said to be inadequately prepared.

Education policy is perceived to be especially important, since a poor educational base is believed to be a threat to both economic and security concerns of the nation. American scientists and engineers traditionally have met the challenge of developing totally new technologies, from the development of the atomic bomb to the creation of the B-2 "invisible" bomber. Similarly, American entrepreneurs from Andrew Carnegie to Henry Ford to William Gates have been associated with advances in productivity in major American industries such as steel, automobiles, and computers. A fear exists that deterioration of America's educational system could slow economic growth because of an insufficient number of the highly skilled workers who are essential for competition in the technologically sophisticated world of today.

Another issue that has occupied the attention of policy analysts is the environment. Ground water pollution, toxic waste, air pollution, global warming, depletion of the ozone layer, nuclear waste disposal, acid rain, solid waste pollution, and water pollution are all concerns that have gained the attention of policymakers in recent years. Perhaps the most striking example of environmental pollution occurred in the 1960s when the Cuyahoga River in Cleveland caught fire as a result of the extensive discharge of flammable wastes into the river. Such environmental degradation is relatively easy to identify. Other environmental problems such as the dangers of depleting the ozone layer (believed to produce higher levels of skin cancer and cataracts) are less visible. While environmental damage represents a clear and present danger to some policy analysts, others are more skeptical of the risks involved. As a consequence of this skepticism, funding levels for environmental programs have been uneven.

Significant challenges are also found in urban and rural locations. Many of these problems can be traced to the inability of residents in both of these areas to secure a viable economic future. Rural areas have been plagued by declining populations brought about by consolidation in the agricultural industry. Many of the nation's smaller farms went bankrupt in the farm crisis of the mid-1980s, and declining numbers of farmers forced the closure of small businesses in many rural communities. Diversification of an area's economic base is perceived to be essential for the revival of such communities.

Lack of economic opportunity in urban areas is often perceived as more dangerous than rural poverty. This is attributed to the higher densities found in cities and the danger of urban violence. The riots in Los Angeles in the early 1990s illustrate the continued volatile condition of urban America. High rates of welfare, rampant crime, lack of job opportunities, poor schools, broken families, drug use, a "culture of poverty," poor transportation, and a shortage of good role models are all cited as explanations for the plight of certain inner-city neighborhoods. Government funding for programs to train, employ, empower, and house inner-city residents are advocated as remedies. Enterprise zones and self-help programs are popular innovations, yet enthusiasm to fund inner-city programs has waned.

Crime and family dissolution have grabbed the attention of policy analysts in the 1990s. Prison populations as well as spending levels for crime prevention grew in the 1990s. Drug abuse, lack of lawful opportunities, an absence of role models, and gang activity all were possible explanations for the incidence of crime. The rise of female-headed households also was viewed with great concern as analysts linked family dissolution with a multitude of societal problems.

Policy and the American Experience

American public policies are compared often to those of other nations and found to be superior or inferior in some regard. Such comparisons hold value, but policy analysis also must consider the context in which American policy is developed. It is a cliché to describe America as a heterogeneous nation of immigrants, yet the fact remains that America is different from more homogeneous polities. Public policy in the United States must account for a multitude of religions, races, and cultures mixing together in an often uneasy amalgam.

The unique composition of American society has developed over centuries, with immigrants coming to the United States for different reasons. Early settlers came in search of wealth, to escape religious persecution, or to reduce prison sentences. Some Americans were transported forcibly as slaves while others came to avoid starvation. Today, immigrants still attempt to come to America both legally and illegally. The contribution of these immigrants to American society today is a source of continual concern. Restrictions on immigrants have been implemented recently, reflecting contemporary perceptions of immigration within American society. Restrictions have been put into place, yet many Americans recognize their immigrant roots and realize that people with vastly different backgrounds have come together to preserve, protect, and defend American policies in times of peace and war.

Public policies in America traditionally have balanced competing demands, such as demands to create unity with demands to protect diversity, or demands to ensure personal liberties with demands to implement the collective will. Some core values conflict with others and resolution of value conflicts may only transpire following shifts in philosophical paradigms. For example, shifts in basic thinking occurred in the 1930s about the usefulness of government (government is essential) and shifts occurred in perceptions of its proper size in the 1980s (government is too big).

Power relationships in the United States also impact public policy. Some groups or individuals have a great ability to influence policy; others have very little. The issue of power also interacts with values. Are core values undermined when concentration of power occurs, or are they reinforced? Are wielders of power likely to use their influence to promote their self-interest, or are they likely to advance policies that benefit the general good?

Policymaking either directly or indirectly helps to establish the norms of society and declare winners and losers in policy struggles. Sensitivity to the diversity that exists in the patchwork nation of America, as well as awareness of various policy inputs, is imperative if policymakers are to meet the challenges that face them.

The ultimate "cop-out" for scholars is the call for more study. We recognize the vacuity of such a call, yet we also believe that further research into underlying forces affecting public policy is needed. We believe that policy analysts should focus not only upon political institutions in order to understand public policy but should look also at how ideological, rational, and power forces drive outcomes.

Notes

1. Steven Koven, "Base Closings and the Politics-Administration Dichotomy Revisited," *Public Administration Review* 52 (5) (1992), pp. 526–531.

2. V. O. Key, Jr., "The Lack of Budgetary Theory," *American Political Science Review* 34 (1940), pp. 1137–1144.

3. Ed Gillespie and Bob Schellhas, *Contract with America* (New York: Random House, 1994); Christian Coalition, *Contract with the American Family* (Nashville, TN: Moorings, 1995).

4. James Q. Wilson, *American Government*, 5th ed. (Lexington, MA: Heath, 1992), p. 398.

5. Ibid., p. 400.

Index